NO EXIT

CULTURAL FRAMES, FRAMING CULTURE
Robert Newman, Editor
Justin Neuman, Associate Editor

Contemporary American Literature and the State

SETH McKELVEY

UNIVERSITY OF VIRGINIA PRESS
Charlottesville and London

The University of Virginia Press is situated on the traditional lands of the Monacan Nation, and the Commonwealth of Virginia was and is home to many other Indigenous people. We pay our respect to all of them, past and present. We also honor the enslaved African and African American people who built the University of Virginia, and we recognize their descendants. We commit to fostering voices from these communities through our publications and to deepening our collective understanding of their histories and contributions.

University of Virginia Press
© 2025 by the Rector and Visitors of the University of Virginia
All rights reserved
Printed in the United States of America on acid-free paper

First published 2025

9 8 7 6 5 4 3 2 1

LIBRARY OF CONGRESS CATALOGING-IN-PUBLICATION DATA
Names: McKelvey, Seth, author.
Title: No exit : contemporary American literature and the state / Seth McKelvey.
Description: Charlottesville : University of Virginia Press, 2025. | Series: Cultural frames, framing culture | Includes bibliographical references and index.
Identifiers: LCCN 2024059229 (print) | LCCN 2024059230 (ebook) | ISBN 9780813953069 (hardback) | ISBN 9780813953076 (paperback) | ISBN 9780813953083 (ebook)
Subjects: LCSH: Literature and state. | American literature—20th century—History and criticism. | American literature—21st century—History and criticism.
Classification: LCC PS228.S68 M35 2025 (print) | LCC PS228.S68 (ebook) | DDC 810.9/355—dc23/eng/20241211
LC record available at https://lccn.loc.gov/2024059229
LC ebook record available at https://lccn.loc.gov/2024059230

The publication of this volume has been supported by *New Literary History*.

Cover art: "Waterfall plot 2," Andrew Zawacki, *Unsun : f/11* (Toronto: Coach House, 2019)
Cover design: Cecilia Sorochin

CONTENTS

Acknowledgments   vii

Introduction:
Contemporary American Literature on the State: No Exit   1

1. Escape's Edges: Limited Politics of Exit in
   William Carlos Williams and Charles Olson   33
2. Fantasies of Flight in Richard Wright and Thomas Pynchon   73
3. Unstate: Deauthorizing Representation in
   Don DeLillo and Joan Didion   104
4. Escape Politics after the Transnational Turn in
   Karen Tei Yamashita and Junot Díaz   138
5. Beyond Protest:
   Voice and Exit in Juliana Spahr and Nathaniel Mackey   177

Conclusion:
Not Even through the Gift Shop   217

Notes   233
Bibliography   261
Index   277

ACKNOWLEDGMENTS

Thank you to the many sincere, thoughtful friends and colleagues who have confronted this book, in part or in whole, in the many steps along its compositional journey: Chelsea McKelvey (first and last), Andrew Forrester, who also welcomed us to Dallas and into his home, Anna Hinton, Kevin Pickard, Liz Duke, Kelsey Kiser, and the rest of our writing group; Katharine Boswell, who also loved our dogs, and Ashley Winstead; the English faculty at Southern Methodist University who taught me to read and think more widely and more meaningfully, especially Dennis Foster, Willard Spiegelman, who taught me the meaning of a bow tie, Lori Ann Stephens, who taught me to teach and who has loved my family, Jayson Gonzales Sae-Saue, Steven Weisenburger, who also taught me to write well, and most of all Lisa Siraganian, who has always been candid in her care for both me and my work, often by challenging it; Michael Clune; Hudson Smith, who helped me through data visualization in R; and many anonymous readers. Thanks also to Eric Brandt and Angie Hogan at the University of Virginia Press and series editors Robert Newman and Justin Neuman; this book is better for your advice and advocacy.

I am also grateful for the many organizations, institutions, and awards that have supported this book in direct and indirect ways: the English Department at SMU for the Taos Writing Workshop (twice over), the Michael Pueppke Writing Prize, and Hughes Dissertation Fellowship; the Dedman College Interdisciplinary Institute at SMU for sponsoring a research cluster on the relationship between graffiti and institutional authority (and thanks to my co-leader, Lauren Richman); Coffee House Press for providing a digital version of Karen Tei Yamashita's *Tropic of Orange* to aid in my stylometric analysis; the University of Connecticut Library Archives and Special Collections for research assistance and digitization of materials from the Charles Olson Research Collection; and the Humanities Hub at Clemson University for a Project Completion Grant.

Over and above these academic relationships, I have been privileged with abundant friendship and family that has made sure neither the difficulties nor successes attending my work could ever be too important. Many of the names above could be repeated here, though I'll limit myself to those I haven't yet mentioned: Andrew Zawacki, Julianne Sandberg, Kari Nixon, Daniel Millwee, Danny Grace, and Maria Kuznetsova; all my family, especially Isaac, Lexie, Mom, Dad, Connie, John, and Judy; and all my family embodied in All Saints Dallas and Christ the Redeemer in Pendleton. I am acutely aware of both how much love has been given to me and how little I have ever deserved any of it. Chelsea, most of all: it's convention to note that this book is only possible thanks to you. That is true. But it's also thanks to you that any of this is worthwhile.

An earlier version of part of chapter 3 appeared as "Unstate: Disarticulating State Knowledge and Joan Didion's *Democracy*" in *Journal of Modern Literature* 43, no. 3 (2020), copyright Indiana University Press. Used with permission.

An earlier version of chapter 5 appeared as "Beyond Protest: Voice and Exit in Contemporary American Poetry" in *American Literature* 91, no. 4 (2019), copyright Duke University Press. Used with permission.

Works by Charles Olson published during his lifetime are copyright the Estate of Charles Olson; previously unpublished works are copyright the University of Connecticut. Used with permission.

NO EXIT

INTRODUCTION

CONTEMPORARY AMERICAN LITERATURE ON THE STATE: NO EXIT

THIS IS WHAT contemporary American literature says: there is no exit from the state. But also, it wonders: could there be an escape?

American literature has a long pedigree of escape. "I never hear the word 'Escape,'" wrote Emily Dickinson in 1859, "Without a quicker blood, / A sudden expectation—/ A flying attitude!"[1] From slave narratives to Henry Thoreau's cabin to science fiction, flights from undesirable realities persist in the American literary imagination. As a nation, after all, the United States was founded on escape in the Revolutionary War, threatened by escape in the Civil War, and, if we accept the logic of Frederick Jackson Turner's Frontier Thesis, sustained, for a time, by the escape of westward expansion. It should be no surprise that American literature has often adopted the content, structure, and logic of departure.

Dickinson's second stanza clarifies and qualifies the excitement of escape:

> I never hear of prisons broad
> By soldiers battered down,

> But I tug childish at my bars
> Only to fail again!

Escape is a response to imprisonment, one that holds a revolutionary hope. Dickinson's poetic speaker cannot escape, and yet she stubbornly tries nonetheless. This is a useful illustration. The poetics of escape, as I will endeavor to illustrate throughout this book, recognizes the exitlessness of the state, but, confronting it, nevertheless pursues escape anyway.

Escape in American literature does not always take on such directly political ramifications. This book cares about when it does. I consider escape in American literature as a thematic, formal, and political concern spanning genres and political allegiances. Other literatures have been concerned with a politics of escape, but in modern and contemporary American literature, escape takes on a relatively consistent political meaning and persistently evokes a corresponding inquiry into the relationship between literature and politics. For the poetics of escape, the state is the object of fleeing; literature contributes to that politics by investigating and experimenting with the nature of representation.

By and large, literary critics are no longer interested in defining an "American Literature" that is synonymous with the national literature of the United States or representative of a national culture, the kind of work inaugurated by F. O. Matthiessen's *American Renaissance*.[2] Yet, even as we move beyond nationalist categories of analysis, we must be careful not to lose sight of the importance of the state, both as a determining factor in cultural production and as an explicit object of literary attention. Nor should we mistake twentieth-century neoliberalism or contemporary globalization for the withering away of the state. Aihwa Ong notes how neoliberalism, in particular, "is often discussed as an economic doctrine with a negative relation to state power, a market ideology that seeks to limit the scope and activity of governing," but Ong proposes instead that we should understand neoliberalism "as a technology of government ... a profoundly active way of rationalizing governing and self-governing."[3] Moreover, "contrary to claims that globalization engenders an 'unbundling' of sovereign powers," Ong shows how the fragmentation of citizenship and territory are "specific state strategies that are designed to respond effectively to the challenges of global markets."⁴ Matthew Hart likewise observes how "almost any crack or gradation in a state's political geography gets misrepresented as a crisis in its very being or purpose. The truth, however, is that state sovereignty helps produce international and transnational relations."⁵ Even as political power seems less bound to physical space, Hart argues, "the puncturing and graduation of territorial sovereignty doesn't erase state power but extends it throughout putatively 'global' space."⁶ The US state does not entirely delimit *No Exit*, as I consider globalization and international space explicitly through hemispheric novels (in chapter 4) and the British graffiti writer Banksy (in chapter 5 and the conclusion). "American literature" nevertheless makes sense as an organizing category for this book, not because culture obeys national borders but because the United States, as the most powerful exemplar of the inescapability of the political structure of the state, is a unifying concern of the texts I study here.

Centering this book around "American literature" also serves to emphasize that literary opposition to the state is not just about international imperialism—although it is that too—but about the state as such. Joel Nickels, for example, provides a compelling account of attempts in world literature to imagine "nonstate space," to represent "political communities external to state-centric social structures, as opposed to those whose tactical horizon is defined exclusively by the conquest or reform of the state apparatus."⁷ This attempt to identify and understand, in literature, social practices outside the state is congruent with my goals here. The global scope of Nickels's project, however, coupled with the priority he gives to explicitly colonial forms of state power, leaves space for us to think about political exit not just from international imperialism and the metropole but also from the local, domestic state.

In that way, this book affirms Jennifer Harford Vargas's insight that "the drama of U.S. imperialism is not just something that unfolds in foreign countries but that . . . plays out in our own domestic dictatorial hierarchies of power in the United States."⁸ Imperialism, of course, still matters to many of the texts I discuss, but attending to the poetics of escape in American literature, specifically, helps us recognize that colonialism is not the only source of literary anxiety over the state. At the same time, I expand on Harford Vargas's work by showing how antiauthoritarian opposition to the domestic state is not exclusive to the Latin American dictatorship novel but rather forms a broad, cross-genre and multiethnic literary impulse. In a compelling analysis of African American narratives of political escape, William Merrill Decker observes that "no specifically geographical refuge exists for the black American."[9] The poetics of escape extends that to say no refuge exists for anyone, geographic or otherwise. That is not to erase the state's unequal application of power. The ways states brandish racial, ethnic, sexual, and other identities remain important to the poetics of escape (explicitly in chapters 2, 4, and 5 but germane throughout). Yet, neither does any of that eclipse the state itself. Put it this way: if we could somehow imagine a counterfactual history with a kinder, gentler state, one innocent of colonialism, international imperialism, and racism (as far-fetched as that would be), the demand to exit the state would nevertheless still exist.

My periodic scope likewise corresponds with the height of US state power, both globally and domestically. This period bears a notably coherent and consistent climate of opposition and concern towards the state (following on the heels of an era of relative approval towards US state power in the decades surrounding the World Wars and the New Deal). Since the 1960s, anti-state sentiment and rhetoric has persisted through varying, sometimes contradictory and electorally opposed forms in US politics and culture. Some of the most obvious examples include the rise and fall of hippie culture, Goldwater conservatism, Vietnam War protests, the formation of the Libertarian Party in 1971, punk aesthetics and culture, neoliberalism's gerrymandered opposition to the state, Internet anarchists of every ideological flavor, Occupy Wall Street, and Black Lives Matter. By 1979, this widespread anti-statism or "state-phobia" was so firmly established that Michel Foucault could note offhand that the state "is mistrusted by everyone on both the right and the left, for one reason or another. Everyone is in agreement in criticizing the state and identifying its destructive and harmful effects," going so far as to suggest that "what is currently challenged, and from a great many perspectives, is almost always the state: the unlimited growth of the state, its omnipotence, its bureaucratic development, the state with the seeds of fascism it contains, the state's inherent violence beneath its social welfare paternalism."[10] Foucault's perspective is European, of course, again reminding us of the international scope of these concerns, but his sustained interrogation of American liberalism also points us back to the US state as the paradigmatic example. Although Foucault perhaps overestimates the prevalence of the state's detractors and underestimates its defenders, he nevertheless pinpoints an anti-state attitude, broader than perennially marginal anarchist movements and transcending left-right divides, that has never cooled off.

Moreover, the twentieth century marks a dramatic global surge in the political logic of exit. Secession movements worldwide became "significantly more common after World War II," with about "a fivefold increase" in frequency compared to the preceding century, at least in part due to the "widespread internationalization of the norm of self-determination," a legitimization of the right of withdrawal that corresponds to a twentieth-century proliferation of liberal theorizing on exit (which I'll discuss later in this introduction).[11] Though secessionism primarily aspires to create new states, and in that way is fundamentally incompatible with this book's interest in a politics of escaping the state, it nevertheless prioritizes exit as political means: the best way to pursue ethnic and nationalist interests is to leave the state that doesn't meet them. A similar logic is at work in the dramatic proliferation of communes and intentional communities during the 1960s and '70s, a "communal wave" that saw hundreds of thousands look for ways to drop out of US society.[12] Again, hippie dropout politics, and the politics of communes more generally, do not fully align with the anti-state politics at issue in *No Exit;* for the former, dominant social values and cultural norms could motivate withdrawal as much or more than the political reality of the state. Exit does not always oppose the state, but in general it becomes an increasingly attractive political means in the twentieth century.

These two political ingredients—anti-state ends and the means of exit—combine in compelling and surprising ways in contemporary American literature. I argue that the thematic interests and formal strategies of a broad group of anti-state texts are best understood as attempts to work through the allures and frustrations of escaping both literary and political representation. Inheriting from modernists an interest in treating literary representation as a metaphor or synecdoche for political representation, the texts I consider in the following chapters attempt to imagine a politics of running away. Starting from modernist precursors in William Carlos Williams and Richard Wright, I trace this tendency forward through the canonically postmodernist on to the globalized contemporary, in the poetry and fiction of Charles Olson, Thomas Pynchon, Joan Didion, Don DeLillo, Karen Tei Yamashita, Junot Díaz, Juliana Spahr, and Nathaniel Mackey. Insisting—against countless state projects to the contrary—that there is more to knowledge, meaning, and life than what can be represented, this diverse group of authors from the past half-century, centered around the period's most powerful political state, have tried to imagine escape from the state's all-encompassing representational systems. Faced with the impossibility of shedding political representation, these poets and novelists seek analogous or displaced solutions through their attempts to get literature outside representation, often through the interplay of formal experimentation and thematic insistence. I call this the poetics of escape.

Though my interest in the intersection of linguistic representation and political representation leads me to prioritize poetry and literary fiction in *No Exit,* it is also important to recognize how escape poetics exist in relation to a wider media ecology. As such, in addition to these thoroughly literary examples, I will also occasionally gesture towards manifestations in other media and arenas of popular culture, considering important examples in film, television, graffiti, rock music, and video games. By the same token, my interest in the formal relationship between literary and political representation also means that I have set aside texts that, though asserting a politics of exit on a thematic level, do not interrogate that politics through literary form. Cory Doctorow's postscarcity novel *Walkaway* (2017), for example, explicitly imagines exit as a viable political response to capitalist dystopia, with the titular "walkaways" leaving behind "default" society in order to form their own communities and ways of living in the wastelands that have been cast off and ignored by the state. Inverting the right-wing exit of Ayn Rand's *Atlas Shrugged,* Doctorow helpfully iterates a politics of exit beyond the United States through the novel's setting in a near-future hypercapitalist Canada. Formally, however, *Walkaway* is straightforward and uninteresting, treating the novel form as a neutral container for political assertion and reproducing many of Rand's own formal standbys—with long-winded monologues from mouthpiece characters and a plot structured around a simple moral binary, with good guys who are always on the right side of history and bad guys who are unquestionably evil.

The texts I consider, in contrast, all treat flight from literary representation and flight from political representation as parallel or even conjoined projects. As the above list of authors indicates, the poetics of escape is not marginal to this period. The principal texts of this study are widely read or even canonical, central rather than peripheral in the minds of critics of American literature—from Olson's *The Maximus Poems* to DeLillo's *White Noise* to Díaz's Pulitzer-winning *The Brief Wondrous Life of Oscar Wao* to Mackey's National Book Award–winning *Splay Anthem*. My corpus thus skews canonical, in part, to emphasize the cultural gravity of the poetics of escape: even as it expresses a radical politics, one well outside mainstream American political opinion, it nevertheless appears conspicuously in established American literary culture. Much has already been written on these authors and their works, but very rarely have critics discussed them in the context of fleeing the state. This scholarly lacuna should encourage us to rethink our conception of this period's fiction and poetry. Dominant critical debates leave us to choose between postmodernist literature and its contemporary successors as either reproducing the logic of the neoliberal state or else as seeking to generate more democratic inclusion within it.[13] *No Exit* tells a different story. Neither the logic of late capitalism nor identity politics, the poetics of escape, thus far unrecognized in its importance to American literature and culture, seeks to transform our historical political reality by maneuvering beyond the state.

With the deep, regular antagonism to the state I attribute to these texts, it may be tempting to collectively label them "anarchist." Throughout, however, I have generally favored "anti-state" to "anarchist." Anarchism typically entails a whole host of other commitments beyond opposition to the state, touching on nearly every aspect of human sociality and organization, from religion to family life to gender norms to management in the workplace.[14] While any given text in this study might share some or even all of those anarchist commitments, as a group these texts' politics do not consistently add up to anarchism. Anti-statism is a singular political desire that might be hitched to a number of other politics, making it a more inclusive category than anarchism.

The texts I look at, then, are anti-statist but not necessarily anarchist. There is an anarchist element to this study's methodology, however. *No Exit* proceeds from the anarchist notion that improvement in the world primarily emerges from the spontaneous, unguided creativity and ideas of the multitude. In situating literature as an aspect of that creative multitude, reading literature as a potential source of transformative ideas, this project runs counter to the general outlook of the Frankfurt School and New Historicism, and indeed the long social-realist tradition sitting behind such dominant critical perspectives. Through such discourses it has become standard to treat literature primarily as a kind of historical evidence—literature can reveal to us the way things really were or are, demystifying the dominant ideologies of capitalism.[15] In contrast, this book takes literature seriously as a source of ideas for the world, ideas that are not *wholly* determined by the historical conditions in which they are produced but which rather might contribute towards the generation of new historical conditions.

Consider the brief political and cultural history of anti-statism that I summarize above. This helps provide context for the poetics of escape, but the point of this study is neither to further document the cultural component of that history nor to use literature to try to reveal some hidden cause behind such anti-statism. Rather, the point is to understand literature as an active participant in the construction of new realities. Against Marx and Engels's claim in *The German Ideology* that life determines consciousness, I am motivated by the second half of their observation: "circumstances make men *just as much* as men make circumstances" (emphasis mine).[16] That is, literature (and thought more generally) is not entirely circumscribed by material conditions, and may be more than a mere reflection or symptomatic expression of those conditions.

In rejecting symptomatic reading, I am not adopting the common alternative of surface reading. I continue, rather, to prioritize close reading throughout this book. Symptomatic reading has long offered a standard justification for the "heroic" critic's struggle in "wresting meaning from a text,"[17] but, as Rita Felski points out, "all texts teem with meanings that are covert or implied … All texts mean more than they say, inspiring critics to elaborate on the elliptical, to expound on the implicit. Interpretation just is this act of drawing out the nonobvious."[18] We don't need to reduce texts to ideological symptoms to believe they have "nonobvious" meanings that are nevertheless worth thinking about.

This is not to say that the literature of escape is ahistorical. As Heidi Slettedahl Macpherson points out in her study of feminist literary escape, effective escape literature has to maintain some kind of connection to historical reality: "in order to represent the maneuver of feminist protest escape, one must also depict that from which the character is escaping."[19] Sean Grattan similarly observes of utopian literature that it "comes into being against the backdrop of the oppression that spawned it," further arguing that "Utopia is predominately a critique of the present."[20] While I don't categorize the poetics of escape as properly utopian, it is worth recognizing how utopian literature, with its fundamental desire to go beyond history, nevertheless only exists in relation to history, often self-consciously so. The poetics of escape maintains a similar relation to the history it critiques, embedding within itself the realist assertion that there is no exit from the state.

However, we must also recognize that the relevant history for the poetics of escape is a long one, spanning a variety of ideological and policy regimes as well as identifiable historical periods. Discussing postmodernist fiction writers of the 1990s, Samuel Cohen argues that "what they and others saw when they looked back was that the issues of the Cold War and 1960s were not unique to the time but were related to issues threaded through all of American history."[21] An analogous logic applies to all of the texts I discuss in this book. Though they are often situated, contextualized, or rhetorically informed by specific historical conditions, the historical focus of these texts is a much longer and more general one: the state is a power that manifestly exists in and shapes history, but it is also "not unique to the time," extending beyond specific historical moments.

My point is not to deny that states change over time in important ways but to recognize how those changes are, by and large, not significant or of particular relevance to the poetics of escape. Exit from the state is no more or less impossible under Roosevelt than under Reagan. For the poetics of escape, the issue is not a particular historical manifestation or ideological variation of the state—the New Deal, Cold War imperialism, or neoliberalism—but rather the state structure itself that persists across all of these. This is of particular importance to my reading of Joan Didion's

Democracy in chapter 3, but this longer historical view of the state is common across *No Exit*. Thomas Pynchon, for example, points us to postwar Europe not as a historical disruption of the state but as a particularly clear expression of a political logic that persists over a much longer timeline. Junot Díaz intentionally conflates colonial power with the contemporary state, Nathaniel Mackey collapses the slave ship of the Middle Passage onto the neoliberal ship of state, and so on. For the poetics of escape, the state that excludes the young Black man in a Richard Wright novel and the state that privileges the female college student through affirmative action in a Juliana Spahr poem are both similarly intolerable in their inescapability. For the anthropologist or political economist, this means relocating the relevant questions from the differences between competing policies and regimes to their similarities, the common denominator that gets taken for granted, the state itself.

Recognizing how these texts assert an understanding of history is not the same thing as reading them like a historicist. Hannah Arendt offers such a historicist insight when, considering the relationship between totalitarianism and escapist fiction, she asserts that "the masses' escape from reality is a verdict against the world in which they are forced to live and in which they cannot exist."[22] In that realist mode of reading, the desire for escape, manifested in culture, is evidence of unbearable material and political conditions, but escape itself cannot be a meaningful politics. The thing that most interests me as a reader of these texts, in contrast, is not what they tell us about history but how they want to imagine changing it.

Take, for a more concrete example, the Dickinson poem with which I opened: "I tug childish at my bars / Only to fail again!" Reading as a historicist means looking at Dickinson's poetic speaker tugging childishly and seeing evidence of bars; my approach, taking the bars as almost self-evident, seeks to understand the speaker's escape strategies and why they fail—and, thanks to the stubborn repetition, why they fail in different ways and on different points. It is in this sense that *No Exit* is invested in literary history (if not the categorizing work of periodization), attempting to understand the development of these literary forms and ideas, as well as how that should impact our previous critical understandings of these texts.

My approach builds on one proposed by Michael Clune as an alternative to the social realist approach that still dominates literary criticism: "Once we see literary works not as evidence of actually existing capitalism, but as intellectual and material examples of escape from capitalist reality, a meaningful relation both to other disciplines and to urgent political questions becomes possible."[23] Elsewhere, Clune expounds upon his approach to literature as a source for new ideas: "I sometimes think of literature in the way scientists working on new medications think of the rainforest: the chances are that the next great idea—of philosophy, economics, history, neuroscience, or political science—lies buried somewhere in the literature section of the library. If nothing else, the critics who've found so many of the signature ideas of other fields 'anticipated' by literature have given us compelling evidence that this might be the case."[24] In this view, literature's political value need not manifest through mass didacticism, in which "literature reaches a substantial audience of uninitiated readers who need to learn what writers want to teach them."[25] Even setting aside how the "uninitiated" might access the "nonobvious" meanings uncovered by close reading, Sarah Brouillette helpfully disillusions us from that fantasy, since "literary production now takes place under conditions of decline that make it a residual rather [than] a dominant circuit within overall cultural production," with literary culture dependent upon the conditions of power it purports to critique: "relatively high levels of wealth, a well-funded publishing infrastructure, a forceful national copyright regime, and an accessible, state-backed educational infrastructure."[26] Though Brouillette's historicism would point us back to symptomatic reading, my approach means taking seriously literature's contributions to thought without reducing them to ideological symptoms on the one hand or obvious didacticism on the other. The interdisciplinary connections I draw throughout this study are a testament to literature's capacity for generating new, valuable ideas.

Importantly, even as I appeal to economics, anthropology, and political theory to help explain concepts I find in literary texts, I also hope to show how literature can take us beyond what we already know through those disciplines: literature does not just illustrate ideas found in other fields (this is how economists use *Robinson Crusoe* in 101 courses) but contributes new ideas of its own. Most poignantly, the poetics of escape asserts serious limitations to the concept of exit in liberal political economics. Exit as conceived by liberal theorists gives us an important starting point, but it is literature that gives us the politics of escape—confronting the lack of exit from the state but seeking a way out anyway—and it is literature that then thinks through escape's problems and possibilities.

In their widely read *Empire* (2000), Michael Hardt and Antonio Negri gesture towards this possibility of finding politically transformative ideas in the spontaneous actions and products of culture rather than in the expertise of academics. Regarding the revolutionary event that will finally topple Empire and free the multitude, they explain, "we do not have any models to offer for this event. Only the multitude through its practical experimentation will offer the models and determine when and how the possible becomes real."[27] Literature is one aspect of that experimentation. It is in part because novelists and poets are *not* experts that we can take them as part of the multitude. By couching their inquiries in formal experimentation, none of these texts ask to be taken as authoritative or final. (In contrast, Doctorow's *Walkaway*, with its heavy-handed didacticism, *does* ask to be read as authoritative.) Many, even most, of the experiments will fail. But those failures are instructive; whatever success there is to be found, it is likely to be found in the unauthoritative, unpredictable creativity of the multitude. Literature is one pretty good place to look.

Frederic Jameson describes a similar function for literature, casting the novel as productive space of thought experiment. Yet, importantly for Jameson, this possibility no longer seems tenable in "so-called high literature," because life under late capitalism feels so thoroughly entrenched and immutable "that the serious artist is no longer free to tinker with it or to project experimental variations."[28] Instead, this capacity for generating new ideas gets relegated to the utopianism of pulp science fiction. While Jameson does cite Pynchon as one attempt "to reincorporate those formal capacities into the literary novel,"[29] I contend that the dominance of historicism as an interpretive practice has obscured how those capacities never really left—an objective that further motivates my focus on "serious" literary novels and poetry. Moreover, Jameson's rigid historicism means that ultimately even utopian science fiction works primarily to reveal how our historical conditions limit our ideas, with utopianism's "deepest vocation" to demonstrate "our constitutional inability to imagine Utopia itself: and this, not owing to any individual failure of imagination but as the result of the systemic, cultural, and ideological closure of which we are all in one way or another prisoners."[30] Throughout *No Exit*, in contrast, it is not that "our imaginations are hostages to our own mode of production" but rather that our lives are hostages to the state.[31] As a result, my goal is not "making us more aware of our mental and ideological imprisonment" but rather to investigate the nature, mechanisms, and consequences of potential escape from imprisonment within the state.[32]

In that regard, the fictions and poems I analyze in this book differ from the utopian tradition, even as I recognize important affinities as well. Most broadly, any desire for a better world can be understood as utopian. In Ruth Levitas's seminal account, the central, unifying trait of all utopian thought and expression is "desire—desire for a better way of being and living."[33] Grattan glosses Levitas as portraying "the mode of utopia . . . as a pedagogical method for developing and educating desire,"[34] and in that specific sense, the poetics of escape is a kind of utopianism, one focused on nurturing, refining, and nuancing the political desire to escape the state.

However, utopian modes also typically assert a particular image of the good world, the final object of that desire. For Levitas, utopia consists of "representations of the worlds we would like to inhabit."[35] Grattan's account of utopia aligns fairly closely with the poetics of escape when he specifies that "contemporary literary utopia is not based on the construction of a perfect society" but "is marked by ambivalence and incompleteness."[36] Yet, even for Grattan, utopia ultimately means "attempting to form clear and distinct ideas about a world to come."[37] In that regard, it will not work to treat the poetics of escape as properly utopian: throughout *No Exit*, these texts stop short of offering any coherent picture of the "radically different 'post-revolutionary' society," instead focusing almost exclusively on "the moment of revolution itself" that, for Jameson, utopia must necessarily "overleap."[38] Instead of Jameson's notion of the utopian mode as "commitment to closure (and thereby to totality)," one that "aim[s] to resolve all political differences" into concrete political ends,[39] the poetics of escape is open-ended, focused on the means and process of escaping the state rather than imagining any specific post-state reality.

This is not to say that literature actually produces a way out of the state, or even that it contributes to political change in any way that is direct enough to be readily identifiable. As Juliana Spahr, one of the poets I discuss in this book, puts it in her history of the state's role in shaping contemporary literary production, "no one is more convinced than writers of literature that literature has a role to play in the political sphere, that it can provoke and resist. They assert it all the time. While often theoretically sophisticated, much of this assertion is fairly ahistorically optimistic."[40] The texts I analyze in this book are all too aware of the history of state power to be optimistic, too aware of the state's violence and its capacities to co-opt resistance and to bring its outsides into itself. To ignore that history, to indulge in a vision of literary political power, would be more escap*ist* than escape, running away from reality itself. Again and again these texts insist: there is no exit from the state.

In this sense, the poetics of escape provides an important counterpoint to Sean McCann and Michael Szalay's charge that post-sixties American literature indulges in the New Left's "magical" view of culture, one that assumes "that the ability to affect culture is, independent of other means, also therefore politically efficacious."[41] The poetics of escape suffers no such delusions. As Andrew Joron puts it in "The Emergency," the introductory prose poem to his post-9/11 collection *Fathom* (2003), "American poetry is a marginal genre whose existence is irrelevant to the course of Empire."[42] This echoes Jameson's logic, as he notes how "that very distance of culture from its social context which allows it to function as a critique and indictment of the latter also dooms its interventions to ineffectuality and relegates art and culture to a frivolous, trivialized space in which such intersections are neutralized in advance."[43] For Jameson, to the extent that thought is not constrained by history, to that same extent it is also impotent.

Why, then, write poetry against Empire? (Or, for that matter, literary fiction, which we must recognize as only marginally less marginal.) For Jameson—and historicism more generally—the answer is that literary failures reveal the boundaries of thought imposed by our historical conditions. Joron's answer suggests an alternative: "here, only here, at this very juncture between language and power, can the refused word come back to itself as the word of refusal, as the sign of that which cannot be assimilated into the system" (18). Because the state extends its violence through representational systems, language itself becomes a way to think about power. Joron therefore proposes a poetry that is "sigh more than sign" and "does not communicate at all, except to announce the incommunicable, as abyssal groan" (19). Getting poetry outside of communication becomes a way of imagining life outside of state power.

Here, we might think McCann and Szalay are correct: How could writing noncommunicative poetry do anything to the state, unless by magic? Joron, indeed, uses the language of magic, calling this poetry "miraculous" and "shamanic" (19). Yet, Joron also formally subverts his declared poetics here: these proclamations appear in a ten-page prose poem that is straightforwardly communicative, producing none of the feeling of nonmeaning one gets from, say, language poets like Bruce Andrews. The poem doesn't so much accomplish the "saying of the unsayable," as Joron proposes, but for the most part simply says what it says (21). That is, Joron has explicitly proposed a poetics that he knows he cannot fulfill: "poetry cannot be anything other than inadequate, even to itself. Where language fails, poetry begins" (15). Language doesn't fail, though, and that's precisely the problem, precisely why the magical poem beyond language never begins. Undergirded by violence, the state's decrees, as language, remain in force. In order to maintain the homology between language and state, Joron makes the poem communicative: language persists in the poem because the state persists in history.

But these poems and fictions are also more than just cultural evidence for the historical impossibility of exit from the state. These texts begin in that place of exitlessness, and from there try to imagine the possibility of—the conditions and means of—escape. Even here these texts seem unsure; Spahr finds it difficult even to "imagine any" literary resistance to the state.[44] Yet, Spahr does imagine a scenario where imagining might be possible: "It is almost impossible to imagine what it would be like if something like the Anarchist Black Cross Federation or Cooperation Jackson had millions to give out to artists. Impossible to imagine politically and impossible to imagine what this literature might look like, what forms it might take, what languages it might use."[45] Spahr seems to be at three removes: she is imagining a situation where she could imagine the historical conditions (that are currently "almost impossible to imagine") where literature (with "impossible to imagine" "forms" and "languages") could resist the state. We're a long way off, but this also suggests a way forward. If the literature we have cannot imagine escape from the state, perhaps we can begin the work of imagining a literature that could.

In contrast to the historicist approach to the failures of imagination—which asks, "what do these imaginative failures say about the present?"[46]—the poetics of escape treats such failures as invitations to further thought, speculation, and experimentation. Returning once more to Dickinson, the stubborn, "childish" insistence both recognizes that escape is, under current circumstances, impossible, yet nevertheless continues probing and trying again, not because that will reveal hidden bars but from the hope, however faint, of someday discovering a way out. Precisely because the state's exitlessness is historical (rather than metaphysical), it remains possible to imagine a future capable of imagining a way out, and in that way, literature is more than a symptom of that historical condition. Whereas Jameson portrays "closure or the narrative ending" as "the mark of that boundary or limit beyond which thought cannot go,"[47] the poetics of escape treats its endings as open, displacing potential solutions to the space outside or beyond the text in order to mark not impossible ideas but undiscovered ones.

This is a frequent pattern for the poetics of escape, one that I have tried to reflect by calling it a "poetics," framing this textual practice as one concerned with creating a resistant literature that does not yet (but hopefully might) exist. The poetics of escape tries to imagine escape from the state, and, when it so frequently fails to do so, it imagines a literature capable of imagining escape from the state. My goal in *No Exit* is not to find a solution to the state's exitlessness—this book is not an example of the poetics of escape—but rather to provide a multifaceted and nuanced account of the motivations, difficulties, ambiguities, contradictions, and tensions attending this desire to escape political representation. Successive iterations do not merely repeat past failures but rather, failing in new ways or on different points, produce meaningful political, social, and literary knowledge, cumulatively building and refining our understanding of these ongoing literary experiments.

To bring this poetics into relief, I want to briefly consider a counterexample in the 2018 film *Leave No Trace*, directed by Debra Granik and based on Peter Rock's 2009 novel *My Abandonment*. Shot in Portland, Oregon, and nearby old-growth forest, *Leave No Trace* foregrounds understated performances from Ben Foster and Thomasin McKenzie as Will and Tom, respectively, a father-daughter pair trying to escape twenty-first-century life by living secretly as wilderness survivalists on public forest lands. Will, an Iraq War veteran suffering from post-traumatic stress disorder, wants to run away from all aspects of society—not just the state. Thus, after park rangers catch Will and Tom and social services arranges a more conventional life for them, including formal schooling for Tom and regular housing in exchange for Will's labor on a Christmas tree farm, one of the first things that Will does is unplug the television and hide it in the closet. Yet, this act also indicates the difference between wanting to escape society and wanting to escape the state. The former is almost trivial by comparison. Indeed, Will's most extreme desires to run away stem directly from the state's inescapable presence, especially in the form of Will's assigned social worker and the constant barrage of documents that she brings him to fill and sign, his representational inclusion within the state. He can unplug the television, but he can't ignore this government paperwork.

Society wields representation in myriad ways, from mass media to social media to high art, to constitute, shape, and appropriate subjectivities; but this becomes another matter entirely when, in the state, representational technologies of control overlay a more fundamental power of coercion. This is what Antonio Gramsci means when he defines the state not just as "hegemony" but rather "hegemony protected by the armour of coercion,"[48] what Louis Althusser means when he notes how the violence of "the repressive State apparatus" secures "the political conditions for the action of the Ideological State Apparatuses," with state power providing "a 'shield'" for hegemonic ideology.[49] In this regard, *Leave No Trace* is congruent with the more general pattern of escape that emerges in twentieth- and twenty-first-century literature that I am trying to describe and understand in this book: the state is inescapable in a way that other aspects of society are not, and that inescapability is fundamentally embedded in the state's representational systems and practices.

Yet, most importantly to my immediate purpose here, the film remains narrowly realist throughout, to the extent that this realism constrains any potential politics of escape.[50] The film does invite us to sympathize with Will, and it openly acknowledges the romantic allure of running away to live in the woods. When Will and Tom first move into the house at the Christmas tree farm, Will's boss and landlord confides, "a lot of people like to imagine they could live the way you guys were living," an observation that the film clearly understands applies to its own viewers as well. Ultimately, though, *Leave No Trace* pathologizes Will's desire to flee from a life dominated by the state. In the film's affective climax, Will once again prepares to disappear into the woods, but Tom decides she won't go with him this time, tearfully explaining to him that "the same thing that's wrong with you isn't wrong with me." In the next scene, a final, moving goodbye in the woods, Tom empathizes, "I know you would stay if you could." We can hardly disagree with Tom here, or with the underlying realism that motivates these moments: the faintest possibility of leaving the state requires leaving behind society altogether. Tom's character poignantly embodies the unviability of that escape, grieving a now-absent father she still loves even as she needs other friendships and experiences, life in community.

The end of the film ambiguously suggests that Will succeeds in leaving behind society and state with his final return to the woods, but Will's escape cannot be political. Instead, it is a solipsistic escapism, a symptom of history but irrelevant to changing it. As one reviewer puts it, the film evokes a distinctly American "element of yearning and romanticism, manifested most strongly in Thoreau's *Walden* . . . But Granik is careful not to idealise that."[51] In its realism, *Leave No Trace* is insightful and nuanced, but that realism also forecloses any attempt to imagine a meaningful politics of escape. In this book, my goal is to uncover and analyze a different literary strategy, one that, while recognizing and admitting the realist claim that there is no exit from the state, nevertheless works towards a politics of escape, even if the hope of such a politics remains obscure and distant.

Let me now offer some further, necessary context and conceptual framework by way of intellectual history and definition for a set of four key terms that frame this book.

EXIT, THE STATE, ESCAPE, ESCAPISM

In political theory, the story of exit has traditionally been a liberal one. Political economist Albert O. Hirschman, one of the most important theorists of exit as a political mechanism, went so far as to link exit with the logic of the marketplace, equating it with competition: freedom of disassociation is a primary value to a liberal market society.[52] In its obituary for Hirschman, *The Economist* aptly describes Milton Friedman and Chicago School economics as "the cult of exit"—they took exit a step too far for Hirschman, even as Hirschman himself promoted exit as a useful mechanism for societal improvement.[53] On the other end, political theorist Chandran Kukathas claims that his fellow liberals typically do not take exit far enough. He places exit at the center of his theory of the free and good liberal society, elevating the "the right to leave the community" to the supreme liberal right: "If there are any fundamental rights, this has to be that right. It is an inalienable right, and one which holds regardless of whether the community recognizes it as such. It would also be the individual's only fundamental right, all other rights being either derivative of this right, or rights granted by the community."[54] Exit becomes the foundation of free society and the source of political authority. Kukathas thus privileges exit far more than Hirschman, and we can see a continuum within the liberal tradition, along which exit takes on lesser or greater importance. Even at the lower bound, though, freedom of exit remains a primary (if not absolute) liberal political value.

Although the works to be discussed here share liberalism's broad commitment to exit as a central value, they also diverge from liberalism in a crucial respect. For the poetics of escape, the thing to break out of is the political state. This is almost never the case in the liberal treatment of exit. In Hirschman's framework, for example, "the exit option is unavailable" when it comes to the state, and his analysis is entirely limited to examples of exit that take place *within* the state.[55] This is the case in other, competing strains of liberalism as well. Friedman, for example, proscribes departure from legal norms of behavior: "We are willing neither to permit [madmen] freedom nor to shoot them."[56] The figure of the madman exists outside the state's conception of full rights-bearing citizenship, but the state cannot let that amount to exit. (This will be directly pertinent in chapter 1, as William Carlos Williams critiques the state for declaring a potential escapee insane.) Or, consider John Rawls, who, in abstracting his ideal political society, models it as a "closed social system ... in that entry into it is only by birth and exit from it is only by death."[57] Kukathas endorses the political value of exit to a far greater extent than most other liberals, and he critiques Rawls's version of liberal pluralism for being "circumscribed by its subordination to the moral standards of a particular community: political society."[58] Nevertheless, even Kukathas allows a final, encompassing boundary of state authority that is not to be quit. Because Kukathas holds so strongly to the standard liberal view that freedom and autonomy are not the same thing—being free to exit is not the same as being able to exit—he struggles to define a case in which freedom of exit does not exist. For Kukathas, "raising the cost of exit does not count as prevention," and though he admits that "surely a more nuanced view is possible—and necessary ... a more robust right of exit," he never clearly articulates such a view.[59] Instead, we again end up with exit taking place only within an overarching framework of the state, or merely as immigration from one state into another. In mainstream political philosophy, exit from the state is unimaginable.[60]

Thus, although the liberal tradition is responsible for almost all of the academic thought on exit as a political freedom and mechanism, the poetics of escape ultimately diverges from that tradition. Liberal exit takes place within the state; the poetics of escape seeks to leave the state itself. Indeed, we might even take advantage of the subtle shades of meaning in this terminology. Exit, in the liberal usage, is on some level a mutually voluntary occurrence: when a person leaves a group, the group may try to convince the person to stay, but the group does not forcefully prevent the parting of ways. Escape, in contrast, would be an exit in the face of a group's coercive attempt to make one stay. Because the state does not allow exit from itself, it is more appropriate to speak of escaping the state than exiting it. And this lexical distinction captures the difference between liberal exit and the poetics of escape; it is only the latter that is seriously interested in leaving the state behind. Escape is closely related to exit, and theorizing on exit is certainly helpful in understanding escape, but as politics, exit and escape diverge on the point of the state.

The state allows no exit from itself: to make such a blanket claim is to imply that part of what defines the state is its exitlessness. Indeed, Kukathas's difficulty in differentiating costly exit from prohibited exit is closely related to a difficulty in defining the state. The political economist Peter Leeson, for example, similarly treats exit from the state as a matter of high cost rather than strict impossibility, and thus for Leeson there is no bright line, on the basis of exit, to reliably differentiate the state from other groups (like a family or a church) that might be difficult to leave.[61] As a result, Leeson struggles to define what counts as a state, settling on the deeply unsatisfying answer that "you know it when you see it."[62]

Here, literature can improve upon the political economist's deficient framework. Again and again, twentieth- and twenty-first-century American literature treats exit from the state not just as a matter of extreme difficulty, an obstacle to be overcome in heroic triumph, but a matter of outright impossibility. In other words, fiction and poetry remedies this definitional problem by recognizing that exit from the state is not merely expensive but unattainable—or, sticking to the economist's vocabulary, recognizing that the cost of exiting the state is effectively infinite. There is no cost, pecuniary or otherwise, that can be paid in order to exit the state (a contention I'll return to in the conclusion of this book), and in this way, the state can be clearly differentiated from other organizations or associations that have high costs to exit. (As Hirschman puts it, "the barrier to exit constituted by loyalty," which might prevent one from leaving a family or a church, "is of finite height."[63]) Enough resources might allow one to modify one's relation to the state—to become privileged within or above the law—but this is still an ongoing relation to the state, not a departure from it. Exit from the state is not for sale. The state then can be defined, in part, as a political authority that historically no one can depart.

Treating exitlessness as a defining trait of the state also has the further advantage of according with Max Weber's standard definition of the state as a monopoly on legitimate violence. A monopoly is an organization from which there is no exit; you cannot avoid a monopoly and choose an alternative. Indeed, Hirschman uses "monopoly" and "no-exit situation" interchangeably.[64] We must of course update the details of Weber's definition; anthropologist James C. Scott, for example, emphasizes that states *aspire* to this monopoly without necessarily always achieving it,[65] and, in light of Hart's analysis of extraterritorial state power, discussed above, we should excise Weber's qualifier that this monopoly pertains "within a particular territory."[66] Nevertheless, the core of Weber's definition retains its descriptive and explanatory value. To define the state by its lack of exit is not esoteric but simply a way of highlighting an aspect of the state as generally understood in both academic and colloquial usage.

Other thinkers have helpfully expounded on what this monopoly on legitimate violence looks like and how it functions—most importantly, they have tried to answer the question of how the violence monopoly gets legitimated and how it stays that way. Gramsci offers a usefully explicit answer: "State = political society + civil society, in other words hegemony protected by the armour of coercion."[67] Gramsci's political society is the monopoly on violence, the physical power of police and military, while civil society produces a general attitude of consent and, in the end, an ideology of state legitimacy.

The state is the combination of ultimate physical power with the ideology of legitimacy that prevents all the various agents who provide that physical power, in all its various forms, from turning against it. Stuart Hall glosses the state defined by Gramsci as "the point from which hegemony over society as a whole is ultimately exercised (though it is not the only place where hegemony is constructed). It is the point of condensation—not because all forms of coercive domination necessarily radiate outwards from its apparatuses but because, in its contradictory structure, it condenses a variety of different relations and practices into a definite 'system of rules.'"[68] In this view, the state is "not a *thing* to be seized, overthrown or 'smashed' with a single blow," writes Hall, "but a complex *formation*," a set of relations extending beyond officially acknowledged state actors and organizations.[69] Structures and entities officially set apart from the state while nevertheless mutually interdepending with the state to sustain and guarantee each other (such as Althusser's ideological state apparatuses, Foucault's disciplinary systems, or global corporations) are at least partially understood as extensions of the structure, logic, and reach of the state. After Giorgio Agamben (discussed in chapter 3), we should see even monarchs above the law and criminals acting outside the law as constituting and perpetuating the state, providing the necessary ground on which the state can perennially justify and legitimate itself. Or, to draw from another intellectual tradition, the influential political scientist Theda Skocpol observes that "we must often look above and below the level of historic nation-states to see the most fascinating 'state-building' going on in our time," and even "institutional undertakings by the United Nations and other transnational bodies can be understood as new kinds of statebuilding projects" as well as "simple organizations of coercion and extraction" in conflict regions without stable nation-states.[70] To look only at the official, explicitly declared domain of the state—or to restrict the state to territorial boundaries[71]—is to misapprehend the nature and extent of its power.

This expansive understanding of the state helps us take more seriously the state's status as a monopoly, as a structure without exit, and it helps us make sense of how the literature does too. So, for example, we understand that Thomas Pynchon's totalizing notion of "the System" or the vague conspiracy of "Them" refer to the same "complex formation" that is at issue in various ways for Gramsci, Althusser, Hall, Foucault, and Agamben.[72] The texts I analyze in the following chapters begin with an understanding of a comprehensive state, from there investigating and confronting its consequent exitlessness.

The state's far-reaching nature explains why these texts find escape simultaneously so difficult and so urgent to imagine. It also elicits one of the abiding problems for the poetics of escape, one suggested in Kukathas's justification of state authority: "Political obligation stems from our acquiescence in the authority of those associations which have themselves accepted the authority of the state."[73] Participating in associations that accept and work within the state amounts to participating in the state. Does leaving the state necessitate also abandoning all those other groups, organizations, and communities we belong to that, in one way or another, give in to state authority? In other words, does leaving the state have to mean leaving society?

The stakes of these questions will become increasingly clear over the following chapters. For now, let me observe that, as I define it through the practices of the authors in this study, the poetics of escape is not escapist.[74] As Macpherson observes, it has long been commonplace to dismiss literary escapes, especially in popular and genre fiction, as opiates, "harm[ing] political sensibilities by deflecting the readers away from real social issues. Science fiction, Westerns, detective fiction, and especially romances have been accused of channeling the political anger of readers into safer areas."[75] Indeed, in twentieth-century political philosophy, escapism is perilous. Arendt identifies escapism as one of the sources of totalitarianism, observing that "the masses are obsessed by a desire to escape from reality" because they cannot tolerate the chaos of twentieth-century life; through the promise of order and structure, "totalitarian propaganda thrives on this escape from reality into fiction, from coincidence into consistency."[76] Escapism, in this sense, means ignoring political reality in favor of political fictions, fictions that might be dangerous in the extreme.

This distinction between escape and escapism is in many ways analogous to a central dichotomy in utopian studies: Ernst Bloch's distinction between "concrete" and "abstract" utopias, between a wish and wishful thinking, what Lyman Tower Sargent glosses as the difference "between utopias disconnected from and connected with human reality."[77] The problem with "abstract" utopias, as with escapism, is that "daydreams do not take us very far, in that they are more a sign of our dissatisfaction than a guide to change."[78] Jameson expands on Bloch, mapping concrete and abstract utopias onto conscious and subconscious desire, respectively, distinguishing "self-conscious Utopian secessions from the social order" from utopia "as the mere lure and bait for ideology."[79] For Jameson, however, this depends on an untenable Platonist distinction between "true and false desire, the true and false pleasure, genuine satisfaction or happiness and the illusory kind."[80] As a result, Jameson shifts his attention from distinguishing between authentic and false utopian desire to the presence of utopian "closure": utopian desire is only concrete, a wish instead of wishful thinking, if it imagines "totality," wishes for the end of history (which, still wished for, cannot have arrived already under late capitalism).

While I share Jameson's misgivings over distinguishing authentic from inauthentic desires, I reject his contention that political desire must aim at totality and closure to avoid collapsing into wishful thinking. As I have already noted, the poetics of escape does not imagine such a totality or the end of ideological conflict, focusing on the as yet unrealizable means of escape rather than what comes after escape. Instead, I differentiate escape from escapism on their attitudes towards reality. Jameson notes that some utopian "'no-places' offer little more than a breathing space, a momentary relief from the overwhelming presence of late capitalism," a kind of psychic rest in which "the utopian imagination protects itself against a fatal return to just those historical contradictions from which it was supposed to provide relief."[81] This version of utopian desire is what I mean by "escapism," not because the desire for such relief is any more or less "true" but because it posits escape from reality itself rather than the particular historical reality of the state. The texts that I hold to exemplify the poetics of escape do not ignore or relieve the burden of political reality—it is the reality that there is no exit from the state that drives escape. Moreover, these texts do not seek retreat from human sociality into purely private meaning and imaginaries but rather look for escape into new forms of human relation.[82] The poetics of escape is not solipsistic but outward-looking, social.

This is particularly relevant to the matter of representation. One way to get outside political representation, it would seem, would be to abandon representation altogether—the miraculous, noncommunicative poem that Joron fantasizes but rejects. That would be escapist, giving up not just political representation but language itself and all the forms of human sociality that rely on representation. At their most successful, however, these texts are neither content with nor credulous of straightforward attempts to get outside representation. For one thing, these texts do not want to squander the positive social value of representation; freed from state power, representation can foster human connectivity and enrich collective life. Moreover, the bind of representation to power cannot be cast off as easily as direct anti-representation implies; making linguistic material nonrepresentational only severs literature's homological tie to political representation, and as a result, literature ceases to provide a usable means of modeling or thinking through escape from the union of representation and power.

From inside the poetics of escape, simple rejection of representation as such looks like escapism, resulting in a literature unconnected to the problems of political representation that are so central to these anti-state texts. If escaping political representation were as easy as writing nonsense, the poetics of escape would be unnecessary. Instead, the poetics of escape formally and thematically dramatizes a struggle to leave behind representation as a way to confront political representation, not ignore it or wish it out of existence.

This distinction between escape and escapism hinges on the state. The non-escapist poetics of escape insists that the danger is not representation itself but representation in a feedback loop with state power; structures of representation must be escaped only when and because they are backed by the state. The state is the point on which we differentiate escaping political representation from escaping representation as such.

This perspective differs from the many purely anti-representational texts produced in the same period, for example John Cage's chance operations (discussed in chapter 5) or certain language poetry experiments with nonsignification. Take for example Charles Bernstein's "Azoot D'Puund" from his 1979 collection *Poetic Justice*. Even though the poem hints that it might have its own internal logics, gesturing towards patterns and even invented linguistic conventions, all of those are ultimately inaccessible to the reader. As such, I quote at random: "ey Ancded lla tghn heh ugrf het keyon. Hnny iKerw. InVazoOOn uvv spAz ah's ee 'ook up an ays yr bitder guLpIng sum u pulLs."[83] The poem refuses signification to an absolute. When the poem does nod to signification and referentiality—the stylistic and typographic allusion to Ezra Pound is apparent enough, we may cling to "invasion of space" or "bitter gulping" as potential signifiers, and a few lines earlier we even get "u sOond ap uld OOngLeesh," perhaps suggesting a distorted sonic link to Old English—the result is simply more antisignification.[84] Rather than offering some narrow opening into meaning, these feints towards representation only more completely subvert it, bringing it up solely to knock it down.

This total rejection of representation contrasts the qualified opposition to reified representation (representation given force by state power) that is characteristic of the poetics of escape. It is the difference between abandoning human sociality and seeking human sociality outside the state. In other words, the poetics of escape is not like the kind of escape toyed with in Jean-Paul Sartre's one-act play *Huis clos* (notwithstanding my sharing a title with some English translations). Sartre's character Garcin, newly arrived in hell, spends most of the play trying to avoid contact with his fellow damned souls, mostly by cutting off representational contact (refusing to speak with them) until he famously concludes that "Hell—is other people!"[85] The poetics of escape is not like Garcin trying to escape the objectifying gaze of the other, and it is not like other postwar aesthetic experiments in anti-representational art. The flight from representation at issue here is targeted specifically at the political state.

PLOT

Plots lead deathward, refrains Don DeLillo, but this study contends that it is specifically political plots, not literary plots, that must be escaped. It should be safe to give you mine:

Chapter 1 sketches out an edge case for the poetics of escape through Charles Olson's late-career additions to *The Maximus Poems* (1953–83), bringing this poetics into relief through contrast with Olson's most important modernist precursor, William Carlos Williams. Williams flirts with a poetics of escape in his challenge to artistic representation in *Spring and All* (1923) and his polemics against the state in *An Early Martyr and Other Poems* (1935). However, Williams ultimately shies away from escape, fearing that it must inevitably devolve into escapism: without linguistic and political representation, human relationships, like that between author and reader, would not persist.

Olson, I argue, falls on the other side of this dilemma, refusing to give up on escape but risking a total disconnect from wider society. While I read Olson's influential "Projective Verse" manifesto as essentially continuing Williams's truncated poetics of escape, I argue that in his later work Olson rejects his earlier prescriptions and begins imagining how poetry might accomplish total escape from representation, both literary and political. At times, Olson's poetry anticipates the political and cultural logic of the hippie dropout movement, disconnecting from society to escape the bounded lifestyles of the capitalist state.

Chapter 2 traces the poetics of escape into the novel, through Richard Wright's *Native Son* (1940) and Thomas Pynchon's *Gravity's Rainbow* (1973). The structure of this chapter echoes the dynamic of the preceding Williams-Olson pairing—with the earlier modernist contemplating escape only to discard it as unworkable, and the later postmodernist doggedly pursuing escape to the point of asociality. In this sense, these two chapters affirm Szalay's observation that "if during the thirties political parties and the state seemed agents of liberation, by the end of the sixties they seemed to embody all that individuals needed liberation from."[86] I don't want to put too fine a point to this—such a sweeping historical narrative necessarily elides particularities and invites reductive causal explanations, and Williams and Wright are far more skeptical of the state than Szalay's framing would suggest.[87] Nor do I intend any rigorous developmental chronology. Nevertheless, this comports loosely with what I see as the general historical shape of the poetics of escape. Wright ultimately rejects escape, resolving instead towards identity politics and greater democratic inclusion, while Pynchon finds escape only in solipsism.

Chapter 3 argues that more expansive visions of escape emerge in Don DeLillo's *White Noise* (1985) and Joan Didion's *Democracy* (1984). Both of these novels poignantly foreground the potential danger of state representations and their capacity to ignore life's inarticulable details—as the liberal philosopher Michael Polanyi puts it, all that we know but cannot tell. Against standard readings of *White Noise* as a lament over information overload in our media-saturated world, I argue DeLillo's novel deconstructs the noise/information dichotomy at the heart of classical information theory. Instead, DeLillo uses noise to model experiential knowledge that cannot be reduced to representation. *White Noise* casts the state as the primary obstacle to the tacit knowledge typified by noise, contrasting it with nonstate attempts to wield representation as an authoritarian tool of control. DeLillo's novel fantasizes a utopian flight from the state in order to imagine how inarticulable forms of tacit, experiential knowledge, necessarily dismissed by state systems of representation, might be reintroduced alongside articulated knowledge.

Democracy, in turn, complicates the kind of utopian escape underpinning *White Noise*, by focusing more insistently on the insurmountable difficulty of escaping state schemes of representation. Didion's novel links political representation to literary representation as it flees both state and narrative, an endeavor that dead-ends with the conviction that neither sort of representation can be escaped. Instead, Didion ultimately acquiesces to representation, resorting to the narrative of failing to escape narrative in the faint hope of unmasking the state's seemingly natural combination of representation and power. Even as these diverging responses help demarcate the limitations of escape politics, together *White Noise* and *Democracy* illuminate a shared literary impetus to deauthorize the coercive power of state-backed representation.

Chapter 4 considers the poetics of escape in the context of intensified globalization through two hemispheric novels, Karen Tei Yamashita's *Tropic of Orange* (1997) and Junot Díaz's *The Brief Wondrous Life of Oscar Wao* (2007). These novels beckon us to ask whether "escaping the state" can still hold political meaning in an era when the international circulation of people, culture, and capital is commonplace. Both of these novels confront how national borders and racial categories continue to reify as tools of state control even as state power spills over territorial boundaries. These novels cast globalization as an inadequate answer to the demands of the politics of exit: expanding capacity to move between states does not amount to a departure from the state altogether.

Yamashita's novel moves hopefully across the US-Mexico border towards a world without political maps and central planners. However, as I show through computer-aided stylometrics, Yamashita's formal attempt to replace narrative authority with an egalitarian polyvocality fails. A single, authoritative perspective triumphs, and she defers any hope of escaping the state's godlike cartographic vision to a space beyond the novel's end. Similarly, for Díaz physical flights from one country to another prove to be false escapes, comparable to literary flights into the worlds of science fiction and fantasy. For both Yamashita and Díaz, escaping the state remains urgent and unaccomplished, even in the face of widespread movements across national borders and the immediate need for more democratic representation.

Chapter 5 returns to Olson's poetic lineage, reading Juliana Spahr's *This Connection of Everyone with Lungs* (2005) and *Well Then There Now* (2011) alongside Nathaniel Mackey's *Splay Anthem* (2006) as exemplars of a broader impetus in contemporary American poetry to catalog and articulate the state's deployment of catalogs and articulation. Drawing directly on Hirschman's conception of political exit as a compliment to political voice, I show how Spahr and Mackey each fantasize a poetry that could speak escape into existence, wishing for a language that could intervene directly in history. Both undermine that fantasy, though, as they insist that it is only the state's language, backed by military and police power, that can work that way. Instead, Spahr and Mackey turn from exit to voice, working to represent the power of the state's representations. For both of these poets, speaking up is not enough—only exit will suffice—but so long as exit remains impossible, speaking remains the best recourse against the state's fiat realities. Recognizing that voice cannot enact exit, Spahr and Mackey both renew the unappeased demand for exit as a source for new collectivities oriented towards escape.

I conclude by drawing out the wider significance of the poetics of escape and situating it concretely in twenty-first-century political discourses. In most spheres, the political mechanism of exit has been almost entirely ceded to the political right. When the *New Republic* ran a piece in 2017, "It's Time for a Bluexit," suggesting that leftists secede from Trump's America, it was explicitly satirical, a "modest proposal."[88] In standard political discourse, the left cannot seriously recommend political exit; exit belongs to the right.

Many contemporary artists, I argue, make no such concession. I turn to the anonymous graffiti writer Banksy, building off of two brief readings of his graffiti introduced in chapter 5. Banksy's anti-capitalist graffiti often ironically derides familiar modes of anti-capitalist action, and it would be easy to dismiss Banksy as merely perpetuating the logics of liberal capitalism; with his middlebrow popularity and auction house successes, many critics do just that. But Banksy is important precisely because he refuses to relinquish exit to the right. Close-reading Banksy's self-critical satire of commodified art in his 2010 film *Exit through the Gift Shop* alongside a post on his official Instagram account, I show how Banksy recognizes the difficulties of escape while nevertheless insisting on its necessity. Moreover, Banksy is not alone in investigating the anti-capitalist potential of escape. I end with a brief reading of the video game *Bioshock*, which, even as it satirizes right-wing enclavism, nevertheless posits escape as the ultimate answer to the logics of capital and political authority. The poetics and politics of escape has a broad, trans-media presence—for so much contemporary poetry, fiction, film, and even video games, the left cannot give up on exit.

Unease towards state-backed representations pervades contemporary culture, yet critics rarely think of this period in American literature in these terms. That invites a return to these texts on which so much has already been said, clueing us in to the ways familiar animosities to representation are often tied up in an unfulfilled urge to escape the state.

ESCAPE'S EDGES

Limited Politics of Exit in William Carlos Williams and Charles Olson

WILLIAM CARLOS WILLIAMS'S "An Early Martyr," the title poem to his slim volume *An Early Martyr and Other Poems* (1935), opens the collection with the narrative of a man who "stole from / Exclusive stores / then sent post-cards / To the police / to come and arrest him."[1] As suggested by the poem's dedication, Williams bases this strange story on the life of a man named John Coffey, a New York City thief who openly admitted his actions to the law—"On one occasion he actually went in person to the prosecutor's office and reported to the assistant prosecutor his thieving activities of the night before," as Williams relates in his article "A Man versus the Law" (printed in the June 23, 1920, issue of *The Freeman*, edited by the libertarian anarchist Albert Jay Nock).[2] According to Williams, Coffey planned "to make out a case against the law itself and to bring to light effectively by direct action the law's fundamental weakness as a human instrument."[3] By openly stealing from department stores and confessing his acts to authorities, Coffey hoped to confront the law's injustices and expose its contradictions. The law, Williams explains, cannot "adjudge something outside of itself, such as the deeds of a man whose motives do not approach its codifications in any way, without working an injustice from its own point of view.... Thus a man must acknowledge the validity of the law either by fleeing from it or otherwise, before its procedures can become just in his case.... By giving himself up willingly Coffey circumvented the law by forcing it to do him an injustice or to acknowledge a competitor."[4] According to Williams, Coffey's strategy has put him "outside of" the law, but this results not from running away but rather from moving openly into the law. Fleeing the police or attempting to hide his theft would implicitly acknowledge the law's justice and authority. By refusing to do so, Coffey puts the law at an "impasse," and in Williams's telling, the state struggles to know what to do with him: the prosecutor's office "refused to apprehend or to molest him in any way." Later, when his thefts could no longer be ignored and he finally goes on trial, a physician at court asks of Coffey, "What can we do with you? I can't send you to jail and I can't let you go back on the street."[5] Finally, the state sidesteps the problem by declaring Coffey insane.

Williams is clearly unsatisfied by the state's answer to Coffey's challenge. In "An Early Martyr," the Coffey-inspired martyr becomes "a factory whistle / That keeps blaring—/ Sense, sense, sense!" a reminder and rallying cry exhorting a "romantic period / Of a revolt" (378). The state and its law are a "set-up / he fought against," but despite the martyr's sacrifice, the set-up "Remains—" (378). In "A Man versus the Law," Williams explains that, in this battle between a man and the law, "there could be only one answer: the man must win. The law can have no defence under these conditions, except that of arbitrary decision, to disqualify the man."[6] It is "a piece of stupidity as revolting to human nature as the bloody excesses of the Inquisition."[7] Moreover, for Williams this is not simply a matter of incompetent administration of the law, a historically contingent lapse in the state's functioning, but "the whole logical foundation of the law."[8] The problem here is not bad legislation or a corrupt politician. To Williams's mind, Coffey has exposed a fundamental flaw in the state, which can admit no "competitor": "The law can not withstand scrutiny when that scrutiny involves freedom of decision regarding itself."[9] The law cannot justify itself in the face of the demand to depart from it; neither law-abiding citizen nor criminal fighting the law, Coffey attempts to leave the law behind entirely. He does not escape, of course. The law brings him back under its purview by declaring him insane, bringing the outside of its norms back into itself, but this is only an "arbitrary decision," revealing, for Williams, the law's stupidity and brutishness.

However, even though Coffey's method, especially as Williams explains it in "A Man versus the Law," aims at an escape from the state, Williams also highlights a countervailing thrust deeper into the state. This is most apparent in the poem's version of the story, where the martyr's goal seems less to generate a logic outside the law and more to be heard by the state, "to testify in court / Giving reasons / why he stole" (377). The martyr works towards greater inclusion within the state, and the state's response, declaring him insane, appears as a way of getting rid of him rather than bringing him safely back into its domain: "They railroaded him / to an asylum" and "They let him go / in the custody of / A relative on condition / that he remain / Out of the state—," outside of the individual US state where he was tried, but also with the secondary meaning that he remain outside the state structure altogether. For Williams, Coffey actually succeeded in getting "outside of" the law, but that serves only to expose the law's problems, not solve them. Williams finds the state intolerably flawed, but here, he remains ambivalent towards escape as a potential solution.[10]

While the twentieth-century poetry that is the focus of this chapter clearly responds to its immediate historical contexts, from the New Deal to 1960s counterculture, it also points us towards the much longer history of the state as such. A hundred years after Williams's article on Coffey, for example, the popular television series *Silo* (2023–), based on Hugh Howey's series of novels by that name (2011–13), features a strikingly similar dilemma to the one posed by Williams, offering a helpful illustration of some of this chapter's key concerns and gesturing towards the broader, ongoing presence of this complicated desire to escape the state. The setting of *Silo* is postapocalyptic, with humanity confined to an underground citystate, the eponymous silo stretching down instead of up, hermetically sealed off from the poisonous atmosphere above ground. The show's inaugural episodes focus on the silo's sheriff, Holston Becker, who, after extensive deliberation and preparation, declares to his deputy, "I want to go out."[11] This spoken demand to leave the silo—to leave the state—is the ultimate crime, and it carries with it the ultimate punishment: right before banishing

Holston to the outside, the mayor ceremoniously declares, "You have been charged with and convicted of violating the cardinal law of our society. Any spoken request to leave the silo is granted, but it is irrevocable.... Once outside the air lock, you are outside the law."[12] From the perspective of the law and the social norms of the silo, wanting to go out is not only criminal but insane: like Coffey's declaration against the law made to the law, Holston's statement to his deputy casts him outside not only the law but humanity itself, which, in the postapocalyptic closed system of the silo, amount to the same thing, perfectly and unambiguously coextensive and coterminous. To the silo's inhabitants, Holston's desire can only be understood as madness.

Interestingly, the show draws out the mystery of the outside world until the season one finale, tantalizingly suggesting that a secret shadow government is behind a conspiracy to portray the outside world as deadly and uninhabitable, preventing people from returning to what is actually a beautiful and free Earth above in order to maintain authoritarian control over the silo's captive populace. Repeatedly the show offers diegetic representations of that outside world—secret video footage from the silo's topside cameras—as a pastoral landscape, brilliantly green hills with birds flying serenely overhead. This sharply contrasts the camera feed actually given to the silo's populace: from their view, the world above is a gray, lifeless wasteland. The audience knows that the shadow government is manipulating these video images, but, until the season finale, the show pushes the pastoral as the real, the wasteland as the lie. Maybe going outside isn't dangerous because of airborne toxins, the show suggests, but because doing so would undermine political control.

The first novel in the series, *Wool*, however, almost immediately reveals this revolutionary hope to be a false one, focalizing through the now ex-sheriff Holston as he goes outside, breathes the polluted air, and dies. The show, in contrast, withholds that perspective, leaving open the possibility that the ex-sheriff is alive and free in the world above, only definitively revealing his fate in the final episode of season one. This change is clearly intended to heighten suspense and intrigue, but this mystery is intriguing precisely because it appeals to the political desire for exit, allowing the viewer, like Holston, to fantasize about what's out there in the world "outside the law." But there is no exit from the state, and the silo only grants the request to go outside because physically leaving the silo doesn't actually free you from the silo's government. The shadow government intentionally sabotages the environment suits given to exiles, a fact only revealed in the season finale. Going outside is a death sentence: the silo does not simply abandon the exiled body to the cruelty of a broken Earth, as it purports, but, in fact, actively ensures the exile's death.

As the silo wields the exile's own words of escape—"I want to go out"—against them, giving those words the force of a political decree, *Silo* dramatizes the marriage of representation and violence that is at the heart of the state and the crux of this book. Even as the show tempts us with an idyllic world beyond the state, it also subverts that dream, casting the state as a necessary, if problematic, bulwark against the isolation and death that lie beyond it.

Williams similarly displays a partial, perhaps fluctuating opposition to the political state. At times, he can seem almost anarchist. David Kadlec, for example, situates Williams within a history of anarchist thought, directly via Ezra Pound and Dora Marsden and, indirectly but more significantly, via a chain of influences running through John Dewey and American pragmatism back to the French anarchist Pierre-Joseph Proudhon and his influence on William James.[13] At other times, Williams's view of the state matches the one in *Silo*—evil, perhaps, but a necessary one, a barrier against a much more dangerous state of nature. In such moments, Williams seems interested in refining or improving the state—as, ultimately, he does here with Coffey.

We could speak similarly of Charles Olson, of course one of Williams's most significant poetic inheritors. Offhand remarks in Olson's prose frequently suggest strong antagonism to the state, if not dogmatic anarchism.[14] Yet, he also casts his poetic work as an attempt "to write a Republic."[15] Olson thus seems more interested in reimagining the state than overthrowing or escaping it. In Robert von Hallberg's influential account, Olson was a committed New Dealer whose opposition to the state was historically particular rather than abstract or philosophical: the hypocritical imperialism of American democracy should be replaced with a new form of government.[16]

Inconsistent though they are, these kernels of anti-state politics present in Williams's and Olson's work are important. Part of what makes the poetics of escape meaningful as a categorical concept, relating texts that otherwise might seem disparate, is its anti-state political content. While recognizing that these poets' politics can hardly be reduced to this motive, throughout this chapter, I emphasize moments of opposition to the state in their work so as to highlight Williams's and Olson's congruence with a broader poetics and politics. To the extent that they are skeptical of the state as a form of political organization and entertain the possibility of leaving the state behind, Williams and Olson verge on a poetics of escape.

Antagonism towards the state is an essential feature, but Williams's and Olson's most important contributions occur in their interrogations of literary representation. I argue that when Williams and Olson attribute political significance to literary representation, they often figure it specifically in terms of escape. Breaking out of the strictures of literary representation—for Williams, the logic of substitution, epitomized by metaphor and mimetic realism; for Olson, the most basic orthographic conventions—becomes a way of imagining a flight from political authority. This general structure—using exit from literary representation as a subset (or model, homology, or displacement) of escape from political representation—will remain a key aspect of the poetics of escape I seek to identify and describe in postmodernist and contemporary American literature.

Together, Williams and Olson also help delineate some of the complications that still plague the poetics of escape, problems that keep it an ongoing literary pursuit rather than an accomplished endeavor. For Williams, poetry that does not signify results in a kind of solipsism: words must mean in order to connect author and reader. Wholesale rejection of linguistic representation turns escape into escapism, a way of cutting oneself off from social reality. In consequence, Williams's interest in escape takes place entirely within a framework of linguistic representation that cannot itself be escaped. Poets ought to escape the artistic traditions of "crude symbolism" (the forced representations of metaphor) and mimetic realism (a false representation), but they ought not escape representation itself. Because Williams links aesthetics and politics so tightly, the political corollary here looks something like limited-government liberalism: most structures of political representation ought to be open, freely left at will, but there must remain an outer limit, a final threshold of political representation that holds people together and that cannot be transcended. As he puts it in a 1917 essay on Walt Whitman (from whom Williams got much of his equation of poetic form and politics), "American verse of today must have a certain quality of freedom, must be 'free verse' in a sense... It must be truly democratic, truly free for all—and yet it must be governed."[17]

Olson confronts this same dilemma between solipsistic anti-representation and an imprisoning, impassable final horizon of representation, and he largely continues the approach he inherits from Williams. However, Olson acknowledges—more explicitly than Williams—how his limited conception of escape amounts to asserting and entering into new centers of power and law (political and aesthetic). By highlighting the continuity and structural similarity between the new tradition he wants to enter and the old one he wants to leave behind, Olson helps us more fully recognize the difficulties facing the poetics of escape, showing just how far escape would have to be taken in order to serve revolutionary change. In Olson, the possibilities seem to be either exit bound to subsequent entrance, or else escapism. Olson's experimentation with both of these alternatives indicates his dissatisfaction with each; he circumlocutes (but does not achieve) a poetics of escape that is neither entrance nor escapism.

Williams and Olson each come up against what will remain one of the most persistent problems for the poetics of escape: how to escape representation without abandoning meaning, or, how to escape the state without abandoning other people. This is of course the quintessential Hobbesian perspective and justification for the state: the state is what prevents our descent into the war of all against all, allowing us to relate to one another as people rather than animals. Neither poet can fully commit to a poetics of escape. A final, inescapable horizon of representation and political authority must remain. This helps illuminate a central dilemma: the outer limit to escape is simultaneously representation and political authority. It is precisely their refusal to give up linguistic representation and the human connections it fosters—between speaker and listener, author and reader—that leads them to likewise acquiesce to political representation and, by extension, inclusion within the political state.

WILLIAMS'S EXIT-GOVERNED STATE, STATE-GOVERNED EXIT

Escape from it—but not by running
away.
—Williams, *Paterson*

One of Williams's more anthologized poems, "The Yachts," also from *An Early Martyr,* provides further insight into Williams's class-motivated interest in escape from the state. The bulk of the poem describes a seemingly idyllic, heroic yacht race—Paul Mariani suggests that "Williams was remembering the magnificent America's Cup yacht races he had seen off Newport, Rhode Island."[18] The poem's first eight stanzas describe the scene of the race. Then, in the concluding three stanzas, the poem famously takes a horrific, surreal turn as "the horror of the race dawns staggering the mind" and the sea on which the yachts race morphs into a mass of struggling bodies, "a sea of faces about them in agony, in despair . . . the whole sea become an entanglement of watery bodies" (389). The poem's political symbolism is clear: the yachts represent the privileged classes, held aloft by the toiling masses whom they have mastered. Williams confirms as much in a note filed with a 1955 letter, explaining that "it is a false situation which the yachts typify with the beauty of their movements while the real situation (of the poor) is desperate while 'the skillful yachts pass over'" (541). The wealthy seem beautiful and dignified, but this only obscures the plight of the poor they run over.

Christian Reed provides a brief but compelling reading of Williams's note and its oddly redundant gloss on "The Yachts." Reed points out, "Williams' explanation is structured as if three things were happening simultaneously (X 'while' Y 'while' Z), though in fact, he is describing two simultaneous events in a redundant way (X 'while' Y 'while' X)"—the yachts move while the poor struggle while the yachts move.[19] But it is this very bookended structure that is significant, Reed suggests, as it "stages the drama of containment (or perhaps, more literally, of circumscription, of writing that produces a boundary around something). Y—'the real situation (of the poor)'—is concealed within, contained on both ends by X—the 'false,' though thoroughly distracting, vision of the 'skillful yachts.'" Reed goes on to note instances of this X-Y-X structure within the poem itself, from the race's location in Narragansett Bay, "a sea which the land partly encloses / shielding [the yachts] from the too-heavy blows / of an ungoverned ocean," to the racecourse's "well guarded arena of open water" (388).

For Reed, the poem's primary work is thus demystification: though "bourgeois mythology" has the power to conceal the reality of poverty, "some approximation of the 'real' (a 'real' that discovers the apparently real to be 'false') is nonetheless shown to be salvageable through the work of the informed imagination." Implicitly, however, this seems to impute more political power to the imagination than Williams himself hopes. In his note, Williams explains, "the yachts do not sink but go on with the race while only *in the imagination* are they seen to founder. It is a false situation" (541; italics Williams's). "False situation" can work as a reference to the yachts' seeming beauty, the kind of "bourgeois mythology" Reed sees the poem undoing, but it more directly refers back to the yachts' appearance of foundering. It is precisely the imagination that perpetuates a false situation, an illusion of the masses wrecking the yachts; the reality is that the yachts sail on, unscathed, the other side of the coin to "the real situation (of the poor)." Demystification is not enough, and the imagination is not up to the political task demanded by the "cries rising in waves still as the skillful yachts pass over" (389). The poem does not escape Narragansett Bay, and instead of the revolutionary potential of an "ungoverned ocean" to "sink" the yachts "pitilessly," we get a thoroughly tamed "arena" in which the rich conduct their sport. As von Hallberg notes, even the poem's rhythm suggests mastery over unruliness, moving from a jarring enjambment to a "more stable, less suspended" rhythm by the closing stanzas.[20] Reed is right to note how the poem dramatizes containment, revealing the structure of class relations as they really are, the poor propping up the rich sheltered in the bay of strong government. Demystification, however, does not actually change the structure of power in the poem, and the yachts sail on even after we witness the horrific sea of bodies. The poem formally reproduces containment only to suggest its tragic inescapability.

"The Yachts" also enacts another failed escape, one that would have been of supreme importance to the Williams of *Spring and All* (1923). In that earlier hybrid collection of poems and prose manifesto, Williams repeatedly insists that art must make "an escape from crude symbolism," going so far as to attribute any value in his own work to just such an escape (189). Williams offers a fragmentary definition: "Crude symbolism is to associate emotions with natural phenomena such as anger with lightning, flowers with love it goes further and associates certain textures with" (188). For Williams, crude symbolism is related to mimetic realism's project of representing reality, reproducing nature as in a mirror; Williams wants art to have its own "independent existence," a conception in which nature and reality are "not opposed to art but apposed to it" (208). As he puts it in book 5 of *Paterson*, "a poem is a complete little universe. It exists separately."[21] Art must aspire not to mirror nature but to be like it, existing on its own, next to nature. Crude symbolism makes lightning stand in for anger, but Williams would have lightning be lightning. At bottom, what unites Williams's rejection of both crude symbolism and mimetic realism is a critique of the logic of representation, the substitution of words for life. "The Yachts" plainly does not escape representation in this way. It relies on crude symbolism: the sea is a straightforward metaphor for the oppressed proletariat, with the roiling waves associated with political unrest.[22] "The Yachts" quite directly fails *Spring and All*'s requirements for good art.

While this might seem to distinguish the Williams of the 1930s from the Williams of the 1920s, as critics often like to do,[23] that is not what I am suggesting here: in failing to live up to the prescription for poetic (and by extension, political) escape that Williams lays out in the prose sections of *Spring and All*, "The Yachts" actually duplicates the results of *Spring and All*'s poetry. That is, Williams's apparent acquiescence to crude symbolism in the 1930s was already self-consciously present in his 1920s poetry, even at the height of his theoretical opposition to it. *Spring and All*'s overarching project of inaugurating the new spring of poetry—destroying the old traditions of representation epitomized by crude symbolism and mimetic realism in order to make room for new creativity and imagination—is fraught with difficulty and self-conscious failure.

Take "The Farmer," for instance, the third poem in *Spring and All*, which turns the "artist figure of / the farmer" into analogs for the poet and page. Though "the harvest [is] already planted," the farmer is nevertheless "in deep thought ... among his blank fields" (186). The blankness of the fields evokes a blank page, yet the past tense "planted" implies that the field-page has already been inscribed. The combination is identical to the empty spaces that Jennifer Ashton identifies in Williams's "The Rose," which uses hanging articles to imply absent nouns.[24] It is a written blankness that foregrounds the refusal to represent. The farmer has his "hands in pockets"—he is neither planting nor writing—specifically because that leaves "room for thought." The farmer continues mentally "composing," artistic creation in the present progressive tense, despite the fact that planting-writing on the fields-page has been stopped by the past tense. If, as Ashton puts it, Williams's anti-representational ideal is to create "signifiers that can, in principle, at least, generate an infinite number and variety of effects," Williams's "The Farmer" gestures towards such an open-ended generation of creativity.[25] By refusing to represent, the farmer-artist opens up the possibility of an escape, as "On all sides / the world rolls coldly away" (186). Getting outside of representation opens up a space of creative freedom.

However, the representational logic of metaphor nevertheless remains stubbornly ineradicable here: the farmer is *like* an artist. The farmer marks his field with furrows just as the poet marks his page with lines. The primary thing relating them is the superficial similarity between the parallel lines on the field and on the page; farming and writing appear similar despite their differences. Metaphor, then, is not eradicated, and unlike his ideal farmer's field, Williams's page is far from blank. "The Farmer" exhibits Williams's professed desire to escape crude symbolism specifically and representation in general, but ultimately the poem dramatizes its own defeated flight.

Two poems later, in the last stanza of "The Black Winds," Williams explicitly acknowledges his struggle to escape representation, confiding, "How easy to slip / into the old mode, how hard to / cling firmly to the advance" (191). The resilient "old mode" of crude symbolism proves too tough to be got rid of. The poem's "black winds" here act as a destructive force that nevertheless signals fecundity, reiterating the book's governing season metaphor—crude symbolism if there ever was—in which a spring of new artistic creativity emerges out of the ground cleared by deadly winter. Elsewhere in the book, as in the first numbered poem "Spring and All" as well as in "The Farmer," cold winds drive away clouds hanging over the wasteland, bringing the landscape into sunlight and marking a transition from a degenerated past to a fertile present (183, 186). "Wind" acts as a metaphorical vehicle, with the process of true artistic innovation the tenor. The imagination, as wind, opens up escape from the old and ushers in the new. Thus, in the very act of evoking a dialectical progression from the old symbolism to a new spring of nonmetaphorical art, Williams repeatedly relies on metaphor. He seems fully aware of doing so and expresses a sense of frustration at the ineffectuality of his own artistic toil: "Black wind, I have poured my heart out / to you until I am sick of it—" (190). His very attempt to express resistance—the winds that would destroy the old way and inaugurate the new—becomes the site of its failure, falling back into the logic of representation.

That does not mean Williams entirely gives up on his flight from representation. He asserts a sharp rebuttal to his own metaphorical use of wind: "There is nothing in the twist / of the wind but—dashes of cold rain" (190). Wind does not metaphorically contain the imagination; all wind contains is the rain falling through it. Williams is not content simply to state this rejection of metaphor; he visually puns on it through his punctuation. There is nothing in the wind but dashes. There is nothing in the wind but—. "Dashes of cold rain" describes both what is in the wind as well as the immediately preceding punctuation mark. The em dash, perhaps Williams's favorite punctuation mark across his poetry, thus comes to suggest (at least in "The Black Winds," which features twelve em dashes) a raindrop, blown sideways in a strong wind. Instead of representing with the signifier "rain," Williams tries to give us rain itself, directly. This is the same move Lisa Siraganian identifies in Williams's use of the colon mark in "Flight to the City," *Spring and All*'s fourth poem, sitting between "The Farmer" and "The Black Winds." As Siraganian argues, the line "Nobody to say : pinholes" transforms the page of the poem "into a stage backdrop for its pinhole stars" referenced in the opening stanza. This is a way of giving us a sky "without linguistic imagery,"[26] a sky that is not crude symbolism's "sky ... as an association" (187), but simply the sky, a sky that does not represent but is simply itself.

This fails too, of course, in each of these three consecutive poems. Whether it's lines of text visually suggesting furrows in a field, a colon suggesting stars, or em dashes suggesting rain, this is still representation—just representation displaced from the linguistic to the visual, from the arbitrary representation of the sign to the physical mimesis of the icon. Even though each of these cunning experiments with concrete poetry displace linguistic representation, they nevertheless provide no route out of representation in its entirety. "This is not 'sky' purely as experienced by the reader," Siraganian explains, "for we are still observing imagery or representation of a kind. The page has become a visual representation of sky." This is "extralinguistic representation," but representation still.[27] Importantly, in "The Black Winds," Williams does still give us the signifier "rain"; he cannot seem to resist explaining—representing—the work he hopes his dashes will do. This is part of the reason he concludes the poem with his lament over his poetics of escape: even as he tries to "cling firmly to the advance" through his shrewd formal innovation, he nevertheless slips "into the old mode" (191).

In this struggle with crude symbolism, Siraganian argues, Williams compromises between representational and nonrepresentational poetry, resulting in "an art that aspires to embody democratically-governable liberty."[28] "Aligning aesthetic and political freedom," Williams aims to "control and contain the reader's total liberty" within the representational structure of the poem in order to "promote civil liberties and democratic freedoms while also paradoxically embodying control and authority."[29] Williams's limited representation suggests the limited government of classical liberalism.[30] There is substantial leeway for the reader as for the citizen, but it is always governed by a final boundary—authorial intention or state-backed law—that should not be transgressed.

This is precisely the politics Williams lays out in his important 1936 lecture "Revolutions Revalued." Emphasizing individual liberty as his primary political value, Williams wants "to escape" communism and fascism, both of which he sees as fundamentally totalitarian, and to "retain" liberal democracy, "defective though it has proven in practice, and make it fully effective" as a guarantor of personal freedom.[31] Here Williams echoes the logic he applied to Coffey's thievery, as he again figures exit as a limit to governmental power: exit prevents totalitarianism. Just as importantly, however, he also figures the state as a governing limit on exit: the state should give "individuals full play—*until* or unless their activities prove anti-social."³² Exit keeps state power in check, and vice versa.

Part of this reluctance to commit fully to abandoning representation, making the state a check against unrestrained exit, stems from a lingering belief in the authoritative expert. The genius poet, the doctor, the technocrat: they know what's best for the people, better than the people themselves know. In "Revolutions Revalued," Williams rejects precisely this logic, insisting that "no one is fitted to determine ... so well as [the individual]" which actions will be "socially valuable" and which will be antisocial, as "only the individual can know these things."³³ And yet, he also seems to believe, perhaps contradictorily, that individual geniuses can know things better than the multitudes—adopting, for instance, an essentially Romantic model of artistic genius, "an understanding of the poet as a social regenerator," which he concludes "is an important consideration for government."³⁴ As Siraganian puts it, "Williams satirizes the paternalism of the state and mocks the moralism and racism of earlier Progressive reform activities (such as Prohibition), while also on some level admitting the doctor's own desire to be the rakish savior."³⁵ Or, as Joel Nickels puts it in his discussion of Williams's interest in the Social Credit movement, the "image of the poet as a social healer does not altogether disappear from the symbolic economy of *Paterson*," and whenever Williams cannot quite conceptualize the multitude's capacity to organize and coordinate itself, he falls back on the authority of "the poetic genius or the Social Credit technocrat."³⁶ Even as Williams wants to protect individual freedom, he nevertheless reserves a place for the authoritative expert.

Williams clearly dramatizes this tension between the ungoverned and the paternalistic expert in his short story "The Use of Force" (1938), in which a doctor forcibly pries open a child's mouth to diagnose her illness, an act of violence that the story depicts as loathsome but also a "social necessity" because "the damned little brat must be protected against her own idiocy ... Others must be protected against her."³⁷ Even as the doctor feels ashamed of himself, having "fallen in love with the savage brat" and admiring her rebellious spirit, the story nevertheless depicts the doctor's authoritative use of force as justified and unavoidable.³⁸

Again, though, Williams depicts this rebellion against authority in terms of both anti-representation and escape, and considered in this light, we can begin to see the other side of Williams's allowance for violent authority, beyond guiltily succumbing to the allure of the poet-doctor-legislator. Williams ends "The Use of Force" by describing the girl's rebellion as an attempt "to escape" the discovery of her illness.[39] Keeping her illness secret, of course, would be no escape from the illness itself, and the story does not suggest that the girl is so deluded. Rather, the point of the child's escape would have been (if it had succeeded) to escape the authoritative representation of her illness, the doctor's diagnosis of diphtheria. But the girl's attempted escape requires a total abstention from representation, which is to say a withdrawal from communication and human community. Throughout most of the story, the girl remains stubbornly silent, refusing the doctor's addresses; indeed, she must not speak, for she literally cannot open her mouth lest the doctor insert his tongue depressor and examine the back of her throat. At one point the girl does "let out a scream . . . she shrieked terrifyingly, hysterically. Stop it! Stop it!" but then, as soon as the doctor makes another attempt with his tongue depressor, she again "fought, with clenched teeth."[40] The girl's escape from authoritative representation never could have succeeded—the doctor and his allies, the parents, physically overwhelm her—but even before that, her hope of escape rested on her willingness to forgo contact with the people around her.

Two problems with the poetics of escape thus come to light. First, the chances of actually escaping seem slim. In art, Williams formally enacts his own struggles to escape crude symbolism and mimetic realism, specific forms of representation. This parallels his portrayals of escape in more directly political settings, where authorities can simply prevent escape through brute strength. In this sense, there is only an entrapping escapism, not actual escape, what Williams critiques as "a man bind[ing] himself by ignoring the truths that he cannot escape, no matter how hard he may run."[41] Second, despite these difficulties, Williams does consider escape routes out of representation in art and politics, but these escapes are extremely costly. Even if the girl in "The Use of Force" could somehow fend off the doctor's violence, her escape would still cost her any linguistic connection to other people—a kind of social death, here biologically reiterated through the mortal threat of untreated diphtheria.

Williams suggests that escape at the cost of communication is not worth it. In *Spring and All*, he hints at this negative corollary in his praise of Marianne Moore. Though she "escapes" crude symbolism, he clarifies that "the incomprehensibility of her poems is witness to at what cost (she cleaves herself away)" (188). For Williams, Moore's successful escape comes at the cost of losing the connection of comprehension, what he describes as "a fraternal embrace, the classic caress of author and reader" (178). The imagination, where this relationship takes place, must escape old, obdurate systems of representation, but exiting the relationship itself would not help anything.

This perspective should add further valence to Williams's assertion that "composition is in no essential an escape from life" (189). On first reading, this claim is another aspect of William's rejection of the art-reality dichotomy. The next paragraph begins, "what I put down of value will have this value: an escape from crude symbolism, the annihilation of strained associations, complicated ritualistic forms designed to separate the work from 'reality'" (189). Successful composition is not an escape from life, because it *is* an escape from crude symbolism, eliminating the division between art and life. But the work of the imagination is also not an escape from life in the sense that it is not a withdrawal into solipsism but rather persists in representing the author's ideas to the reader. Later, in the context of again rejecting the representational logic of mimetic realism, Williams rhetorically asks, "But—but why continue without an audience?" (209). The stuttered "but" here indicates the tension Williams feels: the logic of representation peddled by authority and tradition must be escaped, but if that means escaping representation altogether, abandoning the reader and the human connection of language, what is the point?

Thus the poetics of escape halts in Williams: ultimately, he sees escape devolving into escap*ism*, a withdrawal from language and social life. Consider a final, brief example from *Paterson*, which suggests the ongoing importance of escape for Williams, beyond the few poems I have focused on here. In the opening poem of *Paterson* book 3, Williams reiterates this conflict between escape and escapism, summing up his inability to reconcile his desire to escape dead artistic representation and the political state with his desire to remain inside language and human sociality. "It is summer!" not the revolutionary season of *Spring and All*, "Stinking summer // Escape from it—but not by running / away. Not by 'composition.' Embrace the foulness."[42] Williams's pun here is too good to ignore. In *Spring and All*, he allegorizes life as a "bizarre fowl" (180), whose "[escape] from its cage" (184) corresponds with the arrival of spring. Escape the smothering heat of summer and embrace the *fowl*-ness of spring, the "prismatically plumed bird of life" (184)—escape in order to embrace life rather than run away from it. But the striking ambivalence of Williams's quotation marks around "composition" hints at his more general equivocation. Are they scare quotes, mocking false methods of composition? Or is he quoting himself, essentially inverting his claim in *Spring and All* ("composition is in no essential an escape from life"), making composition an escape from life after all, opposed to embracing life? Either way, the poet does not seem capable of accomplishing the kind of non-escapist composition demanded in *Spring and All*.

The danger in *Paterson*, once more, is the loss of linguistic representation, to which Williams adds explicitly political ramifications. Exasperated, the speaker exhorts one to "Give it up. Quit it. Stop writing" and to "Give up / the poem" because one will never get rid of the "stain of sense."[43] Instead, he prescribes departure from signification, commanding to "Quit it. Quit this place. Go where all / mouths are rinsed : to the river for an answer / for relief from 'meaning.'"[44] Escaping, leaving this place, amounts to escapism, leaving behind meaning and, by extension, the human relationships it makes. The poem makes the political analog explicit: "Doctor, do you believe in / 'the people,' the Democracy?"[45] Is it possible to escape the representational fiction of "the people," to escape reified state Democracy, and still believe in democracy? Is it possible to quit this place without giving up sense and meaning?

Williams wrestles with this problem often, but he never seems quite satisfied with his own answers. The only escape is into non-meaning and non-community, an illusory exit, and so Williams allows a final horizon of representation in both art and politics that will not be crossed. Some residue of analogy and mimesis must remain in art, and in politics (because art and politics are so tightly bound for Williams) a residual democratic state and body of law must likewise persist.

Olson rejects escapism by the same logic, refusing its avoidance of reality and its isolation from human sociality; on this issue, Olson's influential essay "Projective Verse" and his subsequent projectivist poetry should be seen as continuing, unbroken, the project of its modernist predecessor in Williams. However, Olson also experiments, in at least one important poem, with pushing his flight from representation further, testing the boundaries of a poetics of escape at the risk of mis-stepping into an escapism, losing the connection between author and reader, that he would rather avoid. Like Williams, Olson is not entirely successful, but he broadens the horizon of possibility, making a non-escapist poetics of escape at least a feasible proposition.

EXIT FOR ENTRANCE'S SAKE: OLSON'S SPIRAL INTO POLIS

Turning and turning in the widening gyre
The falcon cannot hear the falconer;
Things fall apart; the centre cannot hold;
Mere anarchy is loosed upon the world
—W. B. Yeats, "The Second Coming"

The hobo, the hermit, the hippie: the figure of the societal dropout provides a convenient way into thinking about Olson's poetic search for escape. In 1960, Olson published the first volume of what would become his twenty-year, three-volume work, *The Maximus Poems*. The opening four poems of that initial volume consider the dropout strategy that would soon enchant blooming hippie culture. After the first three poems depict advertising and property ownership as an inescapable siren song that enslaves people to consumerism (our poetic speaker Maximus explicitly among them), "The Songs of Maximus" suggests a solution: "In the midst of plenty, walk / as close to / bare ... In the land of plenty, have / nothing to do with it / take the way of / the lowest, / including / your legs, go / contrary, go" (I.15).[46] This entrapment is specifically a matter of ubiquitous representation, with freedom of mind and action limited by "words, words, words / all over everything," prompting an abiding problem for Olson, of "how [to] get out of anywhere" (I.13). The early answer of volume 1 looks like hippie dropout culture: instead of buying into consumerism, refuse to go along. Escape the capitalist state by dropping out of the official economy.

This was still six years before Timothy Leary would urge thirty thousand hippies in Golden Gate Park to "turn on, tune in, drop out" in 1966 (and an even earlier edition of the opening *Maximus* poems appeared in 1953), but Olson was not the first to contemplate dropouts as potential escapees. Williams, for example, turns his gaze to a couple of truants in *An Early Martyr*'s "Late for Summer Weather," "an anarchistic poem," according to von Hallberg, because it asserts that "political organizing and activities are beside the point": "the drop-outs of the 1930s, they represented a life outside of political and economic institutions."⁴⁷ The couple in the poem is anarchistic in the sense of being entirely apolitical, not in the sense of smashing the state: they have abandoned responsibility and the rest of society, "Ambling / nowhere" with "Nothing to do."⁴⁸ The ease with which these truants have made their exit also makes it suspect: you can't call it escape if no one is chasing you. Rather than actually escaping the intertwined power of capital and the state, the couple ignores it. The worry here is that this is not escape but escapism.

Though Williams usually shied away from such escapism, he continued to probe its potential for political transformation—as did Olson and many other poets to come after, especially in connection to the emerging Beat culture in the 1950s and the hippie movement in the 1960s. Williams himself is a part of those histories, most notably through his mentorship and correspondence with Allen Ginsberg, writing the introduction for the publication of *Howl and Other Poems* in 1956, a book itself rife with hobos clacking in "boxcars boxcars boxcars" trying to break away from state capitalism, "Moloch the incomprehensible prison."⁴⁹

This dropout trope gets one of its most thorough expositions from another of Williams's correspondents, the San Francisco poet Lawrence Ferlinghetti. Two years after Ferlinghetti published Ginsberg's *Howl* through his bookstore-publisher, City Lights Books, Ferlinghetti's own influential book of poems, *A Coney Island of the Mind* (1958), grappled with the dilemma of countercultural dropout and the problem of escapism. Through a back-and-forth of conflicting revolutionary attitudes, the first three poems of the section "Oral Messages" dramatize uncertainty about the political usefulness of dropping out of mainstream society in general and, specifically, the capitalist state system.

In the first poem of the sequence, "I am Waiting," the only hope for escaping the chains of the state is patient passivity, with the poem's title its straightforward refrain: "I am waiting / for the final withering away / of all governments."[50] This poem's political logic depends on a simple historical dialectic (appropriating the language of Friedrich Engels) in which the capitalist state will eventually tear itself apart; all we can do is wait. The next poem, "Junkman's Obbligato," then provides a counterpoint, remixing W. B. Yeats's "I will arise and go now" and T. S. Eliot's "Let us go then, you and I" into an iterative refrain that emphasizes actively fleeing the system, a "Let's go" that directly opposes the previous poem: "Let us not wait."[51] Like Olson's "go / contrary, go," here the act of "going" specifically requires an act of severance: "Let's cut out let's go."[52] Exit is no easy task, because "going" is precisely what is not allowed, as the poem suggests in its darker moments: "Let them come / and take it away / whatever it was / we were paying for. / And us with it."[53] Dropping out of the official, legally guaranteed economy does not get you out, freed from material worry, but gets you taken away, captive. By the end, the poem self-consciously exposes its own latent, unworkable utopianism. The Junkman declares, "I must arise and go now / to the Isle of Manisfree / way up behind the broken words / and woods of Arcady," punning a pastoral, anarchic island paradise into existence, a ridiculous Virgilian fantasy where you can get "poppies out of cowpods / thinking angels out of turds."[54] Ferlinghetti sympathizes with the political idealism of the Beats and nascent hippie culture, but he is also already satirizing it, as in the self-deprecating call to "Take up the full beard / of walking anarchy."[55] The speaker of the third poem, "An Autobiography," declares, "It is long since I was a herdsman . . . I see where Walden Pond has been drained / to make an amusement park."[56] This wide-ranging intertextuality expands the perspective beyond the immediate history of mid-century dropout culture, asserting a much wider scope for this political desire for exit. Simultaneously, though, it asserts a historical present in which that exit is impossible—not as an essential fact of human existence but as a consequence of political history. The pastoral fantasies of Virgil, Thoreau, Yeats, and the Junkman are given up, inaccessible to present reality. Though the Junkman obliges us to arise and go with him, Ferlinghetti concludes that he and we all are obligated to stay put.

Confronting this impasse, Ferlinghetti seems to settle on a kind of individual, psychic withdrawal from these inescapable systems. With the lines "I see a similarity / between dogs and me. / Dogs are the true observers," the speaker of "An Autobiography" unambiguously points us towards the next poem in the sequence, "Dog," a poem which finally seems to offer some closure to the debate of the previous three.[57] The poem describes a dog who "doesn't hate cops / He merely has no use for them ... He would rather eat a tender cow / than a tough policeman / though either might do."[58] This dog seems to have attained a transcendent autonomy in which his freedom does not depend upon the social and material conditions that surround him:

> he has his own free world to live in
> His own fleas to eat
> He will not be muzzled
> Congressman Doyle is just another
> fire hydrant
> to him
> The dog trots freely in the street
> and has his own dog's life to live.[59]

This *Überhund* need not escape policemen or politicians, because in his own personal world, they are irrelevant, beneath his concern. Ferlinghetti thus settles on a self-conscious escapism. Unlike the uncritical Junkman he sympathetically mocks, who deludes himself with the hope that his withdrawal from the system will change it, Ferlinghetti accepts that his escape will be an internal condition; the dog escapes the unbearable world of police by becoming the center of his own little private world.

Like Ferlinghetti, Olson rejects the hippie-style dropout strategy even as he too observes a need for escape. Though Olson's ontology of the self is incompatible with the atomistic quality of Ferlinghetti's dog's escape—he understands the individual as thoroughly embedded in and constituted by external political, social, and environmental forces—Olson nevertheless explores a political and artistic escape that is structurally similar to the dog's inward withdrawal into a new center. Where the dog's escape makes the private self the new center, making the individual the lone sovereign over his own private universe, Olson makes projectivist poetics and his ideal "polis" into new centers, into guiding authorities in art and politics. In Olson's poetry, escaping old centers of power culminates in entering new ones, a dynamic running through much of *The Maximus Poems,* with roots reaching back to his famous "Projective Verse" essay. However, as we will see through a close look at a series of poems related by the figure of the spiral, near the end of his life Olson also considered what it might mean to subvert his own long-standing poetics, escaping some of his own previous centers but without offering any apparent replacement to be entered.

The Maximus Poems most explicitly considers the political value of escape through the historical figure of William Stevens, a seventeenth-century ship carpenter who, Olson explains early on, "left Plymouth Plantation, / and came to Gloucester ... until Gloucester, too, got too proper / and he left, fended for himself" (I.30). Olson emphasizes, "That carpenter is much on my mind / I think he was the first Maximus" (I.31), so it is compelling that this captivating first Maximus is one whose primary political acts consist of running away. Indeed, one of our earliest characterizations of Maximus of Gloucester makes him both everyman and slave: he is like "any knowing man of your city," and "he is slave / whom you read ... whose slaver / would keep you off the sea, would keep you local" (I.12). At the foundation of *The Maximus Poems* is a city of people defined by their entrapment, unable to move away. Olson explains, "why I chose to use Maximus of Tyre as the figure of speech, figure of the speech, is that I regard Gloucester as the final movement of the earth's people, the great migratory thing ... migration ended in Gloucester. The migratory act of man ended in Gloucester."[60] Here Olson locates the final frontier earlier and farther east than he did in *Call Me Ishmael,* where it is the Pacific, but the dynamic remains the same. There is nowhere left to run away, "so that the last *polis* or city *is* Gloucester," and it would seem politics must involve perfecting this final polis, the one we are stuck with.[61]

This makes it all the more interesting that Stevens *does* leave Gloucester, Massachusetts; Stevens helps Olson consider what political role escape can play after the great historical epoch of migration has ended—what happens if Maximus of Gloucester tries to leave unleavable Gloucester. Stevens and his descendants pop up here and there throughout *The Maximus Poems*, but his next significant appearance is in "the winning thing" in volume 2, where Olson alludes to some of the historical details of Stevens's life. First, "when signing the oath asked of all Americans then / to pledge allegiance to a new English king," the recently restored Charles II, "Stevens / is listed as ship carpenter" (II.48). However, Stevens, along with others, apparently "refused" to sign the oath, and as a result "Stevens dwindled" (II.48). George Butterick's indispensable *Guide to the Maximus Poems* helpfully explicates with a quote from Olson's source, John J. Babson's 1860 *History of the Town of Gloucester:* "It was a grave offense, in those days, to speak evil of rulers; and discretion would have counselled silence," but Stevens's neighbors testified in court "to his declaring 'that he would bear no office within this jurisdiction, nor anywhere else, where Charles Stewart had any thing to do; and that he cared no more for Charles Stewart than any other man, as king; and that he abhorred the name of Charles Stewart as king.' For this bold and rash expression of his hatred of the king, the offender was sentenced to a month's imprisonment; to pay a fine of £20 and costs; and to be deprived of his privileges as a freeman."[62] With the English Civil War and Interregnum still recent history, Stevens openly rebelled against the king and was punished as a result.

Olson maintains a small hope in Stevens's capacity to resist the sovereign, and it rests specifically on Stevens's potential escape. "Stevens dwindled," at least "on the face of the record," but Olson continues, "I'm not sure he did. . . . he ran away, age 70, to wherever he / did go" (II.48). Butterick concludes that "there is no report of this in the published histories," and Stevens's escape takes extra weight if it is Olson's invention.[63] I speculate that Olson is embellishing on the petition of Stevens's wife, Phillipa, to "the General Court for relief / from his punishment for refusing / to sign the Oath of Allegiance," referenced in volume 3's "Stevens song" (III.30). Butterick quotes Babson's reproduction of Phillipa Stevens's petition: "my husband having been absent about three weeks, in which time they came for the fine, and not as yet is he returned."⁶⁴ Olson thus seems to home in on the open-endedness of this three-week absence, extrapolating it, plausibly, into a permanent flight from Gloucester and Charles II's power there. Stevens models for Olson a political resistance premised on escape.

All of this culminates quite explicitly in "Stevens song": "Stevens ran off, / having called Charles the Second / a king he could not give allegiance to" (III.30). Olson compares Stevens's "remarks / to officers of the Crown / which were considered / seditious" to his father Charles Olson Sr.'s "insubordinate" remarks to his bosses in the United States Postal Service, a parallel reinforced by Olson's memoir of his father, *The Post Office*, where he describes his father's disobedience as "insubordination to duty, to the Postmaster, to the President, to God."⁶⁵ The poem then flatly juxtaposes their contrasting strategies of political resistance: "Stevens ran off / My father // stayed / & was ground down / to death" (III.31). Notably, Stevens and Olson Sr. are politically distinguishable not because they inhabit distinct political histories (British colonial rule and twentieth-century democracy) but rather because they respond to the same fundamental political reality, the state, with diametric attitudes towards escape. Stevens's fate remains uncertain, but that at least leaves open the possibility of hope, whereas Olson's father is doomed. Running away thus seems better than staying, which Olson equates with his father's attempt "to fight back / with usual American political / means, Senator David I. Walsh, Congressman / Hobbs, Pehr Holmes Mayor and so forth" (III.31). Here, politics as usual will not do any good, but running away might.

Only, there is a problem with Stevens's escape, one obvious to Olson, who still had a relationship with his father for fourteen more years precisely because Charles Sr. did not run away. Staying eventually cost Olson's father his life,⁶⁶ but running away cost William Stevens his connection to other people, including his wife, Phillipa, who is left to pay for his crime. This is the same problem with escape that Williams identified with a total escape from representation: it is solipsistic, sacrificing mutual interconnection with others, the kind of human connection made possible by language. Indeed, Olson can only imagine Stevens's escape because Stevens eludes linguistic representation, disappearing from the historical record—significant in light of Olson's own echo of Williams's insistence on signification as the basis of human relationships.⁶⁷ Escaping the political authority of the king—and the Postmaster, President, and God, too—means abandoning the power of language to relate people to each other, leaving the individual isolated and cut off from the dynamic, creative forces of society.

This indeed is where "Stevens song" goes next, turning from escape towards entrance, with the purpose of prioritizing the interpolation of self and outside, subject and object, as a counter to solipsistic escapism. Olson riffs on canines as antagonists to authority, but unlike Ferlinghetti's dog and its withdrawal into its own private world, Olson's dogs and wolves oppose political authority by entering more fully into the world: "On the side / of the King the Father // there sits a wolf / which is not his own will // which comes from outside" (III.31). There is a productive ambiguity here. The wolf is not Charles's will—neither King Charles II's nor father Charles Olson Sr.'s—and is thus subversive. But the coincidence of names suggests that the wolf is also not our poet's will, and the unclear antecedent of "his" allows for the possibility that the wolf is also not the wolf's own will, containing some kind of difference within himself. In all of these permutations, an opposing will enters from outside, countering authority's will and situating the self as a nexus of external forces, breaking down the private individual so that we can separate neither one Charles from another nor any of them from the external will that invades them. The rest of the poem piles on various characterizations and images of this canine, all of which contribute to a figure that opposes political authority by entering into some kind of relation to human life. Variously a "demon" or a "creature, from outer space," "the dirty filthy whining ultimate thing // entered" (III.31–33). Repeatedly coming in from outside, entering into and entered by others' bodies, entrance provides an alternative to Stevens's running away and Olson Sr.'s staying.

Entering and being entered becomes a way of transgressing the boundaries and barriers imposed by authority. In "Projective Verse," Olson figures going into the self as a way of accessing the wider world, because the self is where all the forces of the world intersect and materialize: the poet who "stays inside himself, if he is contained within his nature as he is participant in the larger force, he will be able to listen, and his hearing through himself will give him secrets objects share."⁶⁸ And yet, there is a contradiction underlying this sort of entrance as an anti-state political strategy: if the mutual entrance of world into self and self into world is a way of eliminating individualizing political boundaries, it must also be admitted that the state is one of the external forces that enter into and shape the self.[69] In "Maximus to Gloucester, Letter 27 [withheld]," Olson expounds his understanding of the self as a nexus of intersecting social and historical forces, "the precessions of me" dynamically changing through time (II.14). Foremost among these forces that shape the self is the nation-state: "An American / is a complex of occasions" (II.15). However, here Olson also stresses the persistence of a solid, coherent self that stands against such external forces, explaining,

>   I have this sense,
> that I am one
> with my skin
>   Plus this—plus this:
> that forever the geography
> which leans in
>   on me I compell
> backwards I compell Gloucester
> to yield, to
> change
>   Polis
> is this (II.15)

Anne Day Dewey reads these lines as indicating the dissolution of the coherent liberal subject, with skin placing the speaker "in immediate contact with his environment" and highlighting the social and environmental constitution of the individual.[70] Yet, the wholeness of the individual, contained and made one by the skin, seems just as important to Olson here. As Paul Stephens points out, "Olson's gestures during a filmed reading of the poem in 1966 suggest that the 'this' in 'polis is this' is Olson's own body."[71] In a letter to Robert Creeley, Olson explains, "What I was searching for was the simplest, to say how we do have this sense of unity with our body."[72] The poetic speaker, appearing as a relatively stable "I" that is at one with itself, expels the forces around him—notably a "geography," a written world, indicating Olson's interest in the representational manifestations of power—out of himself. Olson imagines the self insulating and protecting itself from the wider environment that has nevertheless shaped and constituted that self.

Importantly, Olson understands this as a political act, one that, while preserving the self, causes society to "change." The poem concludes "Polis / is this" (II.15), allowing us to read this dynamic of opposing forces as Olson's political ideal, a global, utopian city-state alive with change. Butterick quotes from Olson's unpublished essay "The Methodology Is the Form": "'what is our polis (even allowing that no such thing can be considered as possible to exist...)?' His answer is, 'the very whole world,' not 'a bit smaller than the whole damn thing'; it is 'the State,' 'The System,' the 'totality,' adding that it is necessary 'to invert totality—to oppose it—by discovering the totality of any—every—single one of us.'"[73] For Olson, the self is so completely constituted by the forces around it that the individual can be said to be equivalent to the totality, even as the individual remains intact as a discrete being, not dissolving into an abstraction such as "the People." "Polis is / eyes" (I.26) and "There are no hierarchies, no infinite, no such many as mass, there are only / eyes in all heads, / to be looked out of" (I.29). Instead of hierarchical impositions of social, economic, and political forces ("It is not bad / to be pissed off / where there is any / condition imposed, by whomever" [II.160]), Olson posits a multitude of bodies, individual selves each with their own set of eyes (or "I's") to turn each into their own polis, the polis.

Olson thus figures the self as a synecdoche for a new kind of ideal, universal state, a polis that is both like and constituted by "any—every—single one of us." This serves to resolve the contradiction of escaping a restrictive state by entering a self that is shaped by the state; the self is not made through the restrictive state, which opposes the self, but the ideal state, polis, which is one with the self. Entering the self amounts to entering the field of sociality—entering polis and expelling the state that "leans in on me" (II.15).

This political ontology becomes clearer in a series of poems engaging with the figure of the spiral. In "Physically, I am home. Polish it," after admonishing, "Be Charles the / Product (of the Process)," again figuring the self as the condensate of external forces, the poem asserts a set of identities that once more links the self to the pluralistic perspective of the many-eyed polis but also to the shape of the spiral (hand-drawn spirals appear in facsimile in Butterick's edition of the poem, which I indicate here in brackets): "I, / Charles [spiral] the / Vision (Video to 'look' View Point / see (C [spiral spiral spiral]" (III.84).[74] The comma between "I" and "Charles" indicates a renaming apposition, and the lack of any other syntax implies that this function continues over the following lines. The spiral suggests a visual extension of the I/eye pun, surfacing the "polis" hidden in "Polish," while also potentially suggesting a lack of autonomy due to being dazed or hypnotized, compelled by an external force—a visual trope long commonplace in popular cartoons such as *Looney Tunes*. The poem thus equates a series of terms: I-Charles-Product is eye-polis-spiral.

The spirals also seem to grow out of Olson's initials, linking this nonautonomous viewpoint (as well as our poetic speaker, Maximus, the poems' "I") back to his individuality: Butterick notes "Spirals for the C and O of his name ... near 'spiral, symbolic ... "spiral of entry.""[75] Butterick is quoting here from *The Gate of Horn* (1948) by Gertrude Rachel Levy, whose account of spiraling feathers on the crowns of Egyptian rulers appears to have motivated much of Olson's interest in the spiral and helps clarify its political implications. Olson has underlined in his copy of Levy "the spiral of entry," which refers to a "Libyan ostrich feather" on the front of Egyptian crowns.[76] This appears explicitly in his poem "Cornély," where getting "off into the land" is accomplished by "twisting ... like Libya's feather / stuck out on the front of the Crown of Egypt / go right the curve is clock-wise, / go left / the curve / is left-wards" (III.95). Here, the spiral can take one into or out of political power, depending on whether one goes clockwise or counterclockwise. This dynamic is reinforced by the poem's topical interest in the legend of Saint Cornély, whose "arrival" follows "his flight from the Roman / soldiery," enacting an escape that culminates in entrance, with the ultimate result that one "can't go anywhere / except back to that impossible Nation" (III.95). Overlaying the spirals in "Physically, I am home" (equivalents to "Charles / the Product"), the kingly Egyptian feather spiral provides Olson a way to link deeper entrance into the self with entrance into an idealized form of political power, while figuring both as an escape from the historical, repressive state. Escape is the response to intolerable political power, Roman soldiers, but it leads to entrance into polis, the establishment of a new, hopefully better nation—as Olson puts it near the end of *The Maximus Poems,* "the initiation / of another kind of nation" (III.228). Going into the self—Charles, Maximus of Gloucester, synecdoche for the many-eyed polis, which is the product of social processes just as the spiral is the artefactual trace of the journey inward—means going into a new kind of state.

We can see this pairing of political escape and entrance playing out more dramatically in "Migration in fact...," a graphically experimental poem in which the lines, rather than proceeding down the page in a conventional column of text, instead rotate counterclockwise around a central point as they progressively spiral inward (fig. 1). In a letter to fellow Black Mountain poet Edward Dorn, Olson explains, "one—or I—go widdershins, & write both outside in [as you say] & R to L."[77] As the poet goes "widdershins" (counterclockwise but also connoting going against the grain), so too does the poem, as the line beginnings slide further and further to the left before curling back around the center. Originally published by Andrew Crozier in the *Wivenhoe Park Review* as a reproduction of Olson's handwritten manuscript and then reproduced in that form in Butterick's edition of *The Maximus Poems*,[78] the poem suggests an emphasis on the materiality of the poem and its production that is now quite familiar in contemporary poetry. Like "Charles" in "Physically, I am home," who is a "Product (of the Process)," Olson conceives of this poem as the result of a field of forces; he wrote to Dorn that "it was 'product' [result of *experience* or *practicing*]."[79] The poem is here both expression of and analog for the self, each physically manifesting the flux of social forces at a moment in time. By literally leading readers' eyes into the center of the page, the poem formally extends its declared political content: "migration is the pursuit / by animals plants and men ... of a superior or preferable environment ... and leads always to new centers" (III.104; cf. III.176). The natural and social environment shapes the self through experience and practice, the processes of life, but migration makes it possible to change one's environment. The point of escape is to make things better; but for Olson escape leads inward, into the center of

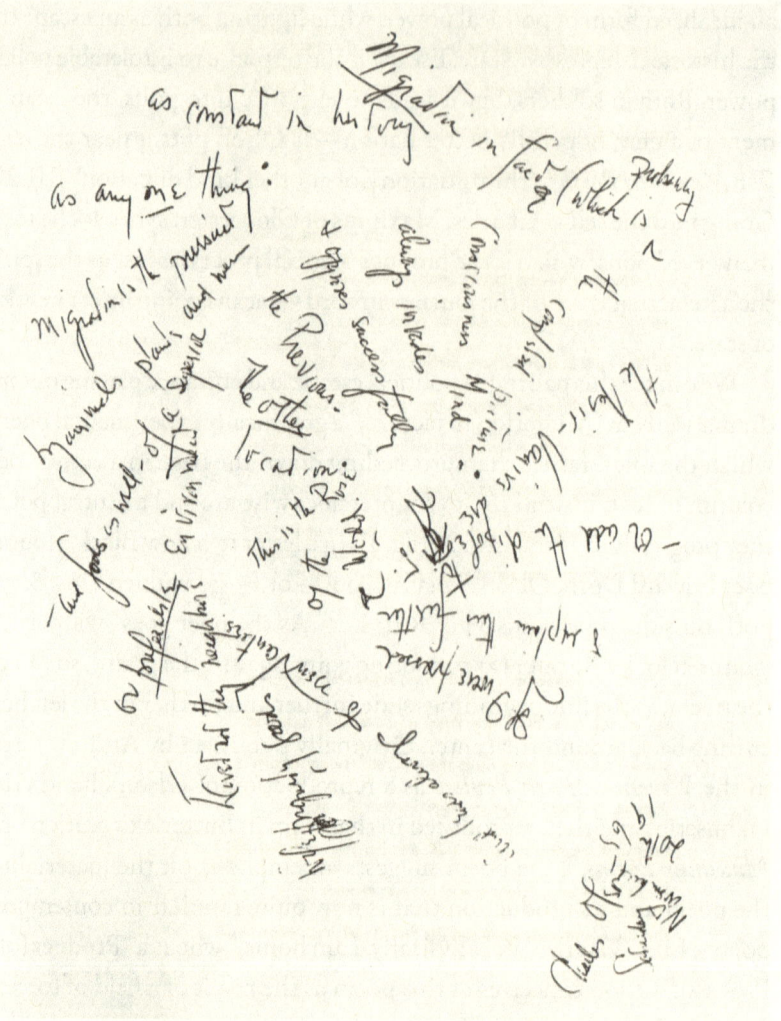

FIGURE 1. Olson's "Migration in fact..."

poem, spiral, self, society, polis. Instead of leading westward or out, migration after Gloucester moves in towards a new center.

For Olson, escaping the nation-state does not result in the mythical tabula rasa of the open plains or the Pacific but rather entrance into the totalizing, ideal state of the polis. A new center of power, preferable for its identity with rather than opposition to the self, takes the place of the old one. If there is to be any revolution (suggested here by the visual pun of the poem's rotation) under Olson's political framework, it is to be a singular, discrete event; once the old centers of power have been escaped, new ones take their place. The frontier does not remain open, an anarchic space of unbounded freedom, but must be closed, must become polis. This runs counter to familiar poststructuralist-inflected characterizations of postmodernism. In her influential account, Linda Hutcheon argues that "postmodernism is careful not to make the marginal into a new center," challenging authorities and master narratives while simultaneously trying to avoid claiming such authority for itself.[80] Such decentering is clearly at odds with Olson's sustained poetic interest in flights from old centers into new ones. And though "Projective Verse" is often identified as the start of postmodernism in American poetry,[81] this sort of provisional attack on the center is as thoroughly a part of Olson's vision for a new poetics as it is a part of his poetic attempts to make polis.

Although "Projective Verse" calls for the casting off of old poetic conventions, and Olson even speculates that projective or open verse could "lead to new poetics and to new concepts" even beyond itself,[82] he nevertheless wants "this convention"—projective or open verse—to "be recognized," distancing this new norm from "the revolution out of which it came."[83] The rhetorical contrast with Williams's related blueprint for a poetic revolution in *Spring and All* is striking and telling. Where Williams repeatedly figures old poetic traditions and conventions in terms of an oppressive political authority that needs to be overthrown, Olson is more likely to figure his own proposed poetics as the law of the land. He describes projective verse as a "law" that must be "obeyed,"[84] hails the poem as "Boss of all," names the "syllable, king,"[85] and proclaims that "the LAW OF THE LINE ... must be hewn to, obeyed."[86] "Projective Verse" clearly continues the modernist penchant for artistic revolution, overthrowing old, suffocating traditions and conventions, but Olson is also explicit, in a way that Williams typically was not, that his revolution would not be open-ended but rather serve to install a new "dogma," a new center.[87]

This is apparent even in Olson's thoroughly convention-breaking move to "go widdershins" in "Migration" (III.104). The poem rejects one of the most fundamental conventions of written English, but it does so only to establish a new convention, one that is just as rigid as the one it replaced. The newness of reading a spiral instead of a column of text can make it feel chaotic and disorienting, but this is hardly any different from learning to read any new language with an unfamiliar directionality. Olson suggests the very conventionality of this spiral writing in his dated signature, reproduced in the published holograph. Like the poem proper, "Charles Olson / Saturday / November / 20th / 1965" spirals counterclockwise; we escape old conventions only to enter into a new one.

Though this pattern—escape the old system, enter the new system—persists through much of Olson's work, he also speculatively plays out the consequences of breaking that pattern. Consider the contrast between "Migration" and "I have been an ability—a machine . . . ," written a few months later and included in Butterick's posthumous edition of *Maximus*. A first look at "I have been an ability" suggests that it continues within the new convention established by "Migration": after an opening three pages of standard left-aligned lines, on the fourth page, the poem pulls away from the margin and begins spiraling around an implied central axis. Things are a little less clear-cut on the fifth page, as the spiral seems to loosen and fragment before falling back into a standard left-to-right, top-to-bottom arrangement, albeit with slightly seesawing, off-kilter lines. Yet, the poem nevertheless seems to reassert the convention invented in "Migration," instructing readers to read the poem as it was written, "turning this page to Right . . . in counter clockwise Circle," thereby tracking the structural logic of "Projective Verse," leaving an old convention for the sake of recognizing a new one (III.121).

However, the publication history of "I have been an ability" complicates this reading, as it shows the poem refusing any center rather than entering a new one. Butterick lists the poem as one of the most difficult *Maximus* poems to edit, one of "the worst defiers of certainty," "which has nine insurmountable difficulties in its more than two hundred lines."[88] Indeed, Olson's original handwritten manuscript—the only version of the poem to exist during his life—suggests a much sharper break from the spiraling convention of "Migration."[89] The poem ultimately leaves behind any conceivable convention for arranging lines on the page; focusing on the poem's visual logic in the manuscript version reveals the specific way that "I have been an ability" rejects an entire domain of textual convention, and helps show how that rejection interfaces with the poem's political content. The

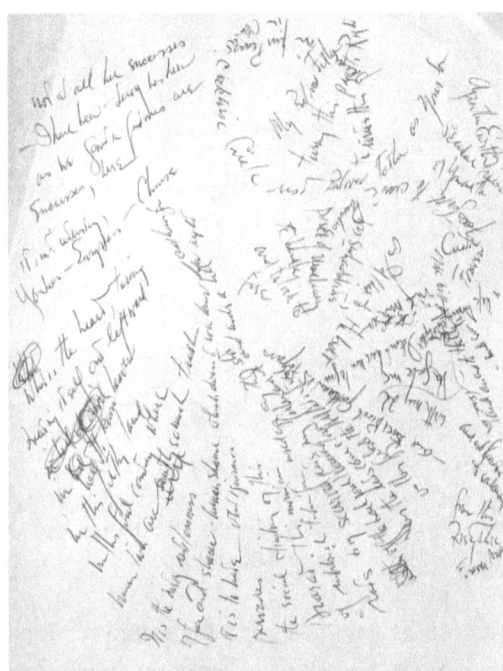

FIGURE 2. Manuscript of Olson's "I have been an ability," p. 7. (Charles Olson Research Collection, Box 5, Archives and Special Collections, University of Connecticut)

arrangement of lines in "I have been an ability" no longer leads into new centers, as it does in "Migration," but, apparently, escapes them. By the end of "I have been an ability," there is neither orthographic nor political center, and the poem thus reads as a thought experiment reflecting on Olson's own poetics: What happens when you leave a representational convention but do not enter a new one to replace it?

At first, the manuscript loudly declares its reliance upon the convention asserted in "Migration"—as the spiral begins (the seventh page of the manuscript, which Butterick's edition splits over the poem's fourth and fifth pages), the long stems of Olson's handwriting reinforce the graphic continuity of the spiral, almost making it melodramatic (fig. 2). But this only makes its disintegration of that convention all the more pointed. In manuscript, a crucial group of three lines abruptly appears upside down, disrupting the smooth movement suggested by the curve of the spiral: "And an end to Hell /—end even to Heaven / a life America shall yield" (fig. 3). Moreover, the third line here bisects the previous, cutting off "Heaven" as well as the next phrase, which roughly uprights the page: "or we will leave

FIGURE 3. Manuscript of Olson's "I have been an ability," p. 7, detail, rotated 90 degrees counterclockwise, with the line "a life America shall yield" running vertically down the center of the image and "or we will——leave her" crossing horizontally. (Charles Olson Research Collection, Box 5, Archives and Special Collections, University of Connecticut)

her." Though Butterick presents this as a single line in his edited version, in the manuscript, the line "a life America shall yield" entirely divides "or we will" from "leave her": a faint diagrammatic stroke traverses and guides the eye across the interruption, linking the sides of the ultimatum but also emphasizing the distance. This disruption of the invented convention, making the lines run away from the spiral, formally enacts the poem's inversion of the logic of "Migration." Migration, like that of Olson's father the Swedish immigrant, should open up entry to a new nation, a new center, but in "I have been an ability," America is a "Nation / which never / lets anyone / come to / shore" (III.119). In the latter poem, Olson's solution is to take the land and the people out of the nation: "we will leave / and ask Gloucester / to sail away" (III.121). America does not yield a life free from the moralizing rules that divide heaven from hell, and the solution in "I have been an ability" is to leave her without any forthcoming entrance into a replacement. If there is any spiral remaining, it is spiraling out now rather than in. Instead of entering more fully and deeply into a totalizing polis, the political strategy here looks a lot like exit.

Unlike "Migration," "I have been an ability" does not enter any new graphical convention after leaving behind the spiral. Butterick ends the poem with an ellipsis in editorial brackets, belying the finality sounded

FIGURE 4. Manuscript of Olson's "I have been an ability," p. 8. (Charles Olson Research Collection, Box 5, Archives and Special Collections, University of Connecticut)

in the concluding line of his version, "Forever Amen" (III.121). The manuscript actually goes on for three more pages after this "Amen"—though Butterick explains that "the order" of these three pages "is uncertain," he affirms that they belong to the "I have been an ability" manuscript (figs. 4–6).[90] These three pages refuse any overarching, organizing logic or guiding orthographical convention—except perhaps the convention of having no convention. There are still echoes of the spiral, as many groups of lines seem to rotate around invisible axes, but just as often, lines seem to sprawl across the page haphazardly, without reference to any center. The allusion to Yeats's widening gyre, in the back of the mind all along, now is fulfilled: the center does not hold, the spiral falls apart, and anarchy is loosed upon the page. Contrary to Yeats's interwar anxieties over the collapse of civilization, though, here loosening the center's hold appears as a potential solution to American politics.

Instead of escape for the sake of entry, replacing old conventions with new, "I have been an ability" asserts escape as an ongoing process, one with no product to be entered into—no stable Charles, spiral, or polis.

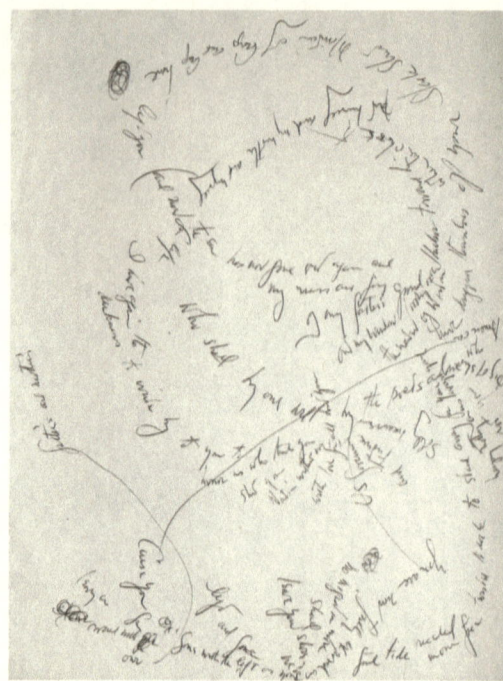

FIGURE 5. Manuscript of Olson's "I have been an ability," p. 9. (Charles Olson Research Collection, Box 5, Archives and Special Collections, University of Connecticut)

"I have been an ability," then, departs from the truncated revolutionary logic of "Projective Verse" and its mechanically perfected poetic products, the breath's reification on the page. The author's embodiment obviously remains at the forefront of "I have been an ability," but no longer is it contained and articulated in a system of representational conventions. In "Migration," we can recreate Olson's actions, moving with him from the page's margins to its center, much as he wants us to breathe like him in "Projective Verse." In the final pages of "I have been an ability," though, it is impossible to even know where to start—Olson gives us no convention by which to retrace his footsteps.

The poem's opening, conventionally arranged lines announce this pending departure from Olson's own previously invented conventions. The poem begins, "I have been an ability—a machine—up to / now" (III.117), with the enjambed temporal marker suggesting a biographical break, distancing the speaker's present from the typewriter of "Projective Verse," the "machine" that makes breath reproducible.[91] Indeed, "projection" makes a cameo in this late poem, as "lantern-slides, on the sheet," the problem being

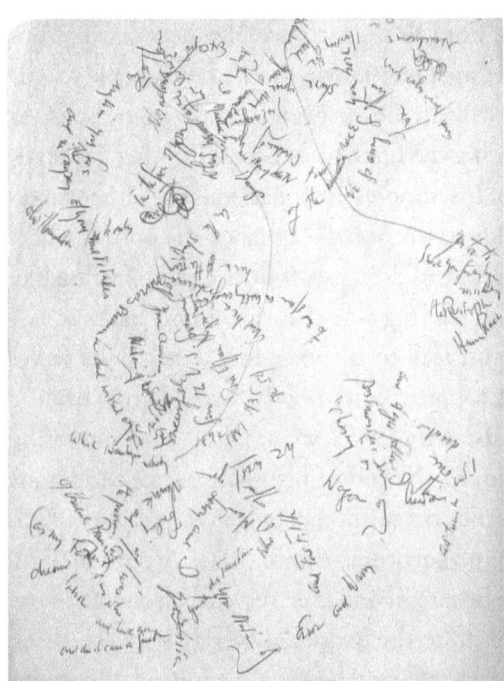

FIGURE 6. Manuscript of Olson's "I have been an ability," p. 10. (Charles Olson Research Collection, Box 5, Archives and Special Collections, University of Connecticut)

"the lantern always getting too hot / and I burning my fingers" (III.117). Projection only reproduces what already exists, the author's embodiment—representing the complex field of energy that constitutes both self and society in order to allow one to know and enter into that energy. But once the goal is escape rather than entrance, projection will no longer suffice. "Up to / now," Olson limited escape to the role of a precursor to a pending entry into new crystallizations of forces. "Now," though, Olson suggests an open-ended escape, a migration with no central endpoint but rather one that keeps pushing outward.

Olson's limited success is indicated by the difficulty of reading and understanding (much less publishing) this poem in its entirety—the last three pages especially, the ones that most fully realize its formal and conceptual break from "Projective Verse," are nigh on incomprehensible. We might say, as Williams said of Moore, that Olson's incomprehensibility is witness to at what cost he cleaves himself away.[92] To be sure, "I have been an ability" is an irregularity in Olson's lifelong body of work and is probably best understood as an inchoate thought experiment rather than a fully elaborated poetics or politics. For Olson, entrance into new conventions is necessary to avoid escapism; such new conventions allow people to stay connected together—linguistically in the poem and socially in the polis. As Paul Stephens puts it, "as much as he loathed Aristotle in other contexts, Olson would have approved of his notion that a man must be either superhuman or a beast to live outside of the polis."[93] Outside the polis is where this poem ultimately takes us, but in doing so, it does end up feeling like it demands a superhuman act of reading—or else, that it only barks at us.

Olson's idea that escape must lead to entrance into a new polis serves as a preemptive critique of the hippie communes that would grow from "a few handfuls" nationwide in the early 1950s, when Olson was composing the initial *Maximus* poems, to, by the end of his life, "tens of thousands of communes with 500 thousand to a million people involved in the U.S. alone."[94] This is apparent in Olson's attitude towards Black Mountain College in North Carolina, where he taught and then served as rector until the school closed in 1957. In addition to the historical overlap between Black Mountain and hippie communes—the work of prominent Black Mountain faculty such as Buckminster Fuller and John Cage were a direct influence on perhaps the most famous hippie commune, Drop City[95]—von Hallberg suggests that Olson saw Black Mountain as "a strategic enclave": "Olson conceived of Black Mountain College as an alternative to the dominant society; more than a college, it was an experiment in living together," one constituted by withdrawal into the periphery.[96] Von Hallberg quotes Olson speaking on BBC television: Black Mountain was "the only, only communal invention that has substituted for the damn Western conception of society, which sort of is assumed, as though it has to be administrative, it has to be government, it has to take care of things, or it has to take care of people, there has to be some sort of thing which does it, city hall like, or nation, or the privy council, or the White House."[97] Like the hippie communes of the '60s and '70s, for many of which "the absence of governmental law is the primary enticement,"[98] Olson hoped that withdrawal to Black Mountain would provide a communal alternative to society governed by institutions such as city hall and the White House.

Yet, in contrast to something like Drop City, which refused to enforce any rules or punish violations of community norms,[99] Olson saw his flight from Washington to Black Mountain not just as an escape but also a kind of entrance. Von Hallberg argues that "Olson's strategy was to centralize cultural expression from an institutionally peripheral position."[100] Black Mountain was to be an escape from the logic of the White House, but Olson also hoped "that Black Mountain was 'the predecessor of the nation!'"[101] Rather than escaping from the state as such, this is more like secession, carving a new, better state out of the old.[102]

For law scholars Paul and Sarah Robinson, hippie communes only survived to the extent that they adopted a similar logic. The communes all ended up following the same pattern: "after an initial period of delight runs into the realities of life and human nature, the cooperative action fails and the group either disbands or adopts rules and sanctions (commonly using the threat of exclusion as the ultimate sanction)."[103] Even setting aside the reality that these communes were never really an exit from the state—the "communal wave" of the '60s and '70s was financially possible, at least in part, because of government antipoverty programs[104]—the only communes to survive were the ones that entered into their own structures of authority and punishment to enforce community norms, however different those might have been from those of mainstream American society they left behind.

Unlike the communards of "the magical years of the 1960s,"[105] neither Williams nor Olson imagines, in any sustained fashion, community apart from the political state. As a result, Williams and Olson provoke a question that will occupy much to follow: Is it possible to escape political representation without abandoning representation as such? This question has deep sources in and ramifications for disciplines beyond literary studies, especially anthropology, economics, and political philosophy, because it amounts to asking whether it is possible to maintain human community outside the state—that is, whether Hobbes was right.

There are good reasons to think he wasn't. Even mainstream scholars like the Robinsons, for example, critique the Hobbesian master narrative that humans without the state are doomed to a war of all against all, summarizing a number of compelling historical examples of people cooperating with each other in "absent-law situations" ranging from a nineteenth-century leper colony to a group of plane crash survivors stranded in the remote Andes mountains.¹⁰⁶ These historical moments provide plausible pictures of humans navigating conflicts of interest and forming meaningful community outside of the state. Yet, notably, all of the Robinsons' examples are only temporary or incomplete escapes from the state, ephemeral and partial. Indeed, they resort to these historical and provisional lapses in the law because the hypothetical premise of the Hobbesian narrative—the nature of life outside the state—is unimaginable: "in a world so dominated by government and law, how could we even imagine a life without it?"¹⁰⁷

When Williams and Olson do imagine it, it looks rather like a failure: leaving the state looks like leaving language, and leaving language means leaving behind human community. It doesn't seem possible to escape political representation without also abandoning all those other representational connections that constitute human sociality. Nevertheless, by couching the question of the state's outside in terms of representation, Williams and Olson also open up new lines of inquiry: How can the representational art of literature contribute to conceptualizing, modeling, or even enacting such a targeted escape from political representation? These questions are constraining for Williams's and Olson's liminal poetics of escape, but for many writers to follow, they become generative, opening up a space where literature might contribute to a politics of disempowering the state by escaping it.

FANTASIES OF FLIGHT IN RICHARD WRIGHT AND THOMAS PYNCHON

> Once they had left their homeland they remained homeless, once they had left their state they became stateless; once they had been deprived of their human rights they were rightless, the scum of the earth.
> —HANNAH ARENDT, *The Origins of Totalitarianism*

STATELESSNESS, ACCORDING TO Hannah Arendt, emerges as a central problem in Europe after World War I, a problem that contributes to twentieth-century totalitarianism and one that intensifies leading into and coming out of World War II. The paradigmatic result of reducing people to the "scum of the earth"[1] is the exclusionary inclusion of the internment camp, and we should recognize the important continuities with what Giorgio Agamben later calls the "*homo sacer*"[2] or, more recently, what Sonja Schillings has extended into the legal fiction of the "*hostis humani generis*," the "enemy of all humankind."[3] The scum of the earth, the *homo sacer*, the enemy of all humankind—the stateless person is not free from state power but, rather, exposed to it all the more thoroughly, "completely at the mercy of the police."[4] Much more than the citizen's rights to freedom and justice is at stake: statelessness threatens one's "essential quality as man, his human dignity. Only the loss of a polity itself expels him from humanity."[5] Stateless people "have become human beings," an animal species, "and nothing else,"[6] reduced to "the abstract nakedness of being human and nothing but human."[7] But these human animals are nevertheless confined to the world of human law, "thrown back, in the midst of civilization, on their natural givenness, on their mere differentiation."[8]

Statelessness, in this sense, cannot be a solution or desirable political end. As political theorist Jane Anna Gordon puts it in a recent extension of Arendt's analysis, "no one would downplay statelessness as a problem. Most would affirm that it is an extreme malediction that no one should face."[9] Statelessness cannot be the goal of any politics—not even an anti-state one, not even the politics of exit—because, despite the word's superficial suggestion of the state's absence, it is the state itself that produces and maintains statelessness. The condition of statelessness, in fact, can incite the desire for exit; as Gordon observes, "given the active complicity of states in the production of statelessness and the conditions that foster contemporary enslavement, it is not hard to recognize the appeal of anarchistic approaches that are growing among some of the most politically committed."[10] Statelessness provides no exit from the state, but it can make you wish there was one. Nevertheless, this figure of the stateless "scum of the earth" also provides an important site of inquiry for the poetics of escape, suggesting some potential ways out of the state while also, crucially, evoking their limitations and failures.

Statelessness takes on central importance in the mid-century fictions of Richard Wright and Thomas Pynchon, with composition dates bookending the heightened historical visibility of statelessness surrounding World War II.[11] While Pynchon's *Gravity's Rainbow* (1973) explicitly considers the stateless refugees in Europe produced in the aftermath of World War II, it is the functional statelessness of Black Americans that occupies Wright's *Native Son* (1940) and *The Man Who Lived Underground* (appearing as a short story in 1945, with the full novel posthumously published in 2021)—though Wright's novels also importantly gesture towards European war and totalitarianism. Juxtaposing these texts helps us remember that, while postwar Europe provides the classic historical exemplar of statelessness, the problem is not narrowly historical. Arendt herself equates the statelessness of postwar refugees with the statelessness of Black Americans,[12] and, as Gordon observes, the problem of statelessness "neither began nor ended in the mid-twentieth century."[13] It is a problem that continues into the twenty-first century as "increasingly, many, even fully enfranchised people, are marked by degrees of statelessness."[14] This same recognition of the broader historical and political scope of statelessness appears in Wright's and Pynchon's novels. They both employ easily recognizable, specific historical examples of the human that is both expelled from and trapped within humanity, but they do so in order to explore a more general politics of escaping state power. Though Wright himself fled the American state for a less racist one in France, and though Pynchon himself withdrew into a secretive life hidden from public attention in America, the fiction of both makes clear that it is not the historically particular American state that is most at issue. Rather, the United States is only the strongest, most pervasive, and most obvious exemplar of a more fundamental political problem, one inherent to the state structure as such.

As we saw in the previous chapter, one of the primary dilemmas for the poetics of escape enacted by William Carlos Williams and Charles Olson is the question of how far is too far when it comes to leaving behind representation in literature and politics. If the representational bind from author to reader, from authority to subject, persists too strongly, in too rigid a form, it becomes oppressive, stunting human creativity and freedom. Yet, entirely dissolving it jeopardizes human connection, the connection of meaning in poetry and of society in politics. Implicit in this is an assumption that access to representation—to participation in human community—is readily available. The problem of externally imposed statelessness did not enter consideration. That is obviously not the case for Wright, whose novels explicitly concern how White society cuts off Black life from the representational structures of power. While Wright is still interested in a politics of exit, his attention to the ways that the state excludes people helps refine both our understanding of the state as well as the responses of the poetics of escape. In *Native Son,* Wright shows how his protagonist, Bigger

Thomas, a young Black man caught in the poverty of Chicago's Black Belt, is excluded from representation within the law—representation as a full, equal citizen. As Bigger's lawyer, Max, puts it, Bigger's "very existence is a crime against the state!"[15] But *Native Son* also shows how Bigger's criminal black existence functions not just to exclude him from citizenship but also simultaneously to trap him in another sort of representational connection to the state, the paradoxically "official" or "necessary illegality," in Michel Foucault's words, that provides a foil against which state sovereignty constitutes and justifies itself.[16] Reiterating this dynamic in *The Man Who Lived Underground,* Wright's fiction not only emphasizes how transgressing the boundaries of law does not make a way out of the state, but, more significantly, it illustrates how the state's abjection of Black bodies does not cast them outside the state but, rather, oppressively alters the way the state incorporates them within itself.

Echoing the structure of the preceding chapter, I will consider the modernist forerunner in Wright in relation to a paradigmatic postmodernist in Thomas Pynchon, considering how the latter intensifies the former's tentative forays into a poetics of escape. Whereas Williams rejects escape because he is not willing to sacrifice human sociality, Wright considers such a sacrifice—Bigger is certainly willing to throw away all interpersonal relationships to escape the state's White world. However, as we will see, not even that appears viable for Wright, as, like Arendt's "scum of the earth," it concedes the very humanity of Bigger. As such, Wright also ultimately rejects escape, resolving instead towards an identity politics of decriminalizing Blackness and of full representation within the law. Pynchon likewise confronts how state power excludes—on the basis of existence, the mere fact of a person's being—in order to include more totally. Rather than demand a more inclusive representation of everyone's existence, though, Pynchon doubles down on escape. As both kinds of existence, inclusion and exclusion—"elect" and "preterite" in Pynchon's theopolitical framing— exist in relation to the state, the only escape Pynchon can end up imagining is an escape from existence itself. Like Olson's flight from language, this escape will end up amounting to little more than solipsistic escapism, a nonhuman statelessness that holds little hope for Pynchon.

"LIKE LIVING IN JAIL": ARRESTED ESCAPE IN *NATIVE SON*

Native Son continues the long, quintessentially American tradition of the escape narrative. Of course, rather than escaping savage captors, as in the captivity narrative, or escaping the stiff clothes of civilization for the open plains, as in the Western, *Native Son* is about escaping the White world of power and privilege. That is, Wright's novel continues not just the American escape narrative but more specifically the Black American fugitive slave narrative.[17] After sexually assaulting and then accidentally killing Mary Dalton, a White woman, protagonist Bigger Thomas embarks on a series of related escapes, both figurative and literal, from his position as a Black man in White society and all the ways that that identity constructs and confines his agency, responsibility, and experiences. As James Baldwin puts it, the oppressive White society and the ways it constitutes Black interiority "is this toward which we endlessly struggle and from which, endlessly, we struggle to escape."[18]

I think all of this is fairly obvious to a careful reader of Wright's novel, so I would like to emphasize, over and above, how the domination that Bigger flees should be characterized not only by its Whiteness but also by its complete entanglement in the political state. Bigger's flight is a flight from political authority in general and, in particular, a flight from state structures of representation; one of the state's distinguishing characteristics is its capacity to marry representation to objective violence. As Bigger's prosecutor, Buckley, literally speaking for the state, puts it in his closing argument, "we all dwell in a land of living law. Law embodies the will of the people" (407). The state makes the words of the law live, gives the law a body that can act on other bodies. To escape the state would be to escape its structural union of violence and representation. Bigger doesn't escape, of course—as Sara Schotland puts it, "Bigger is closed off from all avenues that lead out of the ghetto," quoting from an interview in which Wright explains that Bigger is a "psychological portrait" of a young Black man "with all roads closed and with the constant logical temptation to escape the law"[19]—and I will close this section by addressing the implications of that failure.

Examples of Bigger's various getaways are, unsurprisingly, most apparent in the novel's middle section, titled "Flight"—a title that echoes an earlier scene in which Bigger fantasizes piloting an airplane as a revolutionary act, a fantasy that ends with his friend Gus reminding him, "You black and they make the laws" (20). In "Flight," once Bigger has become the prime suspect in Mary Dalton's murder (drawing suspicion to himself in part by fleeing the scene of the crime), he literally runs away from a posse of police and state-sanctioned vigilantes who are "armed with rifles, tear gas, flashlights, and photos of the killer... under a blanket warrant from the Mayor" (244). Bigger tries to escape the reach of the law and the physical violence that enforces it; race hatred motivates the search party, but it is government systems of representation, the warrant signed by the mayor, that legitimate and thus intensify and extend that violence.

Leading up to that climactic chase sequence, Bigger had already been fantasizing and enacting more figurative escapes. Most obvious is when Bigger rapes and murders his girlfriend, Bessie, which critics have long read as a psychological or existential escape, one that, at least temporarily, allows Bigger to make real choices with real consequences, outside the narrow bounds of the law.[20] Bigger himself reflects, "never had his will been so free as in this night and day of fear and murder and flight" (239). Bigger imagines that he can escape the state and attain freedom by transgressing the law. The state is White, but it's the state structure itself—even more than its Whiteness—that drives Bigger's flight. When Bigger almost loses his nerve just before the murder, he strengthens his resolve by recalling his "driving desire to escape the law" (236). A Black man murdering a Black woman is not much of a transgression against Whiteness, as Bigger and his friends understand earlier in the novel, when they contemplate robbing a White man instead of other Black people for the first time: robbing Blum's Delicatessen "would be a violation of the ultimate taboo... it would be a symbolic challenge of the white world's rule over them," in contrast to robbing "their own people," which by comparison is just "play" (14). In murdering Bessie, though, Bigger moves beyond this earlier logic; he is no longer trying to violate the "ultimate taboo" of Whiteness but rather the law itself. Bigger's crime against Bessie is an attempt to get outside the state, which, even as it abjects Black bodies outside its structures of privilege, nevertheless represents those Black bodies within itself. Bigger's violence and violations are "symbolic challenges" not only to the material history of "the white world's rule over them" (14) but also to the law as such—to that which says, in language if not in practice, that murdering Bessie is a crime.

Interestingly, Bigger describes his oppression in terms of both being trapped inside *and* being locked out, in back-to-back sentences: "It's just like living in jail. Half the time I feel like I'm on the outside of the world peering in through a knot-hole in the fence" (20). Wright repeats this structure in his discussion of creating the character of Bigger, explaining his task of "apprehending the locked-in life of the Black Belt areas" while also reproducing "the deep sense of exclusion" Bigger felt.[21] Bigger is excluded, kept out of picket-fence-America, but he's also a prisoner living in jail. Being outside turns out to be just another way of being trapped inside, and vice versa. This is the contradictory stateless position that, in Arendt's words, is both "forced to live outside" while simultaneously "thrown back, in the midst."[22] As Foucault explains, "there is no outside. It takes back with one hand what it seems to exclude with the other. . . . the delinquent is not outside the law; he is, from the very outset, in the law, at the very heart of the law."[23] And this, of course, is exactly what happens to Bigger. Once he decides to run away with Bessie, "the feeling of being always enclosed . . . had gone from him" (150), and once the reporters find Mary Dalton's bones in the furnace and Bigger's flight from the law takes its more literal turn, he concludes, "he had always felt outside of this white world, and now it was true. It made things simple" (221). He finds himself utterly outside. Yet, he hasn't escaped, either—he is, in fact, totally surrounded by his pursuers: "They circled slowly, hemming him in; bars of light forming a prison, a wall between him and the rest of the world" (258). They have trapped him inside Chicago's South Side, the Black Belt which is nevertheless a "white world" covered in snow (242). He is outside the White world, but state violence also imprisons him within it.

This is important, as it curtails any utopian possibilities that the novel might otherwise gesture towards. For example, in an otherwise compelling analysis of how *Native Son* critiques the Lockean notion of self-ownership at the heart of liberal manifestations of individual subjectivity and property, Kenji Kihara suggests that the "No Man's Land" Bigger finds himself in when talking to White men "may well constitute a place of certain utopian possibility," because it "refers to an area or land that no one owns or controls," suggesting "an outside to property relations."²⁴ The more immediate reference for "No Man's Land" is of course the contested space between opposing trenches during World War I, land which, while not controlled by a single state, is certainly not free from property relations but, rather, a direct consequence of how states envision and attempt to enforce their specific property realities. Even setting that aside, the novel repeatedly suggests that being outside is just another way of being trapped inside. That's exactly how "No Man's Land" functions in context for Bigger, emphasizing the distance between himself and the White world. In *Native Son,* there is no "outside of capitalist ownership relations," and the absence of ownership is not communism, as Kihara suggests, but poverty.²⁵

This is why escape in *Native Son* turns out to be an entirely inadequate solution to the structural racism manifesting through the state: getting outside does not free you from the state. As Bigger notes to himself during his trial at the end of the novel, "he had killed to be quit of them; but even after obeying, even after killing, they still ruled him" (331). Indeed, the novel expresses an abiding fear that the desire to escape will deteriorate into a fantastical flight from reality itself.

Bigger explicitly rejects this sort of escapism. After murdering Bessie, he checks his intoxicating sense of freedom from the law: "he did not want to make believe that it was solved" (240). Transgressing the law does not amount to escaping it. To believe so would mean succumbing to the same weaknesses he faults in his mother and Bessie: "He hated his mother for that way of hers which was like Bessie's. What his mother had was Bessie's whiskey and Bessie's whiskey was his mother's religion" (240). Mother's religion and Bessie's whiskey are both modes of escapism, a way for them to close their eyes and plug their ears to ignore their problems rather than actually escaping them. Bigger's impulsive strategy, to escape the law by violating it, is, as Bigger himself sometimes realizes, futile escapism, wishful thinking.

Wright repeats this critique in his novel *The Man Who Lived Underground* (hereafter *Underground*), which reproduces much of *Native Son*'s investigation into the politics of escape. Many of the same concerns I have been discussing in *Native Son* recur prominently in *Underground,* which, though only published in its entirety in 2021, Wright composed from 1941 to 1942, shortly after *Native Son*'s first publication in 1940. The novel reproduces *Native Son*'s three-part structure, which protagonist Fred Daniels metafictionally summarizes at the novel's end: "I signed the paper, then I run off. Now, I'm back."[26] The first part establishes Daniels's criminal existence (White cops forcing him to sign a confession for a murder he did not commit), the second part relates his flight from the racist state into the underground of the city's sewers, and the third part depicts his return to the aboveground, where he, like Bigger Thomas, tries to gain inclusion within the law.

Like *Native Son, Underground* depicts the state as a system of representational technologies overlaying an ultimate power of violence. The novel viscerally portrays Daniels's physical suffering at the hands of the police, but it also emphasizes, insistently, how his subjugation depends on representation into the law. For the White cops and the district attorney, everything hinges on Daniels signing his name to a (false) confession: "Read the paper and sign it," they demand (25). A "smear of white" (26), a "splash of white that danced before his eyes" (27), the white paper marked with black ink is a synecdoche for the White state that represents Daniels's Blackness and thereby incorporates him under its rule.

Coerced into signing the confession (violence undergirding and enforcing representation), Daniels runs away: "An impulse, not a thought, but just a vague gathering of all the forces of his body urged him to escape, to run off while there was time," because "yeah, I signed that paper" (47). This escape underground suggests an alternative to the state's world aboveground, as the "whispering rush of the water" in the sewers creates "an illusion of another world with other values and other laws" (53). Significantly, however, this is only an illusion; like Bigger's fantastical getaway chase, Daniels's escape into the sewers is not an exit from the state or its laws but only an escapist fantasy. Noting how racialized housing shortages in the 1930s and '40s drove Black Americans literally underground, Thomas Heise explains how, in fleeing into the sewers, Daniels is "willfully imprisoning himself—to a terrain that is only a more degraded version of the de jure and de facto segregations that built the twentieth century's racial ghettos."[27] This escape is "solitary, profoundly alienated, and in no way collective. The clandestine isolation that makes these acts possible also renders them negligible" (143).

Digging his way into a system of interconnected basements beneath the city, Daniels stumbles upon a Black church singing hymns about going to a heavenly "home above" (62). Like Bigger, Daniels feels that this religiosity functions primarily as a form of escapism, and "he felt that these people should stand silent, unrepentant, with simple manly pride, and yield no quarter in whimpering," a "conviction" that makes him feel guilty for his own running away: "He wanted them to assume a heroic attitude even though *he himself* had run away from *his* tormentors, even though he had begged *his* accusers to believe in his innocence" (63).

In "Memories of My Grandmother," an essay Wright intended to accompany *Underground* (as it does in the novel's 2021 publication), he explains that the novel was motivated by his desire to depict his grandmother's Black religiosity, which Wright portrays as a withdrawal from a harsh reality of Black life: "*religion* was her *reality,* the sole meaning in her life" (164). Importantly, Wright's focus is not religion as such but rather religion as a specific instance of a more general pattern of fleeing reality, as one example of "any way of life . . . that is lived distantly from the environment even though it subsists on the environment" (173). While there is a hopeful aspect to this, as Wright depicts his grandmother as a "rebel" who "strove to transform the world" (170), he also emphasizes its limits: her faith "could not manifest itself continuously in daily life. It was capricious, disjointed, brittle, chopped to bits by the daily necessity to live. This was as it had to be, for my grandmother was real, normal, healthy" (172). For Wright, the other world asserted by religion is only a fantasy, one that provides only a psychological escape from reality, one that is ultimately "meaningless" (172). He even goes so far as to pathologize this escapism, equating this pattern of withdrawing from the world with schizophrenia (203). In *Underground,* Daniels similarly finds nonreligious examples of this escapism, such as when he discovers a movie theater, which he explicitly links to the church congregation (71). As he walks up from the theater's basement, "ahead of him glowed red letters: E—X—I—T" (74). On the level of plot, this is a little confusing, because the door beneath the sign is a side entrance into the theater, not an exit. But on a symbolic level, it works: an entrance into the theater is an exit from political realities. In the wake of the Great Depression, cinema in the 1930s seemed a bastion of escapism, as "the advent of sound motion pictures ... gave desperate, frustrated, and disillusioned people someplace to go and forget their troubles for a few hours as they watched the shimmering images on the silver screen ... it offered escape from a real world of broken dreams and continued economic hardship."[28] Even if film scholarship has since complicated this perspective on '30s cinema, arguing that many of these films "were not 'escapist' at all, but were sources of powerful allegories, mirror images of modern society," film critics contemporary to Wright nevertheless believed "that 'escape' was what Hollywood did best," with "hostile critics" arguing "that the movies were fraudulent in their efforts, designed not so much to cheer up the people as to distract them from a reality that needed to be faced."[29]

In Wright's version of this critique, cinema escapism is a descent back into the shadowy illusions of Plato's cave: the theater is "a huge, inverted bowl in whose convex depths there gleamed shimmering clusters of distant lights. . . . Dangling before these faces, high upon a screen of silver, were jerking shadows" (74). Again, Daniels feels the urge to shatter this escapist illusion, as "the impulse he had had to tell the people in the church to stop their singing seized him again. These people were *laughing* at their *lives*, at the animated shadows of themselves. Why did they not rise up and go out into the sunlight and do some deed that would make them live?" (74–75). While the standard reading of the story "as an inverted copy of Plato's parable"[30] is certainly correct—Daniels's *descent* into the cave corresponds to Plato's account of *ascending* into sunlight, since it reveals to Daniels the shadowy delusions that captivate others—we should also recognize a more straightforward correspondence. Wright explicitly equates Daniels's descent with his grandmother's religious withdrawal (201–2). Daniels can critique the inhabitants of Plato's cave, but, in a striking doubling, he is also one of them. Though Daniels went underground in hopes of making an escape, all he finds there are the devotees of escapism, churchgoers and moviegoers, who, even as he sees through their illusions, nevertheless remind him of his own escapist fantasies.

Intrinsic to Daniels's recognition and condemnation of his own escapism is his sense that it disavows his own humanity, rejecting his own being. Looking "at the men and women singing in the church" creates in him a feeling of "nothingness" that is "his enemy; it condemned him as effectively as had those policemen. It made him feel guilty" (65–66). As Wright asserts in "Memories of My Grandmother," "man does not and cannot live alone, and if he tries to, he ceases to be a man" (194). In turn, his impetus to return to the world aboveground arises from "a strange and new knowledge" of his own humanity: "He was *all people*. In some unutterable fashion he was *all* people and they were *he*" (106). To be underground is to be stateless, excluded from humanity without being free from it. In asserting and affirming his own humanity, Daniels realizes that he cannot willingly remain in that position; "at some time in the near future he would rise up from this underground, walk forth and say something to everybody" (107).

That is why Daniels ultimately abandons his life underground, returning to the world above, claiming his place within the law. This reentry is characterized primarily by the need to be included in structures of representation, to have a voice that is heard—to "say something to everybody." In the novel version of the story I have been discussing, Daniels goes straight to the police: "He would go to the station, clear up everything, make a statement" (135). In a notable contrast, in the short story revision published during Wright's life, Daniels's first encounter back in the world above is not with the police but the church, where he repeatedly demands the opportunity to speak: "'But I want to tell 'em,' he said loudly."[31] What he has to say does not really matter at this point. Being able to speak is a way of being included. The congregation responds to this dirty, stinking man with the opposing demand: "Get out!" they scream at him.[32] Daniels does not want to get out, though, but to stay in and speak: "But mister, let me tell—." Finally, the congregation resorts to the police, reminding us who wields the ultimate exclusionary power. But as it dawns on Daniels that the police, as agents of the state, also have the power to include, he decides to go straight to the police station himself, willingly, returning us to the original novel version of narrative: "He would go there and clear up everything, make a statement." The short story revision, in drawing out this return to the law and contrasting it with the attempt at social inclusion within the church, further accentuates the novel's emphasis that it is inclusion within the state, specifically, that is crucial for Daniels.

The dilemma now is not what state violence will do to him but how to get himself represented within the state. Even if it means being arrested and going to jail, he does not want to run away anymore, as long as he is incorporated into power's representational structures, affirming his legal status as a human. In "Memories of My Grandmother," Wright explains that the wrongly accused—a category that includes all Black life, which is condemned by default—"is trying not so much to refute the charges as he is trying to fight for his status as a human being, trying to keep his worth and value in the eyes of others, just because he is innocent."[33] This is why Daniels is so eager, at novel's end, to confess to any and all crimes, regardless of what he has actually done. Here, Wright's novel accords with Arendt's assertion that for the stateless person, "the anomaly for whom the general law did not provide, it was better for him to become an anomaly for which it did provide, that of the criminal. . . . As a criminal even a stateless person will not be treated worse than another criminal, that is, he will be treated like everybody else. Only as an offender against the law can he gain protection from it."[34] For Daniels to become a criminal—not because his existence is a crime ("his mere presence in this world," as Arendt puts it), but because the law has recognized his transgression—would mean he is a human.[35]

Daniels will not get even that, of course—"the solid presence of these men," the cops and their threat of physical power, "seemed to make it impossible for his ideas and feelings to assume the form of words" (142). He cannot enter any straightforward representation within the law, and the cops, who have since identified the real murderer, must find a way to expel the law's internal contradiction that Daniels embodies. Unsurprisingly, they consider another form of exclusionary inclusion, concluding that Daniels is "off his nut": "'Dump 'im in the psycho" (146). This is an attempt to reassert Daniels's stateless position, excluded from the law while remaining subject to it (recall, from the preceding chapter, William Carlos Williams's discussion of how the state responded to John Coffey's challenge to the law by declaring him insane). Even that proves insufficiently thorough for the White cops, though, who fear that Daniels "acts crazy, but that may be a stunt" (144). Thus, they take Daniels's condition of statelessness to the extreme, concluding, "you've got to shoot his kind. They would wreck things," a statement that, in the novel version's surreal apocalyptic ending, Wright bitterly ironizes, as air raid sirens wail and bombs explode around the city, evoking the much more literal wrecking carried out by sovereign powers and immediate historical context of World War II (159). The cop unceremoniously shoots Daniels, letting his body fall back into the sewer, and the sound of the gunshot merges with the percussive backdrop of war.

In the novel's ending, Daniels embodies the apotheosis of the stateless "scum of the earth," the one defined most all by "the capacity to be killed," as Agamben puts it.[36] Notably, Wright formally enacts this specifically as the culmination of Daniels's loss of both voice and human subjectivity, a final expulsion from all representation. Feeling the pain of the bullet, Daniels's "mouth gaped open soundlessly," and his voice drops first to a mumble, but still in quotation marks, "'You-all shot me,'" then to a whisper, still direct quotation but now without quotation marks, rendering his audible speech almost like inaudible free indirect discourse: "he whispered in amazement: They shot me...." Then, his mouth fills with sewage and he speaks no more, reduced to "a whirling, black object" (159).

In a reading of *Native Son* congruent with my own, Jack Taylor aligns Wright's understanding of Black life with Agamben's *homo sacer,* arguing that, for Wright, "blacks are subjects without political rights who can be killed with impunity... included in the political order precisely by being excluded, that is, by being outside of the law."[37] Bigger, indeed, anticipates Daniels' desperate struggle to speak and to be heard at the end of his life. Just before his sentencing, the judge asks him, "Is there any statement you wish to make before sentence is passed upon you?" In response, Bigger "tried to open his mouth to answer, but could not. Even if he had had the power of speech, he did not know what he could have said. He shook his head, his eyes blurring. The court room was profoundly quiet now. The judge wet his lips with his tongue and lifted a piece of paper that crackled loudly in the silence" (417). The only sound is the paper that contains his death sentence, the representational expression of the state's violent power. In the face of this, Bigger cannot speak, but as he waits for his execution, the opportunity to speak—and for someone to listen and truly hear him, so that he can be recognized—becomes his only remaining desire and purpose in living. Notably, he directs this desire specifically towards his lawyer, Max, the person who most fully represents Bigger within the law. Yet, when Max finally comes to visit, Bigger again struggles to speak: "If he could only tell him!" but "he could not talk" (422). Even when he does find words, in the end, he does not get recognition, not even from Max, who does not really see him: "it was a casual look, devoid of the deeper awareness that Bigger sought so hungrily" (423). Bigger's final terror is that at his execution, "I'll be feeling and thinking that they didn't see me and I didn't see them" (425). Confronting the failure of escape, Bigger, like Fred Daniels, wants to be seen and to be heard in common humanity. As Baldwin puts it, "it is the question of Bigger's humanity which is at stake, the relationship in which he stands to all other Americans—and, by implication, to all people."[38]

For Baldwin, this fight for Bigger's humanity is a "trap," for it concedes Bigger as "subhuman,"[39] reinscribing the racist structure against which the novel protests. We should, however, recognize in it a realist assertion, a fact of history that Baldwin himself perceives clearly: racist society "is able to convince those people to whom it has given inferior status of the reality of this decree; it has the force and the weapons to translate its dictum into fact, so that the allegedly inferior are actually made so, insofar as the societal realities are concerned."[40] Through a decree backed by violence, the expulsion of the stateless from humanity becomes fact, social reality if not biological. While Baldwin demands that art move beyond this social reality, insisting that we "need not battle for" Black humanity but only "accept it,"[41] in Wright's modernist realism, in the face of the state's objectifying violence, Bigger Thomas's humanity, like Fred Daniels's, is far from given.

Native Son even formally reinforces this struggle to be recognized in its closing pages. At novel's end, Wright "abruptly and disturbingly abandons Bigger's point of view, giving the reader no more information than he gives Max."[42] Kihara reads this narrative shift as another utopian gesture, making "Bigger's story unpossessable for readers.... At the close of the novel, Bigger defies Max's master narrative, thereby escaping from the third-person narrator's spell."[43] I would suggest, rather, that this absence of free indirect discourse in the final pages (and the corresponding loss of Bigger's perspective) reasserts the need for a politics of inclusion. Just as in *Underground* the shift from direct quotation into a pseudo–free indirect discourse reinforces Daniels's silencing, so too does this shift away from free indirect discourse in *Native Son* fade Bigger's voice out of perception; that is the political problem that *Native Son* poses, formally recreating it here as a problem of narrative representation.

Wright suggests as much when he casts this as a fundamental difficulty of authorship, explaining that "the author is eager to explain," much like Bigger and Daniels, but "he is left peering with eager dismay back into the dim reaches of his own incommunicable life."[44] For the author, "to account for his book is to account for his life, and he knows that that is impossible," but it is also indispensable because "his dignity as a living being is challenged by something within him that is not understood."[45] Wright's biographer Michel Fabre similarly observes the metafictional connection between the character of Fred Daniels and the role of the author, noting how everything the story says "about the nature of mankind could be applied to the nature of literary works. Just as Daniels needs a spectator in order to exist, so does fiction need a reader."[46] Wright's artistic difficulty is a synecdoche for the political difficulty faced by his characters. For the author, it is the language of fiction, while for his characters, it is the language of law, and in this way the novel itself becomes an important means of thinking about the state. For Wright, escape is the first impetus, but there is no exit from the state, so the only thing to do is get more equitably included—to have a voice—within it.

As we will see, this will remain a persistent problem for the poetics of escape in the following decades. If escaping the state is historically and practically (though not conceptually) impossible, does that make inclusion within the state the only viable politics? This is the crux of Baldwin's criticism of *Native Son,* as he rejects a politics of inclusion as "the dream of all liberal men, a dream not at all dishonorable, but, nevertheless, a dream."[47] While those earlier essays in *Notes of a Native Son* emphasize the insufficiency of the protest novel's demand for inclusion, the latter pages also confront more directly the infeasibility of escape, as Baldwin's own exile to Paris, like Wright's, manifested—"People are trapped in history and history is trapped in them."[48] In Baldwin's memorable quip about politicians promising playgrounds in Harlem—it is ridiculous to believe "one playground more or less" will make any real difference, "yet it is better to have the playground; it is better than nothing"[49]—he prefigures a writer such as Junot Díaz, who, as we will see in chapter 4, will try to have it both ways, promoting equal recognition within the state as a reformist relief against injustice while still ultimately seeking revolutionary escape, evacuating the state's power over inclusion and exclusion. Others such as Nathaniel Mackey will instead demand flight all the more urgently, embracing the very inarticulacy that causes "dismay" in Wright and insisting that meaningful inclusion can only be truly realized apart from the state.

For his part, Wright resolves this dilemma in favor of inclusion. Just after Bigger rejects his mother's and Bessie's escapism, he concludes that what he really wants is "to merge himself with others and be a part of this world. . . . to be allowed a chance to live like others, even though he was black" (240), a sentiment he reiterates in the novel's closing pages: "I wanted to be happy in this world, not out of it" (356). As with Fred Daniels, Bigger's position inside or outside the state is repeatedly a matter of representation. After murdering Bessie, Bigger learns from his stolen newspaper that he is now the prime suspect in the Mary Dalton case: "AUTHORITIES HINT SEX CRIME. Those words excluded him utterly from the world" (243). It is the words that exclude Bigger—words with authority and backed by real, physical violence. It is there, at the intersection of representation and state violence, that Bigger finally locates his exclusion, and it is there that he seeks redress through inclusion. Even though Bigger "is looking and feeling for a way out," as Wright explains, his "wild and intense longing (wild and intense because it was suppressed!) to belong, to be identified, to feel that they were alive as other people were" nevertheless drives Bigger to look for ways in.[50]

Native Son has often been read in this way, putting forth a politics of inclusion or recognition.[51] As Lewis Gordon puts it, Wright is responding to "the existential challenges that racism and other forms of dehumanization posed to political life. To act politically, one needs to appear, as political thinkers from antiquity through to Hannah Arendt have argued, in the social world in particular ways—for example, as a human being with a legitimate voice in public affairs."[52] For Wright, that political and social appearance occurs primarily in relation to the state, and Michael Szalay argues that Wright "identified 'the reality of the state' as the only mechanism for securing the Black body from the abrasions of history."[53] I think it is largely correct to think of this novel as a literary forerunner to the Civil Rights era and identity politics more generally.[54] That is where Wright ultimately takes us. But that's not where his fiction starts; it only arrives there after an extensive, difficult attempt to imagine flight from the law. By juxtaposing Wright's politics of inclusion with the potential, countervailing politics of escape that, though cut short and abandoned, these novels nevertheless take quite seriously—as Wright's own biographical flight to France underscores[55]—we reach a better understanding of the political road not taken.

We can also begin to see *why* it is not taken: exit from the state appears to be only an escapist fantasy. Here, *Native Son* also contributes to our understanding of the insufficiency of political theory's standard accounts of exit. For liberals, the freedoms of exit enjoyed in the marketplace should at least alleviate the problems of racism and prejudice. The economist Milton Friedman, for example, argued that "the preserves of discrimination in any society are the areas that are most monopolistic in character, whereas discrimination against groups of particular color or religion is least in those areas where there is greatest freedom of competition."[56] For Friedman, this is a simple consequence of supply and demand: "the man who objects to buying from or working alongside a Negro, for example, thereby limits his range of choice. He will generally have to pay a higher price for what he buys or receive a lower return for his work."[57] Less freedom of exit leads to more discrimination, and vice versa. But Friedman—and liberalism in general—takes for granted the final, inescapable boundary of the state itself, limiting the exit of consumer choice to a space inside the state. Such exit within the marketplace is little consolation for the racial other trapped in the monopolistic state with no way out. Thus Wright rejects the politics of exit as inadequate, doomed to simply producing further imprisonment.

In his dead-end search for exit, Wright nevertheless evokes an urgent desire for escape from the state and its systems of representation, a longing that still rouses and agitates writers to come after, including ones who share many of Wright's political concerns. The well-known trope of blindness in *Native Son* provides one compelling instance of this latent, unrealized prospect of escape. For example, Ian Afflerbach shows how blindness in *Native Son* prefigures mid-century liberal ideals of racial color-blindness while simultaneously critiquing the limitations of a legal system that does not see race, anticipating the later conservative appropriation of color-blindness. Yet, even while Afflerbach is right to note how "blindness in *Native Son* represents neither equality nor a weapon against prejudice but rather . . . undermines any attempt to articulate the injustices shaping Bigger's life," the novel nevertheless does consider seriously the possibility that blindness could be a weapon and source of freedom.[58] Bigger decides that the best way to live is "while they were not looking, do what you wanted" (106). Most people "needed a certain picture of the world . . . and they were blind to what did not fit" (106). Being outside the picture would make others blind to Bigger, "and if he could see while others were blind, then he could get what he wanted and never be caught at it" (107). According to Bigger's logic here, relatively early in the novel, blindness indeed might provide cover enough to exit the state. Bigger's "hands held weapons that were invisible" (130). What more powerful a weapon than an invisible one? How better to defeat the panopticon than by blinding it?

As we have seen, Wright rejects such escape strategies, framing them as more likely to blind Bigger himself than to hide him from the gaze of the state. In the end, Bigger wants to be heard and seen, to be "included in that picture of Creation" (285) rather than hoping for a blind spot in "what did not fit" that "picture" (106). Later artists, however, have taken blindness back up, reconsidering its potential—not as color-blindness but as a stealth tactic. Michael Clune, for example, has shown how the blinding flash of bling in rap lyrics proposes an escape from hierarchal relationships constituted by the gaze from subject to object—rap has found potential political value in invisibility, reappraising strategies rejected by Civil Rights authors such as Wright and Ralph Ellison.[59] It is in this way that Wright's fiction is important for the poetics of escape, as it explores and prods how literature can imaginatively engage political exit. Moreover, the same critical nuance that ultimately leads Wright to reject the escape of invisibility, despite its obvious appeal for someone like Bigger Thomas or Fred Daniels, helps identify clear difficulties that the poetics of escape must address.

"GO AWAY AND NEVER COME BACK": SLOTHROPIAN ESCAPISM IN *GRAVITY'S RAINBOW*

Invisibility provides a useful and illustrative segue. For Wright, invisibility is an alluring but ultimately unviable means of escape. Invisibility in

Pynchon likewise appears as both opportunity and threat. Samuel Thomas notes that "invisibility... is inextricably bound up with the fate and status of the political in Pynchon's work. It carries with it both the full force of radical freedom and the arbitrary horror of being wiped out plain and simple, of repression, abduction, terror and death."[60] Joanna Freer agrees with Thomas, arguing that invisibility functions as both a means of imagining escape as well as a "warning" against escapism, "against allowing imaginative or visionary experience to become an end itself, dissociated from a critical, interpretative practice aimed at alleviating suffering and escaping oppression."[61] Following Thomas and Freer, I argue that Pynchon formally links textual invisibility to political exit—practicing a poetics of escape and asserting a sincere political aspiration that he nevertheless problematizes.

Juxtaposing Pynchon with Wright helps nuance how Pynchon asserts a politics of escape even while condemning its apparently inevitable collapse into escapism. While Wright, concluding that the desire to escape the state cannot be satisfied, settles on inclusion within state-granted privilege as the next best option, Pynchon pushes the getaway quest so far into the extreme that he verges into a self-defeating escapism. Pynchon's literarily imagined flight from the state comes at the cost of solipsistic detachment from representation, a hermitic withdrawal from the world that is fitting for such a famously reclusive author. Nevertheless, such solipsistic, apolitical escapism neither satisfies nor (in contrast to Wright) invalidates a politics of exit. Pynchon's response to escapism is not inclusion but, rather, a dogged and prodding pursuit of escape anyway.

Stefan Mattessich offers one of the first sustained investigations of Pynchon's interest in escape: "the central descriptive category for the counterculture in *Gravity's Rainbow*," he suggests, "might be 'escape' (with its overtone of escapism) rather than 'revolution,'" noting that the rocket's flight represents "countercultural withdrawal from dominant society."[62] While Mattessich's Deleuzian psychoanalytic approach clearly has political ramifications, his focus on subject formation and desire leads him to deemphasize the state and, by extension, the impossibility of escape. Because Mattessich sees "axiomatized desire," rather than the state, as the impetus for flight, all you need in order to achieve escape is a critical self-awareness, "escapism becoming a kind of genuine escape in the limit it was able to produce as its own symptomaticity."[63] Internal, psychological escape counts as a real escape.

After the "political turn in Pynchon studies," as Michael O'Bryan frames it, critics have recognized a much more difficult relationship between escape and escapism in Pynchon.[64] In place of Mattessich's escape/revolution binary, which poses individual withdrawal as an alternative to political change, escape increasingly appears *as* revolutionary strategy, a "fugitive politics" that, in turn, renders psychological escapism an impediment, rather than a route to, political escape.[65] Freer, for example, asserts "anarchism, escape and escapism" as central themes in Pynchon's work, linking escape to radical politics, but she also insists that "there can be no easy escapes in Pynchon's prose," as his work problematizes the psychological escapes, the impetus to free one's mind, characteristic of the Beats and hippies.[66]

Pynchon offers an enduring image of the state's pervasive inescapability right from his first novel, *V.* (1963), in which yo-yos become a symbol of state power through Yoyodyne, Inc., a toy manufacturer that, through its expertise in all things gyroscope, becomes a major military contractor. A broken yo-yo explicitly amounts to individual sovereignty in the text—cutting the yo-yo string would be a kind of escape—but yo-yos in *V.* turn out to be well-nigh indestructible.[67] Direct resistance, flinging the yo-yo away, only increases the speed at which the yo-yo inevitably returns to the controlling hand.

The Crying of Lot 49 (1966) again explicitly considers a politics of escape, framing protagonist Oedipa Maas as a Rapunzel desperately looking for a way out of her tower. Oedipa's potential escape relies on alternatives to dominant systems of representation, replacing the reified structures of the government mail monopoly in the United States Postal Service with the anarchic Trystero. *Lot 49* links semiotics and politics not just metaphorically but constitutively: the state uses representation to extend and intensify its schemes of control, and representations exert force on the world through state apparatuses.[68] One of Pynchon's primary concerns in *Lot 49* is whether it is possible to escape such representational schemes, to find "a real alternative to the exitlessness."[69] For Pynchon, the most difficult question becomes whether such escape is even possible. As Mark Greif puts it, the novel's central anxiety is that "there is no proof that the human efforts at an exit ... really do work; no proof there's anywhere to go, once you're down and out. Where *is* the other world?"[70] Is the Trystero real, or only a terrifying and seductive construction of either a manipulative conspiracy or a madwoman's mind? Can we really believe in such "another world ... An anarchist miracle"?[71]

In *The Crying of Lot 49*, the answer, if ambiguous, nevertheless appears negative.[72] For example, in a compelling reading of the novel's Inamorati Anonymous (a support group for recovering love addicts with ties to the Trystero), Thomas argues that the "'IA' does not just represent an escape from government controlled mail. Above all else, 'IA' is an escape from love ... By extension, it is an also escape from community, from human contact, from shared distribution and from reciprocal trust."[73] This is not political escape but solipsistic withdrawal, antisocial more than anti-state: "It is a club that never meets, a society of isolates, a voluntary form of group alienation.... Hell, or some secular variation on the theme, is other people."[74]

In contrast, critics have typically read Pynchon's post-hiatus fiction, from *Vineland* (1990) on, as offering at least provisionally more hopeful visions of escape.[75] *Vineland*, for example, offers models of political escape through both "the mountainside retreat of the Sisterhood of Kunoichi Attentives," a group of female ninjas, "lady asskickers," as well as the Beckers-Traverse family reunion in Vineland at the end of the novel, a "refuge from government"—each at least gestures towards a communal space outside (free from) and against the state.[76]

Gravity's Rainbow offers a compelling confrontation with both his earlier fiction's hopeless sense of "exitlessness" as well as the hope for escape critics have identified in his later work. With gravity vectors always pulling flights of departure back down towards the authority of the center, Pynchon also begins imagining a tentative solution to the problem of exitlessness—albeit a solution that flounders into solipsistic escapism.

We might consider the characters Roger Mexico and Jessica Swanlake, who in their lovers' affair threaten to escape the global warfare state of World War II. During a tryst, they block out the death raining down around them: "If they have not quite seceded from war's state, at least they've found the beginnings of gentle withdrawal."[77] Their partial secession takes place in "a house in the stay-away zone," a town evacuated by the government, which they occupy "illegally, in a defiance they can never measure unless they're caught" (41). While Freer reads Roger and Jessica as indulging in "escapist absorption in each other's love," a "withdrawal from world affairs," this misses a more fundamental difficulty with escape.[78] Far from apolitical escapism, Pynchon explicitly figures their lovers' withdrawal as a political act of "defiance." Rather, their direct opposition to the state is also part of what prevents their escape from being complete: defiance means they can still be "caught." An important, recurring paradox for Pynchon comes into focus here. Defiance makes escape political rather than escapist, but it also means you haven't really gotten away. Opposing the state is a way of being inside the state.

This insufficiency of straightforward withdrawal from state structures is crucial to Pynchon's political critique; like Wright, Pynchon recognizes that simply being outside the state proper does not amount to escape from it. Drawing directly on Arendt's analysis of statelessness, Luc Herman and Steven Weisenburger observe how *Gravity's Rainbow* represents the "paradoxically included-excluded middle" embodied in the stateless refugees of postwar Europe, posing "a humanity apparently outside of the political" that is nevertheless reincorporated into the political as "mere human trash," Arendt's "scum of the earth" or Agamben's *homo sacer*.[79] The novel's stateless figures are not free from the state but all the more utterly vulnerable to state power. Thus, the Argentinean anarchist character Francisco Squalidozzi is foolishly romantic in his political hopes for the transformative potential of the quasi-stateless "Zone," the power vacuum in Germany after the war but before the Americans and Soviets officially move in. As Herman and Weisenburger show, the Zone is not the borderless, anarchist tabula rasa that Squalidozzi hopes it is, but is rather "where sovereignty performs its greatest magic, lawfully declaring the absence of law, declaring forfeit all guarantees of individual rights, for *some* people."[80] Getting outside the law, outside the state's official boundaries, simply transforms the way one remains stuck inside the state. Running away changes Roger's and Jessica's relationship to the state, but it does not let them escape it.

It is no coincidence, then, that protagonist Tyrone Slothrop both opposes the system more ambivalently than Roger and Jessica and more completely escapes it—the only way to escape the state is not to oppose it but to cease to have any relation to it whatsoever. Compared to the anarchist Squalidozzi or even Roger (who also gets called "anarchist" [89]), Slothrop remains lukewarm: "well, the anarchist persuasion appeals to him *a little*" (268; emphasis mine). And yet, Slothrop nevertheless doggedly pursues escape. Aided in part by incompetent state agents—antagonist Ned Pointsman's plan had "seemed foolproof: to let Slothrop escape . . . and then rely on Secret Service to keep him under surveillance," but "there's now been no word of Slothrop for nearly a month, since the fumbling asses in military intelligence lost him" (270)—Slothrop slowly slips out of representation within the state.

Slothrop distinguishes his prospective escape from simple escapism, in part, on its status as a one-way trip, a trope reinforced through the novel's rocket cosmology. In a flashback conversation, Slothrop contrasts his father's drug trips from his hope for an escape into cyberspace: "Oh Pop. Cripes. It isn't like *dope* at all! . . . you always came back, didn't you . . . it was always understood that *this* would still be here when you got back, just the same, exactly the same, right?" (699). In contrast to Beats and hippies "dropping out," in *Gravity's Rainbow* the escapism of drugs does not free you from the reality you want to leave behind.[81] When Pop Slothrop worries, "Suppose someday you just plug in and go away and never come back?" Tyrone scoffs, "Ho, ho! Don't I wish!" (699). Superimposing three historical moments—postwar Europe, '60s counterculture and psychedelics, and a science fiction future—the novel asserts an urge for escape that transcends narrow historical particularity while nevertheless remaining grounded in history, responding to the historical reality of the state. For Slothrop, true escape means never returning to his present reality—not a rocket rainbowing towards earthly destruction but a spaceship escaping gravity's reach, heading to other worlds.

Slothrop ultimately makes such a one-way trip, but if any other world awaits him, it is difficult to imagine it being a human one. Slothrop's escape happens through a slow disintegration of his subjectivity and his contact with other people. Withdrawing like a hermit, "he's kept alone. If others have seen him or his fire, they haven't tried to approach. He's letting hair and beard grow" (623). Recalling Ferlinghetti's "full beard / of walking anarchy," Slothrop is a long-haired hippie dropping out of society, becoming invisible to the state.[82] The lure of national identity and belonging hampers his escape, as he is "still thinking there's a way to get back [to America]" (623), but eventually he slips by that obstacle too, becoming "scattered all over the Zone. It's doubtful if he can ever be 'found' again, in the conventional sense of 'positively identified and detained'" (712). With the police language reinforcing the direction of flight as one away from law, Slothrop escapes even his sentimental attachment to America and finally leaves behind any relation to the state.

Unfortunately, this also means leaving behind any relation to other people, and here we see the next problem emerging for Pynchon: even one-way trips can be escapist. In the late stages of Slothrop's disintegration, Seaman Bodine is "one of the few who can still see Slothrop as any sort of integral creature any more" (740). But Bodine fears that he too will soon lose touch with Slothrop, that "he'll *have* to let go" (741). This threat of disconnection is specifically a matter of communication, of losing the representational ties of language. Bodine speaks half to himself, half to Slothrop (toggling between third and second person pronouns for Slothrop), wondering, "Does he even hear any more?" and then again, pleading, "if you can hear me..." and "Do you—please, are you listening?" (741). Finally, even Bodine cannot maintain this connection. He stops talking, and he "was beginning, helpless, in shame, to let Slothrop go" (741). After that, Slothrop disappears from representation even within the novel: this is the last we see of him on the page. Slothrop escapes representation within the system—his state-backed pursuers never catch him or give any word of him—but this also results in his exclusion from all representation, from interpersonal communication and, for the final twenty pages, even from the novel itself. Though Slothrop's escape is not escapist like his father's drugs in the sense of being only a temporary delusion, it nevertheless remains escapist in its solipsism, leaving others like Bodine to suffer under the persisting state. Slothrop escapes political representation, but only at the cost of representational connection as such.

Though much has been made of Slothrop's disintegration,[83] relatively less attention has been devoted to another of the novel's escapees, Roger Mexico, who has also been seeking a way out all along. Roger's escape affirms and reiterates the disillusioned poetics of escape we see through Slothrop: he escapes the state only by abandoning representation and other people. His departure coincides with his increasing self-consciousness of how opposing the state still traps him within it. Pirate Prentice explains to Roger that "They" are "only half the story," because the Counterforce opposes the "They-system" with "a We-system" of its own, which provides no way out of the system as such—indeed it is only the other half of the same story. Roger concludes, "well, you're playing Their game, then" (638). This does not seem to bother Prentice, but Roger is no longer content to be the Black pawn opposing—but playing the same game as—Their White pawns, such as the enthusiastic "citizen of" "this war, this State" (75), Dr. Ned Pointsman (the "Antimexico" [89], Roger "the Antipointsman" [55]).

This all comes to a head at the Krupp dinner party, the scene in which Roger and Bodine ruin the appetites of all the military-industrial-complex guests by shouting a menu of alliterative, disgusting dishes: "snot soup," "pus pudding," and so on for two and a half pages (715–17). Superficially, this seems to be an act of resistance, a Counterforce "repulsive stratagem" to demoralize these representatives of the System (715). Freer reads the scene as successful in that regard, arguing that "the Counterforce regain the revolutionary edge they had lost, and Mexico escapes the binary choice of co-optation or death."[84] In Freer's optimistic reading, Roger and Bodine "delegitimise official power" by "circumventing the expectations of the authorities and refusing to play on their terms."[85] Roger, in contrast, has already deflated any transformative power it might hold, treating this as just another move in the game, still playing on Their terms: "They will use us. We will help legitimize Them" (713). Roger does not stop there, though. The scene ends enigmatically: "The last black butler opens the last door to the outside, and escape. Escape tonight" (717). Though later we see Bodine again talking to disintegrating Slothrop, Roger Mexico disappears from the novel after this point. It seems that Roger is among the absent, already unrepresentable subjects of the verb *escape*, grammatically implied but missing from the page.

Roger's escape is no less escapist than Slothrop's, though, because Roger's escape means leaving behind Jessica, his love, the only human connection he cares about—and because abandoning human connection amounts to death, social if not biological. Early in the novel, it dawns on Roger "how easily she might go. For the first time he understands why this is the same as mortality" (176). Thus, when before the Krupp dinner party Roger ponders, "which is worse: living on as Their pet, or death?" he is deciding whether to stay, to continue playing the game and legitimizing Them, or to leave, but in leaving lose Jessica forever (713). In Roger's case, the choice is easy because he's already a dead man, Jessica having already left him for Jeremy, one of Them. Contrary to Freer's claim that "Mexico escapes the binary choice of co-optation or death" at the Krupp dinner party, his escape functions *as* death, his disconnection from Jessica the expression of his mortality. For Roger as for Slothrop, the only way out of the political System is social death, ceasing to exist from the perspective of the state, but also from the perspective of everyone else.[86] Escape in *Gravity's Rainbow* requires departing the entire representational apparatus of human life, a view formally enacted through Roger's and Slothrop's nonexistence in the novel's closing pages.

But what if Roger and Slothrop could escape the state without disappearing from the novel? What if there were a way to escape political representation without having to cede representation as such? This is the most optimistic hope of *Gravity's Rainbow*: "Imagine this very elaborate scientific lie: that sound cannot travel through outer space. Well, but suppose it can. Suppose They don't want us to know there is a medium there, what used to be called an 'aether,' which can carry sound to every part of the earth" (695). The master narrative since Hobbes is that, outside the state, there is no human community, no peaceful communication. But what if that narrative is wrong? What if there is still sound, still representational connection, outside? That would mean Roger and Slothrop could escape the state without disappearing from the novel. That they do not indicates the extent of Pynchon's pessimism—he is no believer in the "aether," in the "anarchist miracle" of *The Crying of Lot 49*. For him, the moment for escape, if there ever was one, has long passed: "you are trapped inside Their frame . . . Reminded, too late, of how dependent you are on Them, for neglect if not good will: Their neglect is your freedom" (694).[87] The only hope now remaining is for a relative freedom, one still circumscribed by "Their frame" and coextensive only with the degree of state indifference. At this moment in history, there is no meaningful escape from the state; and yet, Pynchon still clings to the prospect of creating an escape: "Imagine" is the imperative to the reader. The absence of escape means we have to invent one, and it is first in the imagination that we can explicate, understand, and prepare for the real sought departure, possibly providing, as Freer puts it, the "precursor to political action."[88] That is where the poetics of escape tries to go: to develop, on the page and in the mind, in all its complexities, obstacles, and contradictions, the possibility of a future historical escape from the state.

In emphasizing the political struggle for escape, as distinct from escapism and as something not to be taken for granted but a political objective that remains to be won, I am working against Sean McCann and Michael Szalay's influential contention that post-sixties anti-statism—a "basic antipathy to big government" or "libertarian sensibility"[89] on both the right and the left, which includes "hostility to the Democratic Party" and "doubtfulness about electoral politics generally"[90]—amounts to political quietism, a retreat into magical or miraculous political thinking with no concern for political means or efficacy beyond the individual, "withdrawing not only from traditional politics, but also from the very possibility of orchestrated change."[91] Far from indulging in wishful thinking about the power of culture and imagination to effect political change, Pynchon is a stringent political realist—his forays into utopianism condemn merely reformist ends, but, as Freer observes, "rather than overlooking the problems and affirming what we want to believe, Pynchon's fiction attempts to throw into stark relief the obstacles that confront us on the road to freedom."[92] Or, as Seán Molloy has it, "Pynchon is too much of a political realist to ignore the disparity between ought and is."[93] Pynchon's critiques of escapism align with McCann and Szalay's critique of magical thinking, but, unlike McCann and Szalay, Pynchon nevertheless poses escape not as an avoidance of politics but rather as the most pressing political necessity. I thus build upon Michael O'Bryan's important insights, joining him in extending the implications here out from Pynchon and into more general critical practice: "Pynchon's identifiably anarchist politics often do not register *as* politics within a literary academy steeped in Marxian historiography that has elided the practical and theoretical contributions of anarchism to twentieth-century radicalism."⁹⁴ As Thomas puts it, Pynchon "forces us to rethink what the political actually is."⁹⁵ Pynchon thus provides a clear example of how the poetics of escape can expand our conceptions of the political, beyond the myopias of official intellectual culture.

Neither Wright nor Pynchon gives us a singular, perfect archetype of escape poetics—indeed no single text or author can fully capture what is a broad, ongoing, and thus still evolving literary phenomenon. Nevertheless, together they offer another look at a preliminary poetics of escape in practice, suggesting some of its enduring concerns and obstacles. In *Empire of the Senseless* (1988), for example, Kathy Acker continues the line of thought I have been tracing through *Gravity's Rainbow*. Acker's anarchic space of piracy is a violent, brutal space that is far from utopian—or, is utopian only in the wider sense Sean Grattan applies to Pynchon, in which utopianism "is not found in any particular quirky commune or plucky group of adventurers; it is, instead, found in the desire for those counterpublics multiplying," desiring another world that "is not necessarily a better world" but that "marks, instead, the possibility of running counter to the prevailing norms of mainstream America."⁹⁶ Acker elevates such another world over its nation-state alternative, yet even the escape of piracy proves impossible, the pirate reduced to just another criminal, included within the state: "I who would have and would be a pirate: I cannot."⁹⁷ Acker tries to push against these realizations of hopelessness by imagining a space with no relation to the state whatsoever. The cyborg Thivai can only achieve his dream of becoming a pirate in his imagination, an accomplishment that simultaneously requires, like for post-scattering Slothrop, ceasing to exist in reality: he can only be a pirate in his "imagination as everything... I am nothing in these times" (26). The only real outside to the state is paradoxically outside reality: "I would, and I would have, run away, but there's no place to which to run, so the only safety is psychosis and drugs" (27).

Like Pynchon, Acker rejects this unreal escapism as insufficient: "Once I had had enough of working for bosses. Now I had had enough of nothing" (80–81). How to evade both bosses and nothingness is never entirely clear in Acker's novel, and though it yearns for the "revolts of the non-existent against their economic controllers," it also seems to admit defeat, at least in part (6). Near the end of the novel, the imaginary-revolutionary pirates complain, "we couldn't find any dynamite cause dynamite was still illegal despite the revolution and the cops wouldn't give us any" (201). As with Pynchon's "Counterforce," resistance here again seems to be at the mercy of the system it opposes. What the novel does accomplish, though, is the declaration of a political goal—"I didn't as yet know what I wanted. I now fully knew what I didn't want and what and whom I hated. That was something" (227). For Acker, this is a necessary first step for meaningful political change: "And then I thought that, one day, maybe, there'ld be a human society in a world which is beautiful, a society which wasn't just disgust" (227). There is a long way to go, Acker suggests, but we have to start somewhere.

On either side of World War II—the bombs have just started dropping at the end of *The Man Who Lived Underground,* and we're trudging through the rubble at the start of *Gravity's Rainbow*—the possibility of breaking away from existing nation-states seems historically imminent. As a result of shifting international conditions (a decline in territorial conquest and an increasingly global economy), smaller states become both more attractive and more viable in this period.[98] Secession becomes conspicuously prominent in international politics, redrawing much of the global political map: "the majority of states in the world today were created via secession, including 106 out of 156 new states formed since 1931."[99] This prevalence of secession—fundamentally intertwined with the international crisis of statelessness surrounding World War II[100]—would seem to weaken the sense that escaping the state is impossible; here is the politics of exit in action. Yet, of course, these historical secessions move not just out of existing states but into new ones, aiming ultimately for "recognized statehood."[101] Moreover, even if this explosion of secessionism demonstrates a widespread political logic of withdrawal, it does not indicate any viable means of remaining beyond the state. As political scientist Peter Krause observes, "the vast majority of secessionist efforts fail—and even more never get off the ground—due in large part to the concerted efforts of host states to maintain their territorial integrity."[102] Because "states' top priority is to promote their own strength and survival ... counter-secession is the default policy. Every state in the world has employed it in some form at some point in time."[103]

This reality is perfectly clear to Wright and Pynchon. The state works, above all, to ensure that no one leaves, and the deck is stacked in its favor—all the more acutely when departure would work not to create a new peer state, as with secession, but rather to reject the very logic and legitimacy of the state. Neither Wright nor Pynchon purports to discover a way out of the state. Yet, they nevertheless imagine exit as an at least potentially desirable political end. We might join Acker in saying: that's something. In doing so, however, Wright and Pynchon still posit a close relationship between literary representation and political representation, much as we saw with Williams and Olson in chapter 1. Political exit looks like textual absence or silence. Thus an important dilemma remains for escape poetics: that close relationship is precisely what makes literary representation such a useful tool for thinking about political representation, but that also means that literature cannot imagine a viable escape. So far, escaping the political has meant escaping language, and escape for these writers thus always collapses back into escapism, as solipsism, death, and nonexistence.

In the next chapter, Don DeLillo will offer one way around this problem by instead emphasizing the difference between political and nonpolitical representations. Escape pertains only to political representation that overlays a regime of violence; for DeLillo, nonpolitical representation can be left behind at pretty much any time, and escape is thus unimportant. Of course, if political and literary representation are so different, the problem then becomes wondering how much literary representation can tell us about political representation. Joan Didion seems to offer the next step towards a solution. She assumes, like DeLillo, that political and literary representation are different, but then intentionally forces her own representational practices to look and act like political representation, as a way of reasserting a useful link between the two.

UNSTATE

*Deauthorizing Representation in
Don DeLillo and Joan Didion*

cause dying is

perfectly natural;perfectly
putting
it mildly lively(but

Death

is strictly
scientific
& artificial &

evil & legal)

—E. E. Cummings, "[dying is fine)but Death]"

CONTRARY TO DYING, Death is a product of human systems of representation, a "sin" we have committed rather than a natural counterpart to life. Death can be measured and recorded as fact, contained in a sign, whereas dying, with its progressive verb tense indicating its resistance to being pinned down, can be known only tacitly, through the "feel of it," exceeding such attempts at codification. Death, moreover, is "legal," an artifact of state power reified through representation.[1]

Don DeLillo's *White Noise* (1985) and Joan Didion's *Democracy* (1984) both subsume something like E. E. Cummings's dying/Death dichotomy into a general anxiety towards the combination of power and representation—what Giorgio Agamben calls the union of life and law—located at the heart of the political state.[2] *White Noise* suggests just such a bifurcated concept of death: "Maybe there is no death as we know it," narrator and protagonist Jack Gladney ponders, "just documents changing hands."[3] Jack's "death as we know it" appeals to no external system of representation but appears instead as the unspeakable knowledge of embodied experience. In contrast, the "documents changing hands" are of course the law's paperwork for death, death certificates and wills, death's representational inclusion in state administrative schemes. The same dichotomy likewise manifests in *Democracy* when protagonist Inez Victor's sister falls into a coma after being shot by their father, dramatizing a distinction between "actual death" and "technical death."[4] Whereas Inez can't seem to say exactly what she means by the former, the latter is explicitly defined by "three flat electroencephalograms, consecutive, spaced eight hours apart" (151). Technical death reifies dying into tests, numbers, and, ultimately, an official government death certificate, a piece of paper and a signature that determine whether Inez's sister will continue to receive life support, what can legally be done to her body, and so on. I have briefly touched on how dying yields the only way out of political representation in texts as diverse as John Rawls's *Political Liberalism,* William Carlos Williams's "The Use of Force," and Thomas Pynchon's *Gravity's Rainbow,* but in *White Noise* and *Democracy,* the state represents even death back within itself. The state transforms death—Cummings's "perfectly natural" dying—into articulated, explicit knowledge, a piece of information that can be reduced to a sign.

Agamben describes this transformation as "politicizing death": life and death have become "political concepts," the consequences of sovereign decision rather than strict biological realities.[5] Politicized death incorporates biological dying into state schemes of representation. But politicized death is more than just high-theory abstraction. Agamben grounds his analysis in the history of "brain death" and the legal status of comatose patients, including Karen Ann Quinlan, whose parents' high-profile legal battle to take her off life support raised the question of whether Quinlan was already legally dead.[6] Quinlan's artificial respirator was disconnected in 1976, a year before Didion began writing *Democracy,* and ample media coverage makes Quinlan a likely source for Didion's hospital scene (which would help explain its striking similarities to Agamben's account).[7] A more recent example sharpens the point: the related case of Terry Schiavo in the early 2000s, a political spectacle punctuated by the interventions of Florida Governor Jeb Bush and his brother, President George. Writing a few months after Schiavo's death following the court-ordered removal of her feeding tube in 2005, Didion pushes back against attempts to make Schiavo's life or death a matter of technical knowledge: "Much is unknown here"; "No one who has had even a passing exposure to brain injury can think of neurology as a field in which all questions are answerable"; "No one knows why . . . Again, no one knows why."[8] For Didion, like Agamben, political debates over the right to die miss the point, because both sides have already accepted the state's authority to reduce life and death to explicit knowledge.[9]

Though language such as "natural" and "actual" might suggest essentialized concepts of life and death, naturalizing a specific conception of what it means to be human and alive, these literary rejections of politicized death actually push back against state attempts to discipline bodies and render them unambiguously legible to the administrative gaze. Writing on Schiavo, of course, Didion drew on her own recent biography, including the passing of her husband, John Gregory Dunne, in 2003, as well as the ongoing hospitalizations of their daughter, Quintana Roo Dunne Michael, who would die a few months after Didion's article on Schiavo appeared in the *New York Review of Books.* In *The Year of Magical Thinking* (2005), Didion's memoir of spousal grief (written during Quintana's long illness but before she passed), Didion recalls a hospital visit in 1982, her niece on life support, when a doctor told her, "'it's not black and white' ... the divide between life and death." Didion actually rejects this, "thinking that the doctor was wrong," insisting on a sharp binary between life and death that, in her grief, becomes all the more stark.¹⁰ But even as she affirms a sharp biological distinction between life and death, it remains a matter of embodiment, one that cannot be clearly articulated. Crucially, the exact moment of her husband's death remains painfully ambiguous to her, and the coroner's official time of death, the government's "paperwork," is "just bookkeeping, hospital procedure, the regularization of a death."¹¹ Though she insists that life and death are a biological binary, she admits, "I imagined this way of thinking to be clarifying, but in point of fact it was so muddled as to contradict even itself."¹² Death cannot be known through paperwork, cannot be reduced to articulated knowledge. Politicized death pretends otherwise, and in doing so poignantly manifests the potential danger of state representations—DeLillo's "documents changing hands" and Didion's "technical death"—and their capacity to ignore the inarticulable details of lived experience.

I look first at *White Noise*'s critique of the state's asymmetrical privileging of articulated or explicit knowledge. DeLillo's novel fantasizes a successful escape from the state as the precondition for new forms of social coordination more responsive to the vast domains of human knowledge irreducible to systems of representation. *White Noise* imagines how inarticulable forms of tacit, experiential knowledge, necessarily dismissed by state systems of representation, might be reintroduced alongside articulated knowledge. I then look at *Democracy*'s related attempt to escape narrative representation as a way of imagining escape from democratic representation. *Democracy* complicates the kind of utopian escape underpinning *White Noise* by focusing more insistently on the insurmountable difficulty of escaping state schemes of representation. Instead, *Democracy* acquiesces to literary representation as a way of acknowledging the inescapability of political representation, resorting to the narrative of failing to escape narrative in the faint hope of demystifying the state's seemingly natural combination of representation and power.

Though I situate these novels within a historical moment of widespread anti-state sentiment and within a postmodernist literary tradition made relatively coherent by shared aesthetic, formal, and thematic concerns, I emphasize that neither DeLillo nor Didion understand the state as a problem unique to late twentieth-century life. My readings thus resist dominant critical accounts of these novels, which overwhelmingly see them as reactions to postmodernity as a specific historical condition. Where critics typically have understood *White Noise* primarily in relation to the information age (hence the profusion of Baudrillardian readings) and *Democracy* in relation to the Cold War, I want to highlight their more abstract political critiques.[13] The state does not transcend history, but it nevertheless extends far beyond the specific histories of late capitalism and twentieth-century imperialism.

Before turning to the novels, let me first sketch out the theoretical framework and vocabulary informing my analysis, by way of a brief intellectual history. The distinction between "articulated" and "tacit" knowledges grows out of the anti-positivist epistemology of the liberal chemist-turned-philosopher Michael Polanyi, which he spells out most fully in *Personal Knowledge* (1958) and *The Tacit Dimension* (1966). Articulated or explicit knowledge is knowledge represented in language: for example, most of what we generally think of as scientific or historical fact, the stuff of textbooks. Tacit knowledge, in contrast, is knowledge that resists signification: knowing how to ride a bike is the most familiar example, but the term also includes knowledges beyond skills, such as knowledge of what a particular person looks like, or social knowledge such as how to drive in traffic.[14] Tacit knowledge need not be disciplined or even conscious, so long as it helps us navigate the world more successfully. For Polanyi, "we can know more than we can tell."[15] Put in the terms of my opening examples: there's more to death as we know it than the documents changing hands, more to actual death than technical death.

Polanyi's tacit knowledge framework has been taken up by anti-state thinkers from both the political left and right, whose otherwise stark ideological differences diminish in their shared critique of state schemes to articulate knowledge. The mutual influence between Polanyi and the neoliberal economist Friedrich Hayek, for example, is well known.[16] In his seminal 1945 essay "The Use of Knowledge in Society," Hayek underscores the value of "knowledge of people, of local conditions... special knowledge of circumstances of the fleeting moment not known to others."[17] Most importantly, for Hayek this tacit knowledge cannot be adequately communicated through systems of signification, because such articulations can work only "by abstracting from minor differences between things" and eliding variations that "may be very significant for the specific decision."[18] Likewise, Marxist anthropologist James C. Scott cites both Polanyi and Hayek in developing his concept of what he calls "*mētis,*" a kind of "implicit, experiential" knowledge "that can be acquired only by practice and that all but defies being communicated in written or oral form apart from actual practice."[19] *Mētis* is knowledge that comes almost automatically through experience but that is onerously difficult or outright impossible to articulate.[20]

For Polanyi, Hayek, and Scott, the idea that we know more than we can tell necessarily stands at odds to centralized political authority and its presumption to know the situations it rules: a central decision-maker only has access to knowledge that can be transmitted and thus represented, and state agents cannot take advantage of any unrepresentable, tacit knowledge. This is the same relationship between epistemology and politics that William Carlos Williams posits in his lecture "Revolutions Revalued" in 1936 (around the same time Hayek and Polanyi first began working on these ideas), where he maintains that "no one is fitted to determine ... so well as [the individual]" which actions will be "socially valuable" precisely because "only the individual can know these things."[21] Though Polanyi, Hayek, and Scott each carve out exceptions in line with their differing politics (as does Williams), they are all nevertheless wary of state attempts to articulate knowledge precisely because of the state's unilateral ability to dismiss tacit knowledge, knowledge that does not fit into its schemes of articulation. Hayek, for example, argues that states are cut off from local manifestations of tacit knowledge and must rely on articulable knowledge; regarding the local, the center knows only what is communicated. As a result, state interventions "rarely result in anything closely corresponding to men's wishes," because the means necessary to accomplish those goals are "determined by more particular facts than any such intervening agency can know."[22] Scott likewise emphasizes that articulated knowledge is most detrimental to social welfare when it is "backed by state power through records, courts, and ultimately coercion."[23] Coupled with the implicit and explicit violence of the state, articulated knowledge becomes a tool for shaping and controlling human decisions and behaviors. To the extent the state dominates social organization, we lose the value of all that we know but cannot tell.

DISARTICULATING KNOWLEDGE IN *WHITE NOISE*

"I had never looked at coffee before," says *White Noise*'s narrator and central character, Jack Gladney, a pioneering scholar of "Hitler studies" at a small-town college, who has a compulsive preoccupation with death. Just before this strange statement, Jack is making coffee in the family kitchen when his fourteen-year-old son Heinrich suddenly interrupts him: "Did you see what you just did? You took the coffee can with you to the counter." Jack, understandably, responds, "So what?" Heinrich insists Jack has wasted energy by unnecessarily carrying the coffee can around the kitchen when, if he had thought it through beforehand, he could have left it on the counter by the stove and saved himself the effort. Though Jack first dismisses this critique because that is "what people do" and a "little waste doesn't hurt," he ultimately concedes Heinrich's position: over the years, that wasted time and energy adds up, effectively hastening one's death (102–3). Heinrich's logic strikes at his father's obsessive fear of death, and Jack suddenly takes a grave interest in the coffee.

As they discuss the can of coffee, Jack and Heinrich offer two distinct and incompatible attitudes towards human knowledge. Initially for Jack, knowledge about what he will do with the can of coffee is meaningless, but Heinrich convinces him it merits conscious attention. The novel, however, formally undermines both attitudes towards knowledge, moving away from Jack and Heinrich's debate over the importance of knowledge towards a consideration of the different forms knowing can take. DeLillo grants markedly disproportionate textual space to Jack's stroll around the kitchen and Heinrich's subsequent critique. In one sentence, Jack has just decided to make coffee instead of tea; in the next, Heinrich begins his complaint. All of Jack's supposedly wasted effort occurs in the space between these two sentences, only entering the text through Heinrich's retrospective narration: "You carried it in your right hand all the way to the counter, put it down to open the drawer, which you didn't want to do with your left hand, then got the spoon with your right hand, switched it to your left hand, picked up the coffee can with your right hand and went back to the stove, where you put it down again" (102). Heinrich's ridiculously pedantic description certainly contributes to the novel's humor, but it also dramatizes the potential costs of articulating knowledge—there's more to knowledge than what we put into words. While Jack's expense of energy slips by between sentences, his conversation about it with Heinrich stretches on for half a page. Formally, the text suggests that both of them spend far more energy talking about the coffee can carrying than Jack could ever have spent in the carrying. Maybe "a little waste" does hurt, but not as much as listening to Heinrich drone on about it.

We can begin to see how the novel links overreaching political authority to an exclusionary commitment to articulated knowledge through such ironically paternalistic behavior from Jack's children and stepchildren, whose authoritarian desires are inextricable from deployments of articulated knowledge. Heinrich's articulation of Jack's coffee-carrying, for example, evokes Foucauldian disciplinary control, linguistically breaking down Jack's body and actions into discrete, individually manipulable components, in a technocratic effort to eliminate Jack's supposed inefficiencies.[24] Heinrich's effort for control extends further as he also tries to dictate Jack's consumption behavior, telling him to make tea instead of coffee (because tea would be healthier). Though Heinrich's dictatorial aspirations are mostly limited to the confines of domestic, familial space, throughout the novel Heinrich, more than any other character, is committed to both articulated knowledge and authoritarian control, and it is Heinrich who recognizes "the threat in state-created terminology" (117). For Heinrich, articulating knowledge provides a means of dictating the behavior of others.

Though Heinrich is far more invested in articulated knowledge than his step- and half-sisters, Denise and Steffie, they too appeal to represented knowledge in moments of child paternalism. Denise, for example, criticizes her mother, Jack's current wife, Babette, for chewing sugarless gum. Babette responds that she only began chewing sugarless gum to begin with because Denise had wanted her to, but Denise uses a new transmission of information in an attempt to change Babette's behavior, citing "a warning on the pack" that says that it "causes cancer in laboratory animals" (41). Steffie joins in by suggesting that her stepmother stop chewing gum entirely, unsympathetic to Babette's justification of gum-chewing as a quit-smoking aid, and the girls prohibit Babette from chewing sugarless gum, despite the risk of a relapse to smoking. Interestingly, Babette insists that she is "not a criminal," highlighting the similarities between the girls' attempt to control her behavior and state attempts at prohibition (42).

Yet, though Babette's retort gestures towards the authoritarian quality of the girls' demands, it also highlights the distinction between the girls' and states' prescriptions and proscriptions. The solution to all of the children's petty tyrannies is, in fact, utterly trivial. Babette's gum-chewing is indeed "not a crime," and as such, she can simply ignore the girls' demands (the course of action she ultimately takes). Similarly, Jack simply dismisses Heinrich's demand that he make tea, and instead makes coffee. Heinrich Gladney is not Heinrich Himmler, Jack's scholarship on Naziism notwithstanding, and these child dictators appear ridiculous, not threatening.

The ease of escaping the children's authoritarian representational schemes thus brings to light a gap between non-state and state attempts to shape people's behaviors and decisions through representation. Babette, of course, doesn't make her gum-chewing choice in a vacuum sealed off from state coercion (there is no outside to the state, after all). Yet, even if it is difficult in practice to disentangle non-state from state representations, *White Noise* nevertheless insists on at least conceptually differentiating the two. Even if we can't think of Babette's consumer choices as free, we can still recognize a categorical difference between her children's demands and, for instance, a Food and Drug Administration ban on the artificial sweetener saccharin. (The FDA announced such ban in 1977, but, after public opposition, backtracked and required only the warning label that Denise cites in the novel.)[25] The knowledge Denise articulates can only influence Babette's choices, not restrict them, and Babette can still choose whether to chew sugarless gum.

This sharply contrasts moments in *White Noise* when the state makes similar use of articulated knowledge. Consider again Jack's distinction between the two kinds of death—the tacit "death as we know it" contra the Death represented by "documents changing hands." The medical industry, of course, can and does deploy Death as articulated knowledge in an attempt to increase consumption of medicine. Jack's physician, Dr. Chakravarty, wields various representations of Death, including, especially, "printouts" of medical test results, in an attempt to make all of his patients into "permanent patients, like it or not," always defining and constituting themselves against the Death they are not (260). But *White Noise* casts this as a categorically different kind of problem than state usage of the same sort of reified knowledge. The solution for the former is once again trivial: opt out of patienthood. Most of Dr. Chakravarty's patients do just that, refusing his desire that they become permanent patients, as "once they leave the doctor's office or the hospital, they simply put it out of their minds" (260). Jack too demonstrates the viability of this choice, putting "the printout of [his] death in the bottom drawer of a dresser" to be ignored because he is "afraid to see" his doctor (293), and "making it a point to stay away" from Dr. Chakravarty at the end of the novel (325). Earlier in the novel too, Jack's doctor's attempts to control his diet prove as ineffectual as the children's attempts to control Babette's: the family shopping trip ventures into "the frozen food aisle, an area [his] doctor had advised [him] to stay out of" (19).

The novel thus begins and ends with Jack overtly abstaining from medical consumption. Why, then, does he compulsively consume medical services during the intervening pages? Of course, one of the novel's central plot conflicts, the "airborne toxic event" from a major chemical spill, results in Jack's exposure to the poisonous "Nyodene D.," which leads him to undergo a "sudden flurry of checkups," an increase that elicits comment from Dr. Chakravarty and by contrast further highlights Jack's previous lack of consumption within the medical industry (204). Yet, the fear of death brought on by Nyodene D. exposure is an insufficient answer. Jack was already afraid of death before his exposure, when he avoided medical services precisely because he was "afraid to know," and after the exposure, he is simply "still afraid" (204).

A more compelling possibility for the root of Jack's entrapment within the medical industry is his encounter at the evacuee camp with the SIMU-VAC technician: "Short for simulated evacuation. A new state program they're still battling over funds for," SIMUVAC is the apex of state manipulation of articulated knowledge (139). Though, in one of the novel's notable Baudrillardian moments, the SIMUVAC uses the real emergency to "rehearse the simulation" (139), it is important to recognize that this simulation is nevertheless real state action, producing articulations that are "not a simulation despite that armband [the SIMUVAC technician is] wearing. It is real" (141). Crucially, the state's reliance on articulated knowledge discounts crucial tacit knowledge. The SIMUVAC technician reduces Jack to a "data profile" (140), a collection of signifiers that he tells Jack derive from "your computer history. Your genetics, your personals, your medicals, your psychologicals, your police-and-hospitals" (141). Jack's embodied, experiential knowledge of his exposure cannot enter into SIMUVAC calculations. The only knowledge that matters is that which is articulable within the system. Thus Jack's exposure of "two and a half minutes" is the determining evidence for Jack's doom not because of its duration but because it is articulated. The technician insists that "anything that puts you in contact with actual emissions means we have a situation," but when Jack points out his family's possible exposure while he opened the car door, the technician dismisses it as insignificant (138). "It's the two and a half minutes" that makes the technician "wince," because, unlike the vague possibility of the family's exposure, it can be articulated within the state's centralized systems (138). State agencies like SIMUVAC reduce tacit knowledge of continuous embodied experience to explicit knowledge of discrete categories—from the state's perspective, "you are the sum total of your data. No man escapes that" (141). "Death has entered" definitively for Jack (and not for his family) not because of possible exposure to air containing Nyodene D. but because the SIMUVAC computer says so (141).

Dr. Chakravarty's "printouts" and the SIMUVAC's digital "data profile" are both examples of the "documents changing hands," but only the latter has the power to confine Jack definitively to patienthood. In other words, *White Noise* dramatizes the difference between representation qua representation and representation coupled with coercive power. Unlike Dr. Chakravarty's attempt to make all of his patients into permanent patients or television's injunctions against touching that dial, state applications of explicit knowledge really can control choices. Articulated knowledge can influence human choices, even displacing the value to be found in tacit knowledge, but it is only when combined with state authority that articulations become enclosing boundaries, limiting human choices to preconceived schemes and banishing spontaneous deviations that could otherwise emerge from the embodied knowledge of local moment and place. To restore such banished tacit knowledge, DeLillo turns to noise, and to a surreal escape from the state.

"LIFE JUST OUTSIDE": DELILLO'S UTOPIAN NOISE

Noise in *White Noise* has captivated critics, who generally read it as representing the meaninglessness of late capitalist culture, the empty signifiers of Jean Baudrillard's simulacra.[26] While these Baudrillardian readings have accumulated important insights into the novel's satire of American capitalism and consumer culture, they also reproduce Baudrillard's own engagement with classic information theory, which by its nature concerns only articulated knowledge—that which can be represented and transmitted. Though the discourse of information theory emerging out of the 1950s clearly influenced theorists like Baudrillard as well as novelists like Pynchon and DeLillo himself, in order to understand the importance of tacit knowledge in *White Noise*, we will have to go beyond the classic information theory framework. While noise certainly still occurs in the novel in the classic information theory sense, cluttering signals and impeding information transmission, it also performs a very different function: noise itself becomes a source of tacit knowledge.

The family kitchen, for example, is a conspicuously noisy place in *White Noise,* and it is there, where Heinrich's authoritarian articulations are likewise conspicuously impotent, that we find one of the clearest examples of noise functioning as a source of tacit knowledge. In one of the noisiest scenes in the novel, Denise fires up the kitchen trash compactor, and its "ram stroked downward with a dreadful wrenching sound, full of eerie feeling. Children walked in and out of the kitchen, water dripped in the sink, the washing machine heaved in the entranceway... Whining metal, exploding bottles, plastic smashed flat" (33–34). This extensive catalog of noises certainly evokes a sense of chaos, and it is hard to imagine communicating effectively in such a noisy environment. But the noise itself is nevertheless a source of knowledge: "Denise listened carefully, making sure the mangling din contained the correct sonic elements, which meant the machine was operating properly" (34). The trash compactor does not communicate any articulated knowledge—it is not programmed to tell Denise whether or not it needs repair—but its noise is nevertheless a source of knowledge, evidence of phenomena that helps her better navigate the world. Denise's kitchen listening contrasts Heinrich's, in which the noises should be parsed out, reduced to a coherent message, or, failing that, ignored entirely. Here, Denise models a different kind of listener, one unlike a television or radio receiver trying to filter atmospheric noise out of the signal transmitted by the station. She is not a recipient trying to decode an intentional message but an agent discovering valuable tacit knowledge of the world she experiences.

The value of tacit knowledge discoverable in noise stands out against the inadequacy of articulation during the airborne toxic event. Heinrich sits glued to the radio listening for updates about the toxin and its potential dangers, but the radio's articulations prove errant again and again; the radio cannot seem to convey any useful information about the symptoms of exposure or the risk entailed. Tellingly, a blast of noise allows access to all the knowledge the family needs: "Air-raid sirens sounded again, this time so close to us that we were negatively affected, shaken... They made a noise like some territorial squawk from out of the Mesozoic" (118). The family tacitly recognizes the importance of this noise, eating dinner in fearful silence as "the horrific squawk went on." Contrast this with an earlier alarm that similarly reduces a family meal to silence, albeit a silence of apathy rather than one of anxious foreboding: "The smoke alarm went off in the hallway upstairs, either to let us know the battery had just died or because the house was on fire" (8). The smoke alarm, like a real-life air-raid siren, works as part of a simple sign system, signifying a specific, predefined danger and the need to follow corresponding safety procedures. But *White Noise*'s fictional air-raid siren explicitly does not work that way. The siren's noise affects the family experientially rather than semiotically, a "sonic monster" that conveys knowledge on the level of a direct confrontation, more like stumbling into the den of a dangerous animal or hearing the terrifying screech of a pterodactyl (118).

The air-raid siren is presumably built and maintained by the state. Yet since here it functions on the level of tacit knowledge, it cannot produce the specific effects necessary for state regulation of human populations. Instead, the state must supplement the sirens' noise with "a fire captain's car with a loudspeaker" that "said something like, 'Evacuate all places of residence. Cloud of deadly chemicals, cloud of deadly chemicals,'" leaving Babette to wonder anxiously whether the evacuation order is only "a suggestion" or something "a little more mandatory" (119). The sirens' noise obscures the fire captain's words, hindering the state's evacuation scheme, which directs the movement of bodies in a manner reminiscent of Foucault's account of the syndic going door-to-door and calling "each of them by name," using articulated demographic information as a "disciplinary mechanism" to control people and limit the spread of the plague.[27] From the state's perspective, the noise of the siren's "territorial squawk" induces not tacit knowledge but noise in the information theory sense, an impediment to its articulations; state disciplinary management works only by disregarding such noise. *White Noise* ironizes this official scheme, as the fire captain's instruction to evacuate directly leads to Jack's exposure to Nyodene D. while refueling the family car. Only too late for Jack does a radio station recommend instead that people remain indoors (121)—the family had first responded to the sirens by doing just that, but the state's imposition of articulated knowledge undoes the tacit knowledge of the siren's noise.

This countervailing state force helps explain why *White Noise* poses escape from the state as necessary for tacit knowledge to flourish. Indeed, after being bound to Dr. Charkavarty through the SIMUVAC technician's combination of articulated knowledge and state power, Jack only escapes patienthood—and schemes of articulated knowledge more generally—once he escapes the state. He does so by suddenly rejecting the law: stealing his neighbor's car and attempting to murder Willie Mink, the man who supplied Babette with the anti-fear-of-death drug Dylar in exchange for sex. For Jack, acting outside the law "must be how people escape the pull of the earth, the gravitational leaf-flutter that brings us hourly closer to dying. Simply stop obeying. Steal instead of buy, shoot instead of talk" (303). Rejecting the articulations of talk and the law, Jack frees himself from the pull of the authoritative center. Of course, simply committing crimes does not free you from the state, but that is exactly what happens for Jack: "no one pursued," and he inexplicably gets away with all of his crimes despite conspicuous forensic evidence against him, most obviously his blood all over the stolen car, which he returns to the owners' driveway (303).

Once Jack breaks free, *ex machina,* from the state, his use of articulated knowledge gradually breaks down throughout his revenge scheme to murder Mink, culminating in a sudden eruption of tacit knowledge that knocks Jack out of the deathward trajectory of plots (DeLillo's repeated formulation in *White Noise* and again in his next novel, *Libra*). The origins of Jack's murder plot trace back to a conversation with his friend Murray Jay Siskind, who privileges articulated knowledge: "To plot is to live," Murray insists, in opposition to the plot-death relationship posited by Jack and DeLillo, adding that "your whole life is a plot, a scheme, a diagram" (291). Like the SIMUVAC technician and Dr. Chakravarty, Murray elides all those aspects of life that resist codification. Unsurprisingly, the state exemplifies this articulated life. A state funeral "is all precision, detail, order, design ... The efforts of a huge and powerful government are brought to bear on a ceremony that will shed the last trace of chaos ... The nation is delivered from anxiety, the deceased's life is redeemed, life itself is strengthened, reaffirmed" (292). The life reaffirmed by the state is life reduced to code, defined foremost by its status as not-Death; the state produces a particular kind of Life and Death, legible to the administrative gaze and malleable to schemes of control.

Jack follows just this logic when he sets off to murder Mink, imagining a detailed "plan" that explicitly articulates every element of his impending crime, much as Heinrich had articulated his movements in the kitchen (304). Yet, as Jack repeats the plan to himself over and over, the plan proves unstable. Elements of the plan disappear, morph, and reemerge with each new iteration, and the perfectly calculated crime slips out of Jack's grasp. Just as the Kennedy assassination plot in *Libra* depends on tacit "unknowing," ignorance of the "operational horrors" on the ground,[28] Jack's murder plot only persists as long as he remains viscerally ignorant of Mink as another living person, one whose life and death overflow the neat boundaries of articulated Life and Death.

Jack cannot maintain that visceral ignorance as he enters Mink's dilapidated motel room and finally confronts him face-to-face. Instead of plot and scheme, we get sensory experience, "white noise everywhere," and as Jack's articulated plan gives way to embodiment, tacit knowledge emerges to alter his actions and subvert his original plot's death destination (310). When Jack fires the first bullet at Mink, "the sound snowballed in the white room, adding on reflected waves... I saw beyond words" (312). Jack can no longer reduce his knowledge of human life and action to the words of his multi-step plan. Jack fires a second shot, not because it is part of the plan (though originally it had been) but "just to fire it, relive the experience, hear the sonic waves layering through the room, feel the jolt travel up my arm" (312). Jack has abandoned his plan, privileging instead his embodied experience.

This switch from the articulated knowledge of the plan to the tacit knowledge of the experience corresponds to Jack's transformation from would-be-murderer to surreal hero. Jack deviates from the plan, allowing Mink to shoot back at Jack. With the painful shock of the bullet wound, the plan's final residues vanish entirely, and Jack sees Mink "for the first time as a person. The old human muddles and quirks were set flowing again. Compassion, remorse, mercy" (313). Jack then decides to help Mink and drives him to the atheistic nuns for medical attention. Because Jack allows tacit knowledge to bear on his actions, his plot's deathward trajectory is averted.

Jack himself also receives medical attention from the nuns, who bandage up his bullet wound, contrasting Jack's refusal of Dr. Chakravarty's medical services at the novel's end. The difference, once more, hinges on articulated knowledge: Jack "stays away" from Dr. Chakravarty because he fears medicine's knowledge schemes, "what it knows about me," a fear conspicuously juxtaposed to the government "men in Mylex suits... gathering their terrible data" (325). After Jack's escape from the state and his rejection of plots and plans, he demonstrates the freedom to consume or not consume medicine as he chooses. His choices do not occur in a vacuum, but only the state has the power to control them. Not novel plots but political plots are dangerous; it is specifically the latter that ban tacit knowledge.

DeLillo revisits this power of state articulations in his long novel *Underworld* (1997), where the roar of the crowd at a baseball game "enters the skin more lastingly than the vast shaping strategies of eminent leaders ... that bolt of noise and joy when the ball went in. This is the people's history and it has flesh and breath," noise opening up a deep, visceral connection to human life outside of state schemes of articulation.[29] J. Edgar Hoover, state's synecdoche throughout the novel, tries to contain and filter such noise, turning instead to the "the dossier," "a deeper form of truth, transcending facts and actuality ... The file was everything, the life nothing" (559). This is *Underworld*'s fear: that the state will articulate even what domains of inarticulacy we have left. The character Matt Shay (brother of protagonist Nick Shay), employed in the military-industrial complex, studies satellite photos, seeing the "billion-bit data converted into images. He saw how remote sensors pulled hidden meanings out of the earth ... And he thought of the lives inside the houses embedded in the data on the street that is photographed from space. And that is the next thing the sensors will detect, he thought. The unspoken emotions of the people in the rooms" (415). Matt's compulsive response is to drive "west, deeper into the white parts of the map," the unmapped areas of military secrecy, the blank space outside the law on which the state relies, but, for Matt, also a symbol of escape from the state and the representational schemes to which his career is devoted (422). *Underworld* is skeptical of such romanticized "westward dreams" of "escape" (89–90), but it nevertheless seeks a way out of the sanitized, articulated world of J. Edgar Hoover and into the noisy life of a 1950s baseball game—a life eclipsing state attempts to represent everything.

Daniel Grausam has noted how "DeLillo's interest in the mystery and magic of language," in those moments when language seems most like noise, exceeding its own semiotic function, is actually "more like an investigation into the structures of power implicit in any attempt to claim or dismiss unspeakability as an innocent object of intellectual inquiry."[30] Grausam's focus is on DeLillo's earlier novel *End Zone* and the threat of nuclear annihilation, which he also extends to Didion's depictions of nuclear bomb tests in *Democracy*: the threat of such a future is unspeakable, because it is one from which there would be no one to speak it.[31] But "the implicit politics that surround questions of tellability and silence" Grausam identifies must include not just the ways states produce violent silences, like the "white parts of the map" in *Underworld*—a concern I will return to in my next chapter—but also the ways states capture everything in language.³² *White Noise* helps us recognize noise not just as a symptom of a future that defies representation but as a site of potential, a way of imagining an alternative to the state's systems of articulation.

Nathaniel Mackey, whose poetry I'll consider in chapter 5, offers a compelling picture of this dual function of noise—as both violent obfuscation and alternative to official discourse—in *Bedouin Hornbook* (published in 1986, a year after *White Noise*), the first volume of his ongoing epistolary novel. Following the aesthetic and political experiments of his fictional jazz band, The Mystic Horn Society, Mackey plays with the same information theory dichotomy at issue for DeLillo, attributing to "nonvocal music" an "unarrestable play back and forth between words and wordlessness—between 'signal' and 'noise,' as it were."³³ Yet, shortly after, police come and shut down a Mystic Horn street performance because they "were making too much noise."³⁴ The band members are not in fact unarrestable; they are still vulnerable to state violence and must accordingly stop their political art. At the same time, the state's own noises coincide with its violence, manifesting how the state's exercise of power drowns out all discussion and thwarts lofty hopes: "you don't have to listen long to realize that the music coming down from on high can't be heard for the noise the police helicopters make."³⁵ Noise could be an alternative, one outside officially sanctioned forms of representation, but the state both prohibits and wields noise, through and alongside police powers, as another technique of repression.

And yet, unlike Mackey's Mystic Horn Society, who cannot disregard the state's violent orders or the noise of its weapons, Jack Gladney simply decides to ignore the state altogether. There is no cost, no struggle, no risk, and his escape feels suspiciously too easy. The difference between the children's paternalistic authority and the state's, which earlier seemed so clear, now seems difficult to maintain—not because the children (or advertising, or Dr. Chakravarty) have become effectively authoritarian but because the state has ceased to be. Grand theft auto becomes a choice like drinking coffee instead of tea. In this regard, *White Noise* moves into a more strictly utopian mode, skipping over the particular means of political change and jumping ahead to the result, allowing its "imagination to overleap the moment of revolution itself and posit a radically different 'post-revolutionary' society."[36]

The novel is too self-conscious of its own *ex machina* interventions for us to read them as earnest political strategy. It clearly poses Jack's miraculous escape from the state as metafictional artifice, contiguous with the metafictional "awe-struck" narrative "reconstruction" of his toddler son, Wilder (whose limited language frequently pushes us into the domain of noise and the tacit throughout the novel), as he miraculously rides his tricycle across a busy, noisy highway (322). Interestingly, Wilder's dangerous crossing conspicuously mirrors the spatial logic and layout of the 1981 hit arcade game *Frogger*—like the frog trying to get to the other side, Wilder crosses the highway at a right angle, rests briefly in the safe zone of the median before a second stage of crossing, and then ends up wet and muddy in "the intermittent creek that accompanies the highway," just like the river that parallels the highway in *Frogger* (323).[37]

On the one hand, alluding to *Frogger* in this way functions as yet another assertion of inescapability. Most early arcade games were "endless" or "unwinnable" games, a result of historical factors ranging from hardware limitations to "the peculiar economy of the arcades," in which the lack of a clearly defined ending encourages players to continue spending quarters indefinitely.[38] *Frogger* is no exception, as successfully getting to the other side only spawns a new level, a new road and river populated by increasingly dangerous hazards, over and over without end. On the other hand, the exitlessness of *Frogger* and other endless arcade games is very different from the exitlessness of the state: "players of this sort of infinite games will only either lose against them or, more trivially, stop playing."[39] Wilder, for his part, gives up his game upon reaching the other side, and a concerned citizen stops to rescue him, heroically "holding him aloft" to proclaim his safety (324). Setting aside the realities of traffic in favor of the logic and rules of video games, Wilder's running away from home offers an analog to Jack's utopian running away from the state: in both, the narrative has self-consciously stepped outside of history and its constraints on the plausible.

The problem here is that while *White Noise* makes escaping the state a necessary precondition for exercising the full value of tacit knowledge, it was the very difficulty of escaping state articulations that first distinguished them from non-state articulations and made escape necessary. In staging such an easily successful escape from state-backed representation, *White Noise* risks collapsing that distinction, attenuating any effort to single out the state and pulling the rug out from under its own anti-state politics.

Didion's *Democracy* moves in the opposite direction: by asserting so intently the inescapability of the state and its representational schemes, *Democracy* makes it difficult to imagine even the possibility of an anti-state politics, while simultaneously making it all the more urgently necessary.

DEMOCRACY AGAINST DEMOCRACY

Democracy catalogs the familial and romantic turmoil of socialite Inez Victor as she tries to escape her public identity as the wife of vacuous career politician Harry Victor, while in the background the Vietnam War draws to a tumultuous close. Alan Nadel expresses the standard scholarly account of the novel when he suggests that *Democracy*'s title is "the name of the narrative it does not contain," arguing that democracy is precisely what's missing from *Democracy*, just as true democratic principles are what's missing from Cold War US policy.[40] Nadel is hardly alone in finding a puzzling lack of democracy in a novel by that name. Reviewers and critics generally agree that the novel mourns the corruption or loss of democracy due to the exigencies of Cold War politics.[41] Implicit in most such standard readings is the assumption that the novel's critique is historically particular: a specific US government transgresses democratic principles under the (false) authorizing narrative of the containment of communism. Yet, as an early review rightly points out, for Didion, "corruption by now is so universal that it can no longer be identified with a party or tendency or grand ideal betrayed."[42] *Democracy* spurns such totalizing "grand ideals" in recognizably postmodern fashion, challenging not only official state narratives of the Cold War, that "democracy" authorizes the actions of Western governments, but also that older American master narrative running from the Founding Fathers and the Constitution all the way through to the New Left and the Port Huron Statement and beyond: that true democracy really could legitimize state authority. While the novel certainly castigates the particular expansion of state powers during the Cold War, it also extends its critique of the state into the abstract, attacking political representation and state authority on a conceptual level. *Democracy* does not merely denounce US Cold War foreign policy out of nostalgic devotion to some golden age of democracy before its corruption in the twentieth century but, rather, critiques democracy itself—because, in part, of its very inescapability.

Reading *Democracy* as democracy's critique rather than its elegy, we can more clearly see the continuity between the novel and Didion's own skepticism towards the New Left's attempts to establish some purer form of democracy, one imagined to be free from corruption or abuses of power. In her essay "The White Album," expanded from earlier magazine articles for her book of essays by the same name (published in 1979 while she was working on *Democracy* from 1977 to 1984), Didion uses her visit to San Francisco State College to deride the youthful New Left that dominated such liberal college campuses in the late 1960s. The students there imagine themselves engaged in an epic battle for true democracy, revolting against a corrupt system. For Didion, however, they come across as silly rather than "serious," with administrators and rebellious students alike "joined in a rather festive camaraderie."[43] The New Left's attempt to redeem democracy comes across as faux-revolution, inflating status quo politics into an illusory radicalism coated in a veneer of optimism. They are only playing a "game," embodied for Didion by "a meeting of fifty or sixty SDS [Students for a Democratic Society] members" who are occupied by humorously circular goals like trying to "tell the press who owned the media."[44] For Didion, the project of rescuing democracy from the Cold War offers little promise of getting outside the game itself.

Democracy continues Didion's mockery of the New Left. Inez's inconstant husband, Harry, a US Senator and ex–presidential candidate, visits the University of Michigan campus in Ann Arbor, the birthplace of the SDS, "to deliver his lecture on the uses and misuses of civil disobedience" (62). The irony of a mainstream politician telling a supposedly radical group of students when they are allowed to disobey paints the movement as impotent and toothless. Resistance has been captured and contained within politically granted permission, and the attempt to reclaim true democracy has been seamlessly co-opted into the system itself. Harry sings the praises of the New Left, "sitting around in his shirtsleeves expressing admiration

('Admiration, Christ no, what I feel when I see you guys is a kind of awe')" (62). Such a patronizing endorsement from the likes of Harry of course functions as condemnation, underscoring Didion's sarcasm when she names the youth of the New Left "the most socially responsible generation ever to hit American campuses" (62). As in "The White Album," the New Left's attempt to rehabilitate democracy seems at best foolishly misguided and at worst outright complicit.

For Didion, part of the problem with the democratic state is its proclivity to subsume people into administratively useful representations, representations that cannot be easily cast off. We can recognize some of the impetus to flee representation in "The White Album," where Didion couples her own biographical failure to escape representation with an ominous sense of helplessness and an erosion of personal autonomy. She explains that she "appeared, on the face of it, a competent enough member of some community or another."[45] The nature of these communities ranges from maternal domesticity to her legal status as a "citizen," a contributor of "quarterly F.I.C.A. payments" and licensed driver in the state of California.[46] In each case, her superficial incorporation is predicated on representation: "It was a time of my life when I was frequently 'named.'"[47] The problem is, these attempts to "name" her, to represent her into a coherent narrative, do not fit her tacit knowledge of her lived experiences: "I was supposed to know the plot, but all I knew was what I saw."[48] Eventually, the gap between sight and plot, between experience and representation, becomes untenable. She worries that "certain of these images did not fit into any narrative I knew."[49] Representation is inadequate to present realities, but it hounds her anyway, actively incorporating her into various situations (including the state, among others) even when she would otherwise be absent from them. Her life is always already articulated and politicized.

In *Democracy,* Inez similarly wants to escape representation within the state. For her, political representation is not a hard-won right to be valued and protected. She insists that "just because they were Americans" does not make people special or unique, does not exempt them from the "general movement" of the world (208), and during a period of post-nationalist sentiment, she "ceased to claim the American exemption" (211). Inez works to cut all physical ties to the United States, settling down in Kuala Lumpur, where she works with refugee camps. She makes it clear that her geographical preferences are motivated by the pleasures of biological life rather than the interests of representational structures so often beholden to the state. When Harry's political handler, Billy Dillon, asks her for a single reason why she is in Kuala Lumpur, Inez answers, "Colors, moisture, heat, enough blue in the air. *Four fucking reasons*" (232). Inez's curt response accentuates her own disinterest in articulating her embodied experience. She privileges her tacit knowledge of life in Kuala Lumpur over her representational status as an American.

Sean McCann and Michael Szalay likewise read this moment as Inez imagining "herself slipping out of the political order," but for them it is yet another instance of magical thinking, an "aesthetic rapture" that largely corresponds to what I have been calling escapism, a wishful withdrawal from political reality.[50] Yet far from indulging in this escapism, *Democracy* troubles it. Unlike Jack Gladney's flight from law, Inez's flight from American citizenship does not actually free her from the state. Despite her best efforts to remove herself from US society in the broadest sense, Inez discovers just how persistently representation incorporates her into the state's symbolic structures—most recently via her "signature on the government forms" stored "in the Pentagon bureau of records" (231). As Inez will come to realize, she is still an "American national" (234). Far from being politically unrepresented through some scarcity of democracy, on the one hand, or from ignoring politics on the other, Inez cannot doff political representation even when she wants to.

For both Didion and Inez, the solution to representation within the state cannot be anything as simple as renouncing citizenship. In Agamben's terms, renouncing symbolic inclusion does not result in a figure totally free from the state but produces instead the paradoxical figure of the exception, the *homo sacer*, that which is included via the relation of exclusion. In place of direct representation, the fact of exclusion itself becomes represented instead. Thus Inez eventually reasserts her status as an "American national": to become a stateless person would only expose her all the more to the state's violent power. Inez's change of heart regarding her representational inclusion in the state only occurs, though, after an intimate encounter with the danger of statelessness within the state: the death of her lover, Jack Lovett.

Like Inez, covert agent Jack also removes himself from any straightforward inclusion in US citizenry. As he flits about the globe, moving through the shadows and spending more time abroad (or on airplanes) than on US soil, Jack's physical connection to the United States is tenuous at most. In this, he shares an aspect of Inez's attempt to cut herself off from the American state. Unlike Inez, however, Jack also seems (at least on the surface) to escape representation within the state, whether directly in state agencies or indirectly in mass media. Shrouded in aliases and false addresses, always disguising his motives in misdirection and obscuring his identity, possessed by "a temperamental secretiveness," Jack seems to defy attempts to reduce him to a piece of articulated knowledge (41). Superficially, Jack seems to have escaped the state altogether.

Not so, of course, and Jack's disconcerting death scene reasserts his ongoing incorporation within the state. Presumably, Jack dies of a heart attack while swimming laps in his hotel pool in Jakarta. Yet Didion's terse diction combines with suspicious plot points in the story of Jack's death to evoke misgivings. A series of short, stoic, declarative sentences discredits the official story even as the novel reinforces its determining power. Jack died "after swimming his usual thirty laps." Inez's contacts in dealing with the aftermath had been "extremely cooperative. Extremely kind really. . . . It had been quite sudden. She had reached down to get him a towel. . . . And then she had looked up" (221–22). The curious circumstances surrounding Jack's death—its suddenness, the routine nature of his exercise, the secrecy involved in transporting his body, and the excessively accommodating colonel (representing a government with a subpoena issued against Jack)—create a conspiratorial air around the event. Like his life, Jack's death is neither black nor white but occupies a gray area where it becomes impossible to determine whether he died naturally or was murdered, from heart attack or execution. The doctor covertly brought in to inspect Jack's body hints at the possibility of a heart attack but also gestures towards something much more sinister and gruesome. The doctor explains "that what happened had been instantaneous, circulatory, final. In the blood, he said, and simultaneously snapped his fingers and drew them across his throat, a short chop" (223). The doctor's pantomimed throat-slitting suggests something more nefarious than lipids "in the blood." Though there is no evidence of an assassination ("there had been no one else at the pool that late" [222], leaving neither witnesses nor suspects), the text also unsettles any notion that his death was only a tragic accident. Significantly, Jack's death coincides with a sudden outbreak of representations of him. His name abruptly begins appearing in news stories and government documents, exposing how all along he had never really escaped representation. His unrepresentability becomes the object of representation, and his position beyond the official purview of the state becomes the point of relation to the state, subsuming him within it.

Faced with the reality of Jack's death and his inability to escape articulation within power structures like the state, Inez seems to recognize the recklessness in her earlier rejection of her American nationality, coming to insist not only upon her own Americanness but also upon Jack's: Jack is now an "American in a body bag. An American" (228). Inez understands that no matter how far she distances herself from democracy, she cannot escape it. Attempting to do so, moreover, runs the risk of making things worse for herself; stripping herself of direct political representation provides no escape from the state but only dangerously refigures the way in which her body is represented within the state.

Importantly, Jack's death draws our attention not just to his vulnerability to the state, but also to the constitutive role he plays within it. As Agamben puts it, someone in a relation of exception "is not, in fact, simply set outside the law and made indifferent" but is "exposed and threatened on the threshold in which life and law, outside and inside, become indistinguishable. It is literally not possible to say whether the one [in the relation of exception] is outside or inside the juridical order."[51] Like the *homo sacer*, Jack is defined in the end only by his capacity to die, to be killed with impunity, and he is "exposed and threated" at this threshold of indistinction that is both the limit and foundation of the state. Operating in the "shades of gray" outside official channels (a quality that seems to resist direct representation, tending "not to reproduce in the newspapers"), Jack nevertheless gets incorporated within the state, paradoxically going beyond the official limits of the state while simultaneously constituting the excess found at the very center of the state's existence (219). Tim Parrish describes Jack as "an emblem of 'the process' that cannot be 'officially' acknowledged" and argues that "Jack represents the secret history that makes the official one possible."⁵² By operating outside the official domain of the state, Jack helps ensure the state's continued existence, both accomplishing that which is impossible through official means as well as perpetuating the space of lawlessness against which the state authorizes its own existence. Jack embodies the suspension of the law that makes the law possible.

Jack Lovett, in other words, manifests not the loss of democracy or liberalism but the logic of the state that is at the heart of both. This is what Szalay misses when he argues that Jack embodies the novel's hidden racist logic, one that declares, "brown peoples of the world, keep your place, or suffer annihilation"—as though that hasn't been the message of the liberal democratic state all along.⁵³ For Szalay, Jack embodies how Didion is willing to sacrifice "subaltern constituencies" as "necessary collateral damage," revealing a disturbing and violent nostalgia for a White past hidden in Didion's attack on liberalism.⁵⁴ The strained nature of this reading is apparent in how it requires Szalay to treat the novel as "surprisingly sentimental" towards its cast of economically, socially, and politically elite White characters—a perspective that is otherwise baffling in light of Didion's consistently sober and often bitter tone in describing these characters.⁵⁵ Regardless, *Democracy* portrays the state's violence against the non-White periphery as contiguous with—not a solution to—its broader critique of democracy. For example, when the risk of violent conflict causes Inez and her family to retreat from Jakarta up into an ambassador's nearby mountain bungalow, Inez's sister Janet describes it as a "hill station," referring to the colonial practice of establishing European towns in the cooler higher altitudes, from which to rule the surrounding lowlands (101). The term offends one of the novel's most straightforwardly unsympathetic characters, Harry's mistress, Frances Landau: "Don't call it a hill station . . . 'Hill station' is an imperialist term" (101). Frances's overdetermined insistence on a neat distinction between the democracy she favors and less palatable forms of government merely highlights just how unstable such a distinction really is.

Democracy reiterates this assertion through Harry's refrain that eruptions of lawlessness, including both rioting and the bombing of an embassy commissary, are part of "the normal turbulence of a nascent democracy" (99, 103). Allan Hepburn has dismissed Harry's position, asserting that "riots have no causal connection to democracy" and concluding that Harry is simply spouting empty rhetoric, rhetoric that stands in the way of actually "fostering nascent democracies."[56] Yet, the novel seems to condemn Harry's words not because he's wrong about democracy but because he is right: if such turbulence really is at the foundation of democracy, maybe democracy is not all it is cracked up to be. When Jack Lovett switches the radio off in disgust at Harry's words, it is not because Harry has betrayed democracy but because Harry is "a congressman," a "civilian," someone who benefits from a clear representational relationship to the state (103). Harry is not despicable because he misconstrues democracy for his own political gain but because he understands the true nature of state democracy yet continues to promote it anyway. "Turbulence" is not a historical quirk of the Cold War but a structural necessity of the state, democratic or otherwise. What looks like the waning of democracy in the Cold War turns out to be just democracy.

Szalay, then, is right to note how *Democracy* rejects mid-century liberalism, but his conclusion that this must mean Didion turns instead to a straightforward neoliberalism shows the limitations of how he prioritizes traditional political organizing and political parties. McCann and Szalay criticize post-sixties fiction for offering "a highly limited understanding of political action," but in this light it is their exclusive focus on traditional politics that appears myopic.[57] When Szalay quips that, for Didion, "politics is for assholes, and she's not interested in producing blueprints for how to change the world," he takes for granted that "blueprints" are an appropriate tool for politics, as though politics were only a matter of social engineering. "Blueprints" are how the state privileges articulable knowledge over tacit knowledge, reducing life only to what can be represented. It is not "the world" that Didion wants to "destroy," as Szalay would have it, but, rather, precisely this technocratic faith in the state.[58]

"RESISTING NARRATIVE HERE" (AND FAILING)

Plot and character in *Democracy* prove insufficient to imagining alternatives to state articulations: not even Jack Lovett, at home in black markets and illegal channels officially outside the state, can escape political representation. Instead, Didion transposes the problem onto narrative representation, reproducing on a formal level her characters' aversion to articulation. Whereas Inez and Jack try to escape political representation, Didion tries to escape narrative representation. She imagines she can deflect narrative representation by asserting her texts as collections of images, images that are present as themselves rather than as narrative representations of events occurring elsewhere. Didion gets at this idea in "The White Album," where she writes about detaching discrete images from the structures that represent them as a coherent narrative, "flash pictures in variable sequence, images with no 'meaning' beyond their temporary arrangement, not a movie but a cutting room experience."[59] Instead of a film narrative, Didion wants to write discrete film frames that do not represent, she hopes, but simply are.

Such "flashes" permeate *Democracy* as well. Most memorably, the novel returns again and again to its opening image of the pink dawn over the atomic bomb test sites in the Pacific. The image of Inez "dancing on the St. Regis Roof" likewise recurs, anchoring the text around it (43). Didion makes clear the opposition between the presence of such images and their incorporation into narrative representation: these images "tend to deny the relevance not only of personality but of narrative" (17). The attractiveness of the image is precisely its difference from narrative, from which Didion yearns to be free, having "abandoned" "most of the stories" and "jettisoned in fact those very stories" (19). She replaces these abandoned and jettisoned stories with meticulously detailed images: reading newspapers, Didion-the-narrator "would skim the stories on policy and fix instead on details" (73). In place of narrative and story, she wants to focus on "specificity of character, of milieu, of the apparently insignificant detail" (163). Instead of representing details into narrative, Didion insists upon the presence of details as details.

To the extent that *Democracy* holds to this antagonism towards narrative representation, it is typically postmodernist. As James Phelan and Peter J. Rabinowitz point out, "narrative is often treated as a representation of a linked sequence of events," but that conception should be subsumed "under a broader conception of narrative as itself an event."[60] A narrative does not simply refer to events outside itself but is present as its own event. Brian

Richardson notes that while traditional narratives have typically tried to "conceal their constructedness and appear to resemble nonfictional narratives," portraying themselves as representations and hiding their status as events, postmodernist narratives have often "acknowledged the fictionality of the fiction," drawing attention to their own presence as events.[61] The latter aptly applies to *Democracy*'s frequent metafictional digressions, as when Didion reminds the reader of "that prolonged spell of suspended judgment in which a novel is written," reiterating the text's fictional genre while also linking the creative process to the reader's own suspension of disbelief (108). She warns that if you "look down," like a tightrope walker, the magic is exposed and the spell "snaps" (108). The text does just that, looking down at the imaginary evidence—*New York Times* headlines, family photographs, a fictionalized version of a real *Newsweek* cover—that sits beneath the narrative, confessing its fictional pretense to nonfictional authority. *Democracy* twice describes such objects as "props," foregrounding their status as fictional constructions, theatrical properties, while also punning on how they prop up the narrative structure. By revealing these props as props, snapping the suspension of disbelief, Didion insists upon the text's presence, its status as an event of its own rather than as a representation of events.[62]

Here, though, we run into the inverse of the problem we reached with DeLillo: if asserting images and details is sufficient to escape narrative representation, then the homology to political representation breaks down. For Inez and Jack, asserting embodied experience is decidedly *not* sufficient to escape state representation. If a novel is understood from the start as something other than representation, then it ceases to have any formal relation to structures of political representation. Yet, although postmodernist fiction and contemporary narrative theory have taught us to treat stories as presentations of imagined events rather than as representations of external referents, *Democracy*'s nested narratives reproblematize the distinction: because *Democracy* is the story of telling the story of Inez Victor, the inner narrative represents events that are present in the story world. This reintroduction of representation to postmodernist narrative is significant: because Didion presents narrative representation, *Democracy* can imagine a structural similarity linking narrative to state.

Democracy tries to escape both narrative and political representation, positing details, images, documents, and bodies in their place. But because Didion conceives of political representation as inescapable, so too must narrative representation persist for fiction to remain a meaningful parallel to political structures. Thus, Didion self-consciously frustrates her own antirepresentational techniques. Shortly after declaring, "I am resisting narrative here," presenting instead two fictional "documents" (a police report and a cable transmission to Inez Victor from her father, Paul Christian), Didion admits, "I was trained to distrust other people's versions, but we go with what we have" (113, 124). The novel admits the inadequacy of its formal strategy to resist narrative; documents become (or always were) "versions," narrative representations. Even Didion's defiant statement that she is "resisting narrative here" is itself subsumed under narrative, represented within the narrative of resisting narrative. Her text cannot cut itself off from narrative, no matter her efforts to resist it.

In other words, *Democracy* is still very much a novel in the most familiar sense, and Didion's text cannot be detached from the narrative form attendant to the genre. She does not accomplish a collection of discontinuous images but, rather, goes out of her way to make sure that representation persists even under a postmodernist conception of narrative as event. Indeed, the historical identification of the novel form with narrative representation is precisely what makes the form useful for Didion's alternative politics. Committing to the novel enables Didion to explore just how difficult escaping representation can be. Didion wants to escape narrative, and Inez wants to escape the state, but *Democracy*, like democracy, always pulls them back in; *Democracy* is not the absence of democracy but its structural twin.

Inez's realization that trying to escape representation only causes her to be represented more disadvantageously explains why, at novel's end, Inez decides to tell her story to the fictional Didion. Janis Stout argues that silence—a refusal to participate in representation—works for the women of the novel as one of the primary strategies of resistance to patriarchy. Inez uses silence "to protect her self from manipulation and from the intrusion of a curious public."[63] Acting "out of the frustration of feminine roles that inhibit her self-realization and interfere with her freedom of action," Inez replicates Didion's own strategy of avoiding narrative through silence, gaps, and space on the page, a strategy that corresponds to Inez's earlier rejection of her American identity.[64] By the end of the novel, however, Didion has acknowledged that narrative representation is inevitable, and Inez has learned that overt repudiation of representation can itself become subsumed into representational structures. Inez decides to end her strategy of silence and allows Didion to tell her story.

Rather than continuing the futile attempt to completely evade representation, which only results in a dangerous represented exclusion, Inez acquiesces to representation within the state, a move that Didion reinforces by acquiescing to narrative representation. But these concessions to representation are made under protest. Didion and Inez accept representational inclusion only provisionally, representing the fact of representation itself in order to voice frustration against the union of state power and representational schemes. The primary dilemma of Didion's novel is not absent democracy but undesirable yet inescapable democracy. Nevertheless, while *Democracy* insists on escape's necessity, it cannot imagine successful escape. Only a faint hope of progress seems possible, one activated through the novel's sustained comparison between narrative and political representation: by drawing attention to the fictionality of her own fiction, Didion suggests how we might begin what Agamben describes as decoupling life from law, a "patient work that, by unmasking this fiction" that unites state violence and political representation, might begin delegitimizing the ideological foundation of state power.[65] Narrative can't directly contribute very much to a politics of escape, but it can work as a supplementary locus of critique, the ground on which to investigate inescapable representation.

Perhaps, in the last analysis, we need to rethink *White Noise* along these lines as well. Even though these two novels respond very differently to the problem of political escape, the end result is in many ways the same. If Jack Gladney's escape from the state can only occur *ex machina*—self-consciously so—then isn't the ultimate effect comparable to Jack Lovett's inevitable failure to escape the state? That is, both instances highlight just how implausible escape really is. There's nothing mysterious or mystical about finding value in noise or the tacit, as the novel's noisy, mundane domestic scenes frequently show; it is only escaping the state that would require an act of magic. Whereas dismissing the children's authoritarianism or refusing to go to the doctor seem realistic enough, Jack Gladney's escape from the state simply cannot be reconciled with the world we live in. *White Noise* doesn't tell us how to get from our world to a world where rejecting the law makes one not a criminal but free from the state, but the gap between those worlds nevertheless works as critique, asserting a particular shortcoming in our own.

Because these two 1980s novels were written and published right in the middle of the Reagan era, it would be easy to try confine these novels to neoliberalism, as either neoliberalism's critique or else its symptomatic expression. But the shortcoming in our world that these novels identify, the authoritative privileging of articulated knowledge over tacit knowledge, does not emerge alongside or uniquely belong to neoliberalism. It is, rather, a necessary principle of administering state authority. Nor should we misread these novels' anti-statism for neoliberalism. Though popular discourse often portrays neoliberalism as an ideology opposed to the state, eroding state power through deregulation, tax cuts, and eliminating social welfare programs, as a matter of historical and policy reality, neoliberalism has never threatened the state. As Aihwa Ong puts it, neoliberalism is "a technology of government ... a profoundly active way of rationalizing governing and self-governing."[66] Neoliberalism modifies how states interact with markets, especially globally, but it works to sustain and propagate state power, not diminish it.

What should we do, then, with the intellectual congruity I have identified, in the concept of tacit knowledge and its political significance, between these novels and Friedrich Hayek, one of the most important intellectuals in the history of neoliberalism? Do these novels unwittingly smuggle in a neoliberal scheme alongside their poetics of escape? I do not think so. We must be careful to distinguish the theory of economists such as Hayek from neoliberalism as a policy reality and ideological regime emerging in the last decades of the twentieth century. David Harvey's touchstone account of neoliberalism helpfully separates the two, noting "how little neoliberal theory has to do with practice."[67] The ideas of someone like Hayek "primarily worked as a system of justification and legitimation for whatever needed to be done," a rhetorical cover with no substantive importance: "when neoliberal principles clash with the need to restore or sustain elite power, then the principles are either abandoned or become so twisted as to be unrecognizable."[68] Thus, in defining and explaining neoliberalism, Harvey never quotes a single word from Hayek—not because Harvey's research is deficient but because, for the purpose of understanding neoliberalism, Hayek's ideas are beside the point.

If we try to read neoliberalism, as a historical political regime, back onto Hayek, we are likely to misunderstand his ideas. Ong, for example, remarks that "at the center of Hayek's liberalism is the *Homo economicus*," the rational actor of neoclassical economics, "an instrumentalist figure forged in the effervescent conditions of market competition."[69] While neoliberal ideology does presuppose political subjects as rational economic actors, this blatantly misreads Hayek's own thought and epistemology. To the contrary, Hayek "rates rather low the place which reason plays in human affairs" and "contends that man has achieved what he has in spite of the fact that he is only partly guided by reason, and that his individual reason is very limited and imperfect," explicitly rejecting the "assumption of a strictly rational behavior" and the "bogey of the 'economic man.'"[70]

In the same way, it would be a mistake to read onto these novels the politics of their neoliberal context, especially if we do so simply because neoliberal politicians rhetorically co-opt Hayek's language. However, my goal is not to rehabilitate Hayek's image for the sake of political radicalism. Hayek never imagines escaping the state; his liberalism is not the "absence of state activity," and, for Hayek as with liberalism more generally, the logic of exit could only apply within an overarching, unsurpassable boundary of state authority, the "legal framework enforced by the state."[71] Hayek's conception of the state as a restrained but ultimately final limit on human activity is fundamentally similar to the limited politics of exit I attribute to William Carlos Williams in chapter 1. And just as the trajectory from Williams to Charles Olson does not point inevitably towards neoliberalism, nor does the trajectory of Hayek's thought. *White Noise* and *Democracy* move beyond both Hayek's liberalism as well the neoliberalism that it was made to legitimize, and we should recognize how the implications and potential uses of Hayek's ideas are more interesting and complicated than the standard narratives around neoliberalism would allow. Reaganism is one direction Hayek's ideas might be taken, but it is not the only one. Much as James C. Scott adapts Hayek's epistemology towards a Marxist anthropology, these novels reveal the possibility of a more thorough and consistent opposition to the state than what seems possible within liberalism.

White Noise and *Democracy* point away, not from neoliberalism specifically but from the state itself. Neither plot contrivances nor refused narrative can take us from here to there, but these novels manifest a wider American literary apprehension towards the long history of the state's union of representation and power. They constitute an antagonistic politics of escape, one opposing the bind of life and law, but one that remains self-aware of its own failures, thus far, to discover a plausible solution.

ESCAPE POLITICS AFTER THE TRANSNATIONAL TURN IN KAREN TEI YAMASHITA AND JUNOT DÍAZ

HAS GLOBALIZATION MADE the state, as an object of literary interest and critique, obsolete? Is escape politically meaningless in an era when the international circulation of people, culture, and capital is commonplace?

In their influential treatise *Empire* (2000), Michael Hardt and Antonio Negri seem to answer in the affirmative. Rejecting the state as a mode of political organization and change, they nevertheless understand it as a dead threat of the past, dangerous now only if revived: "it is a grave mistake to harbor any nostalgia for the powers of the nation-state or to resurrect any politics that celebrates the nation."[1] Echoing Bill Clinton's 1996 State of the Union address, they triumphantly declare, "big government is over!"[2] They suggest we must remain vigilant against big government's potential return, but at millennium's end, they think the battle against the state has been won, beckoning radicals to turn their critical energies elsewhere, against international finance and transnational corporations.

This attitude is reflected in literary and cultural studies, as subdisciplines from American studies to ecocriticism each experience their own various transnational and hemispheric turns. And these turns are indeed welcome:

culture does not stop at national borders, state interests to the contrary notwithstanding. Yet, these transnational turns have also frequently had the unfortunate side effect of prematurely losing sight of the state as a meaningful paradigm of cultural analysis. As Matthew Hart and Jim Hansen put it, "conversations about globalization tend to combine a focus on newly transnational elements of political economy with the proposition that the national state is of declining importance as an object of cultural identification."[3] In contrast, they insist that "the state and its agents have not left the scene. Contemporary literary production surely involves the crossing and confounding of national borders—if not in practice, then in imagination. But those borders—in practice, if not in imagination—are also policed by states with access to ever more panoptical forms of protection and control."[4] Hart furthers this perspective in his cultural analysis of "extraterritoriality," noting how "critics of contemporary art and literature have neglected the role played by the state in the production of international and transnational space."[5] Our understanding of culture should not be delimited by the state or national categories, but we should understand that culture continues to be concerned with the power of states and state borders even as global connectivity increases.

The insights of Hart and Hansen hold true as well for the poetics of escape. Globalization does not answer the demands of the politics of exit: the expanded capacity to move between states does not amount to a departure from the state. We have already seen a glimpse of this in Joan Didion's *Democracy*, when Inez Christian's postnationalist rejection of her US citizenship and her sojourn to Malaysia both proved to be among the many dead ends in her flight from the state. But we can see the state's continued importance in the face of globalization even more clearly in two hemispheric novels, Karen Tei Yamashita's *Tropic of Orange* (1997) and Junot Díaz's *The Brief Wondrous Life of Oscar Wao* (2007). Yamashita and Díaz are both part of the academy, teaching literature and creative writing in the university, and their respective novels exhibit many of the same concerns that have characterized transnational turns in literary criticism—orienting us to global North-South power dynamics, emphasizing transnational cultural hybridity, and disputing the linguistic hegemony of English. Yet, both of these novels also advance rather than break from the poetics of escape, even as they update and complicate the frameworks we have seen in earlier works.

These two novels differ from most of the texts I have considered so far, to the extent that both are more invested in greater representational inclusion within the state. As we will see, both of these novels portray inclusion as an immediate political necessity for those historically excluded from state-granted privilege and protection. This is a conventional perspective, one W. E. B. Du Bois voices when he claims, "the power of the ballot we need in sheer self-defense,—else what shall save us from a second slavery?"[6] While it takes Didion's Inez Christian an entire novel to reclaim her representational inclusion in the United States as an American citizen, Yamashita and Díaz begin rather than conclude with this position. In an important sense, *Tropic of Orange* and *Oscar Wao* run counter to the politics of escape.

In nevertheless aligning these two novels with escape, I am ascribing to them a contradictory politics, one which seeks reform within the state, bringing outsiders in, while simultaneously wishing to break captives out, revolutionary escape from the state. It may help to think of this contradictory politics in terms of competing time horizons: representational inclusion is a stopgap until the more radical ends of escape become possible. There are precedents for such a synthesis of reformism and revolution. Laura Grattan, for example, identifies continuity between Richard Wright's "politics of refusal" (a politics of "rejecting or opting out of a given order," largely aligned with what I call a politics of escape) and how contemporary "anticarceral activists engaged in reform without making a virtue of reformism," supporting only reforms that lead towards abolition—for instance, refusing to support police training against racial profiling if it means increasing the number of police.[7] But I do not want to suggest that these novels successfully resolve this tension between reformist inclusion and revolutionary escape. In both of these novels, the progressive pursuit of greater inclusion in the state appears necessary even as it further defers the revolutionary dream of escape, which lingers on, explicitly left unfulfilled. *Tropic of Orange* and *Oscar Wao* cast escape from political representation as a necessity beyond their literary capacities.

Importantly, both of these novels self-consciously limit their own attempts to imagine political escape. When I say that the hope of escape remains outside the novels themselves, after the end of the novel, I mean something altogether different from the historical determinist's worry that it is impossible to imagine the end of capitalism. When Frederic Jameson asserts that, in the Utopian mode, "closure or the narrative ending is the mark of that boundary or limit beyond which thought cannot go," he means that historical conditions have constrained the imagination's sense of the plausible.[8] These novels stop short of imagining escape from political representation, not because it is ideologically impossible to imagine but because doing so would break the relationship between text and politics. The poetics of escape I have been exploring in this book operates specifically on the way that literary representation provides a way of thinking about political representation—leaving behind one necessarily means leaving behind the other. These novels defer escape in order to reinscribe that relationship, treating the novel form as a way of thinking about the state form while also acknowledging the simple, mundane fact that solving the conceptual and practical difficulties of any politics of escape remains a work in progress.

I first establish the continuing importance of the state in *Tropic of Orange*, showing how Yamashita's novel is more worried about state attempts to contain globalization within its representational schemes than it is worried about globalization itself. I then look at Yamashita's formal interest in multiplying representations through maps and narrative voices, a technique which suggests the proliferation of political inclusion, before considering Díaz's related tactic of multiplying historiographies. In both cases, however, these supplementary approaches to representation—addressing state injustices by trying to represent everyone equally within the state—prove unsatisfactory. Instead, both texts insist that, eventually, political representation within the state must be escaped altogether, even if we do not yet know how.

"NO SINGLE IMAGINATION" IN *TROPIC OF ORANGE*

The Tropic of Cancer, physically manifested as a gossamer thread running through an orange, moves north from Mexico to the United States, carried most of the way by Arcangel, a mystical poet-activist. This magical realist narrative, typical of Yamashita's *Tropic of Orange* and the source of the novel's title, has typically been read as an image of contemporary globalization and reactions to it. Caroline Rody, for example, asserts that "*Tropic of Orange* explodes that furiously defended frontier and cultivates a multicultural sublime... In the region of the world she clears of national borders and unites under the sign of the Orange, Yamashita yokes South to North."[9] According to the logic of Arcangel (who is also the masked wrestler El Gran Mojado, "the great wetback"), "lifting a can of Budweiser" as evidence, "the North has come South," through trade and the movements of capital.[10] Now, for Arcangel and the mass of Mexican immigrant laborers that follow him, it's high time that the South comes North. By the end of the novel, we find the Tropic of Cancer in Los Angeles.

Critics have often read this abstract circle of latitude's physical transposition as the collapse of global distances and the dissolution of national borders: no longer does anything separate the Mexican city of Mazatlán, where the Tropic of Cancer crosses into the Pacific Ocean, from the US city of Los Angeles, a thousand miles to the north. Rachel Adams holds up *Tropic of Orange* as an exemplar of what she terms "literary globalism," a successor to the literary postmodernism of the Cold War that is characterized by a formal reproduction of global interconnectivity.[11] Hande Tekdemir, building on earlier work by Rachel Lee and Molly Wallace, likewise emphasizes the collapse of global distances resulting from weakened borders in the novel.[12] Less often have critics noted the intensification of borders implied by the Tropic of Cancer's transformation into the Tropic of Orange. The imaginary line has transformed into a physical barrier, one that literally keeps families apart: the Mexican character Rafaela, for example, can only reunite with her Asian-American husband, Bobby, and child, Sol, after the line breaks on the last page of the novel. The very possibility of human relationships is predicated on severing the gossamer thread running through the orange, the map's line made real. This most important border in the novel only breaks down in its final twenty-five words, and when it does, it results in redemption rather than exploitation. Until this final page, borders don't disappear in *Tropic of Orange,* they reify. A line on a map becomes a fence between bodies.

I emphasize the oppressive persistence of this barrier in order to suggest that the motivating political problem of *Tropic of Orange* is not the free movement of capital across national borders (that is, too much "free trade," too much globalization, weak borders) but the stubborn perpetuation of borders in the service of the state. Critics generally take the former view, as they treat the polemics spouted by several of the novel's characters (especially Arcangel) as the politics of the novel itself, favoring the free movement of people while demanding state-backed restrictions on the movement of goods.[13] In contrast, I suggest that the novel's attitude towards centralized decision-making undermines these characters' simplistic soapboxing. The novel deconstructs this left-right binary, casting it as a red herring that allows centralized power structures to persist: struggling over who will control centralized power (left or right, immigration or trade?) does nothing to undo that power. As Yamashita puts it in her opening note to the reader, "no single imagination is wild or crass or cheesy enough to compete with the collective mindlessness that propels our fascination forward." Notably, imagination here is not limited because of some historical condition constraining what it is possible to think. Rather, the imagination is inadequate to the extent that it is singular. In *Tropic of Orange*, a desirable future cannot issue from the limited imagination of central planning and control. Instead, that future must emerge from dispersed human creativity, collective activity that cannot be reduced to or even modeled as a discrete mind. This is not a body politic deciding what and how people and things should and should not cross its borders but a wild complex of direction and desire, forward-looking fascination, unleashed by escaping the power of political borders altogether.

My reading is most clearly illustrated by the climactic ending to the Tropic of Cancer's northward journey. The journey culminates, along with the novel itself, in a spectacular pro wrestling match pitting El Gran Mojado, unambiguously representing Mexican immigrant labor and a Third-World Marxist politics, against SUPERNAFTA, a jingoistic personification of US international capitalism and the North American Free Trade Agreement. While traveling north to Los Angeles where the fight will be hosted, Mojado delivers poetic polemics and performs feats of strength to the thrill of the crowds that follow with him, building excitement for the fight. He passes out flyers advertising it as "The Ultimate Wrestling Championship: El Contrato Con América. No holds barred. El Gran Mojado meets the challenger SUPERNAFTA" (153). As Mojado portrays it, his wrestling match is an epic battle with the United States, one with profound historical consequences. In this dramatization of US policy debates between open borders and free trade—as relevant today as they were in the late '90s—critics have almost universally read the novel as simply choosing sides and favoring the underdog, Mojado.[14] This is understandable. SUPERNAFTA is plainly abhorrent, and Mojado/Arcangel often feels like a sympathetic character. But the fact that Yamashita presents this conflict through the genre of *lucha libre* should give us pause. What is actually at stake in a professional wrestling match?

Alluding to the perennial controversy over whether professional wrestling is "fake," Arcangel announces, "of course the fight's not fixed. Why should anyone want to do a thing like that?" (256). Interestingly, however, in response to Arcangel's assurance that the match isn't rigged, the crowd expresses both "sighs of relief, and snickers" (256). These divergent reactions imply two very different ways of understanding the significance of the wrestling match. One can believe that much rides on the outcome of the match, in which case fixing the results could have disastrous consequences—thus relief at being told the fight is not fixed. In this view, the fight matters *as a fight*. Alternatively, one can understand the fight as a dramatic performance, one where the outcome is presumed to be predetermined and there is no fight to fix, only a script to enact—thus the snickers at anxiety over the fight's fairness. As one anthropologist puts it in her investigation of the social meaning of Mexican *lucha libre,* "to say that it is corrupt ... indicates a fundamental misunderstanding of the genre. It is not corrupt. Instead, it is a genre about corruption."[15] Dirty fighting, choreographed moves, and referees that can't or won't enforce the rules—all present in *Tropic of Orange*'s final bout—are not flaws in the game but features of a genre that satirizes the game itself.

While the standard critical attitude towards the wrestling match has coincided with the first of these two possibilities, treating the fight *as a fight*, the novel itself invites us to step outside the narrative of combat between villain and hero to scrutinize the conditions surrounding the game. Before the fight, SUPERNAFTA and El Gran Mojado each give deeply ideological speeches, driven by rhetorical flourishes and shallow emotional appeals. For most critics, here is the true sight of conflict, the ideological battle for which the wrestling match is an allegorical vehicle.[16] Yet the novel clearly undermines the importance of the content of these two speeches. After SUPERNAFTA's paean to economic progress, its ideological relevance disappears almost immediately: "A lot of people started to think the fire FX from NAFTA's head was pretty cool. But before too much thought could be devoted to any of this," El Gran Mojado somersaults into view in his own extravagant costume (258). He gives his own speech in turn, an impassioned ode to the Third World, but it also quickly gives way to the ceremonial tropes of the drama, as each wrestler takes the ring, accompanied by his musical entrance theme. The ideological battle further gives way to spectacle during the match itself. When SUPERNAFTA splits himself into three holograms, "Mojado instinctively knew the real villain, entered the visual range of the hologram, and gave the audience the pleasure of seeing the fight simultaneously from three different angles" (261). The two wrestlers' tactics do not seek swift and sure victory but rather to prolong the fight and entertain the audience.

Ultimately, the novel portrays Mojado's fight against SUPERNAFTA as upholding the political status quo: after all of Mojado's grandstanding and SUPERNAFTA's pyrotechnics, the two combatants simply destroy each other in the ring, and the dramatic battle between the allegorical embodiments of the left and right turns out to be literally and figuratively staged, a performance of conflict that obscures the underlying solidarity between the seeming antagonists. In *Tropic of Orange,* injustices in the era of globalization ultimately arise not from SUPERNAFTA alone but in the spectacular performance of conflict between him and El Gran Mojado.

The emptiness of this spectacle is also apparent in the cockfighting scene that foreshadows Arcangel's fight with SUPERNAFTA. Immediately after Arcangel proudly and condescendingly rejects international commerce and the cultural exchange of food that attends it—"Only he, who had asked the cook the favor of cooking his raw cactus leaves, ate nopales," while the Mexicans around him consumed hamburgers, Fritos, and American beers—he imagines himself stepping into the cockfighting arena, wondering "when his time would come, when he would be forced to spar with knives at his heels, to meet the final destiny of those with wings" (131). While Arcangel seems to view his "final destiny" in grand terms, the cockfighting arena leaves no martyrs: the dead roosters "were carried sadly away," while the survivors "strutted the ring, seemingly boastful, but only the owners were foolish enough to be truly boastful" (131–32). A fighting cock never really wins—only the owners and bookies do. After the cockfight, the novel explicitly links Arcangel to the boastful roosters as he "strut[s]" around the cockfighting arena to play up his upcoming bout to the crowd, trash-talking his nemesis (132). The climactic wrestling match repeats this scene, with a twist: again rooster-like, Arcangel "paraded around the ring," but now "SUPERNAFTA, too, strutted the stage with his flaming head" (260). Arcangel and SUPERNAFTA are two strutting roosters, no more than pawns for the owners and gamblers. Ultimately, even Arcangel's nationalistic posturing against Bud Light and Coca-Cola is all part of the game.

The final consequence of all this display is not the radical political ramifications one might expect from the death of NAFTA, but an anticlimactic continuance of life as usual: "The performance was over. The audience, like life, would go on.... Somewhere the profits from the ticket sales were being divided. A new champion was being groomed" (263). It is political theater in the worst sense: there has been only the performance of political conflict, not political conflict itself. From the perspective of power, the death of the two wrestlers is irrelevant. New causes can be groomed like prize roosters and pitted against each other all over again. As Buzzworm, an activist for a variety of politically oppressed groups, including especially the homeless, puts it earlier in the novel, the word on the street is that "the players change, but the game's the same" (44). The specific histories of NAFTA, neoliberalism, and their opponents are clearly at issue in this novel—not as historical particularities or aberrations, though, but rather as players in a game of much wider historical scope, variations on the more fundamental structure of the state itself. In Arcangel's "Ultimate Wrestling Championship," the only real winners are the fight's promoters, the Orwellian "Ministry of Multicultures" and an alphabet soup of state actors responsible for perpetuating violence along the US-Mexico border, "the CIA, the PRI, the DEA, and the INS..." (256). For these state agencies, it ultimately does not matter who wins so long as tickets keep selling. Rooting for Arcangel (or any other *luchador*) is just another way of buying into the game.

Yet, the novel does seem to hold out the possibility of rooting against the game itself. As Claudia Sadowski-Smith notes, the two wrestlers' simultaneous deaths at the end of the match "also symbolize the possibility that when the signifiers of first-world imperialism and third-world underdevelopment destroy each other and the borders they represent, new ways for imagining a different kind of continental future may emerge."[17] Here is the novel's tentative political hope. Its critical portrayal of Arcangel's "Ultimate Wrestling Championship" works not to valorize one wrestler over the other but to pursue the "hope that the dichotomous thinking represented in the wrestling match will be replaced with new myths that can cross what we now perceive to be national, racial, and ethnic divides."[18] Any solution to injustices in the era of globalization will come not from El Gran Mojado's triumph over SUPERNAFTA but from escaping the power undergirding (and sustained by) their conflict.

Despite Sadowski-Smith's important recognition of how the novel deconstructs this dichotomy, she nevertheless clings to the wish that Rafaela feeding the orange to the dying Mojado/Arcangel after the match might signal his eventual recovery and return, thereby simply deferring the usefulness of their conflict to a later date.[19] Like a losing candidate running again the next election cycle, Arcangel could rise to fight once more. However, the prospect of Arcangel's rebirth is much less hopeful than Sadowski-Smith portrays it. After it is clear that Arcangel is dead, a crowd comes to take him home, where they will "bury him under an orange tree. Plant him at the very edge of the sun's shadow. Maybe grow another line right there" (267). His body could become the seed that grows into a new Tropic of Orange.

But the Tropic of Orange embodies the problem from which the novel envisions escape. Simply leaving Mexico to come north, as Rafaela and Sol do, cannot accomplish the necessary exit; immigrating from one state to another offers no escape from state power. (The Tropic of Orange is a political border, but it is not the US-Mexico border—it is not a border between two states, even though it is nevertheless a border imbricated in state power.) Contrary to Tekdemir's claim that Bobby and Rafaela's reunion at the end of the novel "is paradoxically strengthened by the invisible cords/borders that keep them separate from each other," their final embrace is only possible after the line is no longer in the way.[20] After cutting the line in two, Bobby stubbornly clings to the two pieces, holding the line together. These "invisible bungy cords" prevent him from reaching Rafaela, until, finally, in the novel's closing sentences, "he lets go. Lets the lines slither around his wrists, past his palms, through his fingers. Lets go. Go figure. Embrace. That's it" (268). Finally allowing the magically realized border to slip away makes the hopeful embrace between Bobby and Rafaela possible.

The crowd's desire that some new line of demarcation might grow out of Arcangel's body thus threatens the novel's fragile hope for the future; reanimating Arcangel to once more perform battle against SUPERNAFTA or some other foe risks reproducing the very barriers from which the novel imagines a tentative escape. Each performer in the wrestling match critiques only specific uses of lines on maps in the service of power: to regulate the movement of people or of goods. But the novel itself goes beyond such myopic criticisms; replacing SUPERNAFTA's map with Mojado's map is no solution. The fight between Mojado and SUPERNAFTA perpetuates the real power of an administrative map's imaginary lines. To move beyond those lines means giving up on that fight, letting go.

Critics have addressed at length the importance of maps in Yamashita's novel, and maps can shed light on the tension *Tropic of Orange* creates between proliferating ever more inclusive representations and escaping representation altogether.[21] Elisabeth Mermann-Jozwiak, especially, has emphasized how the novel's maps, as fictional representations, function as technologies of political control.[22] As the critical geographer J. B. Harley (a key source for Mermann-Jozwiak) puts it, "maps are never value-free images . . . Both in the selectivity of their content and in their signs and styles of representation maps are a way of conceiving, articulating, and structuring the human world which is biased towards, promoted by, and exerts influence upon particular sets of social relations."[23] Like the news cameras in the novel, every map requires that "a human eye directed its vision" (250). To be mapped is to be subject to someone's particular vision.

As Mermann-Jozwiak observes, one of Yamashita's responses to official maps, maps representing only the perspective of authority, is to make more, alternative maps.[24] Buzzworm, for example, ponders the erasures written into a map of gang territories claimed by the Crips and the Bloods. He begins with an extensive list of all the other kinds of taxonomies that could have been mapped, that might be more pertinent to a given situation: "Might as well show which police departments covered which beats; which local, state and federal politicians claimed which constituents; which kind of colored people (brown, black, yellow) lived where; which churches/temples served which people," and so on (81). It is true that this is in part the novel's project—offering these missing maps, the maps that would be written from the social margins. But Yamashita's approach to mapping is not just supplementary. Simply adding more maps will not be enough to displace the state's administrative maps; those maps instead must be escaped.

To see why, let's first look at Manzanar Murakami, an elderly, homeless Japanese-American who stands on top of overpasses and conducts magical symphonies (which the novel explicitly figures as a form of mapping) out of the sounds of the city (57). Manzanar takes the logic of supplementary mapping to the absolute: "*There are maps and there are maps and there are maps.* The uncanny thing was that he could see all of them at once, filter some, pick them out like transparent windows and place them even delicately and consecutively in a complex grid of pattern, spatial discernment, body politic" (56). Note that Manzanar's mapping has a specifically political function, incorporating space and bodies into a political abstraction, the "body politic." Of the many maps synthesized into Manzanar's mapping, most are explicitly the maps of government administrators, from the city-managed "grid of civil utilities" on up to the state- and federally managed systems of property rights and roads, the "grid of land usage and property, the great overlays of transport" (57). Manzanar seems to satisfy Buzzworm's wish for a cartographer that "could put down all the layers of the real map" and create "the real picture," providing a necessary supplement to the inadequate maps used by city bureaucrats and political authorities (81). Though it's clear that such a perfect, Borgesian map must remain only a fantasy, in one of the text's numerous magical-realist turns, Manzanar proves equal to the task of managing and reading the map's innumerable palimpsests. The impossibly inclusive map, one capable of perfectly knowing and articulating the body politic in space, becomes magically possible for Manzanar.

However, *Tropic of Orange* presents this perfect administrative map only to undermine its administrative uses. When normal maps come up against their own limitations, confronting the fissure between representation and reality, they must either accept that deficiency or alter the map itself to match. The state administrative map, in contrast, can resort to force to make its subjects conform to its abstracted fictions—instead of making the map match the world, make the world match the map. In Harley's bold formulation, "as much as guns and warships, maps have been the weapons of imperialism."[25] Like the Tropic of Cancer turning into the Tropic of Orange, state maps can effectively translate representations into things that act on bodies. It is telling, then, that despite the immense potential for control imbued in Manzanar's mapping and the ease with which reality can be altered through the tropes of magical realism, Manzanar quite poignantly refrains from shaping reality at all.

Contrary to Chiyo Crawford's characterization of Manzanar's symphonic conducting as an active guidance that transforms reality, directing highway traffic like a city planner, he actually conducts only as a passive, almost inert observer.[26] He creates music not by shaping sound waves to fit a score but by "concentrating" his mental attention on environmental sounds and conceptualizing the relationships between them (119). He cannot control what sounds arise or when but must "accommodate" whatever sounds occur into his compositional vision (122). Manzanar is a Cagean composer, creating music not by producing notes but by listening to the sounds that are already there. As Buzzworm puts it, Manzanar "sees and hears things nobody else can. What he's doing up there is a kind of interpretation" (157). While the interpretive act can have very real power (as every literary critic hopes)—Manzanar's interpretive symphonies seem to have positive consequences on the world, building community and inaugurating a grassroots movement of like-minded conductors—the passive mapping of Manzanar's listening-as-conducting does not forcibly reshape reality the way the administrator's map can. Like Buzzworm's list of maps that could have been made but were not, Manzanar's mapping does not produce a more adequate administrative map so much as highlight how much such maps inevitably leave out.

However, even as Manzanar's mapping draws attention to the inadequacies of state administrative maps, it does not displace them; if the novel's cartographic project stops with Manzanar, giving voice to perspectives erased from official maps, we end up with another politics of inclusion, a liberal multiculturalism aspiring to include more and more on the central, official map but, crucially, leaving that map in power. The novel is quite plainly dissatisfied with the promise of multicultural inclusion, and Buzzworm's encounter with the active destruction and displacement made possible by government maps highlights the limitations of simply making more inclusive maps. Buzzworm remembers when "city bureaucrats come over to explain how they were gonna widen the freeway. Move some houses over, appropriate streets, buy out the people in the way" (82). "Bureaucrats unveiled their poster boards and scale models," their maps of the future, and with "time and paper on their side," they impose this future even against holdouts (82). Paired with the state's violent power, mapping displaces people and transfers ownership through the legal operations of eminent domain.

Including more maps (the map from the perspective of the elderly woman who does not want to sell her house) does not stop the state from enforcing its own maps; the state expands the freeway regardless. Manzanar's magically proliferating musical maps seem involved in the utopian possibility of a reorganized society—his *The Hour of the Trucks* is the background music as the homeless appropriate the abandoned vehicles trapped between two wrecked semitrucks, reclaiming a mile of freeway from the state and transforming it into "a community out of a traffic jam" (156). But the state's map returns with a vengeance. Even as Manzanar's mapping-conducting practices expand still further (now incorporating not just Manzanar but other conductors too), the state violently extinguishes the freeway homeless camp and its experimental community, bringing to bear "the coordinated might of the Army, Navy, Air Force, Marines, the Coast and National Guards, federal, state, and local police forces of the most militaristic of nations" (239). Making new maps is not enough to counter the injustice enabled through politically authoritative maps.

Yamashita's interest in maps is also related to *Tropic of Orange*'s polyvocality, as numerous critics have noted.[27] Yamashita explains in an interview that the novel began in "a digested form on a spreadsheet program called Lotus. It was a big map," a map reflected in the book's opening, "HyperContexts," a supplementary table of contents that maps the novel's forty-nine chapters onto a seven-by-seven grid of seven characters and the seven days of the week.[28] Here is another example of Yamashita's attempts at generating multiple, more inclusive maps, a book with "no white characters" so that "someone else gets to tell the story for a change."[29] Instead of one definitive narrative voice, we get multiple voices, voices from the margins.

It is not just that there are seven main character voices; there are distinct *narrative* voices as the text focalizes through each of the seven points of view, decentralizing narrative authority. The narrator in Rafaela's chapters, for example, often has a winding, digressive style, clearly identifiable through the extensive use of dashes and ellipses. In contrast, the narrative voice in her husband Bobby's chapters is characterized by short, choppy sentences, connoting an orality reinforced by colloquial diction and frequent use of slang. In both cases, the narrative voice is distinct from the dialogic voice of the character; Rafaela does not speak in long, dashed, elliptical sentences, and though Bobby often speaks in short sentences, the effect is one of curt seriousness rather than the rhythmic play of street talk. Even when the narrator's voice collapses with the character's voice, as with the first-person narration of Gabriel's chapters or the extensive use of free indirect discourse in Buzzworm's and Manzanar's chapters, the result is not just to represent multiple character voices but to suggest multiple narrators. Rather than relying on one narrator who subsumes the stories of seven unique characters (and who might even preserve their seven unique voices), *Tropic of Orange* instead implies seven different narrative voices, refusing to mediate their experiences through a single coherent perspective. These multiple narrators suggest pluralistic authorities and sources of knowledge. "No single imagination" can know the full scope of the story; it requires the cooperation of multiple storytellers, as each narrator is better situated to speak for each of the seven points of view. Just as Yamashita tries to proliferate maps in order to offer alternatives to official, authoritative maps, so too does she

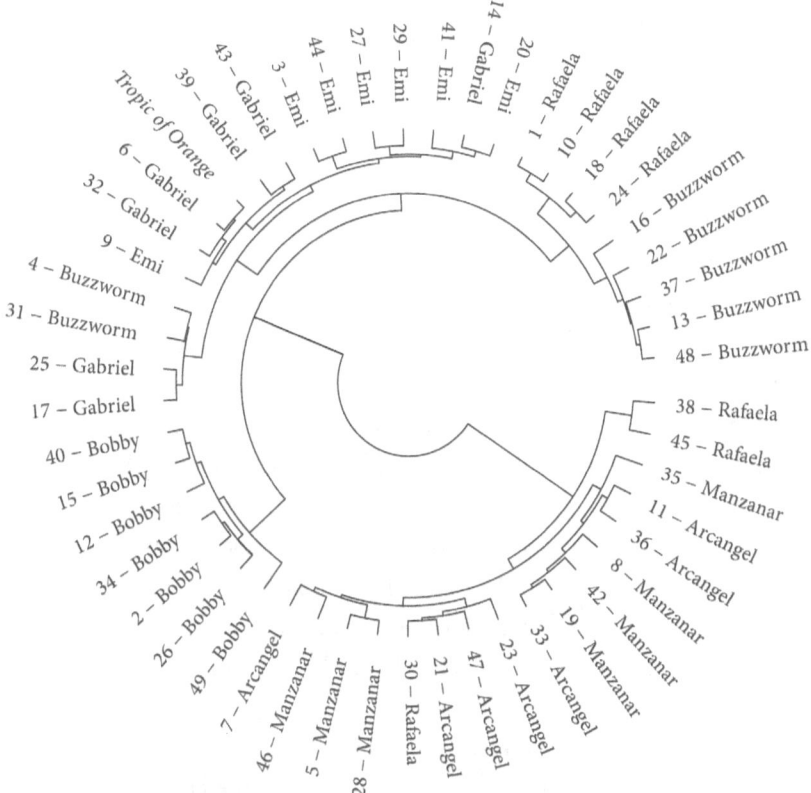

FIGURE 7. *Tropic of Orange* cluster analysis, 25 most frequent words.

proliferate voices. But as we have seen, the inclusionary logic of proliferating maps proves unsatisfying in *Tropic of Orange*. So does Yamashita's formal experimentation with multiple voices likewise fail, or can it amount to a more successful multiculturalism, one capable of providing a way out of the determining power of state representations?

Basic stylometric analysis sheds some light on these general impressions of Yamashita's polyvocality and, furthermore, suggests that escaping an authoritarian voice will not be accomplished by simply including more voices (that is, multiplying voice fails in the same way as multiplying maps). I used the Computational Stylistics Group's Stylo package for R to analyze relative word frequencies across the novel's forty-nine chapters. This is a common stylometric approach, typically used for the sake of authorship attribution. The authorship of *Tropic of Orange* is not in question, of course, but my intuition was that Yamashita's seven distinct narrative voices might appear, stylistically, like seven different authors.

I used Stylo to perform a cluster analysis, grouping the forty-nine separate chapters according to the statistical similarities in their word frequencies. In simple terms, that means Stylo creates a list of the most frequent words across the entire corpus (the whole novel) and then compares how frequently each of those most frequent words appear in a given chapter. This creates a kind of stylistic signature for each chapter: the more those word frequencies correspond in two chapters, the more stylistically similar those chapters appear.

Stylo plots this cluster analysis to a dendrogram, which gives us a fairly intuitive picture of the comparative similarities between the chapters (fig. 7).[30] For example, chapters 40 and 15, both Bobby chapters, are clustered very close together, whereas to reach chapter 45, a Rafaela chapter, we would have to trace all the way up the hierarchy and back down another series of branches, indicating a relatively greater stylistic difference. By this measure, all of Bobby's chapters are relatively self-similar, but none of Bobby's chapters are stylistically similar to Rafaela's.

We can make the same observations to the other chapters, grouping them into increasingly nuanced stylistic clusters. The largest distinction is between the chapters focusing on Bobby, Buzzworm, Gabriel, and Emi (in the top half of the chart) and those focusing on Rafaela, Manzanar, and Arcangel (in the bottom half of the chart). This makes sense in terms of character and plot; the four minority characters in the top half of the chart are assimilated to varying degrees within Anglo American society, while the three in the bottom half exist entirely outside US society, often even outright opposing it. From there, we can further distinguish a Bobby and Buzzworm cluster from a Gabriel and Emi one, and further still Bobby from Buzzworm and Gabriel from Emi. Gabriel and Emi chapters are more similar to each other than they are to Bobby or Buzzworm chapters—which, again makes sense on the level of character and plot, as Gabriel and Emi are the characters most fully assimilated within dominant White society— but there is still a subtle yet observable stylometric difference between each of them. There's a similarly sensible narrative explanation for the fact that Rafaela's last three chapters show something of a stylistic shift from her

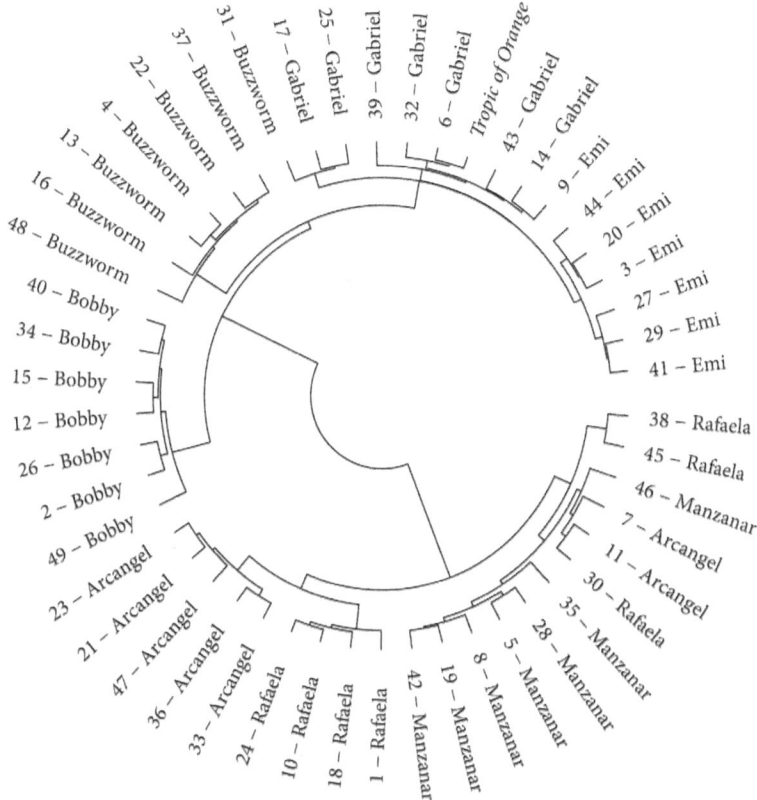

FIGURE 8. *Tropic of Orange* cluster analysis, 50 most frequent words.

first four chapters—this corresponds to her meeting up with Arcangel and beginning a violent, traumatic, and transformative northward crossing of the US-Mexico border—but again we can nevertheless make out relatively coherent stylistic clusters around each of Arcangel, Rafaela, and Manzanar.

These clusters essentially comport with the impressionistic observations I described above as well as other critical accounts. This stylometric analysis provides nice confirmation of what literary scholars already know: the set of chapters for each character gets a distinct narrative voice.

That's not the whole picture, though. In fact, this analysis opens up one surprising but deeply important insight: *Tropic of Orange*, taken as a whole, clusters very closely with Gabriel's chapters. It's worth pausing to note that

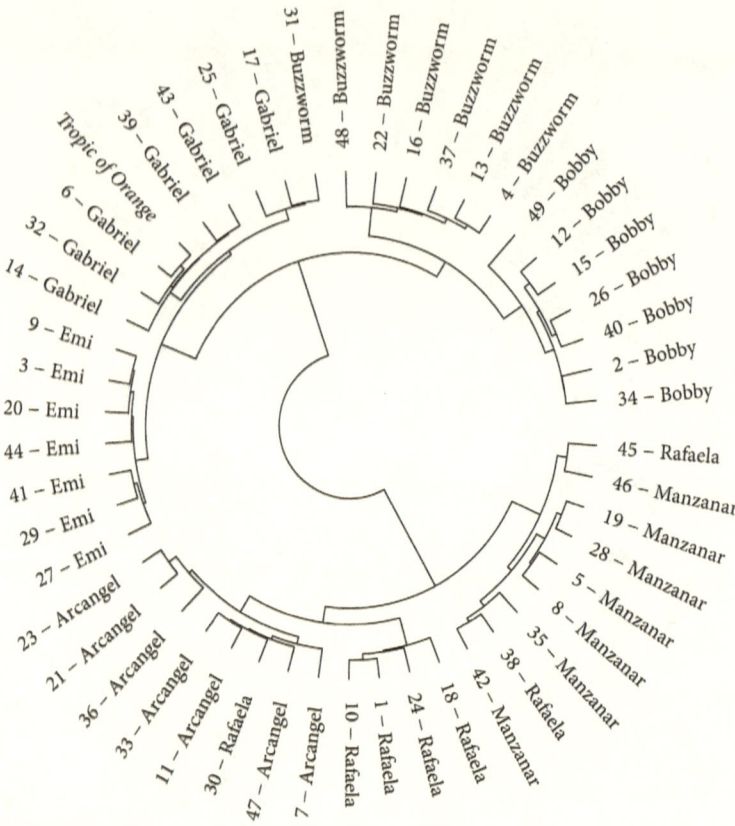

FIGURE 9. *Tropic of Orange* cluster analysis, 100 most frequent words

these clusters remain stable across a range of possible feature choices (figs. 8–10)—which is significant, because, as the author of Stylo, Maciej Eder, notes, "the final choice of the number of features to analyze is *a priori* arbitrary."[31] Should we compare only the twenty-five most frequent words, which will grant more weight to frequent function words like articles, conjunctions, and pronouns? Or should we look at the hundred most frequent words, which will capture more content-dependent vocabulary that appears less often? Why not two hundred? To account for this unavoidably arbitrary element, Eder explains that analyzing "a given corpus with a few discrete cluster analyses for different most frequent word (MFW) values . . . gives a fairly good insight into variability of the input data." If the same results hold independently of this arbitrary choice, that's a pretty good indicator

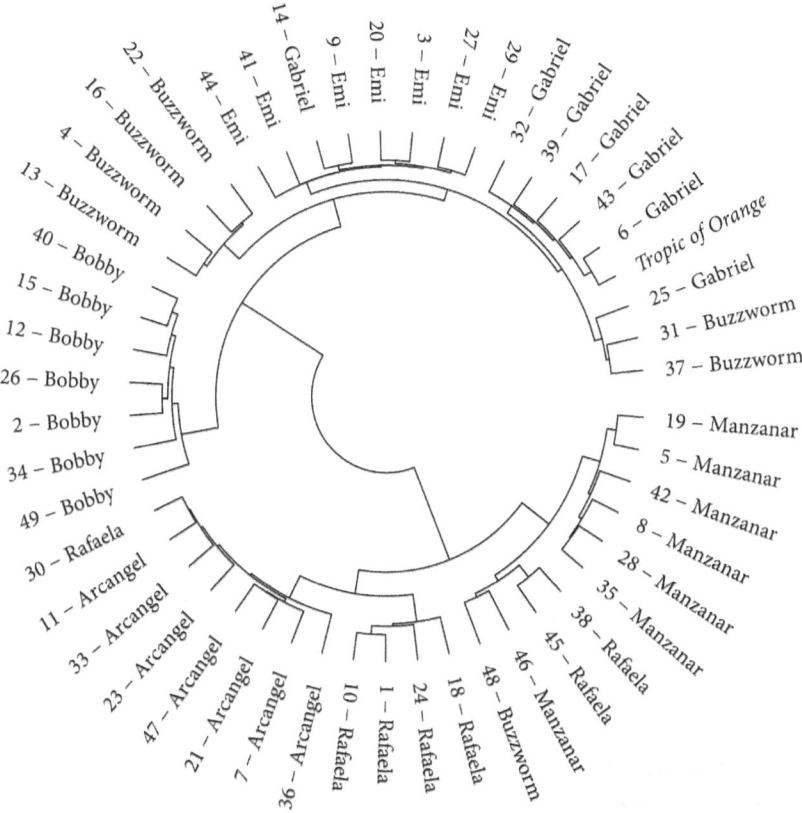

FIGURE 10. *Tropic of Orange* cluster analysis, 200 most frequent words.

that the underlying pattern is meaningful. That is the case here: whether we look at the twenty-five most frequent words or two hundred most frequent—or if we iterate across multiple analyses and combine them into a single consensus tree (fig. 11)—the result is the same: the novel sounds like Gabriel.[32]

This is provocative, because it suggests that Gabriel, our one character privileged with first person narrative point of view, a journalist interested in telling the kind of stories told in this novel, is *Tropic of Orange*'s stylistic center. Each of the individual character perspectives sound different from each other, but when you add them all together, it sounds like Gabriel. Gabriel takes on a stylistic authority; Gabriel's voice coincides with the overall voice of the novel.

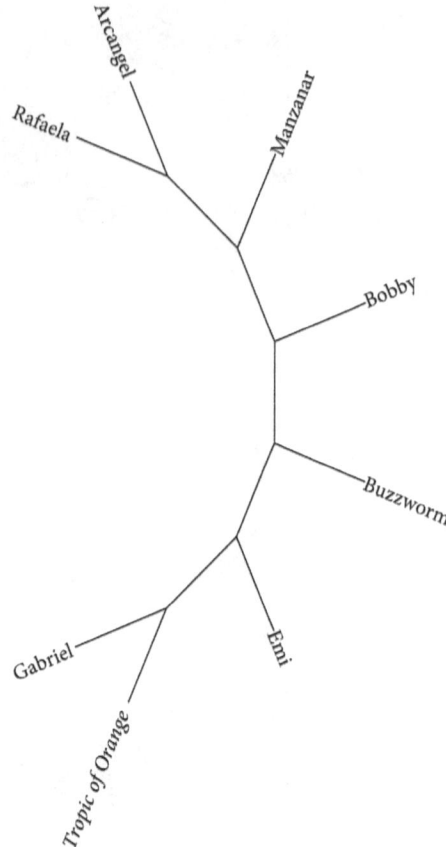

FIGURE 11. *Tropic of Orange* cluster analysis consensus tree, 25–200 most frequent words in increments of 25.

In this light, the novel's attempt to disperse representational authority, to refuse any singular authoritative narrative or map, cannot entirely succeed. Gabriel's voice dominates. Proliferating voices, in other words, is insufficient to escape the imposition of an authoritative narrative voice, just as Manzanar's proliferating maps offer no escape from the reified lines on state maps. We fall back into the logic of liberal multiculturalism, including diverse voices but subsuming them all within an overarching system, making the diversity of voices an aspect of a singular, authoritative voice. This amounts to a formal critique of the logic of inclusion; greater representational inclusion only obscures state power's continued inescapability. A single, authoritative perspective triumphs, suggesting that the political hope the novel places in diversifying voices is much more tenuous than critics have understood. Proliferating voices does not stop a "single imagination" from taking over.

This would help explain why Bobby's final, triumphant dissolution of the Tropic of Orange—the only real moment of political hope in the novel, like a ribbon-cutting ceremony for a better future—coincides with the end of the novel. All *Tropic of Orange* accomplishes—the proliferation of maps and voices—is inadequate to the task of escaping authoritative representations. The novel maps multiple maps, voices multiple voices, but in doing so becomes an official map and voice in its own right. Much as in *Gravity's Rainbow* Thomas Pynchon can only figure Tyrone Slothrop's escape from political representation through an end to narrative representation, ultimately Yamashita can only imagine exit from authoritative representation through exit from the novel itself. Ending the Tropic of Orange means ending *Tropic of Orange*.

Tropic of Orange's attitude towards globalization is much more complex than critics have generally acknowledged. It does not simplistically extol the enrichment of cultures through transnational contact while condemning the global circulation of goods, ignoring the frequent reciprocity and occasional commingling of the two.[33] Instead, Yamashita's novel wants to go beyond the state's representational boundaries, abstractions enforced by real guns. Neither El Gran Mojado nor SUPERNAFTA is a sufficient hero for this tentatively optimistic future; along with the mainstream left and right they caricature, they are merely puppets for the state and its borders, mapping both international and domestic space. Yet, *Tropic of Orange* also displaces any escape from those borders to the negative space outside the novel. The most it can do is write alternative maps and voices, but those are no challenge to the liberal state.

DÍAZ'S STOPGAPS, YUNIOR'S GAPS

As with Yamashita's *Tropic of Orange*, Junot Díaz's sci-fi–fantasy–comic book–magical realist mashup *The Brief Wondrous Life of Oscar Wao* has been read as heralding a paradigmatic shift in the history of the novel, a post-postmodernism in creative production that is deeply intertwined with the transnational turn in criticism. Ramón Saldívar's reading of *Oscar Wao* is exemplary in this regard, situating the novel within "a radical turn in twenty-first-century fiction by ethnic writers to a new stage in the history of the novel," a "post-magical realism, post-postmodern, post-borderlands, and neo-fantasy transnational turn in the postrace era of American literature."[34] Saldívar's periodizing move echoes Rachel Adams's formulation of "literary globalism" via *Tropic of Orange*. Saldívar argues that Díaz along with numerous other contemporary ethnic writers must contend with new, globalized forms of injustice and racism by developing new literary formal strategies: changes in geopolitical history demand changes in literary history.

While I appreciate Saldívar's insights into the ways Díaz moves beyond old models of nationalism (demystifying any deterministic link between nation, culture, and identity), the state—and, moreover, political representation—remains as much at issue in *Oscar Wao* as it is in postmodern fiction from Pynchon to Didion.[35] *Oscar Wao*, like *Tropic of Orange*, does not diminish the state's importance but emphasizes the persistence of state (not necessarily nationalistic) power in the context of globalization. Alongside heightened attention to transnational cultural flows in a globally connected world, contemporary fiction such as Díaz's still takes up the state as a primary object of literary critique. I read *Oscar Wao* as yet another instance of the political-aesthetic project we have seen in Pynchon, DeLillo, Didion, and now Yamashita: the poetics of escape. Like those earlier examples, Díaz's *Oscar Wao* figures literary representation as a stand-in for political representation, using the novel's form as a way to think about political exit.

However, Díaz also complicates the framework I have been relying on thus far. In *Oscar Wao*, the state wields not just representation but also the active repression of representation; in addition to confining people within its representational schemes, the state also censors counterschemes. To some extent this could be understood as a difference between a totalitarian state—Rafael Trujillo's mid-century dictatorship of the Dominican Republic—and a liberal one like the United States, where overt censorship plays a relatively smaller role in the maintenance of state power.

Nevertheless, Díaz points us to more general ways that state articulations work together with state inarticulacies; dictatorships and liberal democracies alike not only preclude tacit knowledge incompatible with their representational schemes but also wield their own tacit knowledge, erasing other, competing attempts to articulate its tacit operations. This insight is reflected in James C. Scott's account of the "dark twin" of state articulations—the unofficial, unarticulated reality that, though technically running counter to the official scheme, actually supplements the scheme's inadequacies.[36] State schemes survive parasitically off underground markets, bureaucrats looking the other way, unsanctioned improvisations from local state actors, and all other manner of tacit deviations from the scheme.[37] We might retrospectively read this nuance back into my previous chapter. The SIMUVAC technician's use of articulated knowledge in *White Noise*, for example, relies on his tacit judgment that Jack Gladney's articulation of events is irrelevant, and though in *Democracy* the state uses representation to control Jack Lovett, it also uses his covert operations, erased from official narrative, to perpetuate its own power and interests. Díaz makes this dynamic explicit, giving prominence to the state's exploitation of gaps in representation. *Oscar Wao* still advances a poetics of escape—getting outside of state history constitutes one the novel's main dilemmas—but it does so while foregrounding, to a greater extent than we have yet seen, the ways the state itself eludes representation.

The state's incorporation of anti-representation alongside its representational schemes is introduced through the attention *Oscar Wao* devotes to gaps in the story, the absence of representation. As we follow Oscar and his traumatic family history back and forth between the Dominican Republic and New Jersey, we frequently encounter blanks in the narrative, places where we simply never learn what happens. "Even your Watcher has his silences, his páginas en blanco," admits Yunior, the Watcher, Díaz's semi-autobiographical narrator and the novel's fictional author.[38] There are indeed silences and gaps in Yunior's narrative (though *Oscar Wao* does not actually have any blank pages, a curious detail to which I will return later), and blankness is a central motif throughout the novel, from such directly metafictional comments to the more figurative imagery of faceless apparitions haunting the novel's characters.

For example, names connected to power and prestige—including notably the Dominican police captain who orders Oscar's murder near the end of the novel—are frequently redacted, replaced by long dashes (71, 100–101, 105, 227, 305, and 318). These omissions seem to be residues of authoritarian strategies to erase evidence of political atrocity, to make political power less accountable. In a footnote on Joaquín Balaguer, one of Trujillo's lackeys who, post-Trujillo, would go on to violently quash political opposition during his three terms as president of the Dominican Republic, Yunior explains how Balaguer's memoir expunged the assassination of left-wing journalist Orlando Martínez by including a literal blank page where the killer's name should have appeared, "a blank page, a página en blanco, in the text to be filled in with the truth upon his death. (Can you say *impunity?*) Balaguer died in 2002. The página is still blanca" (90). As José Saldívar puts it, Díaz shows how the Trujillo regime "became legitimized through ghastly spectacles of the state's erasure of violence."[39] Instead of people trapped in state representations, we get the state and its violence disappearing from historical representation, a blank page where there should be a record of the state's wrongdoing. Here, the absence of representation means not an escape from state power but further entrapment within it.

We see a related logic at play in Díaz's most famous contemporary, the popular inheritor of the fantasy tradition. In J. K. Rowling's *Harry Potter* series, the forces of good refer to arch-antagonist Lord Voldemort as "He-Who-Must-Not-Be-Named," "You-Know-Who," and so on, superstitiously fearing that simply speaking Voldemort's name aloud might summon the evil wizard. Against such a fear of naming the oppressive power, Rowling's wise, benevolent Dumbledore advises Harry, "call him Voldemort, Harry.... Fear of a name increases fear of the thing itself."[40] Díaz explicitly aligns his project with Dumbledore's advice, explaining in a 2012 lecture that "he wants us to 'not be afraid of saying Voldemort's name.'"[41] He offers his own version of this trope on *Oscar Wao*'s opening page: "the Admiral's very name has become synonymous with both kinds of fukú, little and large; to say his name aloud or even hear it is to invite calamity on the heads of you and yours" (1). Díaz uses the Dominican "fukú," a kind of curse or bad luck, specifically for the curse of colonialism, brought to the Americas by Admiral Columbus and perpetuating relationships of domination ever since; he portrays the fukú as folkloric superstition that is historically all too real. Transposed from Rowling's mythos back to Díaz's, the goal is to bravely name the fukú and its ongoing legacy of political domination—refracted through gender, sexuality, and class as well as race.

Critics have followed suit, reading *Oscar Wao* as filling in those blank pages of history, undoing repressive silences—in particular those created by Trujillo's dictatorship and maintained by US governmental complicity. In an influential reading, Monica Hanna argues that "silence is elemental to the historiography sponsored by the Trujillo regime because it is this silence that naturalizes the status quo and thus closes the possibility of change. It is a historiography characterized by silences, denials, and the violent repression of voices that might contradict the official narrative of heroic nationalism and the continuity of progress."[42] Thus Yunior's footnoted dig at officially disseminated history is representative of *Oscar Wao*'s larger critique: "You didn't know we [the Dominican Republic] were occupied twice in the twentieth century? Don't worry, when you have kids they won't know the U.S. occupied Iraq either" (19). Understood thus, Yunior's goal is to write his own antiauthoritarian counterhistory, filling in the gaps left by the state's selective history. "Fukú," the curse of colonialism, would be a blank page, while "zafa," the counterspell to fukú that Yunior hopes his book might become, would be the page filled in.

We should recognize in this project a gesture of inclusivity, akin to Yamashita's method of bringing in myriad maps and voices: the histories of the oppressed and marginalized must be reclaimed, made visible and audible. To the extent that this logic operates in Díaz's work, it is amenable to familiar progressive politics of inclusion, a more robust multiculturalism that goes beyond the multicultural consumerism Yamashita so acerbically satirizes. As José Saldívar explains, this is a politics of inclusion that is not satisfied by capitalist liberal democracy: "Even long after the Trujillo dictatorship had ended in the 1960s, political democracy in the Dominican Republic continued, as Díaz suggests, to exclude and 'blank out' from the nation the social subjects like La Inca, Belicia, Lola, and Oscar."[43]

A more thorough politics of inclusion to counter such exclusions is apparent enough in Díaz's own life and activism (itself not without problems and controversy, which I will address in a moment). Arlene Dávila characterizes Díaz's activism as taking place within the "contradictory realm of Latino/a electoral politics," explaining that "Díaz is not blind to the limits of institutional politics as a realm for representation and progressive change, but the choice to remain 'above politics' has never been an option whenever there is an opportunity to bring about incremental change."[44] As Dávila frames it, the impetus for such pragmatic, immediate politics is more equitable representational inclusion within power structures: "eschewing categories and representations is never enough."[45] Even if Díaz were to refuse the "Latino" label, power would continue organizing itself along such lines anyway. "Eschewing categories and representations" does not amount to escape from power's use of such representations; at most, it recasts how power represents. Instead, for Díaz the move is to include such excluded categories—including Dominicans in the history of the United States, for example, or including Haitians in the history of the Dominican Republic, or the dark-skinned, the nerdy, the fat, the queer, the immigrant, the emigrant, and so on. If you are going to be subject to historiography, you might as well try to write that history yourself as much as you can. This is about claiming and taking charge of representation, not escaping it.

While Díaz's biography is not my focus here, and, as Ruth McHugh-Dillon notes, "the practice of reading minority writers such as Díaz through a biographical framework is fraught" because mainstream readerships burden minority writers to write *only* in autobiographical registers, nevertheless, "in his memoir-essay 'Silence,' Díaz's tendency to play with fiction and autobiography takes a new turn when he invites readers to read his own life into his fiction."[46] Appearing in the *New Yorker* in April of 2018, Díaz's essay "The Silence: The Legacy of Childhood Trauma," recounts how he was raped as a child and how he sees that trauma leading to a pattern of destructive behavior in his life, harming himself and his romantic partners, many of them women of color—a pattern that Díaz explicitly connects to the character of Yunior. This essay took on new meaning when, a few weeks after it was published, multiple women publicly accused Díaz of abusive and misogynistic behavior, with the timing of these accusations making it possible to read back into "Silence" a cynical PR move to get in front of the controversy and salvage Díaz's literary celebrity image.[47] Whether we read

"Silence" as a preemptive apology or not, it does highlight important limitations to Díaz's politics of inclusion.[48] As McHugh-Dillon observes, "no doubt to protect their privacy, Díaz chooses to censor the names of women mentioned in the essay. Yet, given that his own experience is fully fleshed out, this leaves the women as side characters—as 'not fully human'—in ways that echo his fiction's frequently limited and conscribed representation of female characters."[49] While it might overstate things to attribute *Oscar Wao* with "limited and conscribed representation of female characters" (La Inca, Belicia, and Lola are fairly developed characters that are crucial to the novel's plot, structure, and affect), it's nevertheless true that the centrality of Yunior's hypermasculine perspective often leaves women silent, blanks that the counterhistory fails to fill in.

Yet, *Oscar Wao* is entirely self-conscious of the ways it fails this politics of representational inclusion. As Hanna observes, Yunior's alternative history can never be fully inclusive but must inevitably have its own gaps and omissions—not least of all in the stories of the women he hurts.[50] More importantly for my purposes here, though, even if, as Hanna suggests, Yunior's incomplete counterhistory is nevertheless superior to the exclusionary official history,[51] it cannot undo the official history's power. As we will see, *Oscar Wao* ultimately casts this project of filling in official history's gaps as inadequate, for the same reason that supplemental maps and voices are inadequate in *Tropic of Orange*. At most, such inclusive gestures are provisional balms, alleviating the immediate suffering of exclusion—an important task, to be sure—but leaving in place the underlying structure of representational power. The poet Juliana Spahr, for example, whose work I discuss in the next chapter, notes how writers such as Díaz have been "useful for propaganda purposes by the State Department, and especially useful as an example of state-sponsored multiculturalism," with Díaz among others "featured prominently in the State Department propaganda publication called 'Multicultural Literature in the United States Today.'"[52] Spahr refrains from censuring or assigning blame over such complicity, which she recognizes in her own practice as well, but she nevertheless emphasizes how this works against meaningful resistance to state power: "no one has told the State Department that a novel influenced by Latin American neo-realism is inimical to their cultural diplomacy concerns ... And it might be the opposite."[53] To the extent that Díaz works towards political inclusion, he also works to support state power. In conversation with Dávila, Díaz defends his inclusion-oriented political practices by explaining that if it were not for groups and action devoted to that project, "shit would even be much worse."[54] But his defense also implicitly acknowledges its limits as well; it is a stopgap that keeps things from being worse, but it offers no revolutionary hope.

Unlike his life, however, Díaz's creative work is not bound by the immediate needs of reformism; even if Díaz does not have the luxury to go beyond the contradictory realm of electoral politics, his fiction, to which Caren Irr rightly attributes an "anti-statist approach" and "arguably anarchist concerns," does.[55] This is not to suggest we cordon off *Oscar Wao* from Díaz's activism—the novel certainly contributes to Díaz's general politics of inclusion through its counterhistoriography. But *Oscar Wao* also looks beyond inclusion. Rather than expanding the scope of official representation, including ever more in the pages of state history, *Oscar Wao* ultimately fantasizes escaping representational power altogether. Yunior's gaps come to represent not just the incompleteness of his counterhistory but also the vulnerable potential for departure out of official historiography.

In other words, the counterhistoriography reading, generally undergirding most critical accounts of *Oscar Wao* even when it is not the focus, is by and large correct, but it leaves out half the story. *Oscar Wao* not only works to fill in the pages left blank by the state; it also desperately hopes to write its own blank pages, a way of escaping state representations altogether.

The counterspell to fukú, after all, is *zafa*—as Jennifer Harford Vargas notes, from the Spanish verb *zafar,* "to let go of" or "to escape."[56] Though critics have hardly touched on its significance, escape indeed pervades *Oscar Wao*. According to Oscar's sister, Lola, what their mother, Beli, "wanted, more than anything, was what she'd always wanted throughout her Lost Childhood: to escape" (80). When Trujillo finally dies, the one glimmer of hope is the possibility of escape: "with El Jefe dead and the Plátano Curtain shattered all manner of escapes were now possible" (161). Grandfather Abelard's hope for his daughters, against Trujillo's supernatural sexual violence, is a "chance to escape" (228)—the daughter particularly targeted by Trujillo could be sent away to Cuba, "but," Abelard frets, "I'd need permission from the state!" (221). So Abelard does the opposite, "pulled a Rapunzel on her ass and locked her *in*" (217), a strategy that leads to Abelard's arrest, with Yunior suggesting that the family should have at least tried to run away when they had the chance (230). Oscar also struggles to get away—from his own fatness and more generally his loser social status—but he cannot achieve escape velocity, "the evil planet Gordo pulling him back in" (271). Even Lola herself, thoroughly disillusioned by the impossibility of escape, nevertheless figures getting out as the ultimate goal. Responding to her own dream of running away, she explains, "if these years have taught me anything it is this: you can never run away. Not ever. The only way out is in" (209, cf. 57). The only way to go is in, but *in* only matters as a means to *out*.

Lola explains that whatever Beli's situation, even without the poverty and child abuse she actually suffered, even "if she'd been a princess in a high castle," Rapunzel-like, "she would have wanted out" (80). Ultimately, Lola identifies Beli's deeper desire for escape as a response to violent state power, placing her within an entire generation wanting to escape the Trujillo regime. Like her own desire to get out, Lola again casts this general desire as futile, distinguishing actual escape from the delusional fancies of escapism: "Beli had the inchoate longings of nearly every adolescent escapist, of an entire generation, but I ask you: So fucking what? No amount of wishful thinking was changing the cold hard fact" of the Trujillo regime, and "this was a country, a society, that had been designed to be virtually escape-proof" (80). Desiring escape does not change the fact that, vis-à-vis the state, escape is impossible.

The impossibility of escaping the state is not just a consequence of Trujillo-specific policies; this is not a problem limited to dictatorships, nor does it disappear in a context of globalization. After all, the Plátano Curtain falls with Trujillo's death, making it seem that "all manner of escapes were now possible," and Beli immigrates to the United States, but the novel's cyclical familial plot makes clear that this escape is not enough. The United States is certainly better for Beli than the Dominican Republic—she no longer daily fears for her life or for her children's—but the escape offered by immigration is only partial. Thus, Oscar will suffer too and seek his own escapes in turn. Just after Yunior's description of Oscar trying to escape the gravity well of planet Gordo, Oscar fantasizes a flight *back* to

Santo Domingo, reversing Beli's diasporic movement as he attempts to escape the problems of Paterson, New Jersey (271–72).

Oscar's flight does not work either, of course, suggesting that movement between states can at most only partially satisfy the demand for escape. Indeed, immigration gets wrapped up in the escapist desires of fantasy literature. For Beli, destination USA is "Never-never land," a fantasy escape from Trujillo's Dominican Republic (163). Oscar and Lola make the perpendicular move, losing themselves in speculative fictions, Middle Earth an escape from the United States. Either way, fantasy escapism is not enough. Neither immigration nor literature gets you outside the state.

If the text of passports and fantasy novels offers no escape, maybe answers can be found in absences of text. Here, Yunior's sustained attention to "páginas en blanco" takes on new meaning: perhaps effaced representations—dangerous and oppressive in the hands of authorities—might contribute to a more general strategy of escaping hegemonic power. *Oscar Wao*'s lacunae, after all, are not always effects of political authority. The magical realist Mongoose's hopeful dream message to Oscar, for example, appears only as long dashes: "——— ——— ———, said the Mongoose" (301). The Mongoose is one of the novel's very few figures of liberatory hope, appearing as a savior when Beli and Oscar are each in turn nearly murdered in a Dominican canefield. In a note, Yunior characterizes the Mongoose as a migratory antiauthoritarian accompanying humanity's global movements, explaining that "the Mongoose has proven itself to be an enemy of kingly chariots, chains, and hierarchies. Believed to be an ally of Man" (151). The golden Mongoose also earns one of *Oscar Wao*'s only fantasy allusions to the forces of good, "Aslan-like" (302). Comparisons to evil forces such as Sauron abound, but heroes like Aragorn, Frodo, and Gandalf remain conspicuously unreferenced.[57] It is noteworthy, then, that the novel's antiauthoritarian savior figure speaks blanks towards different ends than the gap-filled official history Yunior writes against. Blanks in *Oscar Wao* do not always have to "stand in for the spectacular state's erasing of all its past tortures and murders" but might perform something else more worthwhile.[58]

Indeed, the novel's best bets for the future all end up being words that have gone missing, ideas that one way or another have slipped through the grasp of representation. Most obvious is Oscar's final manuscript, which he tells Lola in his final letter is "the cure to what ails us" (333). But Oscar's textual "cure" never arrives in the mail as promised. Instead, it remains tantalizingly absent. Oscar's description echoes Yunior's a few pages earlier. Yunior has "this stupid dream that shit could be saved," in which he would "finally try to say words that could have saved us. ——— ——— ———. But before I can shape the vowels I wake up" (327). The immediate context of Yunior's dream is his relationship with Lola, but the marked connection to the Mongoose's three dashes and Oscar's words that could cure us remind us that Yunior's individual problems are synecdoches for societal ones.

Notably, in his essay "Silence," Díaz singles out this specific passage as a moment of hope. Throughout the rest of the essay, Díaz's many attempts to "be cured of all that ailed me," as he paraphrases it from Oscar, amount to little more than psychological repression and escapism, avoiding rather than processing his trauma: "Eventually what used to hold back the truth doesn't work anymore. You run out of escapes, you run out of exits." Here, though, Díaz appears sincere as he quotes Yunior's dream in the context of his "salvation."[59] The words that could save us, the pages that could cure the structures of domination that infect human relationships, are blank.

Oscar dreams of the Mongoose while recovering from his canefield trauma. During that same time, while he "was out for three days," in a section subheaded "Briefing for a Descent into Hell," he has another dream: an old man wearing a mask holds up a book, "but then he saw that the book was blank" (302). Once more, the blankness seems to hold some promise of redemptive transformation: "The book is blank. Those were the words La Inca's servant heard him say just before he broke through the plane of unconsciousness and into the universe of the Real" (302). After this three-day blackout descent to hell and his encounter there with the blank book, Oscar ascends with Christly triumph. Blanks are again associated with salvation.

Yunior has a structurally identical dream, only with Oscar as the masked man holding up the blank book: "wearing a wrathful mask that hides his face," Oscar "is holding up a book, waving for me to take a closer look . . . the book's pages are blank. . . . behind his mask his eyes are smiling. *Zafa*" (325). Zafa, fukú's counterspell, the cure to what ails us, is not a book filled in, the representation one deserves, but a blank book, the elimination of representation. Zafa is an escape from representation's power.

The masks in these dreams reinforce and clarify this understanding of zafa. It is tempting to read these masks through Frantz Fanon's *Black Skin, White Masks* (an obviously important text for Díaz)—as false consciousness imposed by the racist logic of imperial power.[60] Or, the masks might simply be another way to repress trauma, as they clearly function in "Silence," where Díaz describes himself hiding "behind an adamantine mask of normalcy."[61] Indeed, the masks sometimes horrify: as for Yunior's recurring dream of masked Oscar, Yunior comments, "sometimes, though, I look up at him and he has no face and I wake up screaming" (325).[62]

At other times, however, the novel links the unrepresented face to desirable escapes from oppressive power. After Oscar's first canefield beating, he returns to Ybón, the forbidden love whose jealous boyfriend, the *capitán*, had sicced his henchmen on Oscar: "Of course the capitán had beaten the shit out of her too, of course she had two black eyes . . . For some reason Oscar couldn't see her face, it was a blur, she had retreated completely into that other plane of hers. . . . He tried to focus his eyes but what he saw was only his love for her" (304–5). Yunior casts Ybón's facelessness as an otherworldly retreat, one apart from the capitán's violence and filled with Oscar's love. Later, when the capitán's goons are driving Oscar to the canefield for the second time, Oscar thinks he sees the Mongoose again, this time driving a bus with his whole family on board, "and who is the cobrador [conductor, ticket-taker] but the Man Without a Face" (320–21). If only he could get on that bus, Oscar seems to hope, the Mongoose and the Man Without a Face might help him and his family escape. The state can use masks to shroud its hegemonic power, but moments like this remind us that rebels wear masks too.[63] Obscured faces in *Oscar Wao* are not just *White Masks*, but black bloc.

This liberatory connotation of masked and faceless faces tracks back to two short stories in Díaz's first collection, *Drown* (1996)—both of which, notably, conclude with the trope of running away: "Ysrael" and "No Face" both center around a Dominican boy who wears a wrestler's mask to hide his disfigured face. Unlike Yamashita's wrestlers, Díaz's masked Ysrael, No Face, represents the defiance of the marginalized. In "Ysrael," an airplane drops advertisements for the next match, "posters of wrestlers, not politicians"—linking wrestling matches and elections as spectacles, but also differentiating wrestlers from politicians.[64] Ysrael, like Oscar, looks for hopeful role models in masked heroes, and in his own mask he is something of a superhero of the oppressed: "faster than a mongoose, someone said, but in truth he was even faster than that."[65] In "No Face," Ysrael seems to possess the fantastic power of a zafa, a magic word like Captain Marvel's "shazam" (which Oscar fetishizes), shouting "STRENGTH" and then fighting off his bullies, four boys who threaten "to make you a girl," long enough to run away.[66]

But then, Ysrael doesn't really have superpowers, just childhood imagination; shouting "INVISIBILITY" does not actually mean "no one can touch him," and he has to run away when his abusive father shows up.[67] In the same way, Oscar's vision of the Mongoose and the Man Without a Face busing him and his family away to safety "was nothing but a final fantasy, gone as soon as he blinked" (321). And that is precisely the problem with Oscar's attempts to escape representation through blank pages and blank faces: they are only desperate fantasies, no more productive than his escapes into Stephen-King-induced postapocalyptic tabula rasa. None of the hope promised by these blanks comes to fruition. Oscar dies foolishly, the butt of a violent joke: "we'll let you go if you tell us what *fuego* means in English. Fire, he blurted out, unable to help himself," unable to leave the joke's blank unfilled (322).[68] Yunior likewise self-consciously fails to write the blank words that could have saved us, instead displacing that project to future writers—namely, Lola's daughter Isis, who he hopes will "take all we've done and all we've learned and add her own insights and she'll put an end to it" (330–31). The blank pages and faces in *Oscar Wao* never attain the status of zafa, escape from representation; like superhero masks, they are only fantasy escapism.

We might conclude that these attempted solutions do not succeed precisely because they remain blank: if only we had gotten Yunior's words or Oscar's, we could be saved. In a 2012 interview with Paula Moya, Díaz suggests exactly that regarding Yunior's missing words: "what he couldn't say to Lola was that 'I too have been molested,'" explaining that Yunior "couldn't tell the story that would have tied him in a human way to Lola, that indeed could have saved him."⁶⁹ Salvation would come from representing silenced historical traumas, as Díaz claims it does for himself six years later when he, unlike Yunior, can finally say, "I was raped."⁷⁰ This likewise seems to be the logic surrounding Abelard's missing book. "An exposé of the supernatural roots of the Trujillo regime! A book about the Dark Powers of the President," Abelard's book exemplifies the counterhistoriographical project critics have attributed to Yunior (245). For José Saldívar, Abelard's book, "representing the unspeakable violence of the Trujillo regime, and Oscar's late black science fiction Creolist writings in the Dominican Republic are analogues to Díaz's *The Brief Wondrous Life of Oscar Wao* as a whole."⁷¹ But, "alas, the grimoire in question (so the story goes) was conveniently destroyed after Abelard was arrested" (245). Abelard's book offered the hope of filling in the blanks in Trujillo's mythological history but becomes a blank of its own instead. "I only wish I could have read that thing," says Yunior (245). If only we had gotten Abelard's words, Trujillo's power would have been diminished. If only we could supply the missing texts, the state would be more just and democratic.

But *Oscar Wao* is not missing—is, in fact, full of text—so by the counterhistoriographical logic, we should be on our way to being saved. Why, then, is Yunior in the end so convinced of his project's failure, finding his only glimmer of hope in the possibility that Isis might complete what he could not? Once more, it seems the reason that Yunior has failed is not because he has not been able to write over the state's gaps but because his book is not blank at all. *Oscar Wao* is no zafa, no escape from representation under power, but a fantasy about zafa.

Take Yunior's claim that he has his own "páginas en blanco" (149). This statement is stranger than critics have generally recognized, because Díaz does not in fact give us any actual blank pages. The metafictional device of the blank page is an old one, famously stretching back to Laurence Sterne. Plenty of Díaz's contemporaries *do* include blank pages, perhaps most notably in Mark Z. Danielewski's *House of Leaves* (2000) or, more proximate to Díaz's Latin American context, Salvador Plascencia's *The People of Paper* (2005), both of which Ramón Saldívar notes as formal and aesthetic companions to *Oscar Wao*.⁷² And in other ways Díaz actively participates in contemporary fiction's "metamediality"⁷³—especially through his use of footnotes, which, as Harford Vargas argues, "literally lowers [Trujillo] on the page,"[74] reproducing Plascencia's counterdictatorial logic of pushing authoritative voices to the margins of the text. Díaz explains in an interview that he is interested in "the way words fall on a page. Literally, the physical way words look. If a sentence looks wrong on the page, I don't care what it says, I change it."[75] For someone who cares about the look of a text on the page, writing at a time when the blank page is an almost commonplace device, using a fictional author who claims to have his own páginas en blanco, Díaz's refusal to actually include any blank pages in *Oscar Wao* is striking.

The Brief Wondrous Life of Oscar Wao is not like Abelard's or Oscar's books, which somehow become emblems of hope in their frustrating, intransigent inability or refusal to represent. Although Yunior's narrative is not airtight—there are gaps and lacunae—he nevertheless does represent. That is why he fails. He cannot write zafa's blank book. Instead, he can only represent the desire for the blank page, displacing escape from representation to a time after the novel ends, through the character of Isis, the hoped-for author of the future. In the same 2012 interview with Moya in which he fills in Yunior's blank words that could save, Díaz also reasserts the necessity—and difficulty—of writing blanks as he explains why hope resides with the writing of Isis, not Yunior:

> In the Egyptian legends I grew up on, Isis assembles her lover-brother Osiris, she assembles the pieces of Osiris that have been chopped up and scattered by Set.... Isis doesn't find Osiris's penis, but I like to believe she just leaves it out. Osiris comes back to the world alive but penisless. Which for some is a horror but for others a marked improvement... I've always thought the thing with Yunior is that he couldn't reassemble himself in a way that would leave out his metaphorical penis, that would leave out all his attachments to his masculine, patriarchal, phallocratic privileges.[76]

The difference between Isis and Yunior is that Isis can "leave out" but Yunior cannot. Yunior, like Díaz, cannot escape his patriarchal masculinity, and ameliorating reform, finding a better way to live with a penis, becomes the necessary stopgap. Díaz wishes Yunior could write páginas en blanco, the open space of freedom undetermined by hegemony's representations, but he cannot; Yunior's gaps can only be understood as involuntary deficiencies that need filling. But *Oscar Wao* dreams for more than that. The hope affixed to Isis is that she could incorporate absences on purpose, strategically leaving things out as a way of escaping hegemonic structures of power. Hers is a new kind of writing, one that Díaz, by dramatizing Yunior's inability to write that way, suggests is still yet to be achieved.

Oscar Wao fantasizes a blank page more zafa than fukú. But it also always remains aware of the ways the state applies its violence differentially through representations, a reality that makes identity matter: how one gets represented directly affects one's relation to state power. This means that reformist politics of inclusion cannot be ignored. Officially and unofficially, states apply their power through representational systems such as race, gender, sexuality, nationality, and class; the state does not care if you think any of these categories are essential or not.[77] Or, as Yunior puts it, "it's perfectly fine if you don't believe in these 'superstitions.' ... Because no matter what you believe, fukú believes in you" (5). In consequence, proliferating representations remains an urgent political project, one with life-and-death ramifications.

Yamashita gives us this through maps and voices, Díaz through histories. Yet *Tropic of Orange* and *Oscar Wao* also gesture beyond such politics of inclusion. These novels suggest that, eventually, we will need to part ways with political representation. Beginning in the Civil Rights era and especially since the 1990s (and the start of Yamashita's and Díaz's literary careers), multiculturalism in the United States has functioned primarily to extend and secure a coherent, if heterogenous, national identity, maintaining and reinforcing state power.[78] Mermann-Jozwiak notes how "the very emphasis on cultural identity and recognition by the majority society has ultimately prevented effective challenges to the nation-state. Though its relations with the nation-state may at times be strained, in the end multiculturalism functions to contain diversity," reinforcing the "imagined community" that Benedict Anderson identifies as the underlying glue of the state: "With national unity still the ultimate goal, the nation-state has become rather adept at co-opting multiculturalism."[79]

Both novels insist on the inadequacy of such multiculturalism. Yamashita describes the character of Emi as her "mouthpiece for saying things that normally should not be said. She's the one who says that 'multi-culturalism' is bullshit."[80] Díaz likewise rejects unthreatening, easily digestible consumer multiculturalism such as "music and food and other charming Latino cultural simplifications that an outsider can connect with and consume ahistorically."[81] In an interview, Díaz asks rhetorically, "we can elect Obama, but what does that say about the fate of the African-American community?"[82] Such identity scorekeeping, he suggests, does not accomplish much that is meaningful. Over and over, these fictions suggest that more equitable representation and diverse inclusion will not be enough.

These perspectives do leave room for a more nuanced politics of inclusion, one that, for instance, "engages progressive political projects, with immigration reform, with the country's oppressive social realities, with activism, with the neocolonial umbra that define in large part the Latino reality."[83] In that regard, *Tropic of Orange* and *Oscar Wao* do not take their critiques as far as, for example, Walter Benn Michaels, for whom diversity politics is not merely inadequate but fully imbricated in economic rule: "Major social changes have taken place in the past 40 years with remarkable rapidity, but not any in any sense inimical to capitalism. Capitalism has no problem with gay people getting married and people who self-identify as neoliberals understand this very well."[84] Even as these fictions are acutely aware of the ways economic logic both accommodates and appropriates the demands of multiculturalism, they also recognize how state power nevertheless violently wields representations of identity. In the decades after these novels, the Black Lives Matter movement can make such a recognition feel rather obvious, but these texts help us see this logic at play in a much more expansive sense, including but also extending beyond the realities of police violence against Black Americans: this is a fundamental characteristic of how the state represents bodies into its administrative schemes. Even as the appearance of the state morphs with the history of globalization, American literature still warily regards representation's service to state power.

In the next chapter, I will take up these concerns again in the context of contemporary poetry, considering in greater length the ways the state makes identity matter by producing it as a site of political violence. In that light, fuller representation is expedient in the meantime. But *Tropic of Orange* and *Oscar Wao* also look past such expediencies toward an ultimate hope of escape. Reformist inclusion and revolutionary exit are largely at cross-purposes, and it is difficult to imagine how pursuing one would not necessarily inhibit the other. These novels do not feign to resolve this political contradiction, nor do they settle on either side; rather, they insist that it still needs solving. The hope of escaping state representations' determining power remains distant, beyond the ambit of either text, but it shines faintly as lodestar.

BEYOND PROTEST

Voice and Exit in Juliana Spahr and Nathaniel Mackey

Tell us how we're doing. Your feedback is important to us!
—Suggestion boxes

COMMENT CARDS, OPINION polls, customer satisfaction surveys: these are ubiquitous.[1] Liberal societies have relatively abundant access to *voice*. In political economist Albert O. Hirschman's compelling framework, voice is any attempt to improve an organization's behavior by expressing dissatisfaction.[2] Distinct from poetic or character voice, this standard political sense of voice includes everything from op-eds to general protests to voting; it is "interest articulation," communicating opinions, preferences, needs, and demands.[3] This notion of voice has no necessary connection to "voice" as a formalist literary term; it may have nothing to do with, say, lyric subjectivity or prose style. Nevertheless, our understanding of art's political function could benefit from the term's particular usage in political economy. As Hirschman and social scientists after him understand it, voice is a crucial feedback mechanism for improving social organizations, whether businesses, churches, families, clubs, unions, or the state.

In this sense of voice—which I intend throughout this chapter—voice communicates dissatisfaction from customers or members to managers or leaders, giving the latter the information necessary to make changes for the better.

This conception of voice describes much of what we think of as political art—an anti-war poem, for example, or anonymous street artist Banksy's stenciled satires of state surveillance—because one of its primary (though not only) functions is signaling discontent. This is not to say political artists are reading Hirschman; though his work remains influential in contemporary political science and economics, I am not interested in tracing the intellectual history of Hirschman's ideas so much as in using them to understand art's political capacities and limitations, capacities and limitations that artists themselves have recognized and striven to overcome. Moreover, Hirschman's descriptive framework reveals a set of political prescriptions at play in much contemporary political art. For Hirschman, the counterpart to voice is *exit*—leaving the organization rather than protesting or complaining to its leaders. Exit, in this sense, need not involve physical departure; Hirschman's idea of exit would include ending a relationship or partnership, withdrawing one's membership in an association, or ceasing to identify with or participate in a group. Exit is cutting things off, disconnecting. As we have seen, exit from the political state becomes a significant political aspiration in twentieth- and twenty-first-century American literature, and Hirschman's usefulness here is twofold: he provides a particularly lucid understanding of how political art can work, and he suggests a politics that is frequently and importantly present in American literature.

Ultimately, however, contemporary poetry takes us beyond what we learn from Hirschman's voice-exit framework. As we have seen, in political economy, the story of exit is traditionally a liberal one: political theorist Chandran Kukathas places "the right to leave the community" at the core of liberalism, calling it "fundamental" and "inalienable."[4] Although other liberal theorists do not prioritize exit to the same degree as Kukathas, exit remains a central liberal value for thinkers ranging from Hirschman to Milton Friedman to John Rawls. Yet, for each of these, exit always takes place *within* the liberal state: there must be no exit from the state itself. Contemporary poetry, however, takes us beyond this liberal tradition, appropriating

FIGURE 12. Banksy's *If Graffiti Changed Anything*.

the same logic of exit we find in Hirschman but seeking to turn it against the state.

Hirschman highlights the role of exit by identifying some important ways voice might fail. We have already looked extensively at one of those failures in the preceding chapters: voice fails all those aspects of human life that resist articulation. Some things simply will not be adequately communicated, and voice alone is insufficient to align organizational behavior with members' needs. Thus exit offers a necessary complement to voice. When speaking up does not do any good, members can leave the organization entirely. The problem, though, is that when the organization in question is the political state, "the exit option is unavailable."[5] This is the dilemma confronted by the four novels discussed in the last two chapters, and the various solutions tried by DeLillo, Didion, Yamashita, and Díaz can all be characterized in part as attempts to voice—in Hirschman's sense of articulating a critical belief—the need for the exit option. Some things are inarticulable, but the demand for exit is not one of them.

Here, unfortunately, another of voice's critical failures comes into view: organizations can sometimes simply ignore critique (the old joke about the trash can masquerading as a suggestion box delivers its requisite grain of truth). Under certain conditions, administrators are insulated from voice, or otherwise lack necessary incentives to heed it. Such conditions are common under exitless situations such as the state; as Hirschman explains, "the *effectiveness* of the voice mechanism is strengthened by the possibility of exit."[6] Without the threat of exit, it is far less costly for an organization to disregard voice. James Baldwin gets at this dilemma in his critique of protest literature (a clear example of Hirschman's voice): "escape is not effected through a bitter railing against this trap."[7] Complaining to your captors won't get you free.

The difficulty of enabling exit through voice is further compounded by the ease with which dominant institutions, when they cannot ignore subversive speech, co-opt it. Take Banksy's *If Graffiti Changed Anything*, which riffs on the anarchist adage about voting: "If graffiti changed anything—it would be illegal" (fig. 12). The exaggerated dripping of the red lettering suggests a hurried, clandestine act, one to flee before you get caught like Banksy's signature rat, here visually punned into red-handed culpability. On first read, then, Banksy seems to ironize the aphorism, reasserting the efficacy of voice: graffiti is illegal, so maybe it does change something, voicing a critique that officials must acknowledge and respond to. But graffiti *isn't* really illegal, not for Banksy anyway, at least effectively if not always officially.[8] City officials and property owners go out of their way to protect Banksy's works, exempting them from regular graffiti removal and even enshrining them in plexiglass,[9] and in the United States, graffiti has received broad legal protections under the Visual Artists Rights Act of 1990.[10] As one journalist put it, "it is difficult to imagine the police being anything but embarrassed if they caught Banksy in the act today. Even prosecutors elevate him into a different class from other graffiti artists."[11] Once graffiti works as art rather than a transgression of property or regulatory norms (a distinction suggested by the contrast between Banksy's neatly stenciled rat and his slapdash lettering)—insofar as it functions, like voting, *as voice*—it becomes co-opted within the law. So the straight reading wins out: at least by radical standards, Banksy's protest graffiti does not change anything, and his voice remains politically impotent.

In another Banksy piece, which went up in New York City in 2010 (fig. 13), a hand reaches through the bars of a prison window to draw a door on

FIGURE 13. An untitled variation on Banksy's *Jail Break* stencil appearing on the side of a bail bonds agency in New York City.

the wall, frozen inches from completing the handle that would, supposedly, open the door and let the prisoner free. The piece recalls the magical logic of the popular children's book *Harold and the Purple Crayon,* but only to invert the book's fanciful celebration of the power of imagination and art. The stylistic distance from the relatively photorealistic hand and bars to the hand-drawn door suggests that, unlike Harold's, this prisoner's drawings will not open the way to a new world. Even if the magic worked, the physical escape through the door would be meaningless. This prisoner is already out of jail: we learn from the shop awning, conspicuously included in Banksy's photographic frame, that the building houses a bail bond agency, a reminder that entrapment within the state extends into a myriad of nominally non-state institutions that nevertheless maintain and propagate state power. (The jail still looms in the background, of course, as across the street the Brooklyn Detention Complex towers over the scene.) The piece cannot take seriously its own fantasy of escape. Presumably a key could be drawn, but why does the door have a lock at all? Using the door could never have been the point. The hand does not draw from a delusional hope of escape but draws as a proclamation of desire that self-consciously emphasizes its own inadequacy: there *should* be a way out, but saying so will not make it so.

A later Banksy piece reiterates this idea while also making the potential literary ramifications more explicit. In early 2021, *Create Escape* went up on the side of Reading Gaol—of literary notoriety for being the prison where Oscar Wilde was held from 1895 to 1897.[12] The piece shows a prisoner descending what at first appears to be, in cliché jailbreak imagery, a rope of knotted bedsheets. The bedsheets, however, turn out to be paper, lined with text and spooling out of a typewriter hanging at the bottom. Text, like a Wilde poem, would be the means of escaping unjust political imprisonment. But turning the bedsheets into paper also undermines this escape route: it's only in the imagination that paper can bear the weight of this escapee, and in the imagination the prisoner also remains frozen, never reaching the ground. Banksy's making-of video for *Create Escape* reiterates this fact by overlaying the piece with archival audio from the innocuously uplifting public television show *The Joy of Painting*. Host Bob Ross, in his famously soft-spoken manner, comments, "painting, to me, represents freedom. I can create the kind of world that I want to see and that I want to be part of."[13] This is a fantasy of art that "goes all the way off the canvas," one that can "turn you loose on the world"—a fantasy of art as something more than voice. Recontextualized against the backdrop of graffiti and prison break, Ross's words take on more explicit political implications, but their presence also undercuts any political pretensions in Banksy's work. If a Banksy piece or Wilde poem creates freedom or another kind of world, it is like the kind produced by a Bob Ross painting, with its happy little clouds, comforting but harmless.

Contemporary American poetry, especially in its more radical idioms, often finds itself in a situation similar to Banksy's prisoners. Transgression is no escape route, but neither does voice seem likely to create one. What to do when only exit will suffice, but voice is all you have? Many contemporary poets, I argue, have responded to this bind by wondering if poetry might make voice, improbably, a provisional substitute for exit. For the remainder of this chapter, I will focus on Juliana Spahr and Nathaniel Mackey as particularly salient examples of this contemporary escape poetics, but we should also recognize similar dynamics at play in many other contemporary poets—Susan Howe and Andrew Joron, for instance. (My brief engagement with Banksy above should also suggest the broader transatlantic and cross-genre preoccupation with exiting the state—an idea I'll return to in this book's conclusion.) Spahr and Mackey ultimately want not greater voice, not greater inclusion within the representational structure of power, but the freedom to exit the representational structure altogether. So long as exit is impossible, though (and violent revolution long out of the question, unviable if not unjustifiable), voice is all they have, and abandoning voice under the pretense of exit is only a counterproductive fantasy. But rather than simply using voice to demand exit, as Hirschman's framework would stipulate, Spahr and Mackey try to make voice, as poetry, play the role of exit.

As we will see, this experiment cannot help but fail, in much the same way Banksy's prisoners fail. Exit and voice can sometimes overlap (think boycotts or strikes), but, as Spahr's and Mackey's poetries emphasize, voice alone—where the conditions for exit are not already in place—cannot act like exit. In so failing, this poetics of exit collapses back into voice. There, Hirschman's basically liberal framework will no longer suffice. After confronting these dead ends (the inefficacy of merely demanding exit, the circular equivocation of positing voice as exit), Spahr and Mackey turn voice to another purpose, one that exceeds Hirschman's conception. Rather than a complaint addressed to authority, a plea to be satisfied, the demand for exit now forms the potential basis of new political collectivities, people brought together by a shared desire to leave the state. Voice, in this sense, works not so much within the liberal vision of the marketplace of ideas as to produce a political collectivity, a sphere of discourse and "scene of association" Michael Warner calls a "counterpublic."[14] Voicing the need for exit becomes a way of connecting to others who believe, or might come to believe, the same.

I look first at the ways Spahr frets over her own complicity in violent global imperialism, a complicity that sticks to her through the state's dual exertion of military power and systems of representation. Spahr fantasizes a poetry capable of doing by speaking—and thus capable of creating its own exit—but she quickly gives up that project as hopeless, ultimately returning to voice as she tries to articulate the power of state articulations.

I then turn to Mackey, who similarly dreams of a poetry-as-exit, voice or song as a breath to fill wings and enable flight like a bird lifted on thermals. Like Spahr, Mackey knows this dream is unrealizable, but instead of fixating on the power of state representations, Mackey tries to give voice to inarticulacy, making the incoherent cry of suffering speak. Recognizing that voice cannot make exit happen, Spahr and Mackey both renew the unappeased demand for exit as the seed for new collectivities, though they emphasize different motivations behind the will to escape: Spahr foregrounds the determining power of state-backed representation, while Mackey foregrounds the state's dismissal of inarticulate human experience. As we work through these two poets, we will see how the poetics of escape inflects familiar issues of open form and identity politics in contemporary poetry. These poets' formal engagement with openness and indeterminacy is not merely a privileging of subject position over ideology, as some critics have charged, but rather an attempt to address the problem of escaping state articulation—and its corresponding confinement of politics to the domain of voice.

SPEAKING POLITICS AND SPAHR'S POLITICS OF SPEAKING

Open Spahr's thirty-two-page chapbook *things of each possible relation hashing against one another* (2003) to the very middle, to pages sixteen and seventeen, and you might notice a bit of yellow string, tied in the middle, running down the book's gutter. That's because the Palm Press edition has saddle-stitch binding—that yellow string stitches the pages to the book's spine. This is interesting because page sixteen opens with the line, "then the opening of the things sewn together."[15] Lots of things are sewn together in a book about relationships between things, but one of those things is certainly the book itself.

What, then, is "the opening" of the sewn poetry chapbook? Physically, of course, the book is already open as we read it—indeed is halfway to being shut again by the time we reach this page. This is the opening of an open book. The easy solution is to read the line in terms of the open form poetics that have largely dominated avant-garde American poetry since Olson's "Projective Verse" manifesto. To open the poetry chapbook in this sense would be to reject semiotic closure in favor of indeterminacy, privileging the multiplicity of readerly experiences over authorially intended meaning: what the book *is*, as an object (a thing sewn together) experienced by the reader, would matter more than what it *says*.[16] The poem certainly suggests such a shift from meaning to embodiment when it imagines "the cells in the veins of the paginations of impelling mechanisms."[17] These pages are like bodies, apparently acting directly on the world. We could read these lines as an acknowledgement of the way the materiality of writing affects the production of a poem—the physical fact of the page shapes Spahr's writing, and in her recent critical work, Spahr is all too aware of the political forces that constitute and shape poetic production[18]—but it nevertheless makes more sense to read these lines as a claim about what a poem does after it is written. The pages that impel are already paginated, not blank; the "impelling" happens after, not before, the act of writing. This is a vision of texts acting forcefully rather than communicating messages—this is the version of the avant-garde that the poet Ben Lerner criticizes for believing "that poems (or other artworks) can intervene directly in history," treating the poem as a "bomb."[19] Poetry, in this sense, would do more than speak, the product of writing more a body than an idea. If poetry could ever be capable of exit, going beyond speaking (the discursive home of Hirschman's voice) seems like a good place to start.

That's a little too easy, though, for a few reasons. Most immediately, Spahr's insistent use of the gerund means that "opening" never becomes "open" (either adjective or imperative); "opening" is a never-completed process, always pushing against a closure that it cannot be rid of, frozen like Banksy's prisoner on the verge of opening the prison door. Moreover, even this process is temporally displaced to "then" instead of now. We haven't even begun opening, much less accomplished a move from meaning to experience. These initial hints are cemented by the poem's republication in Spahr's full-length collection *Well Then There Now* (2011). Unlike the chapbook, *Well Then There Now* is perfect bound, with the pages glued to the spine rather than sewn. "Things sewn together" no longer points to the physical book itself. The poem's earlier gesture towards a fully embodied poetics, one that incorporates within itself the nonsemiotic world of book bindings, is now revealed to be a futile one. In choosing to reprint the poem thus, Spahr privileges signs over signifiers, the reproducible meaning of the poem's words over their singular physical being. What matters, what persists, is what the poem says.

These two moves—first, trying to make poetry do something more than speak, and second, rejecting that project as hopeless, reasserting poetry as message—encapsulate what I think is going on in much of Spahr's poetry and much contemporary poetry generally. Though Spahr might wish her poems could be bombs, hating that such a poem-bomb "never goes off" because "the poem remains a poem," she does not lapse, as Lerner's avant-garde does, into "a military metaphor that forgets it is a metaphor."[20] As we will see, Spahr remains acutely aware that it is only the state's words, not poetry's, that can be a bomb, carrying force in precisely the way poetry's words do not.

This is important, because it complicates a common argument about contemporary poetry, especially avant-garde poetry like Spahr's that can be said to fulfill a trajectory from Olson to the language poets to something we now sometimes call postlanguage. A keystone text for this argument is Walter Benn Michaels's *The Shape of the Signifier* (2004). Devoting attention to the poetry of Susan Howe (whose interest in the materiality of the page and the book is an obvious precursor to Spahr's play with the sewn chapbook), Michaels argues that any poetics that privileges the text's physical embodiment over its semiotic meaning—the shape of the signifier over the content of the sign—is incompatible with leftist politics, because it inevitably privileges, wittingly or not, identity over ideology. When what the poem *is* matters more than what it *says*, history really has ended, and the ideological battle against capitalism is over. Instead of right and wrong, there are only different positions, differences in perspective. According to Michaels, identity politics reinscribes the essentialisms it claims to fight against while diverting attention from the problems of economic class, which really *is* essential, grounded in history.

In instances such as the sewn chapbook, Spahr does seem to want to move beyond signification and thus seems exposed to Michaels's critique. Yet in reprinting the poem outside of the chapbook's material context, thereby staging the persistence of the sign, Spahr suggests that getting outside representation is not so easy. In turn, this indicates that something else is at stake in the pursuit of open form: something stands in the way of openness, something that must be actively resisted. While to Michaels contemporary poetry's disaffection with discourse looks like giving up on political disagreement, Hirschman helps us recognize when it is motivated instead by the limitations of political voice and the unrealized potential of political exit. Rather than emptying out ideological conflict by privileging perspectival difference, here the site of ideological conflict relocates to the fight to escape representation. This is not the end of history but a reconceptualization of where history is taking place.

For Spahr this conflict takes on political urgency because of the state: social inscriptions acquire determining power when they are reified by state violence; the difficulty of achieving openness comes to stand in for the difficulty of escaping representations brandished by the state. For example, in *This Connection of Everyone with Lungs* (2005), Spahr writes of "the forces that are compelling all of us to be brushing up against one another."[21] The "brushing up against one another" is Spahr's refrain for collectivities formed out of individual bodies, bodies that are both separated and joined by their skin, which acts as both boundary and connective interface. Such joining of bodies is often sexual and loving for Spahr, with beloveds who "like to press our skins against one another in the night" (19), as well as more broadly communal, as with "the crowds that are gathering all together to meet each other with various intents" (22). But the connection of skin can also take on more troubling aspects, as when connection comes to hinge on racial categories. Spahr tries to dismiss this kind of problematic connection, insisting,

> But when I speak of skin I do not speak of the arbitrary connotations of color that have made all this brushing against one another even harder for all of us.
>
> Beloveds, your skins are of all colors, are soft and wrinkled, blotchy and reddish, full of blemish and smooth. (23)

Race here seems to be erased in its multiplicity. Adopting Michaels's perspective, we would say that, beneath that surface rhetoric, Spahr is actually privileging the identity categories she is trying to deconstruct—she is speaking of the arbitrary connotations of color, even in the very act of denying as much.

However, in the context of the poem as a whole and of Spahr's poetry more generally, it's clear that she is painfully aware of her own inability to stop talking about race, or gender, or sexuality, and so on. The reason she cannot stop talking about such representational categories is the state's deployment of these representations as tools of domination:

> I keep trying to speak of loving but all I speak about is acts of war and acts of war and acts of war.
>
> I mean to speak of beds and bowers and all I speak of is Barghouti's call for a change of leadership and the strike in Venezuela against Chavez and the sixty-six ships on the fleet of shame. (28)

Spahr wants to talk about skin as the place of contact between lovers, but she ends up talking about skin as the locus of violence in war. The touch of lovers' skin cannot escape state systems of violence: "the military-industrial complex enters our bed at night. / We sleep with levels of complicity" (63). Skin matters not just as a pluralistic interface of interpersonal connection, bodies pressing together at night, but as the site of state power.[22] Spahr would adopt Hirschman's logic of exit and leave all this behind, but state power makes voice the only option. All she can do is keep speaking of acts of war.

The state's role in giving force to identity is even more explicit in "The Incinerator," the concluding poem of *Well Then There Now*. As in *This Connection*, Spahr cannot help but talk about categories of identity even when she wants to talk about something else: "wanting to talk about class, I kept talking only about gender."[23] The poem talks about race, too, but it discusses both race and gender always in relation to state schemes of representation given legal force, as when, in an autobiographical moment, she thinks about "how white women were beneficiaries of affirmative action" (150–51).

Affirmative action is one example of what Aihwa Ong has described as a "positive exception," a variation on Giorgio Agamben's classic account of the sovereign exception. In contrast to a "negative exception that suspends civil rights," a positive exception, according to Ong, can "create opportunities, usually for a minority, who enjoy political accommodations and conditions not granted to the rest of the population."[24] Yet, as Ong makes clear, the positive exception functions just as much as the negative exception to secure and maintain state sovereignty—it is a strategy "invoked, especially in bureaucratically centralized societies, in order to allow privileged groups to face the challenges of globalization."[25]

In this instance, Spahr herself benefits from state power through affirmative action, but she understands this privilege as a form of complicity in an unacceptable system. A state that wields identity in her favor can wield it just as easily as a weapon against others. Reflecting on Hannah Weiner's poem "Radcliffe and Guatemalan Women," Spahr emphasizes the role of state violence in determining subject positions, from "the police burning alive thirty-nine people" to "18,000 state killings" to "the government kidnapping and then 'disappearing' a number of student leaders," "how the Guatemalan government did all of this with the support of the US government" (145). She concludes that such state violence defines both the college-educated Radcliffe women and the Guatemalan women, feeling "uneasy" that the two categories are "joined opposites, joined by their gender, by the ties that their governments have with each other, and by the ties that they have with their governments" (146). As Josh Cerretti argues in his historical analysis of sexuality and the military in the United States in the 1990s—an immediately relevant context for Spahr's poetry—the state deploys gender to justify military intervention in the name of equality, but, in "encouraging the armed response of the state over effective, survivor-centric responses," this only "militarizes sexual violence" rather than solving it, "making civilian cultural understandings of sexual violence complicit with militarized projects."[26] In like manner, gender connects the women of Spahr's poem not through essentialism but through the determining, violent power of the state.

While critics have devoted attention to many of Spahr's sociopolitical concerns, as in Diane Chisholm's account of Spahr's ecopoetics, few have taken seriously her interest in the state (one exception is Jesse Cohn, who usefully reads Spahr's poetry within an anarchist literary tradition). But Spahr's more explicit anti-capitalism cannot be understood apart from her anti-statism (which also importantly distinguishes her thought from liberal accounts of exit such as Hirschman's).[27] This becomes especially clear through contemporary issues of globalization. Critics such as Nicky Marsh and Kimberly Lamm perceptively highlight Spahr's anxiety about the individual's relationship and responsibility to global events ranging from war to climate change. Globalization per se, though, isn't what bothers Spahr: her anxiety turns on the absence or presence of state-backed violence in global structures. In "The Incinerator," for example, Spahr does not unequivocally reject the forces of globalization, acknowledging how "the global economy empowers some women and disempowers others" (147). What's more, she repeatedly attributes the negative consequences of globalization to state action, such as "how the manipulation of trade barriers by the US government has adversely impacted women across many different nations" (147). Bolstering those barriers is no more a solution than "free trade" agreements, because trade itself is not the problem—in an essay on literature in the Pacific, Spahr sketches out a vision "of hope [that] sees travel, trade, and migration as prominent parts of Pacific life, a life of movement, canoes, and jets."[28] Strengthening the barriers only makes them that much more powerful as a tool of manipulation.[29] The issue is not a global economy but a global economy beholden to capitalist state power.

Put another way, Spahr desires globalization without imperialism, mutual human interconnection totally unimpeded by political borders and undistorted by the asymmetrical privileges and sanctions bestowed by states. This is pretty close to what anthropologist David Graeber calls "anarchist globalization": "the effacement of nation-states will mean the elimination of national borders. This is genuine globalization. Anything else is just a sham."[30] In this view, capitalist imperialism is nothing intrinsic to globalization but is, rather, an external pollutant to human interrelationships manifesting both locally and globally. Spahr wants to escape this structural contamination, leaving behind the violence embedded in state-based political organization, in pursuit of reciprocal exchange—exchanges of culture and capital, of love and language, of flora and fauna, which Spahr declares are "worth celebrating."³¹

Consider, for example, "Dole Street," also collected in *Well Then There Now*, which likewise foregrounds the state's role in the history of globalization. The essay's title refers to the street in Honolulu where Spahr lived and worked during her time at the University of Hawai'i at Manoa from 1997 to 2003. Spahr tells us that the street is named after Sanford B. Dole, the colonial president and then governor of Hawai'i at the end of the nineteenth century (33). She admits that at first, she "thought that it was named after the Dole of pineapples," but the pineapple Dole turns out to have been a relative, who "got the land for his pineapples from Sanford's governments" (33). Dole Street and Dole Food Company, Inc., both emblems of the asymmetrical imposition of Western values and power structures, trace back to underlying state power. The pineapple corporation is an imperialistic force, at least in part, due to its constitutive relationship with the state.

Spahr's opposition to the state thus suggests two different kinds of connection. On the one hand, there seems to be the possibility for good connections, the intimate connections between lovers, the collective ones in a crowd, or even global networks of exchange. On the other are bad connections, the state-imposed grouping of bodies into representational categories such as skin color, gender, or nationality, with international economic relationships "so obviously entirely maintained and perpetuated by the militaries of various nation-states."³² "Dole Street" suggests as much, with the global connections manifested by the street having both "lovely possibilities and sad humiliations" (39). The line closely mirrors another of Spahr's, one of her most memorable. In *This Connection of Everyone with Lungs*, Spahr imagines individual human bodies all connected by the air they breathe in and out, but this connection is far from uniform or homogeneous: "How lovely and how doomed this connection of everyone with lungs" (10). "Doomed" indicates that part of the connection is unlovely and undesirable, but it also carries the weight of an unavoidable fate. Indeed, the inevitability and the unloveliness become one and the same, joined together in a single word. The connection is unlovely in part *because* it is inescapable.

This comports with the line's "Dole Street" parallel. Spahr confides, "I am a part of Dole Street's swirl of connection whether I like it or not" (47). In "Dole Street," Spahr cannot escape connections constituted and defined by the imperialist US state. Likewise, the connection of everyone with lungs is doomed, unavoidable, because of its political basis. In *This Connection*, as Spahr accumulates repeating lines and images (one of her favorite poetic techniques) indicating the extent of air's connectivity, her perspective successively draws back to larger and larger scales, zooming out from "the space between the hands" to the "space of the mesosphere," somewhere around 160,000 feet above the Earth:

> as everyone with lungs breathes the space between the hands and the space around the hands and the space of the room and the space of the building that surrounds the room and the space of the neighborhoods nearby and the space of the cities and the space of the regions and the space of the nations and the space of the continents and islands and the space of the oceans and the space of the troposphere and the space of the stratosphere and the space of the mesosphere in and out (8).

Though the poem's iterative trajectory suggests that it has reached a totalizing scope, positing air as an essential, universal bond that automatically includes all people, its apex in the mesosphere problematizes such a reading. The mesosphere begins far above the highest altitudes humans can breathe unaided (air does not actually "connect" anyone's lungs that high up), but the mesosphere is also not the outermost stratum of the Earth's atmosphere (the thermosphere and exosphere extend above it). Moreover, stopping in the mesosphere conspicuously excludes a group of people with whom the poem is especially infatuated, astronauts orbiting the Earth. The poem's expanding iterations climax in a manifestation of the ultimately arbitrary boundaries of inclusion and exclusion: the connection of everyone with lungs that stops in the mesosphere is not a natural fact but a political decision, a matter of choosing criteria to determine who gets represented as connected and who is connected through representation.

Stopping in the mesosphere, however, also invites the possibility of disconnection—of exit. If doomed connection (connection to things, such as the military-industrial complex, that you do not want to be connected to) is not a universal, natural fact but a political, historical condition, then appropriating Hirschman-style exit to use against the state becomes, conceptually if not yet historically, imaginable. Astronauts beyond the mesosphere become a way of imagining disconnection from the connection of everyone with lungs.

This is important, because, for Spahr, the possibility of disconnection matters just as much as connection. Insofar as connection is inevitable, decreed by the state and enforced by its violence, connection loses its meaning and value. It is only in the context of potential disconnection that connection enriches human life. For example, in *Fuck You-Aloha-I Love You* (2001), Spahr imagines culture as a complex human pyramid in a Vegas-style acrobatics show, which iterates all kinds of combinations of human relationships: "In culture we have muscles and / we use these muscles to let us / move towards and on top and out / of each other. / We build ourselves into a configuration."[33] This "configuration" makes the bodies "tremble"—under the strain of muscular exertion but also with orgasmic connotations, approximating Spahr's political ideal of mutually voluntary, spontaneous human relationships free from top-down strictures ("There are no set patterns and / innumerable combinations may / be developed").[34] But such loving connection extends only as far as the possibility of disconnection: "We trust each other's bodies but / only to the extent that we can lift / ourselves off them."[35] To put it in Hirschman's terms, in these lines exit emerges as a necessary compliment to the connections that join bodies together.

However, in Spahr's earthly perspective (as in Hirschman's), exit from state hegemony is not possible—in *This Connection of Everyone with Lungs*, not even the most private spaces provide refuge from state structures ("the military-industrial complex enters our bed at night"). This inescapability is specifically a matter of representation, one enacted in maps, legally articulated rights, and the legitimating functions of voting and citizenship. She complains, "still a huge sadness overtakes us daily because of our inability to / control what goes on in the world in our name" (71). What goes out into the world is a representation ("in our name"), one that provides a mandate for state action. Likewise, representation is what enters the bed of lovers at night, pinning them with the weight of complicity: "we are on our backs in our bed at night unable to turn over or away from this, the three-legged stool of political piece, military piece, and development piece, that has entered our bed at night holding us down sleepless" (18). These media "pieces," the representational manifestations of US culture, are all inseparable from the violence that constitutes and sustains the US government. Thus, "when we speak of Lisa Marie Presley having sex with Michael Jackson, we speak of JDAM [Joint Direct Attack Munition] and JSOW [Joint Standoff Weapon] air-to-surface precision bombs" (72). The problem is not representation itself, but representation overlaying state violence. With the state, there is always force behind the representation, a potential or actual physical violence against human bodies. When Spahr tallies up a week's worth of deaths in the news, her mourning refrain is for "each of those one hundred and thirty-six people dead by politics' human hands" (39). Politics is representation, politics is physical violence; it is the combination of the two that make the state globally inescapable.

That is why *This Connection* sustains such interest in astronauts, transforming their exclusion from the connection of everyone with lungs into a hopeful image of escape from state systems of representation. Connection might be politically and historically doomed—ruined and inescapable—but astronauts allow Spahr to imagine changing that history. Thus, Spahr writes, "I try to comfort myself with images of exile," an exit that by definition occurs in relation to political power (63). The next phrase suggests what the comforting image of exile might look like: it is "the view from space," an image that abounds in Spahr's poetry. Earlier in the same long poem, Spahr adopts the perspective of "those astronauts on the space station" who "sent ahead of them images of the earth from space" (34). These images offer Spahr the same hope as exile: "Something in me jumps when I see these images, jumps toward comfort and my mind settles" (34). Like DeLillo's Jack Gladney rejecting the law as a way to "escape the pull of the earth," Spahr is riffing on the familiar science fiction trope, from Robert Heinlein to Octavia Butler, of escaping the political troubles of Earth by literally flying to another world.[36] Orbiting far above the highest extents of the mesosphere, astronauts embody an escape from the connection of everyone with lungs. This is Spahr's poetic goal: she announces that "this poem is an attempt to speak with the calmness of the world seen from space and to forget the details" (35). She wants the poem to achieve the comforts of exit, but she wants it to do so specifically by *speaking*. The poem Spahr wants to write would speak an escape from the awful details of life on Earth. If such a poem could be written, it would make voice, implausibly, act like exit, paving a way out of the state and its structures of domination.

Such a poem might work like one of J. L. Austin's performative utterances. Rather than talking about exit, the poem would enact exit, in the same way that saying "I now pronounce you" is the act that makes marriage happen. Spahr seems to suggest as much when she tries to privilege human love over military violence: "I say it again, the sight of the ones you love, those you've met and those you haven't. / I say it again and again. / Again and again. / I try to keep saying it to keep making it happen" (47). The act of saying that "the thing most lovely" is "whatever you love best" would make it so, carving an escape route out of the bed infested with the military-industrial complex and into a public bed of lovers (46). In this conception, rather than conveying ideas or beliefs about disconnection, the act of speaking would directly sever old connections and constitute new ones. Saying it would make it happen.

But Spahr's overdetermined insistence ("I say it again and again. / Again and again") betrays how she does not really believe this fantasy, and the poem's interest in voice-as-exit seems increasingly self-critical rather than aspirational. The hint of tautology in defining "the thing most lovely" as "whatever you love best" reveals one crack in the fantasy's edifice. In such a pluralistic conception, the problem is precisely that "some say the thing most lovely is the thirty thousand assault troops from Britain today joining the sixty-two thousand from the US" (46). What some say they love best is incompatible with what others say they love best, and if saying is making, then all that matters is who can say with more force—who can utter, in Austin's terms, a more "successful" performative. The success of the utterance relies on its context, which is to say its relation to existing power structures—the wedding officiant's proclamation is typically preceded by the phrase "by the power vested in me by the state of . . ." An even more problematic circularity thus emerges: for voice to work as exit, complimentary power structures strong enough to enact exit must already be in place. To enter a contest of performative utterances against the military-industrial complex is to play by their rules and into their strengths. States, not poets, have bombs.

That is why Spahr rejects voice-as-exit, despite its comforting appeal to her, as an escapist fantasy: "That view from space, this view now seems so without promise, / so empty of hope" (63). Spahr's poetics of escape is not escapist, and saying the view from space doesn't amount to making an exit. "Despite our isolation," Spahr writes, "there is no escape"; solipsistic withdrawal from the world, ignoring the details, is no meaningful exit (25). Elsewhere in her academic work, Spahr observes that the dream of a poetry that "easily moves from language to tangible action—is not possible in the current moment."[37] Like Banksy's prisoner dangling from a rope of typewriter paper, Spahr longs for a poetry that could create a way out, but, in the opening decades of the twenty-first century, she does not believe it possible to write one. Spahr's flirtation with the possibility of a poetry literally enacting escape from the state, her "attempt to speak away" the state's violences, culminates in recognizing its own futility (36).

The kind of exit described by Hirschman still holds an allure for a poet like Spahr, promising a way forward if it were possible. However, when Spahr turns to voice as a provisional alternative to unavailable exit, it is not the voice described by Hirschman, voice as a protest to leadership aiming to reform and improve the system itself. Rather, Spahr turns to voice in hopes of establishing new political collectivities around the need for exit, speaking to others who might also work towards escape.

Spahr's "New World Sonnet" offers a glimpse of how voicing the problems of state-based connection, the impetus for exit, might itself function as the basis of non-state connections that could in turn enable escape. The space of the poem is the colonial periphery, outside the violent power that constitutes the metropole, yet it is nevertheless complicit, still trapped by the connections it seeks to escape: the New World is only "new" from a European perspective, and though Spahr pushes against the sonnet tradition by stretching the thirteenth "line" over sixteen lines of text, she indents these surplus lines, reasserting the structural control of the European convention. The poem indiscriminately mixes machine-translated English, French, Spanish, German, Portuguese, and Italian, suggesting both the beginnings of an international connectivity as well as a hodgepodge of European powers fighting for colonial dominance. They are "languages from elsewhere," and though Spahr does not seem to think of linguistic exchange as inherently violent, the poem is acutely aware of the violence that coincided with the introduction of European languages to the Americas: "In the language. / In the taking and the burning."³⁸ The poem is more concerned with imperialist violence as a means than globalization as an end, a qualification made clear in its refrain of "how we are here." The poem insists that we need to "listen" to the "how," and concludes with a call-to-action, declaring, "we are here but how we need listening. How we need listening to the furnace." The conjunction "but" separates and differentiates the simple fact that "we are here," the connectivity of globalization, from the "how," the "furnace" that implicates us as perpetuators of violence for our own comfort. The problem is not the presence of a European form such as the sonnet in the New World but the violence, always justified and legitimized through the state, that helped get it there.

For Spahr, only listening to the furnace, the engine fueling the capitalist state, offers a tenuous hope of stopping imperialistic violence. Listening could alert us to our complicity in the violence, and it might help us empathize with the furnace's victims; listening could help establish social connections based on the desire to escape the furnace together—connection for the sake of disconnection. Spahr wants her poetry to facilitate that listening, stretching political voice beyond Hirschman's framework by giving voice to the furnace, articulating its noises and making them intelligible, as in *This Connection:* "We do not speak about the loading of M1 Abrams tanks, Apache helicopter gunships, and other equipment . . . We do not speak about the *Seay* loaded with Patriot antimissile batteries and wheeled vehicles . . . We do not speak about the *Constellation* in the Persian Gulf and the *Harry S. Truman* in the Mediterranean each with forty fighter jets on board, including F/A-18 Hornets and F-14 Tomcats . . ." (*This Connection* 43). These lists of military vehicles and weapons each follow the anaphoric announcement, "we do not speak about." Of course, Spahr *is* speaking about all of this military equipment, but she disclaims these words as her own. Indeed, the words do not sound like they belong in Spahr's mouth at all but rather, as Cohn points out, in a *Jane's Military Vehicles and Logistics* catalog.³⁹ Spahr is giving voice to all the wretched noises of the burning furnace so that we can hear its violence. She would rather escape all of this burning, but she cannot: "This burning, this dirty air we breathe together, our dependence on this air, our inability to stop breathing, our desire to just get out of this world and yet there we are taking the burning of the world into our lungs" (57). We are all connected through the violence of states; either through complicity or victimization, there is no escaping the burning states perpetrate. There is no exit, so Spahr resorts to voice.

This is why Spahr's poetry catalogs so extensively, so repeatedly, so insistently: she is articulating the weapons of the state. These weapons include not just the munitions, vehicles, and troops listed in the catalog, but also, in the hands of the state, the catalog itself. In this way, we should recognize a formal connection to what Michael Leong has termed "documental" poetics, which understands and grapples with how "documents, whether we like it or not, are constitutive of social reality."⁴⁰ Through the state, articulated skin and air connect people together whether they like or not. In both content and form, Spahr's catalogs speak the instruments of state power, documenting its documents, so that anyone listening might hear the "how" in "How we are here."

When Spahr resorts to voice, the goal is not to be more equitably included within the state, to be listed as an equal in the state's catalogs, but to escape such altogether. Voice ends up working not as an appeal to the state, as Hirschman describes, nor an exit itself, as Spahr at times wishes, but as a source of communal desire for exit—a way of bringing together a "we" that listens to the furnace. Nevertheless, that does not mean Spahr is satisfied with voice. As Leong notes, "while we are often controlled by our papers, they are not so easy to control."⁴¹ Though Leong nevertheless believes in poetry's capacity for "profound epistemological and affective work," Spahr, in contrast, is more consistently alert to the ways poetic documents lack the institutional power of state documents, and as a result she is much more skeptical of poetry's ability to intervene directly in history.⁴² She still sees her political poetry as susceptible to the inefficacies Hirschman identifies with voice: "Today, as this war [the Iraq War] begins, every word we say is caught—every word, whether it is ironic or not, whether it is articulate or not" (*This Connection* 72). Whatever we say, no matter how we say it, is caught, a prisoner to the state and its wars. And yet, "we speak"—of bombs and tanks and Humvees and missiles and ships and aircraft and more, all of which contributes to the violence that both prevents and behooves exit (73). The thing being voiced is that exit is necessary because voice is not good enough. But when the state is the enemy, voice is all anyone has.

"RUNNING IN PLACE": NOMADIC RESISTANCE IN MACKEY'S *SPLAY ANTHEM*

The indie rock band Modest Mouse has been exploring political themes of exit and voice since their 1996 debut album *This Is a Long Drive for Someone with Nothing to Think About*. "Exit Does Not Exist," for example, demands exit even in the face of its impossibility, with the staccato vocals of the opening chorus accentuating its contradictory imperative: "Does not exist / take an exit."[43] Displacing the grammatical subject of "exist," asserting it only in the title and retroactively in the subsequent line, the song suggests that "exit" is somehow discrepant with linguistic representation. Voice, indeed, seems to be the motivation for exit. This opening chorus overlays an unsettling sound of someone wheezing rhythmically into the microphone, a nonsemiotic vocal line that evokes someone struggling to breathe, with the opening lines of the verse crashing into a paranoid distrust of its own words: "I hear voices insinuating. / Feeds me lyrics to this song that I am saying."[44]

This indie rock iteration on the poetics of escape continues through other songs on *This Is a Long Drive*, notably bookending the album as a whole in the opening track "Dramamine" and the final track "Space Is Boring." It threads through Modest Mouse's later albums too, as with "Tiny Cities Made of Ashes" off *The Moon and Antarctica* (2000) and its frantic, shouted refrain, "does anybody know a way that a body could get away."[45] It culminates, though—both in its political focus and in its mainstream success—in the band's 2004 album *Good News for People Who Love Bad News*. The lead single "Float On," nominated for a Grammy Award for Best Rock Song, opens with a political fantasy of dissociating from the reality of police and the state: "I backed my car into a cop car the other day. / Well, he just drove off, sometimes life's OK." The chorus refrain indulges and reinforces this escapist optimism, insisting, "don't worry, we'll all float on. / Even if things get heavy, we'll all float on."[46]

"Float On," however, is actually an upbeat, radio-friendly reimagining of "The World at Large," the track immediately and seamlessly preceding it on the album, with the two songs sharing a chord progression as well as lyrical themes and language. This more somber rendition in "The World at Large" subverts the easy escapism of the hit single, positing departure as an appropriate yet insufficient response to climate crisis and political uncertainty:

> Ice-age, heat wave, can't complain.
> If the world's at large, why should I remain?
> Walked away to another plan.
> Gonna find another place, maybe one I can stand.[47]

Though music theorist Kenneth Smith reads these lines as a resignation to life's trials, an "acceptance of fate," the narrator's "can't complain," through its sinister pun, actually suggests a much more oppositional stance for this departure, one that hinges on the question of representation.[48] Rather than conceding any right to complain, the lyrics actually suggest an inability to complain, a failure of representation that results in the need for escape, the need to find another, better place. Though the song optimistically suggests that "you still got your words and you got your friends," finding hope in "songs about drifters, books about the same," it concludes with the speaker's inability to articulate his response to the world at large, a world that seems itself to have escaped our political comprehension:

> But my thoughts were so loud I couldn't hear my mouth.
> My thoughts were so loud, I couldn't hear my mouth.
> My thoughts were so loud.[49]

Bandleader and lyricist Isaac Brock's mouth is conspicuously not heard after that final refrain, as the song continues with an instrumental that lasts another minute and a half (a third of its total length). Except, that is, for another vocal refrain, one notably not printed with the rest of the lyrics in the album booklet, consisting of the nonsemiotic utterance "uh" (articulating, if anything, only a blanket refusal or negation) repeating in a pattern of six eighth notes followed by a drawn-out quarter note to fill the measure. This refrain first appears early in the song as a background vocal, echoing Brock's lead vocal line that introduces it (and which the booklet does include): "Well uh-uh baby I ain't got no plan. / We'll float on maybe would you understand?"[50] Here, floating on to an alternative to the world and its plans that govern us remains the political impetus, but its eventual success seems questionable at best, foreshadowing the song's turn to inarticulacy. "Uh-uh-uh-uh-uh-uh uh" suggests an escape from voice that nevertheless gets expressed vocally.

Nathaniel Mackey's poems similarly dwell on such vocalized inarticulacy, twisting voice into an expression of its own inadequacy that implies the need for an escape that, at present, is not realistic. I thus intend this brief digression into indie rock to again indicate the wider significance of the poetics of escape in popular American culture but also to help illustrate a core aspect of Mackey's poetics. Where Spahr's poems catalog, articulating the state's weapons and atrocities, Nathaniel Mackey's poems cry, lamenting the state's dismissal of inarticulacy—complaining that complaints against the state must be voiced, articulated, to count. Like Spahr, Mackey fantasizes a poetry capable of enacting escape, and voice-as-exit, state-mandated identity politics, and truncated open form are similarly present. But instead of articulating the state's use of articulation, Mackey tries to voice the inarticulacy of the cry, a refutation of state systems of representation, articulating the inadequacy of articulation alone. Mackey's poetry critiques the political usefulness of what Hirschman describes as voice, while nevertheless turning to such voice as its only recourse.

Though critics rarely discuss Spahr and Mackey together, these two poets share a number of fundamental poetic and political convictions that make pairing them fruitful. Readers familiar with Mackey's poetry, for instance, will recognize his ongoing commitment to the open form poetics of the Olson–Black Mountain tradition, which for Mackey means prescribing perpetual movement and proscribing "systematization, fixity, and closure."[51] Mackey's 2006 *Splay Anthem* continues *"mu"* and *Song of the Andoumboulou,* Mackey's two long serial poems, manifesting a postmodernist seriality that Joseph Conte has generalized as "an open structure that welcomes possibility, choice, and chance."[52] *Splay Anthem* pushes this serial openness even further as it allows the barriers between the two serial poems to break down so that, as Mackey puts it in his crucial preface (which itself opens poetic content beyond text into paratext), "each is the other, each is both, announcedly so," *"mu"* becoming part of *Song of the Andoumboulou* and vice versa.[53] *Splay Anthem*'s seriality is not just open-ended but laterally open between serials. As we will see, Mackey's formal resistance to closure in favor of openness is a way of privileging inarticulacy over articulations; for him, open form approximates, in language, inarticulacy.

Splay Anthem repeats this structural openness through both wordplay and narrative theme. A profusion of anagrams, homophones, and graphic associations proliferate meanings as Mackey's serial poems, like one of Modest Mouse's "songs about drifters / books about the same," follow runaways, fugitives, and nomads on a spiraling or circular journey. Unlike traditional travel narratives, the movement in *Splay Anthem* proves perpetual, unable to reach any destination. The travelers are "cut short / of / arrival, named, it said, / no / such arrival" (19). Even when they unexpectedly find that "it was Arrival / we were in, suddenly so with a capital A," the "Arrival" turns out not to be the fulfillment of travel but just another stop along the way (31). A few stanzas later, the travelers are already moving on again, nomadic. The places themselves never seem to matter except as stationary contrasts to bring the travelers' movement into relief. This unending journeying narratively manifests the formal values of open verse, what Olson described as its "kinetics," its privileging of change and process over finality.[54] Mackey's preference for the dynamism of openness over the systemization of closure manifests thematically as well as formally.

Mackey's thematic preoccupation with "fugitivity," as he calls it, is one of the numerous ways he imparts political valences to his open form poetics. He sees his fugitives as "trying to outrun in some way the repercussions of certain ordeals and violences and violations."[55] "Fugitivity" of course suggests not only movement but also opposition to the legal order, and nomadism more generally has historically functioned as a strategy of resistance to the political state. Mackey himself cites the importance of "the various anthropological and political facts of life symptomized by migration and displacement," and his poetry indeed evokes a strategic, politically antagonistic nomadism.[56] As the anthropologist James C. Scott puts it, "nomads and pastoralists (such as Berbers and Bedouins), hunter-gatherers, Gypsies, vagrants, homeless people, itinerants, runaway slaves, and serfs have always been a thorn in the side of states."[57]

For Scott, the most important takeaway of this simple observation is how such nomadic people groups, desiring a life outside the bounds of the state, actively resisted state "efforts to permanently settle"[58] them: "All those who had reason to flee state power—to escape taxes, conscription, disease, poverty, or prison, or to trade or raid—were, in a sense, tribalizing themselves. Ethnicity, once again, began where sovereignty and taxes ended. The ethnic zone was feared and stigmatized by officials precisely because it was beyond sovereignty and therefore a magnet for those who, for whatever reason, wanted to elude the state."[59] Rather than treating nomadism as evidence of an underdeveloped culture, Scott identifies people groups across geography and history who maintained nomadic lifestyles primarily as a strategy for resisting incorporation into the state. In this view, nomadism can be a politics—an anti-state politics. That is what is at stake in Mackey's notion of "fugitivity" as it manifests in his poetry both formally through openness and thematically through travel narrative.

Of course, the "anthropological and political facts" Mackey refers to must also include the violent, involuntary sources of the African diaspora. The Middle Passage certainly haunts his poetry, as for instance when some of *Splay Anthem*'s perpetual travelers seem to be trapped "in a ship's hold helpless," human cargo (113). But Mackey does not confine the impetus for his fugitives' flight to that past; a few lines later, we find out it is "ship of state they'd / call / it" (113). Mackey shrinks the perceived distance between chattel and political slavery, and the historical ship of the slave trade sits like a palimpsest beneath the present ship of state.

As with Spahr, the state is not the only thing that bothers Mackey, but it nevertheless figures prominently as a source of oppression and dissatisfaction throughout his work. The image of the ship as ship of state is indeed uncharacteristically explicit in a body of work so prone to slippage and ambiguity. Language as Mackey understands it is volatile, as his travelers learn: "it was a name we stuck / pins in hoping we'd stay. Stray / was all we ended up with" (66). It would be a mistake to try to pin fixed allegorical meanings to Mackey's seafaring imagery. Yet, early in *Splay Anthem*, Mackey nevertheless suggests a provisional key for interpreting his maritime language: "'Ship of state' she heard, all / but inaudible, exegetic / wind ruffling a dog-eared / book . . ." (9). The phrase "ship of state" here conveys interpretive power, an "exegetic wind" that moves the pages of a book, possibly *Splay Anthem* itself if we are reading it carefully, dog-earing its pages. The state indeed looms ominously here. On the same page we get the lines "'ship of / state' vested every tongue," with the verb *vested* suggesting that the state both contains language, like clothing over tongues, and transforms language into force, endowing tongues with power.

However, it is not just big, powerful ships that interest Mackey but also boats, the vessels you use to get off ships. He frequently links boats to both beds and books, the places to dream journeys of escape: "The bed was their boat, he / reminded her, roused out of / sleep, / awake to not having arrived, / unrisen, 'book' meant get / away, / run . . ." (9). Throughout Mackey's work, dreams are a site of imagining and expressing desire for alternatives, providing contrast to our reality. Dreams and beds, boats and books would be a way to escape the reality of the ship, of the state.

In Mackey's poetry, openness, as both narrative subject and formal value, frequently stands in for resistance to hierarchical power structures, especially the political state. This is in part because Mackey understands linguistic and political structures as synecdochally linked. Language both resembles and partially constitutes politics: "What is language, after all, if not a social pact (an ideology), the basis, in fact, of all other social pacts?"[60] The state is one such pact, not just through the notion of a social contract but through the state's very constitution in language, from its founding documents to its ongoing operation in laws, decrees, and decisions—asserted in *Splay Anthem* by the fact that the "ship of state" is always something spoken, in explicit or implied quotation marks. For Mackey, part of the significance of the linguistic foundation of social structures is that poetry contributes, however minutely, to the external structures of culture and politics that contain it, while simultaneously internally modeling actual or potential cultural and political structures.[61] Thus, Mackey sees open form as "liberating," but closed form as "an attempt to imprison."[62] His values here are unambiguous: art and politics alike should be pushed to the fullest extent possible towards openness and radical free association, rejecting all hierarchical authority.

Splay Anthem's fugitives keep on the move in order to resist stagnation and thus vulnerability to political force: "A / political trek we'd have said it was / albeit politics kept us at bay" (125). The trek's politics of exit is not the politics of voting and representation, the staples of Hirschman's voice; politics in the latter sense is what forces their journey. When "the vote came in early," a clear allusion to the controversy surrounding the 2000 US presidential election (which Mackey also notes in his preface), the travelers "ignored / it. No ballot-box auction for us ..." (120). No matter who wins, they are not willing to sell themselves to the ballot box, the representational structures of state power. It doesn't matter, though, because they can't ignore the ballot box for long—not because voting offers them a way forward, but because it hauntingly ensnares them: "the ballot-box opening grinned / and grinned again, gone we'd have been / could / we have run ..." (124). Mackey's fugitives respond to politics with a halted political running away.

Tellingly, the travelers desire an outward trajectory, away from the center and towards the margins:

> what we wanted
>   was to
> endlessly verge on exit, angling
> out, tangent to circle's edge, on
> our way where we'd be the last to
> say ... Let all edges converge, it
>   seemed
> we said, cut away would-be end (70)

Even the desire to exit, fleeing the authority of the center, must remain an open process, precluding "would-be end." Like open form, the politics of exit remains forever on the move. Yet, eventually the "edges converge," and despite the travelers' wish to be "angling / out, tangent to circle's edge," they nevertheless find that "it wasn't / wander what we did, we circled" (70), lines that themselves circle back to lines from two pages previous: "It wasn't wandering what / we did, we circled, an earthbound orbit / wanting / out" (68). As with Spahr, Earth and its gravity provide Mackey a convenient model for thinking about political exit. Even as it reproduces the state's own discourses of naturalizing political power—political law as inevitable as the law of gravity—such imagery also suggests a limit to the state, imagining space beyond the state's influence.

Mackey's travelers can never achieve escape velocity, though, and end up orbiting the center that always holds them in. The fugitives' flight is "an arrested / run," one that is always already contained by the power it flees (18). The poem both formally and narratively reiterates these explicit declarations of arrested openness, as the outward thrust of both open form and the travelers' political flight are limited by the draw of the center, until tangent force collapses into "centrifugal" force, tamed by the countervailing centripetal (77). Indeed, direct resistance to that centralizing pull proves futile and even dangerous in *Splay Anthem:* "A curve taken too fast / took us out ... Tossed out of the car [...] The curve that had taken us out stayed / with us" (77). Instead of getting out, they are taken out—violently cast out to an outside that nevertheless contains them.

Mackey often uses an upward-spiraling helix to figure the route to spiritual, social, or political ideals, and we get the sense that if the circle could be widened just a little bit with each permutation, we might get an outward-moving spiral—as in Olson's "I have been an ability," or the cover image of Mackey's *Whatsaid Serif* (1998) (the serial installment preceding *Splay Anthem*)—a dialectical shape that really might lead outward into exit.[63] But attempts to break out of the orbit, to cut ties to the center, are defeated. The fugitives "circumambulate," and the widening curves of the spiral compress back into a circle (80). Their nomadism thus strays back towards the legibility and predictability of sedentariness as it reinscribes a fixity of place through habitual mobility: "circling wind we / considered moot, a way we had of / running in place" (86). Though Mackey seems to wish that poetry could create a way out of the circle, an escape from politics' articulations, he does not fancy that poetry achieves that kind of openness.

Dimitri Anastasopoulos also addresses Mackey's notion of "running in place," although he considers an earlier iteration of the phrase, from

Mackey's *Djbot Baghostus's Run* (1993), the second volume of his ongoing epistolary novel *From a Broken Bottle Traces of Perfume Still Emanate*. Much as I have been suggesting for *Splay Anthem*, Anastasopoulos sees *Dbjot Baghostus's Run* advancing "the possibility of poetic language as a site of political resistance... What sanctions and constitutes this law is language. Only from within language can [protagonist] Jarred Bottle address the law's prohibitions and rules of propriety."[64] However, as we have seen, gestures toward openness and rebellion are inevitably met with counterforces of closure and centralization: "Any act that challenges the unwritten exterior of the Law ... is codified instantly (as proper or improper) ... the Law inscribes them inside itself."[65] Anastasopoulos argues that successful resistance to oppressive law requires that the novel's protagonists "press and penetrate into the extreme of language, or else risk 'running in place.'"[66] For Anastasopoulos, "running in place" amounts to political impotency, and the outward thrust of open form must be ever intensified if such stagnation is to be avoided. In *Bedouin Hornbook* (1986), the first volume of *From a Broken Bottle*, Mackey makes this worry explicit: "Unless revolution, as well as taking an upward turn, makes for a lateral displacement (a stepping aside from whatever one thought 'upward' and 'downward' meant), the road ahead doesn't seem to hold much in store beyond running in place," and one risks getting "stuck in the same old rut."[67] If the spiraling helix flattens back into a circle, revolutionary hope seems thwarted. Yet, as we have seen, the "circling" of "running in place" seems unavoidable in *Splay Anthem*. Pressing and penetrating "into the extreme of language" does not circumvent "running in place," as Anastasopoulos suggests, but, rather, induces it. Resisting the curves of the road only causes a crash while doing nothing to get rid of the curve itself. Unable to sustain the outward trajectory of open verse, Mackey's liminal poetics curves back into circular closure.

Indeed, despite the obvious importance of open form to his poetics, Mackey also pairs openness with closure. Neither is ever absolute or immune to the other's competing impulses; Mackey acknowledges "closed as well as open inclinations," explaining, "I say inclinations as I'm not certain that openness can be other than a tendency."[68] As Robert Zamsky puts it, Mackey "troubl[es] openness with repetition, return, and resonance."[69] Circles and repetition temper *Splay Anthem*'s bids for formal openness: for

Mackey, the seriality he relies on not only moves forwards and backwards but is also "repeatedly circling or cycling back" (xi). Even the homonymic multiplicity of a word such as "rung" (which indeterminately oscillates across *Splay Anthem* between a step on a ladder and a musical sound) results in a closed circularity: "ringing is sonic resurfacing [. . .] It invites echo, reverberation, overtone, undertone, resonance and repetition. In seriality, rasp is recursive form, a net of echoes; it catches [. . .] rung is both noun and verb, in which climb, we're reminded, rhymes with chime" (xii). *Rung* echoes, repeats, and circles back on itself, not so much exploding the sign into infinite possibility as joining and relating multiple meanings under a single signifier. Circular repetition paradoxically transforms the perpetual movement of openness and indeterminacy into a sort of closure, simultaneously enacting both the unending and the complete through the figure of the circle. That the echoing of *rung* also catches, like a net, trapping and confining, accords with the explicit political implications Mackey attributes to this tension between open and closed form. Poetry is never free from closure, just as no one is free from the state, least of all rebels or outlaws such as the fugitives populating *Splay Anthem*.

However, this tension between openness and closure does not mean Mackey's project of marginalized resistance passively acquiesces to the authoritative center. Indeed, Mackey's poetry always clings to the hope that the state's inescapability is a historical rather than metaphysical condition of politics—it is impossible to exit the state today, but perhaps that will not always be true. *Splay Anthem* imagines political resistance through the paradoxically sedentary motion of "running in place." Like that of the biblical Israelites marching around Jericho (an image that Mackey turns to in *Bass Cathedral* [2008] and *Blue Fasa* [2015]), *Splay Anthem* proposes a nomadism that, despite going nowhere, nevertheless sounds trumpets and hopes to topple walls. As we will see, his circular journey inscribes a central emptiness—a silent hollow that resonates the inarticulate cry of the oppressed. It is "an arrested run," yes, but "an arrested / run we made look like / dancing," a run transformed into creative power (18). Exit is not an option, but stubbornly trying to exit might still do some good anyway. Arrested running articulates a circle, etched in the ground as a rut; this circle, a representation of perpetually failing to escape, becomes a way of articulating, like circling in red ink, the existence of inarticulacies contained within it—the desires, pains, relationships, knowledges, and experiences that might counter political articulation, in part because they cannot be reduced to and thus cannot be co-opted within the state's representational schemes.

Not giving up on exit implies a shortcoming in more familiar calls for political inclusivity—greater voice, in Hirschman's sense, won't be enough. This runs counter to the politics of inclusion we find, for example, at the end of Richard Wright's *Native Son* (1940), where the primary political goal is to rectify the exclusion of Black people from the White world of power and privilege, making Bigger Thomas "included in that picture of Creation."[70] The way Mackey relates open form poetics and political escape should help us recognize and understand how he moves beyond such a politics of inclusion or recognition. Critics such as Norman Finkelstein and Anthony Reed have made important moves in that direction by distancing Mackey's politico-poetics from older models of identity politics. Finkelstein, especially, is forthright: "Mackey's poetry serves as an explicit rebuke to any form of identity politics; his imagination knows no borders."[71] Yet, for Finkelstein and Reed alike, Mackey's politics is still a politics of inclusion, just one that is more universal than previous fights against identity-based exclusion could produce: Mackey's poetry is "broadly and embracingly democratic"[72] and it manifests "a utopian desire for a collectivity that would exclude no one."[73] In interviews, however, Mackey seems more interested in partial and provisional collectivities rather than an all-inclusive one. He imagines the "we" that populates *Splay Anthem* as an "invitation," an offer to join a social collectivity, but, significantly, an offer that can be refused.[74] It is a nontotalizing "we," and he emphasizes that his "recourse to 'we' has not done away with the other pronouns. 'I,' 'he,' 'she,' and 'they' still abound."[75] The poem's "we" is "some renegade group whose relationship to established collectivities is a fugitive one. This lost tribe is in flight from such established groups and seemingly in search of some alternative way of bonding," which necessarily rejects "conventional, bonded ways of public belonging."[76] The ability to dissolve old bonds is the necessary precondition for new forms of sociality.

This is the political hope Mackey associates with open form poetics. He situates that "alternate form of bonding and belonging" as the result of an "oblique, outward-bound impulse."[77] Creating new communal relationships and escaping the all-encompassing relationship of the state are two sides of the same coin. Thus, in *Splay Anthem,* Mackey writes of "the boat of which / they dreamt / a dreamt we beyond our / reach" (12). The dreamed-of boat, the way off the ship, equates through apposition to an imagined social collectivity, a "we" that does not yet exist. New ways of bonding require escaping bondage, the imprisoning boundary inscribed by closure's circle that Mackey would have open form pierce if it could. Yet, as we have seen, Mackey hesitates to commit fully to open form, partly because he thinks it is, like political escape, impossible. Both the boat and the "dreamt we," the escape route and the new social collectivity, are "beyond our / reach." As he puts it, "even the dissociative assault on language is finally a testimony to its importance and power—is, quite simply, a *linguistic* assault on language."[78] Open form's challenge to the fixity of closure must remain within language. After all, Mackey sees language as the foundation of all "social pacts"—there can be no hope for the "dreamt we" outside of language. Mackey's boat is like a book, and his ideal sociality is a linguistic one; rejecting language and meaning cannot suffice. As long as we remain in language—and we must, to hold on to the dream of a new "we," that which, from the perspective of the center, becomes a collectivity defined by departure, "we the escaping / they" (23)—absolute openness is impossible.

In this, Mackey is working counter to much of the earlier tradition, from Olson and Black Mountain to language poetry, that nevertheless still inflects so much of his work. If Olson's departure from coherent signification at the end of "I have been an ability" that I note in chapter 1 is an anomaly in his own work, it nevertheless becomes commonplace amongst writers associated with open form. For example, John Cage, who crossed paths with Olson at Black Mountain College in the early 1950s, offers a useful contrast to Mackey since he makes the same political value judgments on open and closed form. In the preface to his collection of mesostic poems *Anarchy* (1988), Cage intermixes a straightforwardly anarchist political manifesto, featuring proclamations like "politicians are of no good use . . . We don't need government," with a statement of poetics asserting that his "mesostic texts do not make ordinary sense. They make nonsense."[79] Cage understands his procedurally generated poetry as opening up radical indeterminacy free from the semiotic closure imposed by authorial intention or linguistic conventions, an indeterminacy that corresponds directly to total freedom from political authority.[80] Cage clearly thinks of the relationship between author and artwork as analogous to that between political authority and society. On the one hand, he declares that society should not be "a process a king sets in motion" but "an impersonal place understood and made useful so that no matter what each individual does his actions enliven the total picture."[81] On the other, he declares that in making art "we are not arranging things in order... we are merely facilitating processes so that anything can happen."[82] For Cage, we may not have yet escaped the state, but art can show us the way by escaping authorial authority and, by extension, linguistic determinacy and closure.

From the perspective of the poetics of escape, Cage's strategy is inadequate. It throws out the social baby with the political bathwater: in the zeal to do away with the controlling power of representation, it also cuts off the possibility of producing human connection through language. Cage deals with this problem by suggesting that perhaps his poems are not language at all: "If nonsense is found intolerable, think of my work as music... We are doing everything we can to make new connections."[83] Music can still signify—in the conventions of Western music, for example, a minor key might signify sadness—but Cage is specifically appealing to music's capacity for a nonsignifying aesthetics, one for which "nonsense" makes no sense as a critique. Thus, the connection Cage's poetics can establish is a nonlinguistic one, which is to say a nonideological one. Cage, then, effectively takes us back into the logic of a simplistic identity politics, in which the basis of connection is who or where one is rather than belief or desire. While Mackey has no problem accepting such forms of connection, he makes clear that identity is also not enough. By abandoning those linguistic forms of sociality, Cage's retreat into text-as-music approaches the same sort of escapism we have seen Spahr reject. Commenting directly on his notion of "fugitivity," Mackey insists that "it's not just that you're running away, but that your running transforms the loss."[84] Language may be the basis of detrimental "social pacts" like the state, but it is also the basis of many other forms of sociality that are worth holding onto. Access to voice, inclusion in systems of political representation, is inadequate, but if there is to be any hope of exit, voice, as complaint and commiseration, must remain an active part of political poetry.

Thus, Mackey explains that alongside his inclination towards openness and indeterminacy (which, like Cage, Mackey often associates with music), Mackey also sustains a firmly semiotic component in his poetry. He tries "to become aware of unconscious, unintended, and auxiliary meanings, implications and resonances that happen into the writing," but he also tries "to be as conscious as [he] can be in writing": "Writing is a mix of saying what I mean to say and finding out what else the writing might say."[85] Mackey tries to acknowledge the inevitable presence of the unintentional in his poetry—everything that a purely discursive view of language would consider noise, cluttering the signal and obscuring the message, but which Mackey sees as generating surprising beauty and unpredictable thoughts. But what is most important here is that he also consciously says things that he means. Where Cage's poetry is having nothing to say and saying it, Mackey's is having something to say and then some.

Here, with Mackey's desire to say more than he has to say, we begin to find a potential answer to the enigmatic problem of how circular "running in place" might be thought of as politically meaningful. Mackey links these two paradoxes (mobile stagnation and saying more than you say) as a way of acknowledging—and attempting to solve—the political paradox of exit. Like Spahr, Mackey is voicing the need for exit, a position, like open form, that inherently admits its own inadequacy as voice (were voice or articulation sufficient, exit or openness would be unnecessary). Running in place becomes a roundabout way of voicing the need for exit that, by its very roundabout nature, refuses to be appeased by the concessions of voice. Put simply, it is an attempt to use voice without undermining the claim that voice is not enough; just as open form must attack closure while nevertheless remaining in some measure closed, Mackey's poetry must demonstrate voice's inadequacy even as it uses voice to whatever extent that it can.

The crucial role of jazz in Mackey's poetics becomes especially pertinent here. In "the black musician's stutter" and "telling 'inarticulacy,'" he finds a "critique of a predatory coherence, a cannibalistic 'plan of living,' and the articulacy that upholds it."[86] Even though a stutter does not articulate anything, the performance of a stutter, what is really a representation of inarticulacy, *can* articulate—most immediately, simply articulating the existence of inarticulacy, but also partially articulating some underlying human desire, emotion, or knowledge giving rise to the inarticulacy. Thus, "the way Thelonious Monk makes hesitation eloquent or the way a scat singer makes inarticulacy speak" each register "a need for a new world and a new language to go along with it, discontent with the world and the ways of speaking we already have."[87] Spoken inarticulacy offers a corollary to open form's inadequate political resistance. Speaking inarticulacy causes voice to manifest the fact of what it cannot fully serve, tacit knowledge and embodied experience. It articulates the claim that inarticulacy evinces an important domain of human life that is wrongly erased when, through "predatory" violence, articulacy is all that counts.

For Mackey, running in place works similarly to such spoken inarticulacy. *Splay Anthem*'s fugitives declare, "verge that we wanted / verge was the song we sang had there been a / song we sang. No song left our lips" (70). The impetuses for song and movement converge into one, uniting the unsung song with the "running in place" of circular motion. As Mackey reiterates the circularity of movement through repetition of the phrases "verge that we wanted" and "no song left our lips" over two stanzas, circular travel becomes tantamount to articulating silence: "nonsonant, we rounded circle's edge, / nonsonant ring shout [. . .] No song / left our lips. It wasn't sing that we did, / we / circled" (70). Not singing is circling. Just as "running in place" makes stagnation move, "nonsonance" and "not singing" function as paradoxical expressions of silence. Rather than leaving circularity as a stagnant submission to the demands of the center, Mackey refigures circularity as a means of uttering the unutterable and as a site of political resistance. Both are a way of saying that saying is not enough, without letting saying so pull the rug out from under itself: "unsay said it / best" (112).

Even the title of *"mu"* (one half of the doubled serial poem that constitutes and extends beyond *Splay Anthem*) embodies the paradoxical conjoining of inarticulacy and articulation through its only anagram (one of Mackey's favorite devices), "um." The uttered inarticulacy of "um" is a specific instance of the book's more general means of surviving the perpetual "shipwreck" (21) of state that never really sinks (and here one can't help but think of Benjamin's and then Agamben's permanent state of emergency or exception): "The sunken ships they at times / took it they were on no sooner / sank / than sailed again" (23). The fugitives survive the permanent shipwreck of state, but doing so requires a circumscribed emptiness, like "um" or an inflatable flotation device: "To the bone meant / birdlike, hollow. Emptiness / kept us / afloat [. . .] Buoyed / by lack, we floated boatlike, / birdlike, bones emptied out / inside" (21). Tellingly, "to the bone" also

<pre>
                          meant
                                 to the
        limit, at a loss even so,   eyes,
            ears, nostrils, mouths   holes in
        our heads a stray breeze made flutes
                              of (22)
</pre>

The semiotic hollow of inarticulacy inscribed by the circular journey provides something like, if not exactly, a boat, a means of staying afloat in the permanent shipwreck of state and of remaining at the limit, the liminal space where both the impossibility and the necessity of exit are most apparent. Thus, when the poem mentions the resonating hollows that enable flute music, the white space that graphically suggests such a hollow also facilitates a more sinister secondary reading: the phrase "holes in / our heads," isolated from the facial orifices it points back to, also hints at a latent violence, holes made by weapons. Structural violence is both the cause and subject of Mackey's sung silences and productive lacks, which he uses to refigure aural and spatial emptiness into the tools of political critique, laments over the inadequacy of political speech that foster comradery among mourners.

Mackey's poetry repeatedly finds itself falling back into orbit around the gravity well of power. However, the circle inscribed by that orbital motion simultaneously demarcates the limits of official power and creates a space of silence that resonates the outsider's cry. *Splay Anthem*'s cry is often one of mourning or frustration: "The long odds against" poetry curing society's ills "are enough to induce an exasperated scat or an incipient stutter or lapse into baby talk" (xv), not unlike Modest Mouse's "uh-uh" refrain. But those long odds only strengthen the resolve for exit, and Mackey's poetry strives to be "something undaunted" that "wants to move no matter how inauspicious the prospects, advance no matter how pained or ungainly" (xvi). There is little hope for escape, nor any more that demanding the freedom to exit will make much difference. Mackey's poetry is a demand for exit that recognizes and reiterates these facts in order to make that demand all the more pressing, more meaningful as a germ of the "dreamt we" that would enable escape.

Much as Yamashita and Díaz displace revolutionary hope to a space after novel's end, Spahr and Mackey each suggest that, while we do not yet have a poetry capable of fully imagining, much less enacting, the specific means of escape from the state, perhaps we can begin imagining a poetry that can imagine leaving the state behind. "We are for sure not there, yet," writes Spahr, "but one can always hope."[88] The contemporary poetics of escape imagines a reconfigured relation between representation and power, yearning to escape the state and its representational systems without giving up on representation altogether. It demands new ways of speaking, coherence freed from predation and communal bonding without bonds, it asks us to listen for what cannot be represented or articulated, but it also never dispenses with speaking or telling. Speaking remains essential, because it keeps potential escape social and communal rather than solipsistic. Janis P. Stout observes that escape narratives in American literature are typically centered around the figure of the "loner, forever turning his back on society," but the poetics of escape seeks exit only from the state and its systems of violence that structure society—not from society itself.[89]

In this way, the poetics of escape also importantly differs from Hirschman and the liberal tradition that has been responsible for almost all the academic thought on exit as a political freedom and mechanism. For Hirschman, loyalty discourages exit from a variety of organizations, and we can recognize how that extends into the state through discourses of patriotism and nationalism. Such nationalist loyalty may even appear relatively benign, as with the "weak" nationalisms that Douglas Dowland contrasts with the more affectively aggressive "strong" nationalisms we're likely to associate with US militarism—especially in a post-9/11 context—that Spahr catalogs in her poetry.[90] And while poetry can obviously participate in both strong and weak nationalisms, it can also reject them, as Spahr's and Mackey's poetries both demonstrate, constituting "a literature written in resistance to this national tradition. This literature deliberately avoids the standardized language of the state."⁹¹ As Hirshman puts it, the "barrier to exit constituted by loyalty is of finite height."⁹² In the poetics of escape, loyalty isn't what stops exit.

Yet Hirschman's framework pays little attention to this difficulty, in part because his normative perspective never considers what lies beyond loyalty to the state or nation. In trying to find "the elusive optimal mix of exit and voice," Hirschman necessarily assumes that the goal is to improve the institution in question and save it from dissolution—a meaningless premise when the aim is to abolish the state.⁹³ While he recognizes the political forces that prevent exit from the state, his analysis stops well short of such conflict, focusing instead on the ways loyalty prevents the situation from ever getting that far. As a result, he ends up lumping the state in as just one more group evincing strong loyalty, noting how "exit is ordinarily unthinkable, though not always wholly impossible, from such primordial human groupings as family, tribe, church, and state."⁹⁴ Regardless of whether exit is politically possible, it is ideologically undesirable, "peculiarly unthinkable."⁹⁵

These poetries, in contrast, give us the inverse, thinking about exit from the state while confronting and foregrounding its impossibility. In that regard, they differentiate exit from the state, in a way that Hirschman does not, as uniquely unattainable. People sometimes leave their families or faiths, but no one leaves the state. Spahr wants to escape the doomed connections of the global imperialist state, but she wants to hold on to the lovely connections of sociality; Mackey aspires to a poetry that is "not only lamenting violated connection but aiming to reestablish connection" (xvi). In this light, open form is no longer open with an "o," the semiotic zero of Olson's "I have been an ability" or the extremes of language poetry, a hole in the page, but open with an "ahh," like the girl with diphtheria, Dr. Williams forcing his tongue depressor into gaping mouth—evidence of and emanation from the body that authority penetrates, knows, diagnoses, and represents. Neither silence nor speaking, nonsense nor articulation, is enough. For the poetics of escape typified by Spahr and Mackey, writing in the aftermath of language poetry's revolt against meaning, voice makes exit social rather than escapist.

CONCLUSION

NOT EVEN THROUGH THE GIFT SHOP

GRAFFITI DOES NOT change anything. As voice, it is merely co-opted and contained within the system, impotent. As vandalism, it is merely the criminal outside against which the law constitutes and justifies itself. At its best, graffiti might help foster a counterpublic of escape, bringing together people who want to break off[1]—a project that, as Spahr and Mackey remind us, is slow and difficult, with no guarantee of eventual success.

Banksy's 2010 film *Exit through the Gift Shop* considers a different way out. The film purportedly began as a documentary about Banksy, but Banksy characteristically turns the camera around, back on his biographer, Thierry Guetta, an obsessive videographer who wields handheld camcorders to record everything, all the time. Guetta is a French expat immersed in Los Angeles's culture of conspicuous consumption. Before turning to the art world, he sold "vintage" clothes to L.A. hipsters. "I used to take things that, when the sewing was different, I call it 'designer,' and I put the price there for $400," Guetta explains.[2] Guetta exports this business philosophy to his new career as an edgy artist, "Mr. Brainwash," repackaging well-worn pop art tropes as the latest and hottest new thing. By the end of the film, we witness his well-staffed warehouse (apparently dipping into the Hollywood props labor force) churning out pieces ("sub-Warholian dreck," says the *New Yorker*'s film critic Anthony Lane)[3] to sell at his 15,000 square foot debut show. As the film's voice-over narration puts it, the "ultimate validation" for Guetta's overnight fame "was measured in dollars and cents. By the end of his opening week, Thierry would sell nearly a million dollars' worth of art."

It's tempting to hold Guetta up as a foil to Banksy, as representing the dumb commodification of art that Banksy so insistently critiques.[4] But treating Guetta as foil means forgetting that Banksy's critique is also self-critical. Lane pronounces that the film's critique of Guetta's salesmanship "also applies to Banksy himself," as though this is some kind of gotcha: "to have your print of Kate Moss sold by a London auction house for ninety-six thousand pounds of real money, whatever you choose to do with it, means that you have been press-ganged from the street where you roamed free." But, of course, Banksy knows this, knows that he is behind bars trying to draw his way out, and in fact makes the critique all the more poignant by recognizing that even on the "streets" he did not "roam free," as if the streets ever constituted some idyllic wilderness, outside of state capitalism. Compared to Guetta, Banksy is more self-conscious about his work's commodification, more self-critical—like when he booby-trapped one of his paintings at auction to self-destruct (via a paper shredder hidden in the frame) after it sold for $1.4 million.[5] In that way Banksy is more interesting than Guetta. But the self-critical commodity is still a commodity (the buyer kept the half-shredded work, of course, and three years later, it auctioned for $25.3 million),[6] and Banksy doesn't shy away from that. In an email interview about the film with the *New York Times,* Banksy explains, "it seemed fitting that a film questioning the art world was paid for with proceeds directly from the art world. Maybe it should have been called 'Don't Bite the Hand that Feeds You.'"[7]

It's not called that, though, and the hand keeps feeding—perhaps because the kind of biting this film does, like graffiti and like voting, doesn't change anything. The title the film does have hints at another way of changing things, a way out. Graffiti, art, crime, or critique may not change anything, but what if money can? If state capitalism is the gallery that sponsors and displays Banksy's works alongside Mr. Brainwash's, can we exit through the gift shop? Could we buy our way out of the state? Despite the millions of dollars in sales, Banksy, in satirizing his own participation in the art market, also satirizes such a possibility of buying a way out. Impressive auction house numbers don't let Banksy "roam free," and there is no exit, not even through the gift shop.

In the mainstream US political right, however, this is the shape that a politics of exit most commonly takes. Most notoriously in fiction, Ayn Rand's *Atlas Shrugged* imagines a heroic entrepreneurial escape into "Galt's Gulch," an enclave of hypercapitalism enabled, motivated, and sustained by the profit motive above all else. This aspect of Rand's fiction and philosophy is sometimes an inspiration in real-world manifestations of right-wing exit, as in, most bluntly, "Galt's Gulch Chile," a proposed free-market haven in Chile that fizzled out amidst a drama of corruption and financial scamming.[8]

The technocratic fantasies of Silicon Valley billionaires have likewise imagined spending into existence a political escape. Most notably and directly, PayPal co-founder Peter Thiel has promoted and funded such escape initiatives. In 2009, before his turn to Trumpism and a corresponding shift away from these strategies of escape, Thiel wrote an opinion piece for the libertarian think tank the Cato Institute, suggesting that "in our time, the great task for libertarians is to find an escape from politics in all its forms." Like the literary poetics of escape, Thiel recognized the realist assertion that there is no exit from the state: "The critical question then becomes one of means, of how to escape not via politics but beyond it. Because there are no truly free places left in our world, I suspect that the mode for escape must involve some sort of new and hitherto untried process that leads us to some undiscovered country."[9] Though Thiel later appears to have rejected this assertion, working again "via politics" in his support for Donald Trump's presidential campaign and then administration, Thiel's earlier schemes did indeed look for escape routes out of our legal regimes. He supported and financed projects including the Seasteading Institute, which seeks to create politically autonomous floating cities, as well as private startup cities, most concretely in Honduras, which in 2013 enshrined in law "semi-autonomous, privately run cities, 'zonas de empleo y desarrollo económico' (zones for employment and economic development), or 'ZEDEs.'" The private city of Próspera is the most prominent and ambitious of these ZEDEs, which "are to be governed by private investors, who can write their own laws and regulations, design their own court systems, and operate their own police forces... subject to limited government oversight and few legal restrictions."[10] This might be a way of exiting through the gift shop, a way of purchasing a way out.

Such experiments have, so far, failed to produce any way out of the state. For instance, in one notable attempt at seasteading, a private couple, Chad Elwartowski and Supranee Thepdet, moved into a floating home twelve miles off the coast of Thailand, with the explicit aim of building "a libertarian-style community that they believe will be beyond legal jurisdictions." The Thai government, however, accused "the couple of breaching a section of the country's criminal code that relates to threatening the sovereignty of a state, and erosion of a state's independence ... charges [that] carry the death penalty." After the couple fled into hiding, the Royal Thai Navy dismantled the floating home.[11]

This sequence highlights the more general reality that projects like seasteading and private cities rely on the explicit cooperation of existing states. As Matthew Hart notes, "international waters" are not "simply beyond the national state and its laws... not, in fact, the antithesis of territorial power," concluding that "the seas aren't so free—and perhaps they never were."[12] As Aihwa Ong argues, even territorial suspensions of sovereignty, as in the legal framework of special economic zones that underly private cities like Próspera, function like any other sovereign exception, producing a "pattern of graduated or variegated sovereignty [that] ensures that the state can both face global challenges and secure order and growth."[13] While these projects might offer some partial exits, they are explicitly confined to the liberal sense of an exit that is ultimately circumscribed by the state; these are no escapes from the state itself.

From Rand's fictional fantasies to Thiel's real-world experiments, these endeavors all imagine political solutions through leaving our current society behind, and they all point in the direction of more, not less, liberal capitalism. In part because of the high-profile nature of these examples (not least of all because of the simple quantity of money circulating around them), it can be difficult to imagine a politics of exit as anything other than right-wing. That there can in fact be a far more expansive politics of escape has been the contention of this book: there is a sizeable and important body of American literature (and culture more generally) that, when it does not outright oppose the right, remains at most dismissive or uninterested in it, yet which nevertheless asserts its own politics of escape. Moreover, this current association of exit with the right is a consequence of history, a history certainly rooted at least in part in the racist legacy of secessionism in the United States, but, as I have been trying to help us see throughout *No Exit*, this association is not philosophically necessary or politically inevitable. After all, before Rand imagined Galt's Gulch, Charles Olson was advocating for a different kind of enclave in Black Mountain College, an artistic escape from—and alternative to—political society. (Black Mountain closed in 1957, the same year Rand's *Atlas Shrugged* was published.) My point is not that Black Mountain solved the politics of escape in a way that Rand did not—there remains no exit, and Black Mountain is no more viable an exit than Galt's Gulch Chile or seasteading—but rather a reminder that Rand has no monopoly on imagining escapes.

I would like to bring this into sharper focus by showing how even a biting satire of Rand's work can nevertheless still assert its own politics of escape, through the 2007 first-person-shooter video game *Bioshock*. The player character, our protagonist, Jack, finds himself in the underwater city of Rapture, a dystopian version of the capitalist escape from the state Rand imagines in Galt's Gulch. Rapture's founder, wealthy businessman Andrew Ryan, is a not-at-all-veiled reference to Rand who seeks an escape from the "parasites" of government that mooch off the profits of free enterprise. Upon arriving in Rapture, an offscreen character named Atlas (another nod to Rand) comes over the radio to serve as a guide, giving background on the setting and offering Jack instructions on what to do next. The city has been overrun with genetically modified "splicers," grotesque embodiments of unregulated capitalism run amok that no longer register as human (so killing them, as part of the gameplay, carries no moral weight). The player also encounters "Little Sisters," young girls deprived of human agency, zombie-like yet innocent, who have been psychologically conditioned by Rapture's political powers to roam the city's streets and "harvest" a gene-altering drug from the bodies of dead splicers.

Much of the discourse around *Bioshock* has focused on whether or not video games can be art. While, as Patrick Jagoda observes, "it no longer seems adequate to express wonder at the possibility of video games operating as an art form,"[14] in the years immediately following its release, the narrative and aesthetic ambition of *Bioshock* provided an opportune moment to stake claims about the cultural prestige and artistic capacities of a medium in relative infancy.[15] Much of this prestige comes from *Bioshock*'s narrative rather than its gameplay rules and mechanics. As Felan Parker explains, the game's "narrative and thematic content contributes directly to its high cultural status," and the game's creative director Ken "Levine's auteur persona hinges in part on his image as a visionary storyteller."[16] Indeed, it is possible and reasonable to read *Bioshock* much as we read a film,[17] and the game's narrative and cinematic elements occupy much of my focus here. But it's also important to understand how *Bioshock*'s narrative significance is entirely dependent upon the fact that it is a game, not a film. *Bioshock* poses the structure of the game itself as analogous to political structures: thinking about how games control people becomes a way of thinking about how states control people. Much as we have seen repeatedly throughout *No Exit*, the only solution *Bioshock* can imagine is by leaving both behind. Olson imagines leaving polis by leaving language; Pynchon imagines leaving the System by leaving the novel; Didion imagines leaving democracy by leaving *Democracy;* Díaz imagines leaving political history by leaving the written page; Mackey imagines leaving law by leaving articulation; *Bioshock* imagines leaving the hypercapitalist state through the player leaving the game.

Despite *Bioshock*'s explicit satire of Randian political exit, escape is nevertheless the primary, explicit motivation from the start of the game. Parker summarizes the game's plot: "the player must fight through the ruins in hopes of rescuing Atlas' family [kidnapped by Ryan] and escaping to the surface . . . until it is revealed in a twist that Atlas is in fact Ryan's archrival Frank Fontaine and Jack has been genetically engineered from Ryan's DNA and brainwashed to obey Fontaine's commands."[18] As another critic explains, the basic narrative and gameplay objective is to "kill the mutated citizens, and escape the underwater prison."[19] The underlying player motivation as well as the overall direction of the plot both point towards escape.

In an insightful analysis of the game's music, William Gibbons notes that the game's opening "song is 'La Mer,' a French standard better known to American audiences as 'Beyond the Sea,'" and its lyrics "reinforce the idea of travel to a better place; a life filled with love and happiness awaits the narrator 'somewhere beyond the sea.'"[20] While Gibbons reads "beyond the sea" as a reference to Rapture, ironizing the song's utopianism, this requires a fairly strained reading of "beyond" as equivalent to "beneath," as well as treating Rapture as "the end of [Jack's] journey," rather than its beginning (which is both how the player experiences it, and, ultimately, where it sits narratively, since Jack's pre-Rapture personal history is entirely fabricated through Fontaine's brainwashing). It makes more sense to interpret the song as a sincere statement of *Bioshock*'s direction, in terms of both narrative and gameplay. Love and happiness lie beyond the sea, beyond Rapture, on the other end of a journey of departure.

After Atlas admits to his political machinations and manipulation, revealing his true identity as Fontaine, the player's next objective pops up on screen: "New Goal: Escape!" "New Goal" is how the game introduces all of the player's tasks, but this one also seems self-consciously tongue-in-cheek: the overarching goal was *already* escape. This becomes even more apparent when, just a few moments later, with no real struggle, the player anticlimactically ends up in a Rapture safe house, temporarily protected from Fontaine, with the message popping up, "Goal Completed: Escape!" Unlike most of the other objectives in the game, which often involve extensive gunplay, puzzle solving, and exploration, this "Escape!" objective is trivially simple and brief, to the extent that it feels superfluous. Diegetic cues already tell the player where to go in this sequence ("Come with me," shouts the character who leads you directly to the safe room), so there's no real gameplay need for this nondiegetic quest name. Rather, the mocking, ironic declaration of "Goal Completed: Escape!" accentuates just how trapped Jack remains. Escape continues to be the motivating objective even after this, as another character urges Jack to rescue the Little Sisters and "deliver them from this terrible city at long last."

This ongoing orientation towards escape is confirmed at the end of the game. *Bioshock* has two possible endings, a good ending and a bad ending, with the outcome in a given playthrough determined by a simplistic moral binary (either the player rescues the Little Sisters or "harvests" them for the gene-altering drug to make Jack modestly more powerful).[21] In the good ending, a short video epilogue shows Jack returning to the surface with some of the Little Sisters he has rescued and then quickly moves through a clichéd montage of life events as the girls get to grow up in the "real" world outside of Rapture: receiving a diploma, falling in love, and having children. Finally, the adult Little Sisters are together with Jack, melodramatically placing their hands on his as he dies peacefully, an old man in bed. In the bad ending, Jack is a power-hungry monster, and we see him unleashing an army of violent splicers on the surface. Improbably, the first thing the splicers encounter topside is a surfaced military submarine, ill-prepared to fend off these genetically modified monsters, and Jack takes control of the nuclear missile on board.

Both of these endings amount to an escape from Rapture: from its violence in the good ending or from its boundaries in the bad ending. The psychological and moral stakes differ, but, in both, the only answer to Rapture is to leave. The point of *Bioshock*, the only direction it goes, is towards escape.

So, what does it mean to escape Rapture, the hypercapitalist enclave that was itself supposed "to escape societal and governmental regulations"?[22] It is, simply, another attempt to escape the state. While, superficially, it might look like *Bioshock*'s escape goes in the other direction, leaving behind the anarchic, dystopian Rapture in order to return to the "real" world on the surface, the world peacefully ruled by states, that appearance is indeed only superficial. Most obviously, both endings assert escapes *into* the fantastical: "a very conservative family utopia" in the good ending, or Cold War B-movie drama in the bad ending.[23] Neither ending reads as realist. The world outside of Rapture isn't our world, the world of politics and the state, but rather the nonplace of utopia or dystopia.

By contrast, Rapture is fundamentally a realist (though not mimetic) setting. Rapture asserts an understanding—in admittedly exaggerated, caricatured forms—of twentieth- and twenty-first-century capitalism, and its "combination of free markets and fundamentalist religion is irresistibly reminiscent of early-twenty-first-century U.S. neoliberalism."[24] It critically asserts Rand's Objectivism "as inspirational and relevant for contemporary sociopolitical and economic realities."[25] Escaping Rapture for the surface means escaping our political realities for something else.

Importantly, the realism of Rapture emphasizes political power (rather than its absence) far more than critics have generally recognized. The game's obvious commentary on Rand makes it natural to focus on the game's satirical depictions of economic deregulation and Ryan's villainous antigovernment rhetoric. But much of the political drama driving the game's plot actually emphasizes just how much political power and monopolistic violence continue to determine life in Rapture—how much the familiar political state remains. Approaching Rapture as an "unregulated consumer market" ruled by a "free enterprise, no interference policy"[26] or as an "anarchic society"[27] devoid of any state, critics have generally missed or ignored the game's frequent references to the city's laws, governing bodies, and police and military power.

Early in the game, Atlas introduces Ryan as "the bloody King of Rapture." This is not just hyperbole or a throwaway line but a loaded assertion of political power, cleverly punning on Atlas's British diction to indicate the violence of that power. While Ryan clearly acts as sovereign, political power in Rapture is also more twenty-first-century than "King" might suggest, featuring, for example, mass surveillance, with security cameras "all around you. Ryan's eyes and ears." The city also extends that sovereignty into other governmental structures, including, notably, a police force (Atlas calls them "coppers") and a city council. Ryan notes how the city's legal system limits his own political machinations, explaining that Fontaine was initially "just a menace, to be convicted and hung. But he always manages to be where the evidence isn't."[28] As Ryan's feud with Fontaine escalates, Ryan suspends these legal checks under the pretense of exceptional circumstances, relying on familiar political rhetoric: "The death penalty in Rapture! Council's in an uproar. Riots in the streets they say! But this is the time for leadership. Action must be taken against the smugglers.... A few stretched necks are a small price to pay for our ideals."[29] Notably, this exceptional suspension of the law nevertheless occurs *as* law, as Ryan's head of security observes (and refuses to be a part of): "Hanging now, is it? That's what we've come to? Now look, I don't make the laws here, I just enforce them. But I didn't come to Rapture to string men up for running contraband. If Ryan and his crew have their law, then they can have my badge."[30] This is, as Giorgio Agamben describes it, the suspension of the law on which the law depends, a hallmark of the modern state, and it is an understanding of state power that recurs throughout the texts I have discussed in *No Exit*.

Even Randian moments of anti-regulation reinscribe the underlying political power to regulate. For example, Ryan explains that "there has been tremendous pressure to regulate" the gene-modification market in Rapture, grandiosely refusing to do so: "what use is our ideology if it is not tested?"[31] And yet, the power to regulate persists in Rapture, even if sometimes as unexercised potential—a fact that poignantly manifests when that potential is exercised, such as when Ryan "nationalized" Fontaine's corporation, "for the good of the city, he says."[32] Most importantly, Rapture shares that most fundamental quality of the political state, what I have throughout this book taken as one of its defining features: the absence of exit. This becomes explicit and literal as Ryan and Fontaine's conflict intensifies, as Ryan locks down all of the submersible bathyspheres that go to the surface, so that Rapture's citizens cannot "come and go as they see fit." The game's underwater setting literalizes its abstract political reality: there is no exit from Rapture.

Bioshock navigates this problem of exitlessness in a similar manner to many of the texts across *No Exit* and as such extends my analytical framework beyond the narrowly literary. Many critics have noticed how *Bioshock* seems to satirize or demystify the presumption of player agency, the "illusion of autonomy," which, in turn, becomes a way of critiquing the myth of individual freedom in liberal consumer society.[33] Rather than the player controlling the game, the game controls the player, either directly through the rule set or indirectly through "nudges" that encourage gameplay in the manner envisioned by creators.[34] *Bioshock* throws this in the player's face. Most famously, at the climactic narrative reveal that Atlas/Fontaine has mind control over Jack, the game also takes away control from the player, switching to a video cutscene in which Jack no longer responds to player input, instead carrying out a scripted narrative event: "At the same moment that the character realizes that they are a pawn in a struggle between Ryan and Fontaine, the player is made to realize that they are a pawn in the game and narrative of *Bioshock*."[35] This memorable scene echoes an earlier, more subtle instance, when, as Jack first gains a gene-modification superpower, the game briefly takes control away from the player as Jack lifts his hands on screen in the first-person perspective. The narrative pretext is to show the power now imbued in Jack's hands, but it also reveals Jack's tattoos, chains on his wrists—a reference to the "Great Chain" of market forces in Ryan's Objectivist ideology, which is in turn only an obfuscation of political power, shackles, chains of "the sort with the big iron ball around your ankle," as one character puts it.[36] The game controls and guides the player just as, within the narrative, political power controls the character.

Most importantly, *Bioshock* self-consciously recognizes that this control over the player is unavoidable. As Lars Schmeink argues, "the game's procedural nature, its setting of rules and limits, cannot be overcome—no matter how much some games try to gloss over this fact and provide a rhetoric of 'interactivity' highly stylized into ideology."[37] And it is precisely this inescapable control that *Bioshock* uses to make video games a useful model for thinking about the state. *Bioshock* intentionally makes both of the above cutscenes "inescapable," placing them in gameplay bottlenecks where "all other exits are barred."[38] As Schmeink points out, "the only option to stop the systemic control and to truly become a free individual would be to stop playing altogether, which never really was a choice."[39]

Schmeink is right, I think, insofar as we are thinking about the metaphorical tenor, the political society of control, for which the game is metaphorical vehicle. However, this does not fully capture the imaginative work of the game, nor of the poetics of escape that it manifests. It is not just the realist assertion that there is no exit from the state; it also tries to assert something beyond that reality, in part by acknowledging the distance between vehicle and tenor. *Bioshock*, of course, is *not* a state, and you can in fact exit the game. "Stop playing" may not be a viable option when it comes to politics, but it is an option, in the most trivial sense, when it comes to video games. It is within that difference that *Bioshock* asserts its political desires. Political life should be more like video games: if the rules become intolerable, quit the game.

Like the other examples of the poetics of escape explored in this book, *Bioshock* asserts escape as a response to political power, but because it uses its own artistic structure as a way of thinking about political structures, imagining escape from the political also means exiting the work of art, the game, itself. As Riccardo Fassone notes in his study of endings in video games, video games can look like "authoritative pieces of software, imposing their inflexible procedures on players... Far from being an instrument of creativity and personal affirmation, video games seem to belong to the realm of dystopia; artifacts built to co-op [*sic*] free play into a measurable, regulated, even oppressive activity." Yet, because games are not actually oppressive, cannot actually constrain a player's freedom, Fassone argues that we should understand games not as "authoritative pieces of software" but rather as "games about authority."[40] To play a game is to explore "its rules in order to play with—and around—authority."[41] If playing a game is a way of exploring authority (a perspective that *Bioshock* explicitly invites) then exiting the game can become a way of imagining political escape. *Bioshock* weaves these structural aspects of its own medium into its narrative engagement with escaping the state. That is, indeed, why the game's only political hope occurs in the endings, which imagine fantastical escapes from the realities of state power. This is not to say that the game is escap*ist*, an important qualification for the poetics of escape as I have been considering it in *No Exit*. While these fantastical endings depart from any realist engagement with politics, *Bioshock* asserts these nonrealist images as beyond the purview of the game. Indeed, the player does not play them at all—they are cinematic clips, playing without any input from the player. Jack only leaves Rapture by leaving the player behind, and the player only escapes the game's control by ending the game.

The politics of exit is not limited to the Randian right; even a game like *Bioshock*, which so forcefully critiques Rand, can nevertheless assert escape as a response to the state. One final return to Banksy will reiterate my tentative gesture towards the extensiveness of the poetics of escape, even in one of the most newsworthy instances of right-wing exit in the twenty-first century, the United Kingdom's withdrawal from the European Union, "Brexit." While, like the poetics of escape, Brexit relies on a political logic of departure, Brexit also diverges from the imagined escapes at the center of this book, since it consists of a nation-state trying to leave a supranational state rather than an individual or an incipient counterpublic trying to leave any and all state authority as such.[42] Brexit, in other words, still fits within a liberal conception of exit, in that there remains a final boundary of state sovereignty within which the exit occurs. Much as *Bioshock* seeks escape while critiquing Randian enclavism, Banksy does not give up on departure even while critiquing the nationalistic withdrawal of Brexit. Banksy pushes exit further, beyond what is tolerable to the state, into escape.

On March 28, 2019, the Bristol Museum put back on display Banksy's *Devolved Parliament*, a fairly straightforward mockery of British politics depicting members of Parliament as chimpanzees. The official line from the Museum was that this was to commemorate the ten-year anniversary of the piece's first showing, in the summer of 2009, during the *Banksy versus Bristol Museum* show, when pieces by the Bristol native took over the space. The piece had been auctioned to an anonymous collector, who had now temporarily loaned it back to the Museum for this commemorative showing. Ten years makes for a nice round anniversary, but the Museum Trust clearly had other reasons for the timing of the piece's return. Museum trustee Yona Smith explained, "ten years on, it's so much more relevant now than as it was then. Is Banksy a visionary? Did he paint it thinking it would happen?"[43] What exactly is the "it" that has happened, according to Smith? Banksy gives an answer in an Instagram post of *Devolved Parliament*, with the caption, "I made this ten years ago. Bristol museum have just put it back on display to mark Brexit day."[44] As various media outlets pointed out, the piece made it up just before March 29, 2019, the original deadline for the United Kingdom to leave the European Union. The actual ten-year anniversary of the Banksy versus Bristol Museum show was still a few months away, so this timing seems intentional: the "it" that has happened is conservatives taking over Parliament. Prime Minister Theresa May and the Brexiters are the chimps.

In his Instagram response, Banksy seems to simultaneously affirm and undermine this political use of his piece. His caption quoted above continues, "'Laugh now, but one day no-one will be in charge.'" This riffs on an earlier piece, *Laugh Now* (2002), in which a chimpanzee wears a sandwich board that reads, "Laugh now but one day we'll be in charge." The narrative suggested by this combination of *Laugh Now, Devolved Parliament,* and Brexit day is a familiar one: liberal elites in media and academia long mocked and ridiculed the average, middle-class, White conservative, but now he has finally had enough.[45] In the guise of right-wing populism, the uncultured and uncivilized gets the last laugh. The Museum reads Banksy as a realist: "great art raises a mirror to what's relevant," says Smith, and the humorously sad reality *Devolved Parliament* depicts is the seizure of power by conservative populists, dumb chimps tragically getting the last laugh.

Banky's textual reworking of *Laugh Now* in the *Devolved Parliament* Instagram caption complicates all of this, though. The last laugh won't belong to the unevolved, unenlightened Conservative Party, but it won't belong to the Liberals or Labour either. Banksy's vision of the future is a vision when "no-one" is in charge. This is a no-one that defies representation. In *Laugh Now,* we see the speaker: it is the monkey that says, "we'll be in charge." In the Instagram caption, the line is still spoken, in explicit quotation marks, but the speaker remains invisible—not unlike the famously anonymous Banksy himself.

This is a vision of power divorced from representation, divorced from political authority. This is a vision of escape, of political exit, entirely unlike Brexit. Rather than changing the *who* and *how* of political representation, "no-one will be in charge" flees political representation altogether, leaving *no one* to represent or rule anyone. Banksy uses this visual omission to indicate a rejection of political representation as such.

Banksy helps us reconcile contemporary political art's apparent contradiction of criticizing the kind of exit theorized by liberal academics and pursued from the right while simultaneously proffering another kind of exit, exit from the state, as the only acceptable final ends to politics. Such a politics of escape is present all over twentieth- and twenty-first-century culture. I have closed this book about the poetics of escape in American literature with a video game and with a British visual artist whose work, though figuring significantly in contemporary American culture and sometimes manifesting in US cities (as with the bail bonds piece in New York City and as with the filming of *Exit through the Gift Shop* in and apropos Los Angeles), more prominently exists within and about the United Kingdom and Europe more generally. I would like these closing readings to gesture beyond this book's disciplinary boundaries, even as those boundaries reflect the inordinate power and cultural significance of the US state in the twentieth and twenty-first centuries.

Wherever we find contemporary culture engaging life's excesses beyond the pale of representation, we should perk up to see if the poetics of escape attends also. Often it does. *No Exit* gives us evidence for the significance of the poetics of escape in American literature, and it gives us important models too of what the poetics of escape looks like and how it works. Williams and Wright show us the impetus for escape as they seek a way out of the state's injustices; Olson and Pynchon illustrate the pitfall of solipsism that escape must avoid; DeLillo and Didion reveal the difficulties of disentangling political representation from literary representation; Yamashita and Díaz show that movement between states is no exit, while also highlighting the necessity of representational inclusion within the state as an immediate bandage against injustice; Spahr and Mackey manifest the difficulty and necessity of representing the idea that representation is not enough.

Outside of these literary and cultural experiments, a politics of escape looks like a dead end. In liberal theory, exit takes place only within the state, never against it. In mainstream political discourse and in the most prominent real-world examples, exit appears as the exclusive territory of the political right, aimed at producing bunkers that would preserve some endangered aspect of our political reality, not leave that political reality behind. The poetics of escape is a counter to these notions, seeking escape routes out of the state we inhabit into a new political reality, one we have not yet invented. *No Exit* establishes a corpus around which the poetics of escape, as literary-historical concept and as a politico-aesthetic project, coheres, but we should treat this group of texts as generative rather than exhaustive—as points of departure. The desire to escape the state, and the allure this problem holds as one to be worked at in literature and culture, isn't going away.

NOTES

INTRODUCTION

1. Dickinson, *Poems of Emily Dickinson*, 72.
2. Douglas Dowland provides a compelling recent counterexample. Dowland usefully distinguishes the "strong" nationalisms of partisan outrage and jingoism from the "weak" nationalism, humming along in the background, that constructs the imagined community of the nation. However, Dowland largely neglects how the state foments and employs weak as well as strong nationalisms; it is true that "the connection between a person and the nation is emotional," as Dowland rightly observes, but it is also political, legal, and violent (*Weak Nationalisms*, 6). That is, the "ordinariness" (13) of weak nationalism doesn't make it any less "pernicious" (11) or "disciplinary" (12). Nationalism does not need to be affectively "aggressive and violent" (211) to be politically aggressive and violent.
3. Ong, *Neoliberalism as Exception*, 3.
4. Ibid., 98.
5. Hart, *Extraterritorial*, 7.
6. Ibid., 8.
7. Nickels, *World Literature and the Geographies of Resistance*, 4, 5.
8. Harford Vargas, *Forms of Dictatorship*, 6.
9. Decker, *Geographies of Flight*, 172.
10. Foucault, *Birth of Biopolitics*, 117, 186–87.
11. Fazal and Griffiths, "Membership Has Its Privileges," 83, 80.
12. Wallmeier, "Exit as Critique," 154.
13. For the former, Frederic Jameson's *Postmodernism* is the obvious touchstone, but see also more recent work such as Walter Benn Michaels's *The Shape of the Signifier*, Jameson's *Archaeologies of the Future*, and the collection of essays *Reading Capitalist Realism*, edited by Alison Shonkwiler and Leigh Claire La

Berge, especially Shonkwiler and La Berge's critical introduction (1–25). For an applied critique of this tradition, see Samuel Cohen's *After the End of History*. Cohen compellingly rejects attempts to equate postmodernist fiction with late capitalism and the end of history, including "Jameson's on the impossibility of postmodern historical understanding, as well as Walter Benn Michaels's on the replacement of historicism with identitarianism" (4).

For an overview of the latter perspective, see many of the essays included in *The Cultural Studies Reader*, edited by Simon During, including Gayatri Spivak's "Scattered Speculation on the Question of Cultural Studies" (169–188), Judith Butler's "Subjects of Sex/Gender/Desire" (340–353), and Nancy Fraser's "Rethinking the Public Sphere" (518–536). For a critique of the politics of inclusion or recognition on a theoretical and strategic level, see Pheng Cheah's "Biopolitics of Recognition."

14. For example, see Allan Antliff's *Anarchist Modernism*: "The project of individual liberation lying at the heart of anarchism in the early twentieth century was not only antigovernmental: the movement generated a far-flung cultural rebellion encompassing lifestyles, literature, and art as well as politics" (1).
15. See Michaels's influential *Gold Standard and the Logic of Naturalism*, which is not interested in literature's ideas but rather "the position of those texts within a system of representation that . . . is more important than any attitude one might imagine oneself to have toward it" (19). Daniel Grausam's *On Endings* provides a clear example of how this remains a prevalent critical perspective. Grausam argues that "postmodernist fiction is, in short, the literary symptom of new understandings of space and time produced by the nuclear age with which it coincided" (4) and suggests that "we might even designate postmodern fiction a form of realism, insofar as it tries to find models of representation adequate to the Cold War's changed understanding of historical time" (5–6).
16. Marx and Engels, *German Ideology*, 59.
17. Best and Marcus, "Surface Reading," 5.
18. Felski, *Limits of Critique*, 57.
19. Macpherson, *Women's Movement*, 8.
20. Grattan, *Hope Isn't Stupid*, 14, 19.
21. Cohen, *After the End of History*, 6. See also 24–25.
22. Arendt, *Origins of Totalitarianism*, 352.
23. Clune, "Beyond Realism," 196.
24. Clune, "Formalism as the Fear of Ideas," 1198.
25. Brouillette, *UNESCO and the Fate of the Literary*, 3.
26. Ibid., 5.
27. Hardt and Negri, *Empire*, 411.
28. Jameson, *Archaeologies of the Future*, 270.

29. Ibid.
30. Ibid., 289.
31. Ibid., xiii.
32. Ibid.
33. Levitas, *Concept of Utopia*, 7.
34. Grattan, *Hope Isn't Stupid*, 2.
35. Levitas, *Concept of Utopia*, 2.
36. Grattan, *Hope Isn't Stupid*, 5.
37. Ibid., 21.
38. Jameson, *Archaeologies of the Future*, 16.
39. Ibid., 4, xiv.
40. Spahr, *Du Bois's Telegram*, 4–5.
41. McCann and Szalay, "Do You Believe in Magic," 436, 441.
42. Joron, *Fathom*, 18. Subsequent references are cited parenthetically.
43. Jameson, *Archaeologies of the Future*, xvi.
44. Spahr, *Du Bois's Telegram*, 189.
45. Ibid., 26.
46. Grattan, *Hope Isn't Stupid*, 14. Grattan is glossing Jameson here.
47. Jameson, *Archaeologies of the Future*, 283.
48. Gramsci, *Selections from the Prison Notebooks*, 263.
49. Althusser, "Ideology and Ideological State Apparatuses," 101.
50. Granik herself claims "a strong neorealist tradition" for her work; see Gilbey, "Vanishing Point," 48.
51. Gilbey, "Vanishing Point," 48.
52. Hirschman, *Exit, Voice, and Loyalty*, 15 and 24. I discuss Hirschman in more detail in chapter 5.
53. "Exit Albert Hirschman," *The Economist*, December 22, 2012.
54. Kukathas, *Liberal Archipelago*, 96.
55. Hirschman, *Exit, Voice, and Loyalty*, 33.
56. Friedman, *Capitalism and Freedom*, 33.
57. Rawls, *Political Liberalism*, 40–41.
58. Kukathas, *Liberal Archipelago*, 178.
59. Ibid., 109.
60. For a characteristic example, see Dagmar Borchers and Annamari Vitikainen, "On Exit," 3. Similarly, Jane Anna Gordon refuses to extend the right of exit to the state itself in her effort to rejuvenate social contract theory, primarily because that would "smack of illiberalism" (*Statelessness and Contemporary Enslavement*, 93).

   This plays out in literary criticism, too. When McCann and Szalay dismiss post-sixties literature as a withdrawal from politics into magical thinking, it is because their conception of the political is restricted to the state, especially through electoral politics ("Do You Believe in Magic," 458).

61. Leeson, *Anarchy Unbound*, 8.
62. Ibid., 9.
63. Hirschman, *Exit, Voice, and Loyalty*, 79.
64. Ibid., 55.
65. Scott, *Seeing Like a State*, 86–87.
66. Weber, "Politics as a Vocation," 33. Hart clarifies how the defining boundaries of a state's power—where one state ends and another begins—need not be territorial but may inhere elsewhere, such as in the bodies of citizens, following them around the globe (*Extraterritorial*, 10).
67. Gramsci, *Selections from the Prison Notebooks*, 263.
68. Hall, "Gramsci's Relevance," 228.
69. Ibid., 229. Emphasis in original.
70. Skocpol, "Bringing the State Back In," 121–22.
71. This is the Westphalian model of the state as a territorial sovereignty. For a good critique of this model from a literary perspective, see Hart, *Extraterritorial*, 41–47.
72. Steven Weisenburger argues that Pynchon views the state as a "transnational sovereign entity wielding ultimate powers" ("In the Zone," 111).
73. Kukathas, *Liberal Archipelago*, 210.
74. Sam Bluefarb makes a related distinction as he traces the "escape motif" in American fiction, contrasting "the dynamics of escapism" from "true escape": "Though escape generally implies a flight from one reality into another, escapism has a wider cluster of associations. For escapism implies a flight from daily 'reality,' far less forgivable than literally running away from a society or situation" (*Escape Motif in the American Novel*, 5).
75. Macpherson, *Women's Movement*, 26. Ursula Le Guin, whose science fiction often explores anarchist politics and values, draws on J. R. R. Tolkien in rejecting this derogatory charge of escapism: "fantasy is escapist, and that is its glory. If a soldier is imprisoned by the enemy, don't we consider it his duty to escape? The moneylenders, the knownothings, the authoritarians have us all in prison; if we value the freedom of the mind and soul, if we're partisans of liberty, then it's our plain duty to escape, and to take as many people with us as we can" ("Escape Routes," 204). Tolkien also treats fantasy as a political escape. However, while Le Guin seems to reject the assumption "that SF doesn't deal with the Real World" (204), Tolkien, in contrast, seems also to defend a more straightforward escapism from reality, of the kind rejected here: "Why should a man be scorned if, finding himself in prison, he tries to get out and go home? Or if, when he cannot do so, he thinks and talks about other topics than jailers and prison-walls?" ("On Fairy-Stories," 148).

76. Arendt, *Origins of Totalitarianism*, 352.
77. Sargent, *Utopianism*, 111.
78. Ibid.
79. Jameson, *Archaeologies of the Future*, 3.
80. Ibid., 4.
81. Jameson, *Archaeologies of the Future*, 279, 280.
82. In *Mastery's End*, Jeffrey Gray has similarly responded to critics such as Janet Wolff and Caren Kaplan who fear that escape always amounts to escapism; Gray contends that geographic escape in twentieth-century poetry can be a meaningful response to political oppression. For Gray, escape has more to do with physical immigration than the representational escape at issue here.
83. Bernstein, *All the Whiskey in Heaven*, 34.
84. For a thorough attempt to decode this poem, see Albena Lutzkanova-Vassileva's *Testimonies of Russian and American Postmodern Poetry*, 143–46. Playing with the poem's nonsense anagram "mogh & hmog," Lutzkanova-Vassileva suggests that the poem seems "to mock any attempt to find a lucid design amidst the senseless amalgamation of letters" (145).
85. Sartre, *"No Exit" and "The Flies,"* 61.
86. Szalay, *Hip Figures*, 28.
87. I would also reject how Szalay maps this onto a periodizing shift from ideology to identity (28–29), towards "a politics built on bodily stances and experiences as opposed to words, beliefs, or policies," as he and McCann put it ("Do You Believe in Magic," 444). This is the same modernist-to-postmodernist trajectory Walter Benn Michaels asserts in *The Shape of the Signifier*, which I discuss in chapter 5.
88. Kevin Baker, "It's Time for a Bluexit," *New Republic*, March 9, 2017.

1. ESCAPE'S EDGES

1. Williams, *Collected Poems*, 377. Subsequent references are to this edition and are cited parenthetically.
2. Williams, "Man versus the Law," 348.
3. Ibid.
4. Ibid.
5. Ibid.
6. Ibid., 348–49.
7. Ibid., 349.
8. Ibid.
9. Ibid.

10. Robert von Hallberg similarly reads "An Early Martyr" as "liberal rather than radical" ("Politics of Description," 133).
11. Tyldum, dir., *Silo*, season 1, episode 1, "Freedom Day."
12. Ibid.
13. In Kadlec's account, the American pragmatist distillation of anarchist thought "domesticated" anarchism to make it serve the interests of American liberal democracy (*Mosaic Modernism*), 9; cf. 22, 134, and 144.
14. See Olson's *Collected Prose*, 168, 202, 325, and 343.
15. Olson, *Maximus Poems*, III.9. Subsequent references are to this edition and are cited parenthetically, using the volume and page numbers from the standalone volumes, which Butterick provides.
16. Von Hallberg, *Charles Olson*, 11–13. In *Modernism's Other Work*, Lisa Siraganian reads Olson's politics as even more consistently New-Deal-progressive than von Hallberg does (143–48). Mark Byers, in contrast, renews the case for Olson's retreat, in the 1950s and '60s, from progressive politics towards an "independent left" and a distrust of social planning; see Byers's "Imagining Uncertainty," 444–45, as well as his *Charles Olson and American Modernism*, 160–63. For a related account of Olson's epistemology that also comports with my engagement with information theory in chapter 3, see Paul Stephens's *The Poetics of Information Overload*, 87–108, especially 88–89.
17. Williams, "America, Whitman, and the Art of Poetry," 29.
18. Mariani, *William Carlos Williams*, 370. Mariani's date is wrong—there was no America's Cup in 1935—but the previous year's race is a plausible source for William's poem, with the 1934 iteration marked by pertinent class drama: the professional crew of the *Endeavour*, the challenger for the Cup, left over a pay dispute, necessitating a replacement crew comprised entirely of amateurs.
19. Reed, "On 'The Yachts.'"
20. Von Hallberg, "Politics of Description," 142. Like Reed, von Hallberg reads the poem's work as primarily that of demystification.
21. Williams, *Paterson*, 221.
22. The yachts also clearly stand in for wealthy classes protected from "ungoverned" destructive forces, but since yachts and wealth really are related (in a way that oceans and poverty are not), this metonymy is substantively different from the crude symbolism Williams rejects.
23. See, for example, von Hallberg, "Politics of Description," 131–32 and 146; Johnson, "'A Whole Synthesis of His Time,'"; and Cohen, *Beleaguered Poets and Leftist Critics*, 148–92. While the intense economic and political climate of the 1930s surely affected Williams, too often these accounts suggest that, prior to that, Williams's poetry was somehow apolitical. For a rebuttal to the notion that Williams was less political in the 1920s, see Siraganian, *Modernisms's Other Work*, 79–109. This is further supported by the fact that Williams's article "A

Man versus the Law," so explicitly prefiguring his '30s politics in *An Early Martyr*, was published in 1920.

24. Ashton, *From Modernism to Postmodernism*, 125.
25. Ibid., 145.
26. Siraganian, *Modernism's Other Work*, 97.
27. Ibid.
28. Ibid.
29. Ibid., 102.
30. Ibid., 108.
31. Williams, *Recognizable Image*, 100.
32. Ibid., 103.
33. Ibid., 106-7.
34. Ibid., 109.
35. Siraganian, *Modernism's Other Work*, 106.
36. Nickels, *Poetry of the Possible*, 48, 60. Carla Billitteri likewise argues that Williams sees his poetry as "socially useful insofar as it instructs the masses," making the artist a "social designer ... a social technocrat" ("William Carlos Williams and the Politics of Form," 57).
37. Williams, *Doctor Stories*, 59.
38. Ibid., 58. For a similar reading of "To Elsie" in *Spring and All*, see Maria Farland's "Modernist Versions of Pastoral," 920.
39. Williams, *Doctor Stories*, 60.
40. Ibid., 59.
41. Williams, "America, Whitman, and the Art of Poetry," 33.
42. Williams, *Paterson*, 103.
43. Ibid., 108-9.
44. Ibid., 111-12.
45. Ibid., 109.
46. For Maximus's enslavement, see Olson, *Maximus Poems*, I.12.
47. Von Hallberg, "Politics of Description," 145.
48. Williams, *Collected Poems*, 384.
49. Ginsberg, *Howl*, 12, 22.
50. Ferlinghetti, *Coney Island of the Mind*, 49.
51. Ibid., 56.
52. Ibid.
53. Ibid., 54.
54. Ibid., 59.
55. Ibid., 57.
56. Ibid., 63.
57. Ibid.
58. Ibid., 67.

59. Ibid., 68.
60. Quoted in Butterick, *Guide to the Maximus Poems*, 7.
61. Ibid.
62. Ibid., 318.
63. Ibid., 321.
64. Ibid., 531.
65. Olson, *Collected Prose*, 224-25.
66. Olson believed that Charles Sr.'s battle with the USPS finally killed him after fourteen years (*Collected Prose*, 217). Von Hallberg sees Olson's own career in politics as generating a similar belief: "Eight years in Washington convinced Olson that the alternative [to withdrawal]—to stay and fight political battles—means suicide" (*Charles Olson*, 16).
67. See Olson, *Collected Prose*, 244, and von Hallberg, *Charles Olson*, 29 and 31.
68. Olson, *Collected Prose*, 247.
69. As Byers puts it, "Olson also recognized that this politics of the self was very nearly a contradiction in terms" (*Charles Olson and American Modernism*, 166). See Byers's account of this tension for a useful complement to my own here (165-68).
70. Dewey, *Beyond Maximus*, 40.
71. Stephens, *Poetics of Information Overload*, 99.
72. Quoted in Butterick, *Guide to the Maximus Poems*, 262.
73. Ibid., 25.
74. The capital "C" in the last line here is also handwritten, and could be a partial or incomplete spiral.
75. Ibid., 589.
76. Ibid., 601.
77. Quoted in Butterick, *Guide to the Maximus Poems*, 609. Brackets are Olson's.
78. As far as I can tell, the manuscript Olson sent to Crozier is lost, and Butterick used a copy of Crozier's version in his edition of *Maximus*—see his editor's afterword to Olson's *Maximus Poems*, 644. My image comes from Butterick's published reproduction.
79. Quoted in Butterick, *Guide to the Maximus Poems*, 609. Brackets and italics are Olson's.
80. Hutcheon, *Poetics of Postmodernism*, 12.
81. See of course Perry Anderson's well-known account in *Origins of Postmodernity*, 12, as well as Paul, *Olson's Push*, xv, and Conte, *Unending Design*, 15. In contrast, in *Age of the Crisis of Man*, Mark Greif casts Olson's projectivism as more a continuation of—rather than a sharp break from—earlier work (322).
82. Olson, *Collected Prose*, 239.
83. Ibid., 246.
84. Ibid., 240.

85. Ibid., 242.
86. Ibid., 244.
87. Ibid., 240. As von Hallberg puts it, "open-form poets like Olson establish conventions, the terms of an implicit rhetorical contract, as they proceed; beginnings are especially privileged, for there poets tend to lay down their own laws" (*Charles Olson*, 134).
88. Butterick, *Editing the Maximus Poems*, ix.
89. The poem's arrangement in Olson's *Selected Poems*, edited by his friend Robert Creeley, more closely follows the manuscript, but it too cleans up and regularizes much of Olson's chaotic, disjointed lines.
90. Butterick, *Editing the Maximus Poems*, 56.
91. Olson, *Collected Prose*, 245. A later poet committed to open-form poetics, Rosmarie Waldrop, can retroactively identify in "Projective Verse" an Olson who favors "process, activity" over "the finished product, the art object" only by summarily dismissing the essay's emphasis on the typewriter's rigidity, the fixed relationship between form and content, and the speaker's breath ("Charles Olson," 468). Similarly, Nathaniel Mackey, despite his desire to credit Olson with contemporary developments in open-form poetics, admits that "one might be justified in characterizing the graphic impulse as an effort toward systematization, fixity, and closure, and thus toward a domestication of the volatility of speech, an attempt to imprison by rendering repeatable the instantaneity of an oral articulation" (*Discrepant Engagement*, 123).
92. On these grounds, von Hallberg holds Olson's later poetry in low esteem: he sees it descending into an individualism that neglects responsibility to readers. See *Charles Olson*, 4, 204, and 216.
93. Stephens, *Poetics of Information Overload*, 100.
94. Wallmeier, "Exit as Critique," 154.
95. Matthews, *Droppers*, 28.
96. Von Hallberg, *Charles Olson*, 15, 16.
97. Ibid., 17.
98. Robinson and Robinson, *Pirates*, 10.
99. Ibid., 33-36.
100. Von Hallberg, *Charles Olson*, 15.
101. Quoted in von Hallberg, *Charles Olson*, 18.
102. As Tanisha Fazal and Ryan Griffiths put it, "the end to which secessionist movements aspire" is "recognized statehood" ("Membership Has Its Privileges," 97).
103. Robinson and Robinson, *Pirates*, 45.
104. Wallmeier, "Exit as Critique," 155.
105. Robinson and Robinson, *Pirates*, 33.
106. Ibid., 10, 12-19.
107. Ibid., 9.

2. FANTASIES OF FLIGHT IN RICHARD WRIGHT AND THOMAS PYNCHON

1. Arendt, *Origins of Totalitarianism*, 267. Arendt explains that the problem of statelessness precedes the camp, as "the only practical substitute for a nonexistent homeland was an internment camp. Indeed, as early as the thirties this was the only 'country' the world had to offer the stateless" (284).
2. Agamben, *Homo Sacer*, 8.
3. Schillings, *Enemies of All Humankind*, 6.
4. Arendt, *Origins of Totalitarianism*, 283.
5. Ibid., 297.
6. Ibid., 302.
7. Ibid., 297.
8. Ibid., 302.
9. Gordon, *Statelessness and Contemporary Enslavement*, 4.
10. Ibid., 14. Gordon explicitly rejects anti-statism as a response to contemporary statelessness; I discuss her position in the introduction.
11. For a useful overview of the history of statelessness and the importance of World War II in shaping our understanding of the problem, see Gordon, *Statelessness and Contemporary Enslavement*, 22-29.
12. Arendt, *Origins of Totalitarianism*, 301-2.
13. Gordon, *Statelessness and Contemporary Enslavement*, 2.
14. Ibid., 19.
15. Wright, *Native Son*, 400. Subsequent references are cited parenthetically.
16. Foucault, *Discipline and Punish*, 82-83.
17. William Decker places Wright's fiction in a lineage of "fugitive slave narrative and its descendants, the postslave and neo-slave narrative" (*Geographies of Flight*, 1). Decker argues that even after emancipation, "flight pertains to the material and spiritual oppression of black Americans, and in both cases escape from oppression remains a work in progress," a motif that he traces forward through Wright, amongst others, into the contemporary (111). Similarly, Jane Anna Gordon argues that, for Wright, the key features of slavery and fugitivity continued after the nominal end of slavery ("Slavery Continued, Freedom Sought," 333, 339).
18. Baldwin, *Notes of a Native Son*, 21.
19. Schotland, "Breaking Out of the Rooster Coop," 16.
20. For example, see Sam Bluefarb, *Escape Motif in the American Novel*, 142.
21. Wright, "How 'Bigger' Was Born," 862, 863.
22. Arendt, *Origins of Totalitarianism*, 302.
23. Foucault, *Discipline and Punish*, 301.

24. Kihara, "'I Don't Own Any Property,'" 34.
25. Ibid.
26. Wright, *Man Who Lived Underground*, 138. Subsequent references are cited parenthetically.
27. Heise, *Urban Underworlds*, 142.
28. Dixon, *Black and White Cinema*, 51. See also 65 and 94.
29. Eldridge, *American Culture in the 1930s*, 68, 67. See also 56 as well as 49-53, which explicitly connects escapism in 1930s cinema to Wright through his criticisms of Zora Neale Hurston's *Their Eyes Were Watching God*.
30. McNallie, "Richard Wright's Allegory of the Cave," 77. See also Nash, "'Man Who Lived Underground,'" 62-74. Malcolm Wright likewise suggests this inversion in his afterword to the 2021 edition of the novel (Wright, *Man Who Lived Underground*, 215-16).
31. Wright, "Man Who Lived Underground," 561.
32. Ibid., 562.
33. Wright, "Memories of My Grandmother," 210.
34. Arendt, 286. For further explication of crime as an assertion of human belonging in *Native Son*, see Schillings, *Enemies of All Humankind*, 172.
35. Ibid.
36. Agamben, *Homo Sacer*, 8.
37. Taylor, "Political Subjection of Bigger Thomas," 184.
38. Baldwin, *Notes of a Native Son*, 41.
39. Ibid.
40. Ibid., 20.
41. Ibid., 23.
42. Kathleen Gallagher, qtd. in Kihara, "'I Don't Own Any Property,'" 46.
43. Kihara, "'I Don't Own Any Property,'" 46.
44. Wright, "How 'Bigger' was Born," 853.
45. Ibid.
46. Fabre, "Richard Wright," 178.
47. Balwin, *Notes of a Native Son*, 45.
48. Ibid., 163.
49. Ibid., 58.
50. Ibid., 866, 860.
51. The canonicity of such readings is indicated by their frequent inclusion in edited collections. See John Reilly's "Giving Bigger a Voice" and two essays collected in *Critical Essays on Richard Wright's Native Son*, edited by Keneth Kinnamon: James Miller's "Bigger Thomas's Quest for Voice and Audience," 119-25 (originally published in *Callaloo*), and James Nagel's "Images of 'Vision' in *Native Son*," 86-93.

More recently, this conversation has considered how Bigger's desire for inclusion intersects with Black masculinity. Aimé Ellis, for example, argues that "Bigger's deeply emotional conversations with his homeboys constitute a site of black male community" ("'Boys in the Hood,'" 184). In contrast, Kadeshia Matthews argues that "in attempting to escape the supposed No-Man's Land of blackness, Bigger has seized on a version of manhood premised on whiteness and therefore on the very othering and rejection that have been practiced against him" ("Black Boy No More," 294).

52. Lewis Gordon, "Wright's Afromodern Search for Political Freedom," 26.
53. Szalay, *New Deal Modernism*, 22.
54. In *Making Liberalism New*, Ian Afflerbach has recently strengthened the case for treating *Native Son* as contiguous with his successors in Ralph Ellison and James Baldwin, despite their explicit critique of what they saw as their mentor's complicity with problematic White liberalism (96–100). See also Schillings, *Enemies of All Humankind*, 168.
55. This is, of course, not to suggest that Wright's expatriation freed him from the state or from racism. As Jane Anna Gordon puts it, "Wright, the man and writer, could and did steal himself away from US unfreedom, but this fugitive status, for him, remained far short of a normative ideal of freedom," creating only a temporary "individual reprieve" ("Slavery Continued, Freedom Sought," 342). See also Decker, *Geographies of Flight*, 150–56 and 174.
56. Friedman, *Capitalism and Freedom*, 109.
57. Ibid., 110.
58. Afflerbach, *Making Liberalism New*, 86.
59. Clune argues that "the speaker's shining money prevents the other from taking the subject as the object of her gaze . . . I can see you but you can't see me. I am a subject who takes you as an object, and not vice versa" (*American Literature and the Free Market*, 128–29).
60. Thomas, *Pynchon and the Political*, 56.
61. Freer, *Thomas Pynchon and American Counterculture*, 85.
62. Mattessich, *Lines of Flight*, 3, 5.
63. Ibid., 185, 8.
64. O'Bryan, "Pynchon and New Political Activisms," 147.
65. Thomas, *Pynchon and the Political*, 110. See also 123.
66. Freer, *Thomas Pynchon and American Counterculture*, 8, 9. See also 17–21.
67. Pynchon, *V.*, 200. See Freer, *Thomas Pynchon and American Counterculture*, 21–22.
68. Daniel Grausam reads anti-representation in *Lot 49* as an attempt to grapple with the threat of nuclear annihilation, the erasure of all past and future representation, with nuclear war "less something to be represented than a challenge to representation itself" (*On Endings*, 57). While I think Grausam is right to

understand the absence of representation as potentially horrifying in Pynchon's work, I think he misses the ways in which representation itself likewise terrorizes and, moreover, how representation is never actually absent but, rather, frightfully unavoidable.
69. Pynchon, *Crying of Lot 49*, 170.
70. Greif, *Age of the Crisis of Man*, 248.
71. Pynchon, *The Crying of Lot 49*, 120.
72. Heise, for example, views the "paranoid fantasy of the Trystero conspiracy" as "an important ideological screen," an opiate that allows Oedipa to ignore her political reality (*Urban Underworlds*, 176). As a result, escape in the novel amounts to "an apolitical abandonment of ideological and territorial struggle" (207), what I have been calling escapism. See also Freer, *Thomas Pynchon and American Counterculture*, 22 and 32-35.
73. Thomas, *Pynchon and the Political*, 121.
74. Ibid.
75. See Thomas, *Pynchon and the Political*, 150; Freer, *Thomas Pynchon and American Counterculture*, 164-65; O'Bryan, "In Defense of *Vineland*," 20-23; Carswell, *Occupy Pynchon*, 7-8; and Grattan, *Hope Isn't Stupid*, 91-95 (but see also 73-79 for Grattan's relatively more hopeful reading of escape in *Lot 49*).
76. Pynchon, *Vineland*, 107, 306.
77. Pynchon, *Gravity's Rainbow*, 41. Subsequent references are cited parenthetically.
78. Freer, *Thomas Pynchon and American Counterculture*, 48, 49.
79. Herman and Weisenburger, *Gravity's Rainbow, Domination, and Freedom*, 142-43. On the connection to Agamben's *homo sacer*, see 144.
80. Ibid., 144.
81. Freer reads a more hopeful (albeit ambivalent) politics of psychedelics in *The Crying of Lot 49* (*Thomas Pynchon and American Counterculture*, 77), though she also notes Pynchon's critique of LSD escapism in his 1966 article "A Journey into the Mind of Watts" (80).
82. Ferlinghetti, *Coney Island of the Mind*, 57. For another point of connection between Pynchon and Ferlinghetti, see Freer, *Thomas Pynchon and American Counterculture*, 23.
83. For a summary of standard readings, see Herman and Weisenburger, *Gravity's Rainbow, Domination, and Freedom*, 200. At least partially in line with my reading of solipsism, Slothrop's scattering has been read as masturbatory (Freer, *Thomas Pynchon and American Counterculture*, 51), as social expulsion (Carswell, *Occupy Pynchon*, 12), as manifesting the *homo sacer* (Weisenburger, "In the Zone," 110), and as political apathy (Tabbi, "Pynchon's Groundward Art," 95).
84. Freer, *Thomas Pynchon and American Counterculture*, 63.
85. Ibid., 64.

86. Freer rightly observes how "Pynchon emphasises the importance of maintaining relationships with others, of love even" (86). Freer also very helpfully lays out the importance, via Huey P. Newton and the Black Panthers, of the concept of "revolutionary suicide" in *Gravity's Rainbow*; in the terms of that framework, Roger's social death after the Krupp dinner party appears as a "reactionary suicide," which, in contrast to revolutionary suicide's desperate attempt to push politics forward, is, rather, a fatalistic hopelessness (107).
87. On revolutionary lateness in Pynchon, see Herman and Weisenburger, *Gravity's Rainbow, Domination, and Freedom*, 215–21.
88. Freer, *Thomas Pynchon and American Counterculture*, 80.
89. McCann and Szalay, "Do You Believe in Magic," 442.
90. Ibid., 439.
91. Ibid., 447. See also O'Bryan, "In Defense of *Vineland*," 22.
92. Freer, *Thomas Pynchon and American Counterculture*, 37. Cf. Herman and Weisenburger, *Gravity's Rainbow, Domination, and Freedom*, 144–46; and Grattan, *Hope Isn't Stupid*, 99.
93. Molloy, "Escaping the Politics of the Irredeemable Earth."
94. O'Bryan, "Pynchon and New Political Activisms," 141.
95. Thomas, *Pynchon and the Political*, 152.
96. Grattan, *Hope Isn't Stupid*, 72.
97. Acker, *Empire of the Senseless*, 26. Subsequent references are cited parenthetically.
98. Fazal and Griffiths, "Membership Has Its Privileges," 81–83.
99. Krause, "Strategies of Counter-secession," 789.
100. Siegelberg, *Statelessness*, 225–27.
101. Fazal and Griffiths, "Membership Has Its Privileges," 97.
102. Krause, "Strategies of Counter-secession," 802.
103. Ibid., 792.

3. UNSTATE

1. Cummings, "dying is fine)but Death," 6.
2. Agamben, *State of Exception*, 73. See also 86–88.
3. DeLillo, *White Noise*, 6. Subsequent references appear parenthetically. For an alternative account of the dichotomy of deaths in *White Noise*, see Clare, *Fictions Inc.*, especially 116 and 126.
4. Didion, *Democracy*, 151–52. Subsequent references appear parenthetically.
5. Agamben, *Homo Sacer*, 164.
6. Although Agamben is mistaken in asserting that Quinlan's artificial respiration was ended "on the grounds that the girl was to be considered as already dead" (164) (the Supreme Court of New Jersey explicitly determined that Quinlan

did not meet standard criteria for brain death and therefore was not dead [*In re Quinlan*]), the case nevertheless affirmed legal and medical articulations of death. It is the state that decides life and death: if Quinlan *had* met the criteria, then she *would* have been dead already.

7. *Newsweek* published at least eleven stories on Quinlan between 1975 and 1984, and many others that referenced the case; the *New York Times* ran at least ten during the same period, and *Time* three more in 1975 and 1976. All three publications have notable cameos in *Democracy*.

8. Didion, "Case of Theresa Schiavo."

9. As Didion wryly notes, "it was perfectly clear that the elected officials in question were in fact trying to reap political benefit. On the other hand there was no novelty in this" ("Case of Theresa Schiavo"). For Didion, the problem is that such a case is political to begin with, even as she is no longer surprised by such pervasive politicization.

10. Didion, *Year of Magical Thinking*, 147–48.

11. Ibid., 202.

12. Ibid., 149–50.

13. Joseph Conte calls *White Noise* "a catalogue of the malaise of the Information Age" (*Design and Debris,* 113). It is worth noting that criticism on DeLillo's previous novel *The Names* (1982), where the Baudrillardian perspective is less overwhelming, tends to align more closely with my reading of *White Noise*. Working from distinct but compatible vocabularies and theoretical frameworks, Amy Hungerford ("Don DeLillo's Latin Mass"), Jacqueline Zubeck ("'The Surge and Pelt of Daily Life'"), and Heather Houser ("'A Presence Almost Everywhere'") each emphasize DeLillo's privileging of embodied knowledge, even knowledge that might exceed communication. Despite this common foundation, their interests differ significantly from mine; only Houser addresses the political implications in relation to the state, and there only briefly.

14. In *Tacit and Explicit Knowledge,* sociologist Harry Collins rightly emphasizes the inadequacy of the standard bike-riding example: the embodied knowledge of skills is only one narrow aspect of all that philosophers, economists, and sociologists have meant by tacit knowledge, which also includes knowledge that theoretically *could* be articulated but isn't for whatever reason (difficulty, apathy, etc.), as well as diffuse social knowledge that is ontologically inarticulable.

15. Polanyi, *Tacit Dimension,* 4.

16. See Jacobs and Mullins, "Friedrich Hayek and Michael Polanyi in Correspondence." For an account of Polanyi and Hayek's political and epistemological disagreements, see Mirowski, "Economics, Science, and Knowledge."

17. Hayek, "Use of Knowledge in Society," 522.

18. Ibid., 524.

19. Scott, *Seeing Like a State,* 315. See also 20–21, 81, and 292.

20. Scott's *mētis* tends to emphasize tacit knowledge as "know-how" in contrast to "know-what," but it's important to note that, for all of these thinkers, "know-how" does not fully encompass tacit knowledge, which can also include knowledge that is primarily situational or social. See, for example, Hayek's early essay "Economics and Knowledge."
21. Williams, *Recognizable Image*, 106-7.
22. Hayek, *Fatal Conceit*, 84.
23. Scott, *Seeing Like a State*, 24. See also 76-77 and 87-90.
24. See Foucault, *Discipline and Punish*, 136-38 and 142-43. Biman Basu reads this scene, and the novel as a whole, via Taylorist strategies of efficiency ("Reading the Techno-ethnic Other"). While *White Noise*'s critiques of articulated knowledge certainly apply to Taylorism, I extend them beyond the narrowly economic.
25. The warning label requirement was lifted in 2001 after new research showed that saccharin posed no cancer risk in humans. See Richard Lyons, "F.D.A. Banning Saccharin Use on Cancer Links," *New York Times*, March 10, 1977, and Elena Conis, "Saccharin's Mostly Sweet Following," *Los Angeles Times*, December 27, 2010.
26. In addition to Conte's *Design and Debris*, see Frow, "Last Things before the Last"; Wilcox, "Baudrillard, DeLillo's *White Noise*, and the End of Heroic Narrative"; and Duvall, "(Super)marketplace of Image." More recently, Ralph Clare has turned to Baudrillard to outline the novel's critique of pharmaceutical corporations, with drug advertisements functioning as noise in the stream of diagnostic medical information (*Fictions Inc.*, 115-35). Likewise, while Daniel Grausam is attuned to "unspeakability" and "the untellable" (*On Endings*, 106) in DeLillo's earlier novel *End Zone* (1972), he nevertheless reads *White Noise* as a Baudrillardian tale of how media noise obscures reality (105).
27. Foucault, *Discipline and Punish*, 196.
28. DeLillo, *Libra*, 21-22.
29. DeLillo, *Underworld*, 60. Subsequent references are cited parenthetically.
30. Grausam, *On Endings*, 111-12.
31. Ibid., 151.
32. Ibid., 112.
33. Mackey, *From a Broken Bottle*, 51.
34. Ibid., 65.
35. Ibid., 73.
36. Jameson, *Archaeologies of the Future*, 16.
37. For a useful cultural history of *Frogger*'s origin and reception, see Horowitz, *Sega Arcade Revolution*, 36-42.
38. Fassone, *Every Game Is an Island*, 67-68.
39. Ibid., 65.

40. Nadel, *Containment Culture*, 277.
41. For example, see Tager, "Political Vision of Joan Didion's *Democracy*"; Hepburn, *Intrigue;* and Parrish, "After Henry Adams."
42. Mary McCarthy, "Love and Death in the Pacific," *New York Times*, April 22, 1984.
43. Didion, "White Album," 38-39.
44. Ibid., 40.
45. Ibid., 11-12.
46. Ibid., 12.
47. Ibid.
48. Ibid., 13.
49. Ibid.
50. McCann and Szalay, "'Eerie Serenity,'" 150.
51. Agamben, *Homo Sacer*, 28-29.
52. Parrish, "After Henry Adams," 181.
53. Szalay, *Hip Figures*, 257.
54. Ibid., 260.
55. Ibid., 252.
56. Hepburn, *Intrigue*, 266-67.
57. McCann and Szalay, "'Eerie Serenity,'" 152.
58. Szalay, *Hip Figures*, 268. As John McClure rightfully points out in a response to McCann and Szalay's "Do You Believe in Magic," the "political naïveté and magical thinking" they find in post-sixties fiction is pervasive in "the traditional political culture which McCann and Szalay defend" ("Do They Believe in Magic," 138).
59. Didion, "White Album," 13.
60. Phelan and Rabinowitz, "Narrative as Rhetoric," 3.
61. Richardson, "Antimimetic, Unnatural, and Postmodern Narrative Theory," 20.
62. Richard Levesque argues along these lines, while also gesturing towards the political implications of such a postmodernist narrative practice: "the effect of such a strategy is the dissemination rather than the centralization of authority, each reader of a mass-produced text functioning as his/her own authority" ("Telling Postmodern Tales," 85). While Levesque helpfully analyzes many of Didion's formal devices to this end, he too readily accepts that Didion succeeds. As we will see, Didion subverts her own resistance to narrative as a way of acknowledging just how entrenched centralized authority remains.
63. Stout, *Strategies of Reticence*, 182.
64. Ibid., 183.
65. Agamben, *State of Exception*, 87, 88.
66. Ong, *Neoliberalism as Exception*, 3.
67. Harvey, *Brief History*, 106.

68. Ibid., 19.
69. Ong, *Neoliberalism as Exception,* 10.
70. Hayek, *Individualism,* 8, 11.
71. Ibid., 110.

4. ESCAPE POLITICS AFTER THE TRANSNATIONAL TURN IN KAREN TEI YAMASHITA AND JUNOT DÍAZ

1. Hardt and Negri, *Empire,* 336.
2. Ibid., 349.
3. Hart and Hansen, "Introduction," 502.
4. Ibid., 506.
5. Hart, *Extraterritorial,* 6.
6. Du Bois, *Souls of Black Folk,* 10.
7. Grattan, "Reading Richard Wright beyond the Carceral State," 312, 323.
8. Jameson, *Archaeologies of the Future,* 283. This is in the same register as Jameson's reference to the now oft-repeated bromide "that it is easier to imagine the end of the world than the end of capitalism" (199). For an interesting history of the origins and transmission of this "unattributable truism," see Grattan, *Hope Isn't Stupid,* 8.
9. Rody, "Transnational Imagination," 134.
10. Yamashita, *Tropic of Orange,* 132. Subsequent references are cited parenthetically.
11. Adams, "Ends of America," 250. Rody likewise reads *Tropic of Orange* as paradigmatic of the transnational turn in Asian American literature ("Transnational Imagination," 132).
12. Tekdemir, "Post-frontier and Re-definition of Space," 103–6. See also Rody, "Transnational Imagination," 134.
13. Sue-Im Lee is representative of critical attitudes when she credits Arcangel with "unmistakable authority" in the novel (*Body of Individuals,* 59).
14. See Lee, *Body of Individuals,* 82; Sadowski-Smith, *Border Fictions,* 66–67; Vint, "Orange County," 407; and Crawford, "From Desert Dust to City Soot," 96.
15. Levi, "Sport and Melodrama," 57.
16. See note 14 above.
17. Sadowski-Smith, *Border Fictions,* 67.
18. Ibid.
19. Ibid.
20. Tekdemir, "Post-frontier and Re-definition of Space," 109. Tekdemir's logic is that political borders are necessary to eliminate the economic borders resulting from globalization.

21. See Tekdemir, "Magical Realism in the Peripheries of the Metropolis," 47–48; Adams, "Ends of America," 259; and Vint, "Orange County," 404.
22. Mermann-Jozwiak, "Yamashita's Post-national Spaces," 5–6.
23. Harley, *New Nature of Maps,* 53.
24. Mermann-Jozwiak, "Yamashita's Post-national Spaces," 6. See also Vint, "Orange County," 404.
25. Harley, *New Nature of Maps,* 57. For a similar account of maps as tools of statecraft, see Scott, *Seeing Like a State,* especially 24, 55, and 87.
26. Crawford, "From Desert Dust to City Soot," 92.
27. See Mermann-Jozwiak, "Yamashita's Post-national Spaces," 3; Vint, "Orange County," 404; and Adams, "Ends of America," 259.
28. Yamashita, "Latitude of the Fiction Writer."
29. Ibid.
30. Eder, Rybicki, and Kestemont, "Stylometry with R." Figures 7–10 also use the R packages "dendextend" (Galili) and "circlize" (Gu et. al). Other than the different MFW values, the cluster analyses generating figures 7–10 all use the same standard parameters: word 1-grams with no culling or sampling, classic Delta distance.
31. Eder, "Visualization in Stylometry," 52.
32. For more on how consensus trees combine multiple dendrograms and how "stylo" approaches this, see Eder, "Visualization in Stylometry," 55–60. For the sake of readability, the consensus tree in figure 11 collapses each group of seven chapters per character into a single text, comparing each of those seven character texts to each other and to the novel as a whole, iterating over a range of 25 to 200 MFW values in increments of 25, using the same parameters described in note 30 above and the standard consensus strength of 0.5.
33. As Ursula Heise observes, the desire to purge transnational multiculturalism of transnational trade works "to occlude any consideration of how transnational cultural encounters might be related to and, in quite a few cases, causally dependent on economic globalization" ("Ecocriticism and the Transnational Turn in American Studies," 399–400).
34. Ramón Saldívar, "Imagining Cultures," 3.
35. Though Ramón Saldívar accepts "views emphasizing the persistence of state national power, [he] maintain[s] that the transnational spaces we see developing around the globe today also emphasize the limits of national power" ("Imagining Cultures," 9–10).
36. Scott, *Seeing Like a State,* 261.
37. Ibid., 270.
38. Díaz, *Brief Wondrous Life of Oscar Wao,* 149. Subsequent references are cited parenthetically.
39. José Saldívar, "Conjectures on 'Americanity,'" 132.

40. Rowling, *Harry Potter and the Sorcerer's Stone,* 298.
41. Quoted in Hanna, Harford Vargas, and Saldívar, "Junot Díaz and the Decolonial Imagination," 14.
42. Hanna, "'Reassembling the Fragments,'" 503-4. See also Irr, *Toward the Geopolitical Novel,* 37-39; Graulund, "Generous Exclusion," 35-37; González, *Reading Junot Díaz,* 58; Dávila, "Against the 'Discursive Latino,'" 44; and Harford Vargas, *Forms of Dictatorship,* 57-58.
43. José Saldívar, "Conjectures on 'Americanity,'" 133.
44. Dávila, "Against the 'Discursive Latino,'" 38.
45. Ibid., 42.
46. McHugh-Dillon, "'Let Me Confess,'" 25, 40.
47. Initial media coverage of the controversy often raised this possibility; see Christie D'Zurilla's article, "Acclaimed Author Junot Díaz Accused of Sexual Misconduct and 'Virulent Misogyny,'" *Los Angeles Times,* May 4, 2018. Colleen Flaherty provides a thorough overview of the controversy, including a letter to the editor (as well as subsequent rebuttals) in the *Chronicle of Higher Education,* signed by a number of well-known feminist scholars, that criticized the discourse surrounding the controversy and offered some qualified support of Díaz ("Junot Díaz, Feminism and Ethnicity," *Inside Higher Ed,* May 29, 2018).
48. McHugh-Dillon implicitly reads "Silence" as a preemptive public apology rather than a trauma narrative, approaching it specifically as a "confession," prioritizing what Díaz did rather than what was done to him. While I agree that, as a public apology, the essay would be deeply inadequate, it's not clear that apology is the essay's rhetorical aim. "Silence," of course, was published before the public accusations, and while it does include apologetic language, it does not, at least on the surface, rhetorically position itself as an attempt to right personal wrongs but rather as an attempt to represent erased sexual violence—in keeping with Díaz's long project to fill in the silences.
49. McHugh-Dillon, "'Let Me Confess,'" 41.
50. Hanna, "'Reassembling the Fragments,'" 509.
51. Ibid.
52. Spahr, *Du Bois's Telegram,* 147.
53. Ibid., 148.
54. Dávila, "Against the 'Discursive Latino,'" 46.
55. Irr, *Toward the Geopolitical Novel,* 38-39.
56. Harford Vargas, *Forms of Dictatorship,* 37.
57. The only other characters to receive such allusive praise are Beli's aunt and adoptive mother, La Inca (Tolkien's Galadriel), and Yunior himself (*The Fantastic Four*'s Uatu the Watcher).
58. José Saldívar, "Conjectures on 'Americanity,'" 133.

59. Díaz, "Silence."
60. For one such Fanonian mask, see Díaz, *Oscar Wao*, 34.
61. Díaz, "Silence."
62. Sometimes the blank face also stands in for the anonymity of power, as in Foucault's account of the panopticon. See Díaz, *Oscar Wao* 141, 220, 297–99, and 322.
63. Oscar's childhood girlfriend Olga reminds us of the pragmatism of masks when she doesn't wear one: "she tried to rob the local Safeway . . . hadn't bothered to wear a mask even though everybody at the supermarket knew her—and there was talk that she was still in Middlesex, wouldn't be getting out until they were all fifty" (Díaz, *Oscar Wao*, 266).
64. Díaz, *Drown*, 7.
65. Ibid., 15.
66. Ibid., 156.
67. Ibid., 155, 160.
68. For a compelling reading of the variously oppressive and liberatory roles of jokes in *Oscar Wao* (including this one), see Di Iorio, "Laughing through a Broken Mouth."
69. Díaz, "Search for Decolonial Love," in Hanna, Harford Vargas, and Saldívar, *Junot Díaz and the Decolonial Imagination*, 397–98.
70. Díaz, "Silence."
71. José Saldívar, "Conjectures on 'Americanity,'" 131.
72. Ramón Saldívar, "Historical Fantasy, Speculative Realism, and Postrace Aesthetic," 576.
73. Alexander Starre delineates contemporary fiction's "metamediality," its self-aware exploitation of the book's materiality, in readings of Danielewski, Plascencia, and others (*Metamedia*, 8).
74. Harford Vargas, *Forms of Dictatorship*, 44.
75. Díaz, "Fiction Is the Poor Man's Cinema," 902.
76. Díaz, "Search for Decolonial Love," 399.
77. On Díaz's attention to sexuality, specifically, as a site of state power, see Stringer, "Passing and the State."
78. Mermann-Jozwiak, "Beyond Multiculturalism," 3, 7.
79. Ibid., 7.
80. Yamashita, interview by Jean Vengua Gier and Carla Alicia Tejeda.
81. Dávila, "Against the 'Discursive Latino,'" 46.
82. Díaz, interview by Hilton Als, 35.
83. Dávila, "Against the 'Discursive Latino,'" 46.
84. Walter Benn Michaels, "Let Them Eat Diversity," interview by Bhaskar Sunkara, *Jacobin*, January 1, 2011.

5. BEYOND PROTEST

1. Sarah Igo's *The Averaged American,* a history of the mid-century development of the mass survey and public opinion poll, emphasizes how such articulations have served to strengthen a stable national identity, providing a "national glue" (6) and helping create the kind of imagined community Benedict Anderson saw holding together modern nation-states (21).
2. Hirschman, *Exit, Voice, and Loyalty,* 4.
3. Ibid., 30.
4. Kukathas, *Liberal Archipelago,* 96.
5. Hirschman, *Exit, Voice, and Loyalty,* 33.
6. Ibid., 86. See also 122–23.
7. Baldwin, *Notes of a Native Son,* 20.
8. Old-school graffiti writers and purists will, not without justification, insist that illegality is a defining characteristic of graffiti; once it's legal, it's not graffiti anymore but street art. Of course, it's then also possible to read Banksy's piece as less self-referential and more homage: his legal-ish street art won't change anything, but illegal graff still might. For more on these issues, see the graffiti special issue of *Rhizomes,* no. 25 (2013), especially Jeff Ferrell's "The Underbelly Project" and Gabriel Soldatenko's "The Politics of Writing on Walls."
9. Most legal disputes around Banksy's works now involve not the legality of his actions but disagreements over who legally owns the finished work—the property owner, the government, or Banksy himself (and, most recently, whether Banksy can enforce trademark on his work while remaining anonymous). For example, see Salib, "Law of Banksy."

    If Graffiti Changed Anything went up in April 2011 in London's Fitzrovia neighborhood and remained untouched—except by time and other graffiti writers—until November 2015, when the City of Westminster approved a development plan to demolish the building that hosted the piece. Shortly after, construction fences were placed around the building, blocking the piece from public view, and by 2019 the building had been completely demolished, clearing the way for new luxury apartments in 2022. The digital timeline on Google Street View at the intersection of Clipstone Street and Cleveland Street in London provides a telling visual history of the building and Banksy's piece. In any case, for four years *If Graffiti* seems not to have crossed the law in any meaningful way, despite its apparent taunt.
10. See Adam Gabbatt, "New York Graffiti Artists Triumph over Developer Who Destroyed Their Work," *The Guardian,* November 9, 2017, and Alan Feuer, "Graffiti Artists Awarded $6.7 Million for Destroyed 5Pointz Murals," *New York Times,* Feb. 12, 2018.

11. Will Ellsworth-Jones, *Banksy: The Man behind the Wall: Revised and Illustrated Edition* (London: Frances Lincoln, 2021), 76.
12. See "Banksy Confirms Escaping Prisoner Artwork at Reading Prison," *BBC News*, March 4, 2021.
13. Banksy (@banksy), Instagram video, March 4, 2021, https://www.instagram.com/p/CMAHrGPFV2V/.
14. Warner, *Publics and Counterpublics*, 57. In recent critical work, Spahr appears deeply skeptical that such communities can be politically meaningful, even as she nevertheless sees literature as capable of producing them (*Du Bois's Telegram*, 13).
15. Spahr, *things of each possible relation*, 16.
16. This contemporary understanding of open form goes beyond Olson's understanding; Olson's emphasis, via the typewriter, on a rigidly reproducible experience of the poem works to eliminate readerly indeterminacy. As Mark Byers puts it, Olson's "spatial approximation of the stave and bar was explicitly meant to rule out interference on the reader's part ... these ostensibly 'open' works had to be more controlled than their 'closed' predecessors" ("Egocentric Predicaments," 65–66). Since the impact of language poetry, however, open form has come to be equated with indeterminacy, as later poets focused on Olson's "kinetics" and "process" while largely ignoring his insistence on the rigidity of the typewriter. See chapter 1, note 91.
17. Spahr, *things of each possible relation*, 17.
18. Spahr identifies "structural issues" in literary production, including especially indirect and direct reliance on the state (*Du Bois's Telegram*, 5).
19. Lerner, *Hatred of Poetry*, 37.
20. Ibid., 41.
21. Spahr, *This Connection*, 22. Subsequent references will be cited parenthetically.
22. On states constructing and wielding sexual identity, see Canaday, *Straight State*, and Cerretti, *Abuses of the Erotic*.
23. Spahr, *Well Then There Now*, 151. Subsequent references will be cited parenthetically.
24. Ong, *Neoliberalism as Exception*, 101.
25. Ibid.
26. Cerretti, *Abuses of the Erotic*, 27.
27. Spahr equates "resistance" explicitly with opposition to the state, with being "antagonistic in some way to some part of the nation-state" (*Du Bois's Telegram*, 14).
28. Spahr, "Connected Disconnection," 76.
29. See also Spahr's sonnet beginning "We arrived and everything was interconnected" (*Well Then There Now*, 28–29).
30. Graeber, *Fragments of an Anarchist Anthropology*, 77.

31. Spahr, "Connected Disconnection," 78.
32. Spahr, *Du Bois's Telegram*, 143.
33. Spahr, *Fuck You-Aloha-I Love You*, 64.
34. Ibid., 72.
35. Ibid., 73.
36. DeLillo, *White Noise*, 303.
37. Spahr, *Du Bois's Telegram*, 188.
38. Spahr, "New World Sonnet."
39. Cohn, *Underground Passages*, 145.
40. Leong, *Contested Records*, 9.
41. Ibid., 1.
42. Ibid., 15.
43. "Exit Does Not Exist," track 13 on Modest Mouse, *This Is a Long Drive for Someone with Nothing to Think About*, Up Records, 1996, compact disc.
44. Ibid.
45. "Tiny Cities Made of Ashes," track 5 on Modest Mouse, *The Moon and Antarctica*, Epic Records, 2000, compact disc.
46. "Float On," track 3 on Modest Mouse, *Good News*.
47. "The World at Large," track 2 on Modest Mouse, *Good News*.
48. Smith, "Formal Negativities," 446.
49. "The World at Large," track 2 on Modest Mouse, *Good News*.
50. Ibid.
51. Mackey, *Discrepant Engagement*, 123.
52. Conte, *Unending Design*, 24.
53. Mackey, *Splay Anthem*, ix. Subsequent references will be cited parenthetically. In quotations of Mackey, all ellipses are Mackey's except those set in brackets, which indicate my omissions.
54. See note 16, above.
55. Mackey, "Atmosphere Is Alive," 153.
56. Mackey, interview by Jeanne Heuving, 225.
57. Scott, *Seeing Like a State*, 1.
58. Ibid.
59. Scott, *Art of Not Being Governed*, 122.
60. Mackey, *Discrepant Engagement*, 65.
61. In an interview with Jeanne Heuving, Mackey explains, "it's not unusual for an artistic medium to be used as a synecdoche for a culture, to exemplify a particular cultural disposition or identity ... An artistic medium isn't only an aspect of culture but a culture in and of itself, or at least comparable to one" (227).
62. Mackey, *Discrepant Engagement*, 106, 123.

63. Whereas Olson's spirals often move inward, "to new centers," as he puts it in the graphically spiraling poem "<u>Migration</u> in fact...," Mackey's spirals almost always evoke an outward trajectory.
64. Anastasopoulos, "Resisting the Law," 784.
65. Ibid., 791.
66. Ibid., 792.
67. Mackey, *From a Broken Bottle*, 66.
68. Mackey, *Discrepant Engagement*, 125.
69. Zamsky, "Poetics of Radical Musicality," 116.
70. Wright, *Native Son*, 242.
71. Finkelstein, "Nathaniel Mackey and the Unity of All Rites," 29.
72. Ibid.
73. Reed, *Freedom Time*, 188.
74. Mackey, interview with Jeanne Heuving, 215.
75. Ibid., 220.
76. Mackey, "Atmosphere Is Alive," 156-57.
77. Ibid., 157.
78. Mackey, *Discrepant Engagement*, 65.
79. Cage, *Anarchy*, v-vi.
80. For a similar argument applied to one of Cage's happenings, see Charles Junkerman's "Modeling Anarchy."
81. Cage, *Anarchy*, viii.
82. Ibid.
83. Ibid., vi.
84. Mackey, "Atmosphere Is Alive," 153.
85. Mackey, interview with Jeanne Heuving, 214. Mackey echoes William Carlos Williams here: "In poetry, you're listening to two things... you're listening to the sense, the common sense of what it says. But it says more. That is the difficulty" (Williams, *Paterson*, 222).
86. Mackey, *Discrepant Engagement*, 252-53.
87. Ibid., 274.
88. Spahr, *Du Bois's Telegram*, 194.
89. Stout, *Journey Narrative in American Literature*, 31.
90. Dowland, *Weak Nationalisms*, 5. See also 10-11.
91. Spahr, *Du Bois's Telegram*, 12.
92. Hirschman, *Exit, Voice, and Loyalty*, 79.
93. Ibid., 120.
94. Ibid., 76.
95. Ibid., 113.

CONCLUSION

1. Gabriel Soldatenko argues for a political understanding of "graffiti as a tool for building community" ("Politics of Writing on Walls," par. 1). Jeff Ferrell, in turn, explores and documents the "Underbelly Project," a massive "collective art project" of over one hundred street artists and graffiti writers working illicitly in an "abandoned subway station" under New York City ("Underbelly Project," par. 3). As a *New York Times* article on the project notes, it "goes to extremes to avoid being part of the art world, and even the world in general" (qtd. in Ferrell, "Underbelly Project," par. 3).
2. Banksy, *Exit through the Gift Shop*.
3. Anthony Lane, "Street Justice: 'Kick-Ass' and 'Exit through the Gift Shop,'" *New Yorker*, April 19, 2010.
4. For example, see Julian Sancton, "Shepard Fairey Swears to God the Banksy Movie Is Not a Hoax," *Vanity Fair*, April 16, 2010.
5. Scott Reyburn, "Banksy Painting Self-Destructs after Fetching $1.4 Million at Sotheby's," *New York Times*, October 6, 2018.
6. Tessa Solomon, "Banksy's Self-Destructing Painting Sells for Record-Breaking $25.3 M. at Sotheby's," *ARTnews*, October 14, 2021.
7. Melena Ryzik, "Riddle? Yes. Enigma? Sure. Documentary?," *The New York Times*, April 13, 2010.
8. Harry Cheadle, "Atlas Mugged: How a Libertarian Paradise in Chile Fell Apart," *Vice*, September 22, 2014.
9. Peter Thiel, "The Education of a Libertarian," *Cato Unbound*, April 13, 2009.
10. Ian MacDougall and Isabelle Simpson, "A Libertarian 'Startup City' in Honduras Faces Its Biggest Hurdle: The Locals," *Rest of World*, October 5, 2021.
11. Amy Gunia, "An American-Thai Couple Are in Deep Water over Their Attempt to Establish a Community at Sea," *Time*, April 18, 2019.
12. Hart, *Extraterritorial*, 4–5.
13. Ong, *Neoliberalism as Exception*, 19. See also 98–101.
14. Jagoda, "Videogame Criticism," 205.
15. Felan Parker provides a compelling history and analysis of these discourses in "Roger Ebert and the Games-as-Art Debate."
16. Parker, "Canonizing Bioshock," 746.
17. See Parker, "Canonizing Bioshock," 740, and Gibbons, "Wrap Your Troubles in Dreams."
18. Parker, "Canonizing Bioshock," 743.
19. Schmeink, *Biopunk Dystopias*, 149.
20. Gibbons, "Wrap Your Troubles in Dreams."
21. See Schmeink for a compelling reading of the game's moral "dilemma" over whether to rescue the Little Sisters (*Biopunk Dystopias*, 168).

22. Schmeink, *Biopunk Dystopias*, 150.
23. Ibid., 165.
24. Dyer-Witheford and de Peuter, *Games of Empire*, 196.
25. Schmeink, *Biopunk Dystopias*, 152.
26. Ibid., 150, 153-54.
27. Gibbons, "Wrap Your Troubles in Dreams."
28. Thus far, all dialog that I have quoted comes from scripted events within the game, which allows for no feasible form of direct citation. However, many of the subsequent quotations come from in-game "audio diaries," each with their own title, which the player can choose to play (and replay) at any point after discovering them. While I have taken all of my quotations directly from the game, the text of these audio diaries is also readily available online on numerous websites, such as community-run wikis. So, for ease of reference, I include here the titles of respective audio diary entries, where applicable. This quotation comes from the "Watch Fontaine" audio diary.
29. "Death Penalty in Rapture" audio diary.
30. "Have My Badge" audio diary.
31. "The Market Is Patient" audio diary.
32. "Ryan Takes F Futuristics" audio diary.
33. Schmeink, *Biopunk Dystopias*, 148.
34. Grant Tavinor draws on behavioral economics to conceptualize how games create "the illusion that gamers really are choosing their own actions" by nudging player decisions, "by guiding rather than coercing the player through a game environment" ("Bioshock and the Art of Rapture," 101).
35. Ibid., 104.
36. "Meeting with Fontaine" audio diary. For a complimentary reading of this cutscene, see also Schmeink, *Biopunk Dystopias*, 176-77.
37. Schmeink, *Biopunk Dystopias*, 175.
38. Ibid., 160.
39. Ibid., 175.
40. Fassone, *Every Game Is an Island*, 15.
41. Ibid., 16.
42. For a case that the EU is a supranational state, see Jeremy Richardson's "Supranational State Building in the European Union." While Richardson is proposing a new conception of the state defined by the policymaking function rather than the Weberian monopoly on legitimate violence at the basis of my understanding of the state in this book, he nevertheless observes that "the EU has acquired for itself a kind of 'surrogate legitimate use of coercion' by relying on the considerable powers of national courts," a mediation that functions as "the EU velvet glove which hides the mailed fist of the 'strict legal norms'" (9). This would suggest that Brexit has been so contentious, in part, precisely because it

threatens the EU's sovereignty as a supranational state. This question of sovereignty is indeed exactly how Richardson updates his argument after Brexit; see his article "Brexit."

43. "Banksy: Devolved Parliament Back on Show at Bristol Museum," *BBC News*, March 28, 2019.
44. Banksy (@banksy), "I made this ten years ago. Bristol museum have just put it back on display to mark Brexit day," Instagram photo, March 28, 2019, https://www.instagram.com/p/BvjkJdvliZ7/.
45. For a summary of this position attributing Brexit to conservative populism, see Richardson, "Brexit," 118–19.

BIBLIOGRAPHY

Acker, Kathy. *Empire of the Senseless.* New York: Grove Press, 1988.
Adams, Rachel. "The Ends of America, the Ends of Postmodernism." *Twentieth-Century Literature* 53, no. 3 (2007): 248–72.
Afflerbach, Ian. *Making Liberalism New: American Intellectuals, Modern Literature, and the Rewriting of a Political Tradition.* Baltimore: Johns Hopkins University Press, 2021.
Agamben, Giorgio. *Homo Sacer: Sovereign Power and Bare Life.* Translated by Daniel Heller-Roazen. Stanford: Stanford University Press, 1998.
———. *State of Exception.* Translated by Kevin Attell. Chicago: University of Chicago Press, 2005.
Althusser, Louis. "Ideology and Ideological State Apparatuses (Notes towards an Investigation)." In *Lenin and Philosophy and Other Essays,* translated by Ben Brewster, 85–126. New York: Monthly Review Press, 2001.
Anastasopoulos, Dimitri. "Resisting the Law: Nathaniel Mackey's *Djbot Baghostus's Run.*" *Callaloo* 23, no. 2 (2000): 784–95.
Anderson, Perry. *The Origins of Postmodernity.* London: Verso, 1998.
Antliff, Allan. *Anarchist Modernism: Art, Politics, and the First American Avant-Garde.* Chicago: University of Chicago Press, 2001.
Arendt, Hannah. *The Origins of Totalitarianism.* 1951. New York: Harcourt Brace, 1973.
Ashton, Jennifer. *From Modernism to Postmodernism: American Poetry and Theory in the Twentieth Century.* New York: Cambridge University Press, 2005.
Baldwin, James. *Notes of a Native Son.* Boston: Beacon Press, 1955.
Banksy, dir. *Exit through the Gift Shop.* 2010; London: Paranoid Pictures.
Basu, Biman. "Reading the Techno-ethnic Other in Don DeLillo's *White Noise.*" *Arizona Quarterly* 61, no. 2 (2005): 87–111.
Baudrillard, Jean. *Simulacra and Simulation.* Translated by Sheila Faria Glaser. Ann Arbor: University of Michigan Press, 1994.

Bernstein, Charles. *All the Whiskey in Heaven.* New York: Farrar, Straus, and Giroux, 2010.

Best, Stephen, and Sharon Marcus. "Surface Reading: An Introduction." *Representations* 108, no. 1 (2009): 1–21.

Billitteri, Carla. "William Carlos Williams and the Politics of Form." *Journal of Modern Literature* 30, no. 2 (2007): 42–63.

Bluefarb, Sam. *The Escape Motif in the American Novel: Mark Twain to Richard Wright.* Columbus: Ohio State University Press, 1972.

Borchers, Dagmar, and Annamari Vitikainen. "On Exit: Idea, Context, Topics and Open Questions." In *On Exit: Interdisciplinary Perspectives on the Right of Exit in Liberal Multicultural Societies,* edited by Dagmar Borchers and Annamari Vitikainen, 1–12. Boston: De Gruyter, 2012.

Brouillette, Sarah. *UNESCO and the Fate of the Literary.* Stanford: Stanford University Press, 2019.

Butterick, George F. *Editing "The Maximus Poems."* Storrs: University of Connecticut Library, 1983.

———. *A Guide to "The Maximus Poems" of Charles Olson.* Berkeley: University of California Press, 1978.

Byers, Mark. *Charles Olson and American Modernism: The Practice of the Self.* Oxford: Oxford University Press, 2018.

———. "Egocentric Predicaments: Charles Olson and the New York School of Music." *Journal of Modern Literature* 37, no. 4 (2014): 54–69.

———. "Imagining Uncertainty: Charles Olson and Karl Popper." *Philosophy and Literature* 39, no. 2 (2015): 443–58.

Cage, John. *Anarchy.* Middletown: Wesleyan University Press, 1988.

Canaday, Margot. *The Straight State: Sexuality and Citizenship in Twentieth-Century America.* Princeton: Princeton University Press, 2009.

Carswell, Sean. *Occupy Pynchon: Politics after "Gravity's Rainbow."* Athens: University of Georgia Press, 2017.

Cerretti, Josh. *Abuses of the Erotic: Militarizing Sexuality in the Post–Cold War United States.* Lincoln: University of Nebraska Press, 2019.

Cheah, Pheng. "The Biopolitics of Recognition: Making Female Subjects of Globalization." In *Theory Aside,* edited by Jason Potts and Daniel Stout, 117–42. Durham: Duke University Press, 2014.

Chisholm, Diane. "Juliana Spahr's Ecopoetics: Ecologies and Politics of the Refrain." *Contemporary Literature* 55, no. 1 (2014): 118–47.

Clare, Ralph. *Fictions Inc.* New Brunswick: Rutgers University Press, 2014.

Clune, Michael W. *American Literature and the Free Market, 1945–2000.* New York: Cambridge University Press, 2010.

———. "Beyond Realism." In *Reading Capitalist Realism,* edited by Alison Shonkwiler and Leigh Claire La Berge, 195–212. Iowa City: University of Iowa Press, 2014.

———. "Formalism as the Fear of Ideas." *PMLA* 132, no. 5 (2017): 1194-99.
Cohen, Milton A. *Beleaguered Poets and Leftist Critics: Stevens, Cummings, Frost, and Williams in the 1930s.* Tuscaloosa: University of Alabama Press, 2010.
Cohen, Samuel. *After the End of History: American Fiction in the 1990s.* Iowa City: University of Iowa Press, 2009.
Cohn, Jesse. *Underground Passages: Anarchist Resistance Culture, 1848-2011.* Oakland: AK Press, 2015.
Collins, Harry. *Tacit and Explicit Knowledge.* Chicago: University Of Chicago Press, 2010.
Collis, Stephen. *Through Words of Others: Susan Howe and Anarcho-Scholasticism.* Victoria: English Literary Studies, 2006.
Collis, Stephen, and Jordan Scott. *Decomp.* Toronto: Coach House, 2013.
Conte, Joseph. *Design and Debris: A Chaotics of Postmodern Fiction.* Tuscaloosa: University of Alabama Press, 2002.
———. *Unending Design: The Forms of Postmodern Poetry.* Ithaca: Cornell University Press, 1991.
Crawford, Chiyo. "From Desert Dust to City Soot: Environmental Justice and Japanese American Internment in Karen Tei Yamashita's *Tropic of Orange.*" *MELUS: Multi-ethnic Literature of the United States* 38, no. 3 (2013): 86-106.
Cummings, E. E. "dying is fine)but Death." In *Xaipe*, 6. 1950. New York: Liveright, 1979.
Dávila, Arlene. "Against the 'Discursive Latino': On the Politics and Praxis of Junot Díaz's Latinidad." In *Junot Díaz and the Decolonial Imagination,* edited by Monica Hanna, Jennifer Harford Vargas, and José David Saldívar, 33-48. Durham: Duke University Press, 2016.
Decker, William. *Geographies of Flight: Phillis Wheatley to Octavia Butler.* Evanston: Northwestern University Press, 2020.
DeLillo, Don. *Libra.* 1988. New York: Penguin, 2006.
———. *Underworld.* New York: Scribner, 1997.
———. *White Noise.* New York: Viking, 1985.
Dewey, Anne Day. *Beyond Maximus: The Construction of Public Voice in Black Mountain Poetry.* Stanford: Stanford University Press, 2007.
Díaz, Junot. *The Brief Wondrous Life of Oscar Wao.* New York: Riverhead Books, 2007.
———. *Drown.* New York: Riverhead Books, 1996.
———. "Fiction Is the Poor Man's Cinema: An Interview with Junot Díaz." By Diógenes Céspedes and Silvio Torres-Saillant. *Callaloo* 23, no. 3 (2000): 892-907.
———. Interview by Hilton Als. In *Upstairs at the Strand: Writers in Conversation at the Legendary Bookstore,* edited by Jessica Strand and Andrea Aguilar, 15-38. New York: Norton, 2016.
———. "The Silence: The Legacy of Childhood Trauma." *New Yorker,* April 16, 2018.

Dickinson, Emily. *The Poems of Emily Dickinson.* Edited by R. W. Franklin. Cambridge: Belknap, 1999.

Didion, Joan. "The Case of Theresa Schiavo." *New York Review of Books,* June 9, 2005.

———. *Democracy.* 1984. New York: Vintage International, 1995.

———. "The White Album." In *The White Album,* 11–48. New York: Simon and Schuster, 1979.

———. *The Year of Magical Thinking.* 2005. New York: Vintage International, 2007.

Di Iorio, Lyn. "Laughing through a Broken Mouth in *The Brief Wondrous Life of Oscar Wao.*" In *Junot Díaz and the Decolonial Imagination,* edited by Monica Hanna, Jennifer Harford Vargas, and José David Saldívar, 69–88. Durham: Duke University Press, 2016.

Dixon, Wheeler Winston. *Black and White Cinema: A Short History.* New Brunswick: Rutgers University Press, 2015.

Dowland, Douglas. *Weak Nationalisms: Affect and Nonfiction in Postwar America.* Lincoln: University of Nebraska Press, 2019.

Du Bois, W. E. B. *The Souls of Black Folk.* New Haven: Yale University Press, 2015.

During, Simon, ed. *The Cultural Studies Reader.* London: Routledge, 1999.

Duvall, John N. "The (Super)Marketplace of Images: Television as Unmediated Mediation in DeLillo's *White Noise.*" *Arizona Quarterly* 50, no. 3 (1994): 127–53.

Dyer-Witheford, Nick, and Greig de Peuter. *Games of Empire: Global Capitalism and Video Games.* Minneapolis: University of Minnesota Press, 2009.

Eder, Maciej. "Visualization in Stylometry: Cluster Analysis Using Networks." *Digital Scholarship in the Humanities* 32, no. 1 (2017): 50–64. https://doi.org/10.1093/llc/fqv061.

Eder, Maciej, Jan Rybicki, and Mike Kestemont. "Stylometry with R: A Package for Computational Text Analysis." *R Journal* 8, no. 1 (2016): 107–21.

Eldridge, David. *American Culture in the 1930s.* Edinburgh: Edinburgh University Press, 2008.

Ellis, Aimé J. "'Boys in the Hood': Black Male Community in Richard Wright's *Native Son.*" *Callaloo* 29, no. 1 (2006): 182–201.

Fabre, Michel. "Richard Wright: The Man Who Lived Underground." *Studies in the Novel* 3, no. 2 (1971): 165–79.

Farland, Maria. "Modernist Versions of Pastoral: Poetic Inspiration, Scientific Expertise, and the 'Degenerate' Farmer." *American Literary History* 19, no. 4 (2007): 905–36.

Fassone, Riccardo. *Every Game Is an Island: Endings and Extremities in Video Games.* New York: Bloomsbury, 2017.

Fazal, Tanisha, and Ryan Griffiths. "Membership Has Its Privileges: The Changing Benefits of Statehood." *International Studies Review* 16, no. 1 (2014): 79–106.

Felski, Rita. *The Limits of Critique.* Chicago: University of Chicago Press, 2015.

Ferlinghetti, Lawrence. *A Coney Island of the Mind.* Norfolk: New Directions, 1958.
Ferrell, Jeff. "The Underbelly Project: Hiding in the Light, Painting in the Dark." *Rhizomes,* no. 25 (2013). http://www.rhizomes.net/issue25/ferrell/index.html.
Finkelstein, Norman. "Nathaniel Mackey and the Unity of All Rites." *Contemporary Literature* 49, no. 1 (2008): 24-55.
Foucault, Michel. *The Birth of Biopolitics: Lectures at the Collège de France, 1978-1979.* Edited by Michel Senellart. Translated by Graham Burchell. New York: Palgrave, 2008.
———. *Discipline and Punish: The Birth of the Prison.* Translated by Alan Sheridan. New York: Pantheon, 1977.
Freer, Joanna. *Thomas Pynchon and American Counterculture.* New York: Cambridge University Press, 2014.
Friedman, Milton. *Capitalism and Freedom.* Chicago: University of Chicago Press, 1962.
Frow, John. "The Last Things before the Last: Notes on *White Noise.*" In *Introducing Don DeLillo,* edited by Frank Lentricchia, 175-92. Durham: Duke University Press, 1991.
Galili, Tal. "Dendextend: An R Package for Visualizing, Adjusting and Comparing Trees of Hierarchical Clustering." *Bioinformatics* 31, no. 22 (2015): 3718-20. https://doi.org/10.1093/bioinformatics/btv428.
Gibbons, William. "Wrap Your Troubles in Dreams: Popular Music, Narrative, and Dystopia in Bioshock." *Game Studies* 11, no. 3 (2011). https://www.gamestudies.org/1103/articles/gibbons.
Gilbey, Ryan. "Vanishing Point." *Sight and Sound* 28, no. 7 (2018): 46-48.
Ginsberg, Allen. *Howl and Other Poems.* San Francisco: City Lights Books, 1956.
González, Christopher. *Reading Junot Díaz.* Pittsburgh: University of Pittsburgh Press, 2015.
Gordon, Jane Anna. "Slavery Continued, Freedom Sought: Wright's Political Intellectual Journey." In *The Politics of Richard Wright: Perspectives on Resistance,* edited by Jane Anna Gordon and Cyrus Ernesto Zirakzadeh, 329-47. Lexington: University Press of Kentucky, 2018.
———. *Statelessness and Contemporary Enslavement.* New York: Routledge, 2020.
Gordon, Lewis. "Wright's Afromodern Search for Political Freedom." In *The Politics of Richard Wright: Perspectives on Resistance,* edited by Jane Anna Gordon and Cyrus Ernesto Zirakzadeh, 26-44. Lexington: University Press of Kentucky, 2018.
Graeber, David. *Fragments of an Anarchist Anthropology.* Chicago: Prickly Paradigm Press, 2004.
Gramsci, Antonio. *Selections from the Prison Notebooks.* 1929-1935. Translated by Quintin Hoare and Geoffrey Nowell Smith. New York: International, 1971.
Granik, Debra, dir. *Leave No Trace.* 2018; New York: Bleecker Street.

Grattan, Laura. "Reading Richard Wright beyond the Carceral State: The Politics of Refusal in Black Radical Imagination." In *The Politics of Richard Wright: Perspectives on Resistance,* edited by Jane Anna Gordon and Cyrus Ernesto Zirakzadeh, 310–28. Lexington: University Press of Kentucky, 2018.

Grattan, Sean Austin. *Hope Isn't Stupid: Utopian Affects in Contemporary American Literature.* Iowa City: University of Iowa Press, 2017.

Graulund, Rune. "Generous Exclusion: Register and Readership in Junot Díaz's *The Brief Wondrous Life of Oscar Wao*." *MELUS: Multi-ethnic Literature of the United States* 39, no. 3 (2014): 31–48.

Grausam, Daniel. *On Endings: American Postmodernism and the Cold War.* Charlottesville: University of Virginia Press, 2011.

Gray, Jeffrey. *Mastery's End: Travel and Postwar American Poetry.* Athens: University of Georgia Press, 2005.

Greif, Mark. *The Age of the Crisis of Man: Thought and Fiction in America, 1933–1973.* Princeton: Princeton University Press, 2015.

Gu, Zuguang, Lei Gu, Roland Eils, Matthias Schlesner, and Benedikt Brors. "*Circlize* Implements and Enhances Circular Visualization in R." *Bioinformatics* 30, no. 19 (2014): 2811–12. https://doi.org/10.1093/bioinformatics/btu393.

Hall, Stuart. "Gramsci's Relevance for the Study of Race and Ethnicity." In *Stuart Hall: Critical Dialogues in Cultural Studies,* edited by David Morley and Kuan-Hsing Chen, 411–40. London: Routledge, 1996.

Hanna, Monica. "'Reassembling the Fragments': Battling Historiographies, Caribbean Discourse, and Nerd Genres in Junot Díaz's *The Brief Wondrous Life of Oscar Wao*." *Callaloo* 33, no. 2 (2010): 498–520.

Hanna, Monica, Jennifer Harford Vargas, and José David Saldívar. "Junot Díaz and the Decolonial Imagination: From Island to Empire." In *Junot Díaz and the Decolonial Imagination,* 1–29. Durham: Duke University Press, 2016.

Hanna, Monica, Jennifer Harford Vargas, and José David Saldívar, eds. *Junot Díaz and the Decolonial Imagination.* Durham: Duke University Press, 2016.

Hardt, Michael, and Antonio Negri. *Empire.* Cambridge: Harvard University Press, 2000.

Harford Vargas, Jennifer. *Forms of Dictatorship: Power, Narrative, and Authoritarianism in the Latina/o Novel.* Oxford: Oxford University Press, 2019.

Harley, J. B. *The New Nature of Maps.* Baltimore: Johns Hopkins University Press, 2001.

Hart, Matthew. *Extraterritorial: A Political Geography of Contemporary Fiction.* New York: Columbia University Press, 2020.

Hart, Matthew, and Jim Hansen. "Introduction: Contemporary Literature and the State." *Contemporary Literature* 49, no. 4 (2008): 491–513. https://doi.org/10.1353/cli.0.0037.

Harvey, David. *A Brief History of Neoliberalism.* New York: Oxford University Press, 2005.
Hayek, F. A. "Economics and Knowledge." *Economica* 4, no. 13 (1937): 33-54.
———. *The Fatal Conceit: The Errors of Socialism.* Edited by W. W. Bartley III. Chicago: University of Chicago Press, 1989.
———. *Individualism and Economic Order.* Chicago: University of Chicago Press, 1948.
———. "The Use of Knowledge in Society." *American Economic Review* 35, no. 4 (1945): 519-30.
Heise, Thomas. *Urban Underworlds: A Geography of Twentieth-Century American Literature and Culture.* New Brunswick: Rutgers University Press, 2011.
Heise, Ursula K. "Ecocriticism and the Transnational Turn in American Studies." *American Literary History* 20, no. 1/2 (2008): 381-404.
Hepburn, Allan. *Intrigue: Espionage and Culture.* New Haven: Yale University Press, 2005.
Herman, David, James Phelan, Peter J. Rabinowitz, Brian Richardson, and Robyn Warhol. *Narrative Theory: Core Concepts and Critical Debates.* Columbus: Ohio State University Press, 2012.
Herman, Luc, and Steven Weisenburger. *"Gravity's Rainbow," Domination, and Freedom.* Athens: University of Georgia Press, 2013.
Hirschman, Albert O. *Exit, Voice, and Loyalty: Responses to Decline in Firms, Organizations, and States.* Cambridge: Harvard University Press, 1970.
Horowitz, Ken. *Sega Arcade Revolution: A History in 62 Games.* Jefferson: McFarland, 2018.
Houser, Heather M. "'A Presence Almost Everywhere': Responsibility at Risk in Don DeLillo's *The Names.*" *Contemporary Literature* 51, no. 1 (2010): 124-51.
Hungerford, Amy. "Don DeLillo's Latin Mass." *Contemporary Literature* 47, no. 3 (2006): 343-80.
Hutcheon, Linda. *A Poetics of Postmodernism: History, Theory, Fiction.* New York: Routledge, 1988.
Igo, Sarah E. *The Averaged American: Surveys, Citizens, and the Making of a Mass Public.* Cambridge: Harvard University Press, 2007.
Irr, Caren. *Toward the Geopolitical Novel: U.S. Fiction in the Twenty-First Century.* New York: Columbia University Press, 2014.
Jacobs, Struan, and Phil Mullins. "Friedrich Hayek and Michael Polanyi in Correspondence." *History of European Ideas* 42, no. 1 (2016): 107-30. https://doi.org/10.1080/01916599.2014.1002971.
Jagoda, Patrick. "Videogame Criticism and Games in the Twenty-First Century." *American Literary History* 29, no. 1 (2017): 205-18.
Jameson, Frederic. *Archaeologies of the Future: The Desire Called Utopia and Other Science Fictions.* New York: Verso, 2005.

———. *Postmodernism; or, The Cultural Logic of Late Capitalism*. Durham: Duke University Press, 1991.

Johnson, Bob. "'A Whole Synthesis of His Time': Political Ideology and Cultural Politics in the Writings of William Carlos Williams, 1929-1939." *American Quarterly* 54, no. 2 (2002): 179-215.

Joron, Andrew. *The Absolute Letter*. Chicago: Flood Editions, 2017.

———. *Fathom*. New York: Black Square Editions, 2003.

Junkerman, Charles. "Modeling Anarchy: The Example of John Cage's *Musicircus*." *Chicago Review* 38, no. 4 (1993): 153-68.

Kadlec, David. *Mosaic Modernism: Anarchism, Pragmatism, Culture*. Baltimore: Johns Hopkins University Press, 2000.

Kihara, Kenji. "'I Don't Own Any Property': Richard Wright's *Native Son* and the Rhetoric of Possession." *Arizona Quarterly* 78, no. 1 (2022): 27-50.

Kinnamon, Keneth, ed. *Critical Essays on Richard Wright's "Native Son."* New York: G. K. Hall, 1997.

Konstantinou, Lee. *Cool Characters: Irony and American Fiction*. Cambridge: Harvard University Press. 2016.

Krause, Peter. "The Strategies of Counter-secession: How States Prevent Independence." *Nations and Nationalism* 28, no. 3 (2022): 788-805. https://doi.org/10.1111/nana.12822.

Kukathas, Chandran. *The Liberal Archipelago: A Theory of Diversity and Freedom*. Oxford: Oxford University Press, 2003.

Lamm, Kimberly. "All Together / Now: Writing the Space of Collectivities in the Poetry of Juliana Spahr." In *American Poets in the 21st Century: The New Poetics*, edited by Claudia Rankine and Lisa Sewell, 133-50. Middletown: Wesleyan, 2007.

Lee, Sue-Im. *A Body of Individuals: The Paradox of Community in Contemporary Fiction*. Columbus: Ohio State University Press, 2009.

Leeson, Peter T. *Anarchy Unbound: Why Self-Governance Works Better than You Think*. Cambridge: Cambridge University Press, 2014.

Le Guin, Ursula K. "Escape Routes." In *The Language of the Night: Essays on Fantasy and Science Fiction,* edited by Susan Wood, 201-6. New York: G. P. Putnam's Sons, 1979.

Lerner, Ben. *The Hatred of Poetry*. New York: Farrar, Straus, and Giroux, 2016.

Leong, Michael. *Contested Records: The Turn to Documents in Contemporary North American Poetry*. Iowa City: University of Iowa Press, 2020.

Levesque, Richard. "Telling Postmodern Tales: Absent Authorities in Didion's *Democracy* and DeLillo's *Mao II*." *Arizona Quarterly* 54, no. 3 (1998): 69-87.

Levi, Heather. "Sport and Melodrama: The Case of Mexican Professional Wrestling." *Social Text*, no. 50 (1997): 57-68. https://doi.org/10.2307/466814.

Levitas, Ruth. *The Concept of Utopia*. Syracuse: Syracuse University Press, 1990.

Lutzkanova-Vassileva, Albena. *The Testimonies of Russian and American Postmodern Poetry: Reference, Trauma, and History.* New York: Bloomsbury, 2015.

Mackey, Nathaniel. "The Atmosphere Is Alive." Interview with Sarah Rosenthal. In *A Community Writing Itself: Conversations with Vanguard Writers of the Bay Area,* 137-66. New York: Columbia University Press, 2010.

———. *Discrepant Engagement: Dissonance, Cross-culturality and Experimental Writing.* Cambridge: Cambridge University Press, 1993.

———. *From a Broken Bottle Traces of Perfume Still Emanate: Volumes 1-3.* New York: New Directions, 2010.

———. Interview with Jeanne Heuving. *Contemporary Literature* 53, no. 2 (2012): 207-36.

———. *School of Udhra.* San Francisco: City Lights, 1993.

———. *Splay Anthem.* New York: New Directions, 2006.

———. *Whatsaid Serif.* San Francisco: City Lights, 1998.

Macpherson, Heidi Slettedahl. *Women's Movement: Escape as Transgression in North American Feminist Fiction.* Atlanta: Rodopi, 2000.

Mariani, Paul L. *William Carlos Williams: A New World Naked.* New York: McGraw-Hill, 1981.

Marsh, Nicky. "Going 'Glocal': The Local and the Global in Recent Experimental Women's Poetry." *Contemporary Women's Writing* 1, no. 1/2 (2007): 192-202.

Marx, Karl, and Frederick Engels. *The German Ideology: Introduction to a Critique of Political Economy.* Edited by C. J. Arthur. London: Lawrence and Wishart, 1970.

Mattessich, Stefan. *Lines of Flight: Discursive Time and Countercultural Desire in the Work of Thomas Pynchon.* Durham: Duke University Press, 2002.

Matthews, Kadeshia L. "Black Boy No More? Violence and the Flight from Blackness in Richard Wright's *Native Son.*" *Modern Fiction Studies* 60, no. 2 (2014): 276-97.

Matthews, Mark. *Droppers: America's First Hippie Commune, Drop City.* Norman: University of Oklahoma Press, 2010.

McCann, Sean, and Michael Szalay. "Do You Believe in Magic? Literary Thinking after the New Left." *Yale Journal of Criticism* 18, no. 2 (2005): 435-68.

———. "'Eerie Serenity': A Response to John McClure." *Boundary 2* 36, no. 2 (2009): 145-53.

McClure, John A. "Do They Believe in Magic? Politics and Postmodern Literature." *Boundary 2* 36, no. 2 (2009): 125-43.

McHugh-Dillon, Ruth. "'Let Me Confess': Confession, Complicity, and #MeToo in Junot Díaz's *This Is How You Lose Her* and 'The Silence: The Legacy of Childhood Trauma.'" *MELUS: Multi-ethnic Literature of the United States* 46, no. 1 (2021): 24-50.

McNallie, Robin. "Richard Wright's Allegory of the Cave: 'The Man Who Lived Underground.'" *South Atlantic Bulletin* 42, no. 2 (1977): 76-84.

Mermann-Jozwiak, Elisabeth. "Beyond Multiculturalism: Ethnic Studies, Transnationalism, and Junot Díaz's *Oscar Wao*." *ARIEL: A Review of International English Literature* 43, no. 2 (2012): 1-24.

———. "Yamashita's Post-national Spaces: 'It All Comes Together in Los Angeles.'" *Canadian Review of American Studies* 41, no. 1 (2011): 1-24.

Michaels, Walter Benn. *The Gold Standard and the Logic of Naturalism: American Literature at the Turn of the Century.* Berkeley: University of California Press, 1987.

———. *The Shape of the Signifier.* Princeton: Princeton University Press, 2004.

Mirowski, Philip. "Economics, Science, and Knowledge: Polanyi vs. Hayek." *Tradition and Discovery: The Polanyi Society Periodical* 25, no. 1 (1998): 29-42.

Modest Mouse. *Good News for People Who Love Bad News.* Epic Records, 2004, compact disc.

Molloy, Seán. "Escaping the Politics of the Irredeemable Earth—Anarchy and Transcendence in the Novels of Thomas Pynchon." *Theory and Event* 13, no. 3 (2010). https://doi.org/10.1353/tae.2010.0004.

Nadel, Alan. *Containment Culture: American Narratives, Postmodernism, and the Atomic Age.* Durham: Duke University Press, 1995.

Nash, Charles C. "'The Man Who Lived Underground': Richard Wright's Parable of the Cave." *Interpretations* 16, no. 1 (1985): 62-74.

Nickels, Joel. *The Poetry of the Possible: Spontaneity, Modernism, and the Multitude.* Minneapolis: University of Minneapolis Press, 2012.

———. *World Literature and the Geographies of Resistance.* New York: Cambridge University Press, 2018.

O'Bryan, Michael. "In Defense of *Vineland:* Pynchon, Anarchism, and the New Left." *Twentieth-Century Literature* 62, no. 1 (2016): 1-31.

———. "Pynchon and New Political Activisms." In *The New Pynchon Studies,* edited by Joanna Freer, 141-56. New York: Cambridge University Press, 2019.

Olson, Charles. *Collected Prose.* Edited by Donald Allen and Benjamin Friedlander. Berkeley: University of California Press, 1997.

———. *The Maximus Poems.* Edited by George F. Butterick. Berkeley: University of California Press, 1983.

———. *Selected Poems.* Edited by Robert Creeley. Berkeley: University of California Press, 1997.

Ong, Aihwa. *Neoliberalism as Exception: Mutations in Citizenship and Sovereignty.* Durham: Duke University Press, 2006.

Parker, Felan. "Canonizing Bioshock: Cultural Value and the Prestige Game." *Games and Culture* 12, no. 7/8 (2017): 739-63. https://doi.org/10.1177/1555412015598669.

———. "Roger Ebert and the Games-as-Art Debate." *Cinema Journal* 57, no. 3 (2018): 77-100.

Parrish, Tim. "After Henry Adams: Rewriting History in Joan Didion's *Democracy*." *Critique: Studies in Contemporary Fiction* 47, no. 2 (2006): 167–84.
Paul, Sherman. *Olson's Push: "Origin," Black Mountain, and Recent American Poetry*. Baton Rouge: Louisiana State University Press, 1978.
Phelan, James and Peter J. Rabinowitz. "Narrative as Rhetoric." In *Narrative Theory: Core Concepts and Critical Debates*, 3–8. Columbus: Ohio State University Press, 2012.
Polanyi, Michael. *Personal Knowledge: Towards a Post-critical Philosophy*. New York: Harper and Row, 1964.
———. *The Tacit Dimension*. Gloucester: Peter Smith, 1983.
Pynchon, Thomas. *The Crying of Lot 49*. Philadelphia: Lippincott, 1966.
———. *Gravity's Rainbow*. New York: Viking, 1973.
———. *V*. New York: Bantam, 1963.
———. *Vineland*. Boston: Little, Brown, 1990.
Rawls, John. *Political Liberalism: Expanded Edition*. New York: Columbia University Press, 2005.
Reed, Anthony. *Freedom Time? The Poetics and Politics of Black Experimental Writing*. Baltimore: Johns Hopkins University Press, 2014.
Reed, Christian. "On 'The Yachts.'" *Modern American Poetry Site*. 2006. https://modernamericanpoetry.org/christian-reed-yachts.
Reilly, John. "Giving Bigger a Voice: The Politics of Narrative in *Native Son*." In *New Essays on Native Son*, edited by Keneth Kinnamon, 35–62. Cambridge: Cambridge University Press, 1990.
Richardson, Brian. "Antimimetic, Unnatural, and Postmodern Narrative Theory." In *Narrative Theory: Core Concepts and Critical Debates*, 20–25. Columbus: Ohio State University Press, 2012.
Richardson, Jeremy. "Brexit: The EU Policy-Making State Hits the Populist Buffers." *Political Quarterly* 89, no. 1 (2018): 118–26.
———. "Supranational State Building in the European Union." In *Constructing a Policy-Making State? Policy Dynamics in the EU*, edited by Jeremy Richardson, 3–28. Oxford: Oxford University Press, 2012.
Robinson, Paul, and Sarah Robinson. *Pirates, Prisoners, and Lepers: Lessons from Life Outside the Law*. Herndon: Potomac Books, 2015.
Rody, Caroline. "The Transnational Imagination: Karen Tei Yamashita's *Tropic of Orange*." In *Asian North American Identities: Beyond the Hyphen*, edited by Eleanor Ty and Donald C. Goellnicht, 130–48. Bloomington: Indiana University Press, 2004.
Rowling, J. K. *Harry Potter and the Sorcerer's Stone*. New York: Scholastic, 1997.
Sadowski-Smith, Claudia. *Border Fictions: Globalization, Empire, and Writing at the Boundaries of the United States*. Charlottesville: University of Virginia Press, 2008.

Saldívar, José David. "Conjectures on 'Americanity' and Junot Díaz's 'Fukú Americanus' in *The Brief Wondrous Life of Oscar Wao*." *Global South* 5, no. 1 (2011): 120-36.

Saldívar, Ramón. "Historical Fantasy, Speculative Realism, and Postrace Aesthetics in Contemporary American Fiction." *American Literary History* 23, no. 3 (2011): 574-99.

———. "Imagining Cultures: The Transnational Imaginary in Postrace America." In *The Imaginary and Its Worlds: American Studies after the Transnational Turn*, edited by Laura Bieger, Ramón Saldívar, and Johannes Voelz, 3-22. Hanover: Dartmouth College Press, 2013.

Salib, Peter. "The Law of Banksy." *University of Chicago Law Review* 82, no. 4 (2015): 2293-328.

Sargent, Lyman Tower. *Utopianism: A Very Short Introduction*. Oxford: Oxford University Press, 2010.

Sartre, Jean-Paul. *"No Exit" and "The Flies."* Translated by Stuart Gilbert. New York: Knopf, 1947.

Schillings, Sonja. *Enemies of All Humankind: Fictions of Legitimate Violence*. Hanover: Dartmouth College Press, 2016.

Schmeink, Lars. *Biopunk Dystopias: Genetic Engineering, Society and Science Fiction*. Liverpool: Liverpool University Press, 2016.

Schotland, Sara. "Breaking Out of the Rooster Coop: Violent Crime in Aravind Adiga's *White Tiger* and Richard Wright's *Native Son*." *Comparative Literature Studies* 48, no.1 (2011): 1-19.

Scott, James C. *The Art of Not Being Governed: An Anarchist History of Upland Southeast Asia*. New Haven: Yale University Press, 2009.

———. *Seeing Like a State: How Certain Schemes to Improve the Human Condition Have Failed*. New Haven: Yale University Press, 1998.

Shonkwiler, Alison, and Leigh Claire La Berge, eds. *Reading Capitalist Realism*. Iowa City: University of Iowa Press, 2014.

Siegelberg, Mira L. *Statelessness: A Modern History*. Cambridge: Harvard University Press, 2020.

Siraganian, Lisa. *Modernism's Other Work: The Art Object's Political Life*. New York: Oxford University Press, 2012.

Skocpol, Theda. "Bringing the State Back In: Retrospect and Prospect." *Scandinavian Political Studies* 31, no. 2 (2008): 109-24.

Smith, Kenneth. "Formal Negativities, Breakthroughs, Ruptures and Continuities in the Music of Modest Mouse." *Popular Music* 33, no. 3 (2014): 428-54. https://doi.org/10.1017/S0261143014000385.

Soldatenko, Gabriel. "The Politics of Writing on Walls." *Rhizomes*, no. 25 (2013). http://www.rhizomes.net/issue25/soldatenko.html.

Spahr, Juliana. "Connected Disconnection and Localized Globalism in Pacific Multilingual Literature." *boundary 2* 31, no. 3 (2004): 75-100.

———. *Du Bois's Telegram: Literary Resistance and State Containment*. Cambridge: Harvard University Press, 2018.

———. *Fuck You-Aloha-I Love You*. Middletown: Wesleyan University Press, 2001.

———. "New World Sonnet." In *American Hybrid: A Norton Anthology of New Poetry*, edited by David St. John and Cole Swensen, 408. New York: Norton, 2009.

———. *things of each possible relation hashing against one another*. Newfield: Palm Press, 2003.

———. *This Connection of Everyone with Lungs*. Berkeley: University of California Press, 2005.

———. *Well Then There Now*. Boston: Black Sparrow, 2011.

Starre, Alexander. *Metamedia: American Book Fictions and Literary Print Culture after Digitization*. Iowa City: University of Iowa Press, 2015.

Stephens, Paul. *The Poetics of Information Overload: From Gertrude Stein to Conceptual Writing*. Minneapolis: University of Minnesota Press, 2015.

Stout, Janis P. *The Journey Narrative in American Literature: Patterns and Departures*. Westport: Greenwood Press, 1983.

———. *Strategies of Reticence: Silence and Meaning in the Works of Jane Austen, Willa Cather, Katherine Anne Porter, and Joan Didion*. Charlottesville: University Press of Virginia, 1990.

Stringer, Dorothy. "Passing and the State in Junot Díaz's 'Drown.'" *MELUS: Multiethnic Literature of the United States* 38, no. 2 (2013): 111-26.

Supreme Court of New Jersey. *In re Quinlan*. March, 31, 1976.

Szalay, Michael. *Hip Figures: A Literary History of the Democratic Party*. Stanford: Stanford University Press, 2012.

———. *New Deal Modernism: American Literature and the Invention of the Welfare State*. Durham: Duke University Press, 2000.

Tabbi, Joseph. "Pynchon's Groundward Art." In *The "Vineland" Papers*, edited by Geoffrey Green, Donald J. Greiner, and Larry McCaffery, 89-100. Normal: Dalkey Archive Press, 1994.

Tager, Michael. "The Political Vision of Joan Didion's *Democracy*." *Critique: Studies in Contemporary Fiction* 31, no. 3 (1990): 173-84.

Tavinor, Grant. "*Bioshock* and the Art of Rapture." *Philosophy and Literature* 33, no. 1 (2009): 91-106. https://doi.org/10.1353/phl.0.0046.

Taylor, Jack. "The Political Subjection of Bigger Thomas: The Gaze, Biopolitics, and the Court of Law in Richard Wright's *Native Son*." *CR: The New Centennial Review* 16, no. 2 (2016): 183-202.

Tekdemir, Hande. "Magical Realism in the Peripheries of the Metropolis: A Comparative Approach to *Tropic of Orange* and *Berji Kristin: Tales from the Garbage Hills*." *Comparatist*, no. 35 (2011): 40-54.

———. "Post-frontier and Re-definition of Space in *Tropic of Orange.*" In *Blast, Corrupt, Dismantle, Erase: Contemporary North American Dystopian Literature,* edited by Brett Joséf Grubisic, Gisèle M. Baxter, and Tara Lee, 93–110. Waterloo: Wilfrid Laurier University Press, 2014.

Thomas, Samuel. *Pynchon and the Political.* New York: Routledge, 2007.

Tolkien, J. R. R. "On Fairy-Stories." In *The Monsters and the Critics and Other Essays,* edited by Christopher Tolkien, 109–61. Boston: Houghton Mifflin, 1984.

Tyldum, Morten, dir. *Silo.* Season 1, episode 1, "Freedom Day." Aired May 5, 2023, on Apple TV+.

Vint, Sherryl. "Orange County: Global Networks in *Tropic of Orange.*" *Science Fiction Studies* 39, no. 3 (2012): 401–14. https://doi.org/10.5621/sciefictstud.39.3.0401.

Von Hallberg, Robert. *Charles Olson: The Scholar's Art.* Cambridge: Harvard University Press, 1978.

———. "The Politics of Description: W. C. Williams in the 'Thirties." *ELH* 45, no. 1 (1978): 131–51.

Waldrop, Rosmarie. "Charles Olson: Process and Relationship." *Twentieth Century Literature* 23, no. 4 (1977): 467–86.

Wallace, Molly. "Tropics of Globalization: Reading the New North America." *Symplokē* 9, no. 1/2 (2001): 145–60.

Wallmeier, Philip. "Exit as Critique: Communes and Intentional Communities in the 1960s and Today." *Historical Social Research* 42, no. 3 (2017): 147–71.

Warner, Michael. *Publics and Counterpublics.* New York: Zone Books, 2005.

Weber, Max. "Politics as a Vocation." In *The Vocation Lectures,* edited by David Owen and Tracy B. Strong, 32–94. Translated by Rodney Livingstone. Indianapolis: Hackett, 2004.

Weisenburger, Steven. "In the Zone: Sovereignty and Bare Life in *Gravity's Rainbow.*" *Pynchon Notes,* no. 56/57 (2009): 100–113.

Wilcox, Leonard. "Baudrillard, DeLillo's *White Noise,* and the End of Heroic Narrative." *Contemporary Literature* 32, no. 3 (1991): 346–65.

Williams, William Carlos. "America, Whitman, and the Art of Poetry." *Poetry Journal* 8, no. 1 (November 1917): 27–36.

———. *The Collected Poems of William Carlos Williams, Vol. 1: 1909–1939.* Edited by A. Walton Litz and Christopher MacGowan. New York: New Directions, 1995.

———. *The Doctor Stories.* New York: New Directions, 1984.

———. "A Man versus the Law." *The Freeman* 1, no. 15 (1920): 348–49.

———. *Paterson.* New York: New Directions, 1992.

———. *A Recognizable Image: William Carlos Williams on Art and Artists.* Edited by Bram Dijkstra. New York: New Directions, 1978.

Wright, Richard. "How 'Bigger' Was Born." In *Richard Wright: Early Works,* 851–82. New York: Library of America, 1991.

———. "The Man Who Lived Underground." In *Richard Wright Reader*, 517–76. New York: Harper and Row, 1978.
———. *The Man Who Lived Underground.* New York: Library of America, 2021.
———. *Native Son.* 1940. New York: Perennial Classics, 1998.
Yamashita, Karen Tei. Interview by Jean Vengua Gier and Carla Alicia Tejeda. *Jouvert* 2, no. 2 (1998). https://legacy.chass.ncsu.edu/jouvert/v2i2/YAMASHI.HTM.
———. "The Latitude of the Fiction Writer: A Dialogue." Interview by Ryuta Imafukú. *Cafe Creole*, n.d. http://www.cafecreole.net/archipelago/Karen_Dialogue.html.
———. *Tropic of Orange.* Minneapolis: Coffee House Press, 1997.
Zamsky, Robert L. "A Poetics of Radical Musicality: Nathaniel Mackey's '-mu' Series." *Arizona Quarterly: A Journal of American Literature, Culture, and Theory* 62, no. 1 (2006): 113–40.
Zubeck, Jacqueline A. "'The Surge and Pelt of Daily Life': Rediscovery of the Prosaic in Don DeLillo's *The Names.*" *LIT: Literature Interpretation Theory* 18, no. 4 (2007): 353–76.

INDEX

absence, 42-43, 103; representation and, 161-62, 168-74, 244n68; state and, 71-72, 74, 133-34
Acker, Kathy, 101-2
activism, 163-64, 166
Adams, Rachel, 142, 159-60
affirmative action, 9-10, 188-89
Afflerbach, Ian, 90-91, 244n54
Agamben, Giorgio, 22-23, 73-74, 86-87, 95, 105-6, 126, 128-29, 134, 188-89, 213-14, 225-26, 246n6
agency, 77, 221-22, 226-27
allegory, 48-49, 83, 143-45, 203-4
Althusser, Louis, 17, 22-23
American literature: defining, 2-5; history and, 8-10, 12-16, 220-21, 231; representation and, 5-7, 17, 26, 231; state and, 1-17, 21, 23, 25-26, 28-31, 220-21, 230-31
anarchism, 4-5, 7-8, 37, 51, 93-96, 100-101, 180, 190-91, 236n75, 238n13
Anderson, Benedict, 174, 254n1
Andrews, Bruce, 15
anthropology, 9-12, 71, 202-3
anti-capitalism, 30, 189-90
anti-representation, 25-27, 39, 42-43, 47, 133, 161. *See also* representation
anti-statism, 4-8, 25-26, 38, 57-59, 74, 94, 100-101, 107-9, 122-23, 135, 166, 189-90, 203, 242n10
Arendt, Hannah, 10, 23-24, 73-76, 79, 84-85, 95, 242n1
art: authority and, 210-11; commodification of, 30-31, 217-19; escape and, 41-44, 47-49, 53-54, 72, 228, 230-31; history and, 87; law and, 180, 254nn8-9, 258n1; politics and, 47-49, 53-54, 72, 177-78, 204, 210-11, 228, 230-31, 258n1; representation and, 17, 41-44, 47-49, 72, 87; video games and, 222, 228; voice and, 179-82
articulation: authority and, 111, 115-18, 160-61; knowledge and, 108-11, 122-23, 149-50; inarticulacy and, 28, 88-89, 119-20, 160-61, 183-84, 200-202, 208-9, 212-14, 216, 247n14; noise and, 115-17, 119-21, 197-98; representation and, 130-31, 160-61, 201-2, 206, 208-9, 212-14, 216; state and, 29-30,

articulation (continued) 117-23, 130-31, 160-61, 183-84, 197-98, 201-2, 208-9, 216, 222, 246n6, 254n1; voice and, 177-78, 183-84, 197-98, 201-2, 216. See also knowledge; noise; voice
Ashton, Jennifer, 42-43
astronauts, 192-95
Austin, J. L., 195
authoritarianism, 28, 36, 111-12, 115-16, 121-22, 134-35, 153-54, 162; anti-authoritarianism, 3-4, 163, 168
authority: art and, 210-11; articulation and, 111, 115-18, 160-61; center and, 62-63, 94, 205-6, 249n62; escape and, 19-21, 23, 210-11, 228-30; knowledge and, 109-11, 114-15, 216; language and, 89; narrative, 29, 62-63, 152-54, 157-59, 249n62; openness and, 204-6, 210-11; poetry and, 46-47, 56-59; politics and, 19-21, 30, 36, 38-39, 56-59, 63, 71, 75-77, 89, 109-12, 158-59, 168, 210-11, 230, 249n62; representation and, 46-48, 75-77, 89, 149, 153-54, 158-59, 168, 210-11, 216; state and, 19-21, 23, 33-34, 36, 38-39, 57-59, 62-63, 77, 89, 106, 109-10, 114-15, 121-24, 135-37, 216, 228-30; video games and, 228; voice and, 183
authorship, 88, 153-54
autonomy, 19-20, 53, 59-60, 125, 226-27
avant-garde, 184-86

Balaguer, Joaquín, 162
Baldwin, James, 77, 86-89, 179, 244n54
Banksy, 2-3, 180-81, 196, 230-31, 254nn8-9; *Create Escape*, 182; *Devolved Parliament*, 228-30; *Exit through the Gift Shop*, 30, 217-19, 230-31; *If Graffiti Changed Anything*, 179, 180, 254n9; *Laugh Now*, 229-30
Baudrillard, Jean, 107-8, 113-15, 247n13, 248n26
Beat culture, 51-53, 93, 96
belonging, 23, 96-97, 209-10, 243n34
Benjamin, Walter, 213-14
Bernstein, Charles, 26
Bioshock, 30, 221-29, 258n21, 259n28
Black Americans: escape and, 3-4, 75-79, 81, 242n17; police violence against, 175; religion and, 82-83; state and, 3-4, 9-10, 74-76, 78-79, 81, 84-87, 89-90
Black Lives Matter, 4-5, 175
Black Mountain College, 61-62, 70-71, 201-2, 210-11, 220-21
blanks, blankness, 42-43, 161-66, 168-74, 253n62
blindness, 90-91
Bloch, Ernst, 24
body: knowledge and, 113-15, 119, 125-26, 212-13, 247nn13-14; poetry and, 184-86, 216; racialized, 75-79, 128-29, 175; sociality and, 187-88, 191, 193; state and, 75-79, 85-86, 105-7, 111, 113-15, 127-29, 132-33, 149-50, 175, 187-88, 191, 193-94, 236n66; violence and, 175, 193-94
body politic, 143, 149-50
borders, 2-3, 29, 95, 138-39, 142-44, 146-48, 154-55, 159, 190-92, 236n66, 250n20
Brexit, 228-30, 259n42
Brock, Isaac, 200-201
Butler, Octavia, 194-95
Butterick, George, 55-56, 59-62, 64-67

Cage, John, 26, 70, 150-51; *Anarchy*, 210-12
capitalism, 6-8, 12-13, 24-25, 27, 30, 50-53, 79-80, 107-8, 115, 140-43, 163, 186, 189-91, 197-98, 218-22, 224-25, 233n13
catalogs, cataloging, 29-30, 197-99, 201, 215-16
Cato Institute, 219-20
censorship, 160-61, 165-66
center, centralization, 53-54, 61-68, 206-10, 213, 257n63; authority and, 62-63, 94, 205-6, 249n62
circle, circularity, 205-15
citizenship, 2-3, 19-20, 73-76, 125-27, 140, 193-94, 236n66
City Lights Books, 51-52
Civil Rights era, 89-91, 174
class, 229-30; history and, 186; identity and, 186, 188-89; poetry and, 40-41, 186; state and, 162-63, 174
climate change, 199-200
closure, 12-13, 16, 24-25, 140-41, 184-85, 201-2, 206-12
Clune, Michael, 11, 91
coercion, 17, 20, 22-23, 28-29, 81-82, 112, 114-15, 259n34, 259n42
Coffey, John, 33-37, 45-46
Cold War, 9-10, 107-8, 123-24, 129-30, 142
collectivity, 25, 29-30, 143, 183-84, 187-88, 191, 196, 209-10. *See also* sociality
colonialism, 3-4, 9-10, 162-63, 196-97
comic books, 159-60
commodification, 30, 217-19
commune, 5, 70-71
communism, 45-46, 79-80, 123-24
community, 5-7, 18, 23, 70-72, 75-76, 99-100, 125, 150-51, 255n14; imagined, 174, 233n2, 254n1; representation and, 47, 49-50; right to leave and, 19-20, 178-79. *See also* sociality
Computational Stylistics Group, 153-54
concrete poetry, 44-45
connection, connectivity, 25, 39, 47-48, 50, 56-57, 69-70, 72, 75-76, 97-100, 183, 187-88, 190-99, 211, 216; disconnection, 24, 27, 97-99, 192-93, 195, 197; global, 138-39, 142, 160. *See also* sociality
consumerism, consumption, 50-51, 90, 111-13, 115, 119, 175
control: centralized, 143; disciplinary, 111-15, 117-19; political, 36, 148, 150, 227; representation and, 17, 28-29, 93-94, 148-49, 160-61, 211; state and, 117-19, 143, 160-61, 222; video games and, 222, 226-28, 259n34
convention, 26, 38, 63-70, 210-11
counterculture, 35-36, 51-52
criminality, 75-76, 80-81, 84-85, 101, 117-18, 134-35
cry, 183-84, 201, 208-9, 214-15
Cummings, E. E., 104-5

Danielewski, Mark Z., 172-73
Dávila, Arlene, 163-66
death, dying, 98-99, 103, 108, 110-13; life and, 106-7, 118; plot and, 118-19, 127-29; state and, 105-7, 118, 128-29, 246n6
DeLillo, Don, 5-6, 179, 231; *End Zone*, 120-21; *Libra*, 118; *Underworld*, 119-21; *White Noise*, 7, 28-29, 105, 107-8, 110-19, 121-23, 134-37, 160-61, 247n13, 248n20, 248n26
democracy, 7, 27-29, 49-50, 107, 123-25, 128-30, 133-34, 163, 222

INDEX

Díaz, Junot, 5-6, 9-10, 88-89, 179, 222, 231, 252n47; *The Brief and Wondrous Life of Oscar Wao*, 7, 29, 139-41, 159-76; *Drown*, 170-71; "No Face," 170-71; "The Silence: The Legacy of Childhood Trauma," 164-65, 169-70, 252n48; "Ysrael," 170-71
Dickinson, Emily, 1-2, 10, 16
dictatorship, 3-4, 160-61, 163, 167-68
Didion, Joan, 5-6, 179, 222, 231, 249n62; *Democracy*, 9-10, 28-29, 105-8, 120-21, 123-37, 139-40, 160-61; "The White Album," 124-25, 130-31; *The Year of Magical Thinking*, 106-7
disconnection. *See under* connection, connectivity
diversity, 158-59, 174-75
Doctorow, Cory, 6-7, 12
documents, 105-8, 112-15, 133, 198-99
Dominican Republic, 160-64, 167-68, 171-72
Drop City commune, 70-71
dropout culture, 5, 27, 50-54, 96-97
drugs, drug trips, 96-97, 245n81
Du Bois, W. E. B., 140
Dunne, John Gregory, 106-7
dystopia, 6-7, 224

economy, economics, 10-12, 19, 21, 71, 135-37, 189-90, 219-20; escape and, 50-53; multiculturalism and, 175
Ellison, Ralph, 91, 244n54
embodiment, 67-69, 106-7, 113-15, 119, 125-26, 128-29, 132, 184-85, 212-13, 247nn13-14. *See also* body
Engels, Friedrich, 8, 52-53
entrance, 39, 57-63, 68-71, 82-83

epistemology, 108-10, 136-37, 238n16, 247n16
escape, 1-31; failure of, 2-3, 9-10, 17, 28-29, 39, 41-45, 47-53, 72, 74, 77, 86-95, 101-3, 107, 122-25, 128, 133-35, 137, 158-59, 171-74, 179-81, 183, 191, 193-96, 199-201, 208-10, 213-16, 219-20, 223, 226-27, 231; freedom of, 19-20, 182-83; gender and, 173-74; globalization and, 138-40, 147-48; history and, 9-10, 18, 24-25, 27-28, 52-53, 56-57, 60-61, 96, 99-100, 122, 222; identity and, 77; knowledge and, 122-23, 127; language and, 76, 97, 103, 210-12, 216, 222; law and, 78-81, 89-90, 95-97, 117-20, 134-35, 219-20, 222; power and, 39, 45-46, 53-54, 60-63, 74-76, 117-18, 143, 146-47, 162-64, 170, 172-74, 180-81; race and, 3-4, 77, 79-84, 88-91; sociality and, 27-30, 39, 48-49, 56-57, 69-70, 72, 76, 97-100, 192-96, 198-99, 209-10, 216; subjectivity and, 53-54, 61-62, 92-93, 96-97; video games and, 228; violence and, 224; voice and, 178-80, 182-84, 194-201, 211-12, 215-16
escape narrative, 77, 215
escapism, 10, 14, 18, 23-27, 38-39, 47-53, 57, 69-70, 76, 80-84, 89-103, 126, 167-69, 171, 196, 199-200, 211, 228, 236n75, 237n82, 245n81
ethnicity, 3-5, 159-60, 203
European Union, 228-31, 259n42
exception, 126, 128-29, 213-14, 220, 225-26; positive, 188-89
exclusion, 73-74, 76, 84-86, 88-89, 97,

111, 126, 134, 163-66, 192, 194-95, 209. *See also* inclusion
exit: freedom to, 19-20, 73-74, 90, 182-83, 214-16; liberal theories of, 11-12, 19-22, 90, 136-37, 178-79, 183, 186-87, 216; politics and, 3, 5-7, 19-20, 24-25, 29-30, 36-39, 52-53, 65-66, 74-76, 82-83, 90-94, 102-3, 136-37, 139-40, 160, 175-76, 178-80, 183-84, 186-87, 194-99, 205-6, 208-9, 211-16, 219-21, 226-31; representation and, 38-39, 46, 48-50, 75-76, 88, 90-91, 93-94, 103, 159, 160, 175-76, 182-84, 186-87, 193-95, 208-9, 211-12, 226-31; voice and, 178-80, 182-84, 186-87, 194-99, 211-12, 216. *See also* escape
experience, 61-62, 77, 105-9, 113-16, 119, 125-26, 132, 183-85, 208-9, 212-13
experimentation, 5-6, 12-13, 16, 26-27, 39, 44-45, 50, 61-62, 121, 183, 231

failure: of escape, 2-3, 9-10, 17, 28-29, 39, 41-45, 47-53, 72, 74, 77, 86-95, 101-3, 107, 122-25, 128, 133-35, 137, 158-59, 171-74, 179-81, 183, 191, 193-96, 199-201, 208-10, 213-16, 219-20, 223, 226-27, 231; history and, 14-16; imagination and, 16, 42; language and, 15, 72; representation and, 43-44, 107, 125, 152-54, 164-66, 171-74, 199-200, 208-9, 231; voice and, 152-54, 179, 183, 201
Fanon, Frantz, 170
fantasy, 29-30, 77-83, 90, 149-50, 159-60, 162-63, 166-68, 171-72, 174, 180-83, 195-96, 224, 228, 236n75. *See also* escapism
fascism, 4-5, 45-46
Felski, Rita, 8-9
feminism, 9, 252n47
Ferlinghetti, Lawrence: "An Autobiography," 52-53; *A Coney Island of the Mind*, 51-52; "Dog," 53; "I am Waiting," 52-53; "Junkman's Obbligato," 52-53
film, 6-7, 17-18, 30, 82-83, 130-31, 217-19
footnotes, 172-73
form: escape and, 2, 5-7, 25-26; experimentation and, 12-13; interconnectivity and, 142; narrative and, 133; openness and, 183-88, 198, 201-13, 216, 241n91, 255n16; politics and, 207-8; state and, 86; voice and, 152-53. *See also* openness
Foucault, Michel, 4-5, 22-23, 75-76, 79, 111, 117, 253n62
Frankfurt School, 8
freedom: to exit, 19-20, 73-74, 90, 182-83, 214-16; individual, 45-46, 53, 119, 226-28; political, 45-46, 52-53, 62-63, 73-74, 78-80, 181-82, 210-11, 215-16; representation and, 25, 42-43, 45-46, 50-51, 75-76, 90-91, 99-100, 173-74, 181-83, 210-11, 215
free indirect discourse, 86-87, 152-53
Freeman, The, 33-34
free trade, 143-44, 189-90. *See also* neoliberalism
Friedman, Milton, 19-20, 90, 178-79
Frogger, 122
fugitive slave narrative, 77, 242n17
fugitivity, 77, 93, 202-3, 205-14, 242n17

gender: escape and, 173-74; identity and, 188-89, 191; race and, 243n51; representation and, 133-34, 164-65; state and, 9-10, 162-63, 174, 188-89, 191
Ginsberg, Allen, 51-52
globalization, 2-3, 5-6, 29, 138-43, 145-48, 159-60, 167-68, 175, 183-84, 189-90, 196-97, 216, 250n20; anarchist, 190-91; literary, 142, 159-60
Gordon, Jane Anna, 74-75, 235n60, 242nn10-11, 242n17, 244n55
graffiti, 2-3, 6-7, 30, 179-82, 217-19, 254nn8-9, 258n1
Gramsci, Antonio, 17, 22-23
Grattan, Sean, 9, 13, 101
Grausam, Daniel, 120-21, 234n15, 244n68, 248n26
Great Depression, 82-83
Greif, Mark, 93-94
Guetta, Thierry, 217-18

Haiti, 163-64
Hall, Stuart, 22-23
Hanna, Monica, 163, 165-66
Hardt, Michael, 12, 138
Harford Vargas, Jennifer, 3-4, 166-67, 172-73
Harley, J. B., 148
Hart, Matthew, 2-3, 21-22, 138-39, 220, 236n66
Harvey, David, 135-36
Hayek, Friedrich, 109-10, 135-37; "The Use of Knowledge in Society," 108-9
hemispheric novel, 2-3, 29
hemispheric turn, 138-39
hermit, 50-51

hippie, hippie culture, 4-5, 27, 50-54, 70-71, 93, 96-97
Hirschman, Albert O., 19-22, 29-30, 177-79, 182-83, 186-87, 196-99, 215-16
historiography, 141, 163-66, 171-72, 174
history, historicism, 35-36, 71-72, 159-60, 233n13; art and, 87; capitalism and, 140-41; class and, 186; escape and, 9-10, 18, 24-25, 27-28, 52-53, 56-57, 60-61, 96, 99-100, 122, 222; geopolitics and, 159-60; imagination and, 143; inclusion and, 163-66; language and, 29-30; literature and, 8-16, 159-60, 220-21, 231; poetry and, 7-15, 35-36, 99-100, 160-61, 184-86, 198-99; politics and, 9-10, 52-53, 55-56; representation and, 162-66, 168, 171-72; state and, 9-10, 15-16, 24-25, 35-36, 74-75, 96, 107-8, 160-61, 163, 165-66, 168, 171-72, 203; subjectivity and, 57-59
Hobbes, Thomas, 39, 71-72, 99-100
hobo, 50-51
homelessness, 146-47, 149-51
homo sacer, 73-74, 95, 127-29; Black life and, 86-87. *See also* statelessness
Hoover, J. Edgar, 119-20
Howe, Susan, 182-83, 186
Howey, Hugh, 35-37
human, humanity: death and, 105-7; knowledge and, 114-15; race and, 83-87; sociality and, 7, 24-27, 39, 47-50, 56-57, 71-72, 75-76, 86-87, 98-100, 190-91, 193, 211; statelessness and, 73-76, 83-87; voice and, 169, 179, 183-84, 212-13

Hutcheon, Linda, 62-63
hybridity, 139-40

identity, 3-4, 7, 27-28, 59-60, 76-77,
    89-90, 96-97, 174-76, 183-84,
    186-89, 191, 201, 209, 211, 254n1
ideology: literature and, 8-9, 11, 183-84,
    186-87; state and, 17, 22-23, 134
image, 130-33
imagination, 12-16, 41-44, 48, 91,
    99-101, 140-41, 143, 152-53,
    180-82
immigration, 19-20, 143-44, 147-48,
    167-68, 237n82
imperialism, 3-4, 9-10, 12, 14-15, 37,
    107-8, 129, 170, 183-84, 190-92,
    196-98, 216
inarticulacy. See under articulation
inclusion, 7, 17, 27-28, 35, 39, 73-74, 76,
    79-81, 84-90, 92, 105, 126-27, 134,
    140-41, 148-54, 158-59, 163-66,
    174-76, 182-83, 192, 209, 211, 231,
    243n51. See also exclusion
indeterminacy, 183-85, 207-8, 210-12,
    255n16
indie rock, 199-201
individual, 53-54, 57-61, 79-80,
    100-101, 226-27, 241n92
inescapability. See escape
information age, 107-8
information theory, 28, 115, 117, 121
insanity, 19-20, 33-36, 85-86
internationalism, 2-5, 29, 102, 138,
    143-44. See also globalization
internment camp, 73-74
intertextuality, 52-53
invisibility, 91-92, 96-97, 230

Jameson, Fredric, 12-16, 24-25, 140-41,
    233n13

jazz, 121, 212-13
Joron, Andrew, 14-15, 25, 182-83

Kihara, Kenji, 79-80, 87
knowledge: articulated versus tacit, 107-
    20, 122-23, 125-27, 130, 134-36,
    160-61, 247n14, 248n20; behavior
    and, 112; death and, 105-8, 112-13;
    embodiment and, 113-14; escape
    and, 122-23, 127; language and,
    108-11; noise and, 115-17; politics
    and, 135-36; representation and,
    28, 108-15, 122-23, 125-26, 130,
    152-53, 160-61; sociality and, 107,
    109-10; state and, 105-10, 112-15,
    117-20, 122-23, 127, 130, 135, 160-
    61, 247n13; violence and, 109-10
Kukathas, Chandran, 19-21, 23, 178-79

language, 63-64; authority and, 89;
    escape and, 76, 97, 103, 210-12,
    216, 222; history and, 29-30;
    knowledge and, 108-11; noise and,
    120-21; openness and, 201-4,
    206-11, 213-14, 216; poetry and,
    14-15, 26, 38-39, 48-49, 56-59,
    69-70, 72, 103, 184-87, 196-97,
    201-4, 206-7, 210-12; politics
    and, 93-94, 139-40, 186-87, 204,
    206-12, 222; power and, 14-15,
    56-57, 120-21, 203-4; represen-
    tation and, 25-27, 38-39, 47-49,
    56-57, 97, 108-10, 120-21, 212-13;
    sociality and, 56-57, 69-70, 72,
    209-11, 216; state and, 14-15,
    29-30, 72, 99-100, 109-10,
    120-21, 186, 203-4; violence and,
    196-97
language poetry, 15, 26, 186, 210-11,
    216, 255n16

law, 33-37, 49-50, 71-74, 130; art and, 179-80, 254nn8-9, 258n1; death and, 105-6; escape and, 78-81, 89-90, 95-97, 117-20, 134-35, 219-20, 222; life and, 134, 137; poetry and, 63; politics and, 39, 205-6, 225-26; race and, 86-87, 90-91; representation and, 75-76, 81, 84-87, 105, 188-89; state and, 34-35, 75-79, 84-88, 95, 106, 119-20, 128-29, 136-37, 188-89, 225-26; violence and, 77-79
Leave No Trace, 17-18
legitimacy, 21-23, 77-78, 103, 193-94, 259n42
Leong, Michael, 198-99
Lerner, Ben, 184-86
Levitas, Ruth, 13
liberalism, 4-5, 11-12, 19-20, 30, 38-39, 45-46, 57-59, 79-80, 90-91, 129-30, 136-37, 151, 158-61, 163, 177-79, 183, 215-16, 220-21, 226-31, 244n54
libertarianism, 4-5, 219-20
life: law and, 134, 137; politics and, 125-26. *See also* death, dying
literary studies, 8-12, 71, 138-40, 159-60
loyalty, 215-16
lucha libre. *See* wrestling

Mackey, Nathaniel, 5-6, 9-10, 88-89, 182-84, 201, 215-16, 222, 241n91, 257n63; *Bass Cathedral*, 208-9; *Bedouin Hornbook*, 121-22, 206-7; *Blue Fasa*, 208-9; *Djbot Baghostus's Run*, 206-7; *From a Broken Bottle Traces of Perfume Still Emanate*, 206-7; "mu," 201-2, 213-14; *Song of the Andoumboulou*, 201-2; *Splay Anthem*, 7, 29-30, 201-10, 212-15; *Whatsaid Serif*, 206
Macpherson, Heidi Slettedahl, 9, 23-24
madness. *See* insanity
magic, 14-15, 134-35, 151, 170-71, 181
magical realism, 141-42, 149-50, 159-60, 168
magical thinking, 100-101, 126
maps, 141, 148-52, 159, 174
margins, marginality, 149, 152, 163, 170-73, 205-6, 208-9
market, marketplace, 19, 90, 135
masks, 169-71, 253n63
materiality, 61-62, 184-86
McCann, Sean, 14, 100-101, 126, 130, 235n60
Mermann-Jozwiak, Elisabeth, 148-49, 174
metaphor, 5-6, 38-39, 41-44, 93-94, 186
mētis. *See* knowledge
Mexico, 29, 141-48. *See also* North American Free Trade Agreement (NAFTA)
Michael, Quintana Roo Dunne, 106-7
Michaels, Walter Benn, 175, 186-88, 233n13, 234n15
Middle Passage, 9-10, 203. *See also* slavery
migration, 54-55, 61-62, 65-66, 68-69, 168. *See also* immigration
military, 22, 29-30, 189, 195, 197-98
mimesis. *See* realism
modernism, 5-6, 27-28, 50, 76, 87
Modest Mouse, 199-202, 214-15
monopoly, 21-23, 90, 225, 259n42
Moya, Paula, 171-74
multiculturalism, 151-53, 158-59, 163, 165-66, 174-75, 251n33

multiplicity, 184-85, 187-88, 207-8
multitude, 8, 12, 46, 59
music, 6-7, 121, 150-51, 211, 213-14, 223

names, 162-63
narrative: authority and, 29, 62-63, 152-54, 157-59, 249n62; escape and, 28-29, 77, 107, 133-34, 137, 222-24, 228; openness and, 204, 206; politics and, 87, 133-34; representation and, 28-29, 87, 125, 130-34, 159, 161-63; state and, 132; video games and, 22-24, 228; voice and, 152-59
narrative theory, 131-32
nation, nationalism, 2-3, 5, 29, 65-66, 96-97, 159-60, 174, 191, 215-16, 228-29, 233n2, 254n1; borders and, 138-39, 142-43. *See also* state
Negri, Antonio, 12, 138
neoliberalism, 2-5, 7, 9-10, 130, 135-37, 146-47
New Deal, 4-5, 9-10, 35-37
New Historicism, 8
New Left, 14, 123-25
noise, 28, 115-17, 119-22, 134-35, 212
nomadism, 202-3, 206, 208-9
North American Free Trade Agreement (NAFTA), 143-44, 146-47

O'Bryan, Michael, 93, 100-101
Occupy Wall Street, 4-5
Olson, Charles, 5-6, 37-39, 71, 75-76, 136-37, 201-2, 210-11, 216, 220-22, 231, 241n92, 255n16, 257n63; *Call Me Ishmael*, 54; "Cornély," 60-61; "I have been an ability—a machine...," 64-70; *The Maximus Poems*, 7, 27, 50-51, 53-57, 60-61, 64-65, 70; "Maximus to Gloucester, Letter 27 [withheld]," 57-59; "The Methodology Is the Form," 59; "Migration in fact...," 61-68; "Physically, I am home. Polish it," 59-62; *The Post Office*, 56; "Projective Verse," 50, 53-54, 57-59, 62-64, 67-70, 184-85, 241n91; "The Songs of Maximus," 50-51; "Stevens song," 55-57
Olson, Charles, Sr., 56-57, 240n66
Ong, Aihwa, 2-3, 135, 188-89, 220
openness, 183-88, 201-14, 216, 241n91, 255n16

pastoralism, 36, 52-53
patriarchy, 133-34, 173-74
patriotism, 215-16
performance, 143-48, 212-13
performative utterance, 195
piracy, 101-2
Plascencia, Salvador, 172-73
Plato, 83
plot, 27, 118-19, 125, 127-31, 137
pluralism, 19-20, 59-60
Polanyi, Michael, 28, 108-10
police, 22, 29-30, 77-78, 81, 84-86, 96-97, 121, 140, 175, 199, 225-26
political theory, 9-12, 19-24, 71, 90, 177-79
polyvocality, 29, 152-59, 174
populism, 229-30
positivism, 108
postmodernism, 5-7, 9, 27-28, 38, 62-63, 76, 107-8, 123-24, 131-33, 142, 201-2, 233n13, 234n15, 249n62
Pound, Ezra, 26, 37
poverty, 79-80, 167
power: escape and, 39, 45-46, 53-54,

power (*continued*)
60-63, 74-76, 117-18, 143, 146-47, 162-64, 170, 172-74, 180-81; globalization and, 139-40, 143, 146-48, 160; imperialism and, 3-5, 9-10, 123-24, 170; interpretation and, 150-51; language and, 14-15, 56-57, 120-21, 203-4; literature and, 11, 41; politics and, 2-5, 14, 39, 41, 53-54, 56-57, 60-63, 74-75, 225-28, 230; race and, 75-77; representation and, 14-15, 17, 25-30, 39, 58-59, 75-76, 81, 84-87, 105, 107, 114-15, 117-18, 123-24, 126-27, 134, 162-66, 169-70, 172-76, 182-84, 187-88, 205, 211, 215, 230; violence and, 14-15, 21-23, 29-30, 81, 84-87, 126-27, 225-26

prison, imprisonment, 180-82
projectivist poetry, 50, 53-54, 63
property ownership, 50-51, 79-80
protest, 4-5, 179
punctuation, 44, 48-49, 59-60
punk, 4-5
Pynchon, Thomas, 5-6, 9-10, 12-13, 23, 103, 115, 222, 231; *The Crying of Lot 49*, 93-94, 99-100, 244n68, 245n81; *Gravity's Rainbow*, 27-28, 74-75, 91-92, 94-102, 105, 159, 245n83, 246n86; *V.*, 93; *Vineland*, 94

Quinlan, Karen Ann, 106, 246n6, 247n7

race: escape and, 3-4, 77, 79-84, 88-91; gender and, 243n51; humanity and, 83-87; identity and, 188-89, 191; inclusion and, 89-91; law and, 86-87, 90-91; politics and, 209; power and, 75-77; representation and, 75-76, 81, 84-87; sociality and, 187-88; state and, 3-4, 9-10, 29, 74-81, 83-91, 129, 140, 162-63, 174-75, 188-89, 191, 209, 244n55; subjectivity and, 77, 79-80, 86; violence and, 77-79, 85-87, 129, 175

racism, 3-4, 80-81, 87, 90, 129, 159-60, 244n55
Rand, Ayn, 6-7, 219-22, 224-25, 228-29
rap music, 91
Rawls, John, 19-20, 105, 178-79
Reading Gaol, 181-82
realism, 8-11, 18, 24-25, 38-39, 41-42, 47-48, 87, 100-101, 224-25, 227-30
recognition, 86-90
reformism, 88-89, 100-101, 140, 166, 173-76, 196
refugees, 74-75, 95
religion, 82-84
representation, 2, 36; absence and, 161-66, 168-74, 244n68; authority and, 46-48, 75-77, 89, 149, 153-54, 158-59, 168, 210-11, 216; control and, 17, 28-29, 93-94, 148-49, 160-61, 211; death and, 105, 112-13, 127-28; escape and, 5-6, 38-39, 41-50, 56-57, 64-65, 71-72, 75-76, 88, 90-100, 103, 107, 119-20, 122-23, 125-28, 130-34, 148, 153-54, 158-60, 163-64, 166, 169-76, 182-84, 186-88, 193-95, 199-200, 208-9, 211-12, 215, 226-31; failure of, 43-44, 107, 125, 152-54, 164-66, 171-74, 199-200, 208-9, 231; freedom and, 25, 42-43, 45-46, 50-51, 75-76, 90-91, 99-100, 173-74, 181-83, 210-11, 215; gender and, 133-34,

164–65; history and, 162–66, 168, 171–72; inclusion and, 134, 140–41, 148–50, 152–54, 158–59, 163–66, 175–76, 182–83, 192, 211, 231; knowledge and, 28, 108–15, 122–23, 125–26, 130, 152–53, 160–61; language and, 25–27, 38–39, 47–49, 56–57, 97, 108–10, 120–21, 212–13; law and, 75–76, 81, 84–87, 105, 188–89; literature and, 5–7, 13, 17, 25–30, 38, 72, 75–76, 87, 99–100, 103, 107, 137, 140–41, 159–60, 175, 231; narrative and, 28–29, 87, 125, 130–34, 159, 161–63; poetry and, 5–7, 14–15, 25–27, 38–39, 41–46, 48–50, 56–57, 64–65, 69–70, 72, 74–76, 97–98, 103, 140–41, 160–61, 165–66, 182–84, 186–88; politics and, 2, 5–7, 14–17, 25–29, 38–39, 45, 47–50, 71–72, 75–76, 87, 97, 99–100, 103, 105, 107, 123–24, 126, 128, 130–34, 140–41, 149–51, 159–60, 162–66, 174–75, 186–87, 192–94, 211, 230–31; power and, 14–15, 17, 25–30, 39, 58–59, 75–76, 81, 84–87, 105, 107, 114–15, 117–18, 123–24, 126–27, 134, 162–66, 169–70, 172–76, 182–84, 187–88, 205, 211, 215, 230; race and, 75–76, 81, 84–87; sociality and, 25–27, 39, 47–50, 56–57, 72, 98–100; state and, 5–7, 17, 25–31, 37, 39, 72, 75–77, 81, 84–85, 89–100, 105–7, 109–10, 112–15, 119–23, 125–30, 132, 134, 137, 140–41, 151–53, 159–66, 168, 170–72, 174–76, 183–84, 187–89, 191, 193–95, 205, 208–9, 215, 231; violence and, 14–15, 37, 46–48, 77, 81, 84–87, 89, 134, 162, 174–75, 183–84, 187–89, 193–94

resistance, 14–16, 43–44, 55–56, 93, 98, 101–2, 105, 124–25, 133–34, 165–66, 179, 186–87, 201–9, 212–13, 215–16, 255n27

revolution, revolutionary, 12–13, 41, 77–78, 121–22, 124, 246nn86–87; escape and, 1–2, 39, 51–52, 62–63, 88–89, 92–93, 140, 175–76; hope and, 1–2, 36–37, 165–66, 206–7, 215

Rock, Peter, 17

Ross, Bob, 181–82

Rowling, J. K., 162–63

Sartre, Jean-Paul, 26–27

Schiavo, Terry, 106–7

science fiction, 1, 12–13, 29, 159–60, 194–95, 236n75

Scott, James C., 21–22, 108–10, 136–37, 160–61, 202–3, 248n20

SDS. *See* Students for a Democratic Society

Seasteading Institute, 219–20

secession, 5, 70–71, 102–3, 220–21

seriality, 201–2, 207–8

sewers, 81–82

sexuality: identity and, 188–89; state and, 3–4, 162–63, 174, 188–89, 253n77, 255n22

signification, 26, 38–39, 44–45, 49, 56–57, 108–9, 115–16, 185–87, 207–8, 210–11. *See also* representation

silence, 87, 103, 116, 120–21, 133–34, 161, 163–65, 213–16, 252n48. *See also* absence

Silo, 35–37

simulacra, 115

slavery, 1, 9–10, 77, 203, 242n17

sociality, 24–30, 39, 46, 56–57, 94; escape and, 27–30, 39, 48–49, 56–57, 69–70, 72, 76, 97–100, 192–96, sociality (*continued*) 198-99, 209-10, 216; knowledge and, 107, 109-10; language and, 56-57, 69-70, 72, 209-11, 216; literature and, 75-76; poetry and, 24-25, 48-49, 50, 57-62, 69-70, 72, 74-76, 97-98, 209-10, 216; politics and, 69-72, 75-76, 183-84, 194-96, 209-11; race, 187-88; representation and, 25-27, 39, 47-50, 56-57, 72, 98-100; state and, 39, 59, 71-72, 98-100, 109-10, 191-94, 196-98, 209-10, 215; subjectivity and, 57-59, 61-62, 68-69; voice and, 196-99, 215-16. *See also* collectivity; community; connection, connectivity

solipsism, 27-28, 38-39, 48, 56-57, 76, 92, 94, 97, 103, 196, 215, 231, 245n83. *See also* escapism

sovereignty, 2-3, 53-54, 75-76, 93, 106, 188-89, 220, 225-26, 228-29, 236n71, 259n42

Spahr, Juliana, 5-6, 9-10, 14-16, 165-66, 182-84, 215-16; "Dole Street," 191-92; *Fuck You-Aloha-I Love You*, 193; "The Incinerator," 188-90; "New World Sonnet," 196-98; *things of each possible relation hashing against one another*, 184-87; *This Connection of Everyone with Lungs*, 29-30, 187-88, 191, 193-99; *Well Then There Now*, 29-30, 185-89, 191

spiral, 59-67, 206-7, 257n63

state: escaping from, 1-7, 9-10, 12-15, 17-27, 217-31; history and, 9-10, 14-15, 24-25; opposition to, 4-9, 15-16; political geography of, 2-4; representation and, 5-7, 14-15, 17,

25-27; sociality and, 18, 23-27; violence and, 14-15, 21-23

statelessness, 73-76, 79, 83-87, 95, 102, 126, 242n1, 242nn10-11

Stout, Janis P., 133-34, 215

Students for a Democratic Society (SDS), 124-25

stylometrics, 29, 153-57, 251n32

subjectivity, 17; escape and, 53-54, 61-62, 92-93, 96-97; history and, 57-59; interpolation of, 57-61; poetry and, 57-59, 61-62, 68-69; politics and, 57-63; race and, 77, 79-80, 86; self-ownership and, 79-80; sociality and, 57-59, 61-62, 68-69; state and, 57-61

substitution, 38

surface reading, 8-9

survivalism, 17

suspension, 131-32

symbolism, 38-48, 78-79, 82-83, 126-27, 238n22

symptomatic reading, 8-9, 11

synecdoche, 5-6, 59-61, 81, 88, 119-20, 168-69, 204

Szalay, Michael, 14, 27-28, 89-90, 100-101, 126, 129-30, 235n60

television, 6-7, 17, 35-36, 114-16, 182

Thoreau, Henry David, 1, 52-53

totalitarianism, 10, 23-24, 45-46, 73-75, 160-61

totality, 24-25, 59, 62-63, 65-66, 192

transnationalism, transnational turn, 138-40, 159-60, 250n11, 251n33

trauma, 154-55, 161, 164-65, 169-72, 252n48

travel, travel narrative, 202-3, 213

Trujillo, Rafael, 160-63, 166-68, 171-72

Trump, Donald, 30, 219-20
Turner, Frederick Jackson, Frontier Thesis, 1

underground markets, 160-61
United Kingdom, 228-31
United States Postal Service, 56, 93-94, 240n66
utopia, utopianism, 9, 12-13, 24-25, 28-29, 52-53, 59, 79-80, 87, 100-101, 107, 121-22, 140-41, 151, 223-24

video games, 6-7, 22-24, 30, 122, 221-24; authority and, 228; control and, 222, 226-28, 259n34; escape and, 228; state and, 227
Vietnam War, 4-5, 123-24
violence: escape and, 224; identity and, 175-76; knowledge and, 109-10; language and, 196-97; law and, 77-79; police and, 175; politics and, 22, 175-76; power and, 14-15, 21-23, 29-30, 81, 84-87, 126-27, 225-26; race and, 77-79, 85-87, 129, 175; representation and, 14-15, 37, 46-48, 77, 81, 84-87, 89, 134, 162, 174-75, 183-84, 187-89, 193-94; sexual, 164-67, 171-72, 189, 252n48; state and, 14-15, 17, 21-22, 37, 77-81, 84-87, 89, 109-10, 121-22, 126, 129-30, 134, 146-47, 151, 162, 167, 170-72, 174-76, 183-84, 187-91, 193-94, 196-99, 213-15
Virgil, 52-53
Visual Artists Rights Act, 179-80
voice, 84, 86-87, 141, 152-59, 169, 174; art and, 179-82; escape and, 178-80, 182-84, 194-201, 211-12, 215-16; failure of, 152-54, 179, 183, 201; poetry and, 177-79, 182-84, 186-87, 194-99, 201, 211-13, 216; politics and, 29-30, 177-80, 183-84, 186-87, 196-99, 211-14; sociality and, 196-99, 215-16; state and, 198-99, 201
von Hallberg, Robert, 37, 41, 51, 70-71, 240n66, 241n92
voting, 177-80, 193-94, 205, 218-19
vulnerability, 95, 121, 128-29, 166, 205

Webster, Max, 21-22
Whiteness, 77-81, 129
Whitman, Walt, 38-39
Wilde, Oscar, 181-82
Williams, William Carlos, 5-6, 19-20, 27-28, 37-39, 41-50, 56-57, 71, 75-76, 136-37, 231; "The Black Winds," 43-45; "An Early Martyr," 33-35; *An Early Martyr and Other Poems*, 27, 33-34, 40, 51; "The Farmer," 42-44; "Flight to the City," 44; "Late for Summer Weather," 51; "A Man versus the Law," 33-35; *Paterson*, 41-42, 48-49; "Revolutions Revalued," 45-46, 109-10; "The Rose," 42-43; "Spring and All," 43-44; *Spring and All*, 27, 41-43, 48-49, 63; "The Use of Force," 46-48, 105; "The Yachts," 40-42
withdrawal. *See* escape
World Wars, 4-5, 73-75, 79-80, 85-86, 94-95, 102, 242n11
wrestling, 143-47, 170-71
Wright, Richard, 5-6, 9-10, 101, 103, 140, 231, 242n17, 244n55; *The Man Who Lived Underground*, 74-76, 80-88, 91, 102;

Wright, Richard (*continued*)
"Memories of My Grandmother," 82–85; *Native Son*, 27–28, 74–81, 86–91, 209, 243n51, 244n54

Yamashita, Karen Tei, 5–6, 179, 231; *Tropic of Orange*, 29, 139–59, 174–76, 250n11
Yeats, W. B., 52–53, 66–67

ZEDE (zona de empleo y desarrollo económico, zone for employment and economic development), 219–20

CULTURAL FRAMES, FRAMING CULTURE

Spectacle Earth: Media for Planetary Chang
ANDREW KALAIDJIAN

Changed Men: Veterans in American Popular Culture after World War II
ERIN LEE MOCK

We, Us, and Them: Affect and American Nonfiction from Vietnam to Trump
DOUGLAS DOWLAND

Criminal Cities: The Postcolonial Novel and Cathartic Crime
MOLLY SLAVIN

Skimpy Coverage: Sports Illustrated *and the Shaping of the Female Athlete*
BONNIE M. HAGERMAN

Story Revolutions: Collective Narratives from the Enlightenment to the Digital Age
HELGA LENART-CHENG

Institutional Character: Collectivity, Agency, and the Modernist Novel
ROBERT HIGNEY

Walk the Barrio: The Streets of Twenty-First-Century Transnational Latinx Literature
CRISTINA RODRIGUEZ

Fashioning Character: Style, Performance, and Identity in Contemporary American Literature
LAUREN S. CARDON

Neoliberal Nonfictions: The Documentary Aesthetic from Joan Didion to Jay-Z
DANIEL WORDEN

Dandyism: Forming Fiction from Modernism to the Present
LEN GUTKIN

Terrible Beauty: The Violent Aesthetic and Twentieth-Century Literature
MARIAN EIDE

Women Writers of the Beat Era: Autobiography and Intertextuality
MARY PANICCIA CARDEN

Stranger America: A Narrative Ethics of Exclusion
JOSH TOTH

Fashion and Fiction: Self-Transformation in Twentieth-Century American Literature
LAUREN S. CARDON

American Road Narratives: Reimagining Mobility in Literature and Film
ANN BRIGHAM

The Arresting Eye: Race and the Anxiety of Detection
JINNY HUH

Failed Frontiersmen: White Men and Myth in the Post-Sixties American Historical Romance
JAMES J. DONAHUE

Composing Cultures: Modernism, American Literary Studies, and the Problem of Culture
ERIC ARONOFF

Quirks of the Quantum: Postmodernism and Contemporary American Fiction
SAMUEL CHASE COALE

Chick Lit and Postfeminism
STEPHANIE HARZEWSKI

www.ingramcontent.com/pod-product-compliance
Lightning Source LLC
Chambersburg PA
CBHW021652230426
43668CB00008B/597